Praise for *Culture and Mental Health*

"One of the primary goals of psychology as a discipline is the alleviation of human suffering. To this end, it is imperative that we understand the various forms of human dysfunction and psychopathology, so that we can continuously intervene in constructive and helpful ways. As the world becomes smaller and borders more porous, psychologists also have the need to adopt a global perspective on the causes, forms, and treatments of various types of illnesses that afflict so many in the world today. Eshun and Gurung's book represents the latest and best effort to compile the information about culture and mental health available in the field today. They have assembled some of the best scholars in the field to bring to bear their expertise in each of their respective areas. Readers will be enlightened with the exceptional information described in each of the chapters. The text is relevant, well-written, and engaging, and Eshun and Gurung are to be commended for an exceptional effort that will be a standard in the field."

David Matsumoto, San Francisco State University

"Specifically focusing on the work of counselors and clinicians, and especially oriented to students and trainees aspiring to careers in the helping professions, this volume provides a rich introduction to the multitude of ways in which culture shapes everyday life, its various challenges, and their solutions. Far from an abstract and empty notion, Eshun and Gurung's collection adds flesh, bones, and blood to the notion of 'culture' and offer persuasive illustrations of what is meant by the term 'cultural competence.'"

Larry Davidson, Yale University

"Eshun, Gurung, and their contributing scholars provide a broad overview of culture and mental health. The book is well worth considering for graduate courses in counseling psychology and related fields."

Steven Lopez, University of Southern California

"*Culture and Mental Health* comes to grips with the complexities of the field without overwhelming or intimidating its readers. It blends concepts and findings with clinical realities and challenges. Thoroughly documented and up to date, the book is relevant for clinicians and researchers at all levels of training and experience."

Juris G. Draguns, Pennsylvania State University

Culture and Mental Health

Sociocultural Influences, Theory, and Practice

Edited by
Sussie Eshun and Regan A. R. Gurung

A John Wiley & Sons, Ltd., Publication

This edition first published 2009
© 2009 Blackwell Publishing Ltd

Blackwell Publishing was acquired by John Wiley & Sons in February 2007. Blackwell's publishing program has been merged with Wiley's global Scientific, Technical, and Medical business to form Wiley-Blackwell.

Registered Office
John Wiley & Sons Ltd, The Atrium, Southern Gate, Chichester, West Sussex, PO19 8SQ, United Kingdom

Editorial Offices
350 Main Street, Malden, MA 02148-5020, USA
9600 Garsington Road, Oxford, OX4 2DQ, UK
The Atrium, Southern Gate, Chichester, West Sussex, PO19 8SQ, UK

For details of our global editorial offices, for customer services, and for information about how to apply for permission to reuse the copyright material in this book please see our website at www.wiley.com/wiley-blackwell.

The right of Sussie Eshun and Regan A. R. Gurung to be identified as the authors of the editorial material in this work has been asserted in accordance with the Copyright, Designs and Patents Act 1988.

Wiley also publishes its books in a variety of electronic formats. Some content that appears in print may not be available in electronic books.

Designations used by companies to distinguish their products are often claimed as trademarks. All brand names and product names used in this book are trade names, service marks, trademarks or registered trademarks of their respective owners. The publisher is not associated with any product or vendor mentioned in this book. This publication is designed to provide accurate and authoritative information in regard to the subject matter covered. It is sold on the understanding that the publisher is not engaged in rendering professional services. If professional advice or other expert assistance is required, the services of a competent professional should be sought.

Library of Congress Cataloging-in-Publication Data

Culture and mental health : sociocultural influences, theory, and practice / edited by Sussie Eshun and Regan A. R. Gurung.
     p. ; cm.
   Includes bibliographical references and index.
   ISBN 978-1-4051-6983-7 (hardcover : alk. paper) – ISBN 978-1-4051-6982-0 (pbk. : alk. paper)
1. Cultural psychiatry. I. Eshun, Sussie. II. Gurung, Regan A. R.
   [DNLM: 1. Mental Disorders–ethnology. 2. Mental Disorders–psychology. 3. Cross-Cultural
Comparison. 4. Mental Health. 5. Psychotherapy–methods. WM 140 C9685 2009]
   RC455.4.E8C785 2009
   616.89–dc22

                                                          2008028046

A catalogue record for this book is available from the British Library.

Set in 10.5/12.5pt Galliard by SPi Publisher Services, Pondicherry, India
Printed and bound in Malaysia by Vivar Printing Sdn Bhd

1 2009

Contents

Notes on Editors and Contributors

Editors

Sussie Eshun is a licensed psychologist and Professor of Psychology at East Stroudsburg University of Pennsylvania. She has lived in and experienced diverse cultural settings. Born and raised in Ghana, she received a BA in Psychology (with Sociology) at the University of Ghana and MA and PhD in Clinical Psychology at the State University of New York at Stony Brook. She is a dedicated teacher and researcher who has developed and taught several courses in psychology and supervised doctoral dissertations. In addition to her earlier work on culture and pain, she has several conference presentations and publications on topics related to depression, suicide, stress, and culture in journals including *Cross-Cultural Research*, *Psychological Reports* and *Suicide and Life Threatening Behavior*, and has recently published a work book on culture and health psychology. She is a member of the American Psychological Association and the Society for Cross-Cultural Research.

Regan A. R. Gurung is Chair of the Human Development Department and Professor of Human Development and Psychology at the University of Wisconsin, Green Bay. Born and raised in Bombay, India, Dr Gurung received a BA in Psychology at Carleton College (MN), and a Masters and PhD in Social and Personality Psychology at the University of Washington (WA). He then spent three years at UCLA as a National Institute of Mental Health (NIMH) Research fellow. He has received numerous local, state, and national grants for his health psychological and social psychological research on cultural differences in stress, social support, smoking cessation, body image and impression formation, and has published four other books and articles in a variety of scholarly journals including *Psychological Review* and *Personality and Social Psychology Bulletin*.

Contributors

Gilberte Bastien is a doctoral student of Clinical Psychology at the University of Mississippi. She is originally from Haiti but grew up in south Florida. She obtained a BSc in psychology from Xavier University of Louisiana in 2005. Her research interests include acculturation of immigrants and international students, as well as psychological health in migrant farm-worker populations.

Toy Caldwell-Colbert was a long-standing advocate for issues of cultural and ethnic diversity. She served as President of APA Division 45, Society for the Psychological Study of Ethnic Minority Issues and also chaired the APA's Commission for the Recruitment, Retention and Training of Ethnic Minorities implementation task force (CEMRRAT2). Both organizations were instrumental in the approval of the APA Multicultural Competencies and the promotion of empirical research addressing mental health issues of ethnic minority clinical populations.

Jyh-Hann Chang, PhD, ABPP, is a Clinical Psychologist and an Assistant Professor of Psychology at East Stroudsburg University. He is a board certified Rehabilitation Psychologist, who has experience working with diverse ethnic populations.

Joseph P. Eshun, Jr, PhD, is an Associate Professor of Management at East Stroudsburg University. He has extensive global experience from Africa, Europe and the USA. He obtained his PhD in Sociology (with Management) from Columbia University in New York. His research focuses on entrepreneurship and culture. He has also served as panelist and invited lecturer outside the USA.

Evan M. Forman, PhD, is an Associate Professor of Psychology at Drexel University and Director of Clinical Training for the doctoral program in Clinical Psychology. He conducted a specialty fellowship in traumatic stress at Cambridge Hospital/Harvard Medical School. Research interests include the development and evaluation of acceptance-based behavior therapies for mood, anxiety, and weight control; mediators of psychotherapy outcome; and post-traumatic stress disorder.

Judith Gibbons, PhD, is Professor of Psychology and International Studies at Saint Louis University. As a cross-cultural developmental psychologist, her research centers on the lives of adolescents in different societies of the world. She is a former president of the Society for Cross-Cultural Research and the Vice President for North America of the Interamerican Society of Psychology.

Bonnie A. Green obtained her PhD in Experimental Psychology from Lehigh University. She is currently an Associate Professor of Psychology at East Stroudsburg University. She is the co-author of *Statistical Concepts for the Behavioral Sciences*, 4th edition, and conducts research and serves as a consultant on psychometrics.

Michael J. Hirschel graduated from the University of North Carolina at Chapel Hill in 2000, and then worked for several years in the Washington DC area as a consultant before beginning graduate school in Clinical Psychology at the University of Mississippi in 2005. His main research interest is working to reduce prejudice and discrimination, and he has helped facilitate an adjustment group for international students at the University of Mississippi.

Megan Markey Hood is a Clinical Psychology doctoral student at Saint Louis University. She is presently engaged in her internship training as a Psychological Resident at Rush, Chicago, specializing in Health Psychology.

Laura R. Johnson, PhD, is an Assistant Professor of Psychology at the University of Mississippi where she teaches Multicultural Psychology, Intercultural Communication, and Statistics. Dr Johnson has been an international student, Peace Corps Volunteer, Fulbright Fellow and member of the American Psychology Association's Committee on International Relations in Psychology. Dr Johnson studies youth social and environmental action in multiple cultural contexts.

Shiva Khalili, PhD, is a clinical psychologist. She completed her doctoral studies at Vienna University and is the Head of the Science and Religion Interdisciplinary group at the World Religions Research Center, Tehran, Iran. She is Assistant Professor at the faculty of Psychology and Education, Tehran University, and serves as clinical psychologist at the Tauhid Counseling and therapy center, and the Tehran University Clinic for counseling and psychotherapy.

Kevin J. Kelley, PhD, is an Assistant Professor of Psychology at the Pennsylvania State University, Lehigh Valley campus. His research interests include attachment theory and the relationship between empathy and health. Clinically, Dr Kelley focuses on the treatment of children who were severely abused in infancy or toddler hood and who were later adopted.

David Lester, PhD, has doctoral degrees from Cambridge University (UK) in Social and Political Science and Brandeis University (USA) in Psychology. He has been President of the International Association for Suicide Prevention, and he has published extensively on suicide, murder and other issues in thanatology. His recent books include *Katie's Diary: Unlocking the Mystery of a Suicide* (2004), *Suicide and the Holocaust* (2005), and *Is There Life After Death?* (2005).

Jose E. Luvathingal is a Catholic priest from India pursuing a doctoral degree in Counseling Psychology at University of Wisconsin-Milwaukee. He has bachelor degrees in Theology and English Literature, a certificate in Philosophy, and graduate degrees in Journalism and Clinical Psychology. His research interests include religion and spirituality in the context of psychological well-being.

P. S. D. V. Prasadarao, PhD, is a Consultant Clinical Psychologist at the Waikato DHB and lectures at the University of Waikato, Hamilton, New Zealand. He was formerly an Associate Professor at the National Institute of Mental Health and Neurosciences, Bangalore, India and at the USM Medical School, Malaysia. His areas of interest include cognitive behavior therapies, psychology of older persons, culture and mental health, and health psychology.

Paul E. Priester is an Associate Professor at North Park University. He has a PhD in Counseling Psychology from Loyola University, Chicago. His research interests include religious issues in counseling and psychology, multicultural counseling, and the treatment and prevention of addiction. He has three children (Caitlin, Paul, Margaret) and an ever-tolerant wife (Katherine). He also operates a small organic berry and apple farm.

Simon A. Rego, PsyD, is an Assistant Professor in the Department of Psychiatry and Behavioral Sciences at Albert Einstein College of Medicine, an Associate Director in the Psychology Training Internship Program and also a Supervising Psychologist in the Adult Outpatient Psychiatry Department at Montefiore Medical Center (Bronx, New York). He is also the Director of Quality Management and Development at University Behavioral Associate, and has experience working with diverse ethnic and immigrant populations.

Angela Roethel-Wendorf, is a graduate student in the Clinical Psychology PhD program at the University of Wisconsin-Milwaukee. Her clinical and research interests lie within clinical health psychology, centered on understanding the patient experience of chronic illness. She is interested in examining the influence of depression and anxiety on physical health, treatment adherence, patient-provider interactions, and health disparities.

Jillon S. Vander Wal, PhD, is an Assistant Professor of Psychology at Saint Louis University. She is a licensed clinical psychologist whose research and clinical interests include eating disorders, obesity, health behavior change, and cognitive behavioral and interpersonal interventions.

Kristin M. Vespia, PhD, is an Associate Professor of Human Development, Psychology, and Women's Studies at the University of Wisconsin-Green Bay, where she regularly teaches an undergraduate multicultural counseling course.

She earned her PhD in counseling psychology at the University of Iowa. Her recent presentations/publications have been in areas of cultural competence, counselor training, campus mental health services, and the scholarship of teaching and learning.

Peter D. Yeomans, PhD, is a post-doctoral psychology fellow in trauma at the San Francisco Veterans Affairs Medical Center in San Francisco, CA. He has worked for the African Great Lakes Initiative in Burundi and Rwanda in the capacity of training and evaluation. He completed his doctorate in Clinical Psychology at Drexel University.

Foreword

As a long-standing advocate for understanding issues of cultural and ethnic diversity, I have served as President of APA Division 45, Society for the Psychological Study of Ethnic Minority Issues, and currently chair the American Psychological Association's Commission for the Recruitment, Retention and Training of Ethnic Minorities implementation task force (CEMRRAT2). Both of these organizations were instrumental in the approval of the *APA Multicultural Guidelines for Practice* and the promotion of empirical research addressing mental health issues of ethnic minority clinical populations. The expectation to be competent is for all psychologists but especially for those pursuing or engaged in the clinical and counseling psychology fields.

It goes without saying that I am a staunch advocate for multicultural competencies, as are the co-authors of this book, Regan A. R. Gurung and Sussie Eshun. I was most delighted to receive the call asking if I would support their book and write the foreword. I immediately sensed that this edited book, *Culture and Mental Health*, had the potential to propel many students and faculty of psychology into strengthening multicultural competencies, and to make a positive impact on our clinical work with ethnically and culturally diverse clients.

For the past fifteen years I have consulted with organizations and institutions interested in multicultural curriculum development and the recruitment, retention and training of ethnic minority faculty, students and staff. This has been some of my most fulfilling work as an African American female psychologist, and is how I came to know Regan A. R. Gurung. The expertise of Sussie Eshun has also become more poignant to me as a result of our work as co-authors on the chapter addressing mood disorders. She has a wonderful background as a counselor stemming from her work as a private practitioner.

We should all be committed to infusing the study of cultural and ethnic diversity in the psychology curriculum. This infusion promotes cultural understanding in training, and provides pedagogical tools to assist others in their acquisition of a rich knowledge base. This focus was something I was not afforded as a graduate student for a variety of reasons, primarily because of the lack of available books and articles from people of various ethnic and cultural backgrounds who were addressing the issues and bringing that information into training settings. Moreover, at the time of my graduate training the over-arching philosophy of color blindness led to the assumption that issues of ethnic and cultural diversity were irrelevant. As an African American female, I of course did not embrace this assumption, and found myself exploring issues of ethnic and cultural diversity in the field of psychology. I was encouraged in this quest by the support of my major professor, Karen Calhoun.

Having held a faculty position at an international institution, and enjoying new and interesting places, I consider myself a world traveler and an astute observer who continues to grow in understanding and appreciation of cultural differences. As a matter of fact, my first position as a new PhD was at the University of Manitoba in Winnipeg, Manitoba Canada. This experience provided one of my first far-reaching wake-up calls as a psychologist to cultural differences. It opened my eyes in ways that have helped sustain my long time commitment to understanding and appreciating cultural differences.

While at the University of Manitoba as a professor, I felt prepared to address gender differences, keeping in mind that my training had not emphasized cultural or ethnic differences. I was aware that I would be working with Alaska Natives and Eskimo populations, but I was somewhat naïve about how cosmo-politan the entire city would be. I set out to extend my dissertation research using assessment tools primarily validated on European American populations. I thought I would have a more controlled sample and be safe if I excluded from my population the two ethnic groups just mentioned, along with Asian, Latino, and African Diasporic populations. Within the first two weeks of data collec-tion, even after running a small pilot with graduate students, I realized that the words of the survey had different meanings to subjects based upon their cultural background. This is an excellent example of assumed generalization going awry. Or maybe I should say I failed to thoroughly think through all of the fundamental teachings of generalization, research, and cultural diversity despite my good intentions to control the subject pool. Those who may look the same may not be the same!

I drew two lessons from this experience. The first is that an assessment tool does not automatically translate into a valid instrument for all populations – much like what we have learned about the application of IQ testing instru-ments without regard to ethnic or racial differences. The second lesson is that words matter within a cultural context. What means something in one culture may not have the same meaning in another culture. This truth is much like what they say when studying a foreign language. You have only mastered a for-eign language when you understand the idioms and colloquial expressions unique to that culture. As I stated earlier, I continue to grow in my own knowl-edge base and know that I have come a long way since that early research study in a Canadian cosmopolitan urban center.

A major strength of the chapters in this book is that they keep us focused on the importance of growth in our understanding of self and others. The writers add a contemporary richness to the body of literature addressing ethnic and cultural difference in the mental health field. Chapter authors draw on their own knowledge of their culture and their direct work with clients from culturally diverse clinical populations. This book certainly meets the goals as stated by Gurung and Eshun, in that it clearly carves out important knowledge for helping students to become better therapists for their clients as they grow in their understanding and appreciation of cultural and ethnic differences within themselves and others. The authors provide a context in which to examine the psychopathology of different populations in today's growing cultural and ethnically diverse society. Today's democratic society is marked by growth in international immigration to the United States as well as by the growth of various ethnic and cultural populations already here.

Regan and Sussie have assembled a stellar group of authors who introduce some of the most current and relevant content in this book. I am sure it will become a major resource promoting the study of diversity in psychology programs and curricula. The co-authors are clearly committed to multicultural competence and to a curriculum that addresses issues of cultural and ethnic diversity. This commitment is critical for all students preparing to provide direct services as mental health professionals.

If our eyes are wide open to appreciating cultural and ethnic differences we will have a much deeper reach into the profession of mental health service delivery. I wish *Culture and Mental Health* had been available during my time as a graduate student. I think I could have really tipped the world of mental health on its edge much earlier in my career when working with those culturally diverse populations in Canada and providing training to my psychology students. Don't miss this opportunity to strengthen your skills, the training of students and your cultural understanding through the book that Gurung and Eshun have so ably edited. To borrow a poignant statement from chapter author Prasadarao: "Mental illness is of concern to people across the globe." Let's be prepared to meet the challenge by embracing the profound content of this book.

A. Toy Caldwell-Colbert, PhD, ABPP
Provost and Vice President for Academic Affairs and Professor Psychology
Central State University
Wilberforce, Ohio

Preface

You either picked this book because of personal interest in the topic or it was assigned by your professor for a particular course. Whatever the reason might be, it is very likely that you have some basic, but crucial questions, such as, "What is culture?" or "Does culture really influence our perceptions about mental health?" or "Is the role of culture in health merely a politically correct movement?" This book addresses these questions, but also goes beyond these questions and takes a critical look at the research pertaining to some common psychological disorders and conditions, such as depression, anxiety, suicide, and post-traumatic stress disorders. What is culture? Before we proceed to offer various definitions consider the following scenario:

> Mrs B just lost her 14-year-old son. Her son was a healthy athlete who died out of the blue without any obvious cause such as an illness or an automobile accident. She is very distraught, cries constantly, feels helpless, and is scared about the uncertainties of the future. During the funeral, it is apparent that her pain is unbearable. She is surrounded by her husband, immediate family, and many relatives, as well as friends and neighbors, who are doing their best to support and comfort her while she endures this indescribably difficult experience. As she returns from the cemetery, where she faced the finality and reality of actual separation from her son, she bursts out in tears, wailing and crying hysterically. Just when she begins to wail, an older (or should we say more mature) relative comes over and puts her arm around Mrs B to comfort her, but she also keeps repeating in a firm emphatic tone ... "it is a taboo to go back home wailing and crying ... you cannot let the other children see you in this state ... all of the crying ends right here at the cemetery ... you need to stop crying now." After a few minutes, Mrs B reluctantly whispers, "OK" and stops wailing, although she continues to weep silently.

What are your reactions after reading this story? You probably had some questions, such as, what is a taboo and who decides what constitutes a taboo or who is the older relative and what right does she have to say what she said to Mrs B? Furthermore, from a mental health viewpoint you are probably thinking it is unhealthy for the older relative to discourage Mrs. B from expressing her true feelings and pain after the burial. After all, there is quite an extensive body of literature that suggests that it is better to express such emotions in a safe environment. Is Mrs B likely to develop a psychological disorder … perhaps depression, anxiety, adjustment or acute stress disorder? All of these questions and concerns are valid. The question and main focus of this book is would Mrs B's disposition be any different if you were told that she is of Latin, African, or Eastern European descent?

Overall epidemiological, clinical, and other studies suggest a "moderate but not unlimited impact of cultural factors" on mental health (Draguns, 1997). This implies that accurate evaluation and diagnoses of psychological disorders within the bounds of culture is crucial for appropriate and effective treatment and intervention (Arrindell, 2003). However, in spite of efforts in the field of counseling/clinical psychology to include or emphasize cultural influences on psychopathology in our traditional training programs, we are still limited in the depth and breadth of material available. Arrindell (2003) reviewed published papers in some leading psychiatric journals over a two-year period and noted a substantial underrepresentation of articles and studies from the non-western world. This is interesting because although most of the data from which psychological theories and concepts have been developed are from samples from western industrialized nations, it is estimated that approximately 70 percent of the world's population lives in non-western nations (Triandis, 1996).

The key pedagogical goals of this book are to examine how the areas of mental health can be studied from and vary according to different cultural perspectives. We introduce the main topics and issues in the area of mental health using culture as the focus. The book is specifically designed to help the reader understand (a) the extent to which mental health is culture-specific; (b) the meaning of "culture," and (c) how elements of mental health (symptom recognition, reporting, prevalence, and treatment) vary across cultures both within the United States and across the world.

Interest in the field of mental health and in health care in general has grown exponentially. Close to 1000 out of the approximately 1500 four-year colleges in America today offer undergraduate programs in the health professions, and every psychology department has at least one course on mental health or counseling. A majority of psychology majors (the second most common major in America) want to be counseling psychologists. This interest in the field is matched by a growing number of books written for the area. Although this variety of texts provides a good introduction to the theoretical and applied aspects of the field, few directly address the influence of culture (see Kazarian and Evans, 1998, for a notable, though now somewhat outdated example, and

Castillo, 1997). A cursory review of university catalogues shows that courses dealing with mental health and culture are now also on the rise. This increase in "multicultural mental health" courses corresponds to the areas of culture (especially gender and socioeconomic status) that are "hot topics" in the field of psychology. Similarly, even syllabi for counseling psychology courses at the undergraduate level show an increased emphasis on sociocultural issues and culture more broadly defined.

This book on the cultural issues in mental health will satisfy a growing need. The book is intended as a core text for upper level undergraduate courses in Multicultural Counseling Psychology courses or as a supplement to courses in Counseling Psychology, Medical Anthropology/Sociology, Cultural Psychology, Health Care, or culture-oriented courses in other Psychology courses. The book will also serve graduate psychopathology courses, and clinical practitioners.

The goal of this book is to address issues of cultural influences from the perspective of the client as well as the therapist. Each chapter emphasizes issues that pertain to conceptualization, perception, health-seeking behaviors, assessment, diagnosis, and treatment in the context of cultural variations. We begin with an introductory chapter discussing the role of culture in mental illness and also highlighting the widely used *DSM-IV-TR* categorization of culture-bound syndromes (Chapter 1, Eshun & Gurung). This chapter is followed by a series of chapters that discuss issues applicable to a variety of mental health issues. Chapter 2 (Green) reviews and actively encourages the reader to consider issues related to reliability, validity and standardization of commonly used psychological assessment instruments among different cultural groups. Chapters 3 (Gurung & Roethel) and 4 (Eshun & Kelley) discuss the role of stress in general and work stress in particular as they both relate to culture. Chapter 5 (Chang) focuses on the topic of pain discussing culture-specific issues. Chapter 6 (Priester, Khalili, & Luvathingal) provides a discussion on the role of religion in mental health. We then move to look at a bigger picture, focusing on psychotherapy in a culturally diverse world (Chapter 7, Johnson, Bastien, & Herschel), and to an international perspective on mental health (Chapter 8, Prasadarao).

From the general, we focus in on specific disorders. The chapters on mood disorders (Chapter 9, Eshun & Calbert), anxiety disorders (Chapter 10, Rego), Post Traumatic Stress Disorder (Chapter 11, Yeomans & Forman), and psychotic disorders (Chapter 12, Vespia) offer a critical review of cultural differences and/or similarities in the symptoms reported, with consideration of possibility of misdiagnosing mental illness among people who focus on specific symptoms (e.g., somatic) and less on others for varying reasons. Finally, we close with chapters on eating disorders (Chapter 13, Markey Hood, Gibbons, & Vander Wal) and suicide (Chapter 14, Lester).

By the time you get to the end of this book you should be struck by how important culture is and the differences across cultural groups. We often see texts treating culture as a minor factor relegating it to a paragraph here and there, often tacked on to the end of each chapter. Culture is way too important for that, something that motivated us to compile this volume. You are about to be exposed to how culture influences critical issues and topics in clinical psychology. We hope you find it compelling, and useful.

Sussie Eshun and Regan A. R. Gurung

REFERENCES

Arrindell, W. A. (2003). Cultural abnormal psychology. *Behavior Research and Therapy,* *41,* 749–753.
Castillo, R. J. (1997). *Culture and Mental Illness.* Pacific Grove, CA: ITP.
Draguns, J. G. (1997). Abnormal behavior patterns across culture: Implication for counseling and psychotherapy. *International Journal of Intercultural Relations,* *21*(2), 213–248.
Kazarian, S. S. & Evans, D. R. (Ed.) (1998). *Cultural Clinical Psychology: Theory, Research, and Practice.* New York: Oxford University Press.
Triandis, H. C. (1996). The psychological measurement of cultural syndromes. *American Psychologist, 51*(4), 407–415.

Acknowledgments

No project is a solitary effort. First, Regan has been a very productive and nurturing colleague. I learned a lot from his expertise and insight. I am also thankful for the support and love of my husband Joe and daughters Sandi, Philippa, and Jemiah who took care of some chores so that I could write. Special thanks to my mom and siblings for their support; Drs Fred and Marilynn Levine, Ron and Sandy Rouintree, and Peter Haile, who helped me immensely in making appropriate transitions in acculturation; my professional colleagues Drs Marie and Lowell Hoffman; and the faculty and staff of the Psychology Department at ESU. Last, but certainly not the least, thanks to each chapter author for their persistence, diligence, and willingness to make adjustments. Kudos!

Sussie Eshun

Culture has been something that many academics acknowledge is important to feature, but few manage to do enough about it. Sussie first saw the need for this book and made sure we could get it launched. I am grateful for her perseverance. In addition to my thanks to the authors who put up with our editorial quirks, I am also grateful to the many who fueled my own interests in examining the intricacies of culture and its importance. Specifically, Chris Dunkel-Schetter, Hector Myers, and Shelley Taylor (UCLA), Arpana Inman, Nita Tiwari, and Lynn Bufka (SAPNA), and the UW System Institute for Race and Ethnicity. A special thank you to my wonderfully supportive wife, Martha Ahrendt and my son Liam (for whose train set I can now build many more structures).

Regan A. R. Gurung

We both gratefully acknowledge the work of our editor Chris Cardone and her staff at Wiley-Blackwell, as well as Joanna Pyke (project manager) and Martin Noble, for his excellent copy editing.

Part I

General Issues in Culture and Mental Health

1

Introduction to Culture and Psychopathology

Sussie Eshun and Regan A. R. Gurung

Culture and Psychopathology

Both trained psychologists as well as lay people often mean different things when they discuss culture. It is a commonly used and more commonly misused word. Many use the words "culture," "ethnicity," and "race," as if they mean the same thing. Culture is often defined as a way of life of a group of people. However, this definition is quite simplistic; culture is more of a complex, multi-layered concept. The word culture comes from the Latin word *colo –ere*, which means to cultivate or inhabit. The term culture was first used in the social sciences by an anthropologist, Edward B. Tylor in 1871 (Tylor, 1974), who defined culture as "that complex whole which includes knowledge, belief, art, law, morals, custom, and any other capabilities and habits acquired by man as a member of society." Since Tylor's initial definition, various individuals and organizations have offered perspectives that emphasize a more comprehensive view as shown in the examples that follow:

> Culture is a configuration of learned behaviors and results of behavior whose com-ponent elements are shared and transmitted by the members of a particular society.
> (Linton, 1945, p. 32)

> Culture is the collective programming of the mind which distinguishes the members of one category of people from another.
> (Hofstede, 1984, p. 51)

> Culture should be regarded as the set of distinctive, spiritual, material, intellec-tual, and emotional features of society or a social group, and that it encompasses, in addition to art and literature, lifestyles, ways of living together, value systems, traditions, and beliefs.
> (UNESCO, 2002)

These definitions imply that culture is composed of values, beliefs, norms, symbols, and behaviors, which are essentially learned. Thus, culture is defined as a general way of life or behaviors of a group of people which reflect their shared social experiences, values, attitudes, norms, and beliefs; is transmitted from generation to generation, and changes over time. In general, culture has been conceptualized as something that is learned, changes over time, is cyclical or self-reinforcing, consists of tangible and intangible behaviors, and most important of all, is crucial for survival and adaptation. Cultural traits and norms do influence how we think, how we respond to distress, and how comfortable we are expressing our emotions.

Although we rarely acknowledge it, culture also has many dimensions. A broader discussion and definition of culture is important to fully understand the precedents of mental illness. Culture includes ethnicity, race, religion, age, sex, family values, the region of the country, and many other features. Culture can also include similar physical characteristics (e.g., skin color), psychological characteristics (e.g., levels of hostility), and common superficial features (e.g., hair style and clothing). Culture is dynamic because some of the beliefs held by members in a culture can change with time. However, the general level of culture stays mostly stable because the individuals change together. The beliefs and attitudes can be implicit, learnt by observation and passed on by word of mouth, or they can be explicit, written down as laws or rules for the group to follow. The most commonly described objective cultural groups consist of grouping by ethnicity, race, sex, and age. There are also many aspects of culture that are more subjective and cannot be seen or linked easily to physical characteristics. For example, nationality, sex/gender, religion, geography also constitute different cultural groups, each with their own set of prescriptions for behavior. Understanding the dynamic interplay of cultural forces acting on us can greatly enhance how we face the world and how we optimize our way of life. This book will describe how such cultural backgrounds influence the recognition, reporting, treatment, and prevalence of different mental illnesses. In this chapter, we provide a broad introduction to how culture interacts with mental health.

Culture and Mental Illness: Underlying Theoretical Perspectives and Research

Culture influences how individuals manifest symptoms, communicate their symptoms, cope with psychological challenges, and their willingness to seek treatment. It has been argued that culture and mental illness are more or less embedded in each other (Sam & Moreira, 2002) and that understanding the role of culture in mental health is crucial to comprehensive and accurate diagnoses and treatment of illnesses. Castillo (1997) identified several ways in which culture influences mental health. These include:

1. the individual's own personal experience of the illness and associated symptoms;
2. how the individual expresses his or her experience or symptoms within the context of their cultural norms;

3. how the symptoms expressed are interpreted and hence diagnosed;
4. how the mental illness is treated and ultimately the outcome.

The role of culture in mental health is best summarized in a statement by the US Surgeon General's Report on mental health that "the cultures that patients come from shape their mental health and affect the types of mental health services they use. Likewise, the cultures of the clinician and the service system affect diagnosis, treatment, and the organization and financing of services" (U.S. Department of Health and Human Services, 1999).

To have a better understanding of how culture influences mental illness, we first need a brief overview of the underlying theoretical positions in cross-cultural studies. The absolutist view assumes that culture has no role in the expression of behavior. This view implies that the presentation, expression, and meaning of mental illness are the same, regardless of culture. At the other extreme is the relativist position with the view that all human behavior (including the expression of mental illness) ought to be interpreted within a cultural context. The universalist view takes more of a middle position, with the assumption that specific behaviors or mental illnesses are common to all people, but the development, expression, and response to the condition is influenced by culture (Berry, 1995).

In support of the universalist position, an extensive study sponsored by the World Health Organization (WHO) confirmed that whereas respondents from different countries reported sad mood, anxiety, tension, and lack of energy as common symptoms of depression, western respondents reported additional symptoms of feeling guilty, while nonwesterners reported more somatic complaints (Draguns, 1990). Studies like these have led to the conclusion that the vegetative symptoms of depression are somewhat universal, while feelings of guilt may be related to cultural factors such as individualism and religion (see Draguns, 1997 for review).

Classification, Diagnoses, and Meaning

The assumption that the *Diagnostic and Statistical Manual of Mental Disorders – Text Revision – DSM–IV–TR* (APA, 2000) and the *International Classification of Diseases – ICD-10* (WHO, 1992) categorization of mental illnesses applies to all people also stems from a universalist perspective. This notion presupposes that psychological principles derived from research in western societies can be directly applied to nonwestern cultures, which is not necessarily true. As discussed later in this book, more recent editions of the *DSM* emphasize the importance of the cultural context in conceptualization of mental illness. Mental health professionals are encouraged to seek knowledge about the cultural background of their patients and to work towards cultural competence.

Arguing from the viewpoint that culture's influence on symptoms and presentation of mental illness, and following studies that have consistently reported symptoms in particular regions that have not been found in other regions, recent editions of the *DSM* have included a new category known as culture-bound syndromes (APA, 2000). Although culture-bound syndromes may share some similarities with some other mainstream psychological disorders, they are unique in that they are recognized in a specific region (or cultural group) as psychopathological. An example that has been often cited is *shenjing shairuo* or neurasthenia in China, which appears similar to the *DSM* classification of major depression, but patients report more somatic complaints and less sad mood. Other forms of culture-bound syndromes that appear similar to some common *DSM* psychological disorders are, *hwa-byung*, a Korean syndrome similar to *DSM–IV* major depression; and *taijin kyofyusho*, a Japanese disorder similar to *DSM–IV* social phobia. Several other culture-bound syndromes are discussed throughout this book.

It is worth mentioning that many nonwestern cultural groups have their own informal as well as formal ways of classifying, diagnosing and treating mental illness. One such example is the *Chinese Classification of Mental Disorders (CCMD)*, with the most recent edition *CCMD–3* published in 2001 by the Chinese Society of Psychiatry (Chen, 2002). The *CCMD–3* is similar to the *ICD* and *DSM* in categorizations, but certain symptoms and conditions that are unique to that particular culture are emphasized as in the case of *shenjing shaijo*, discussed earlier. Also several psychological illnesses that are unique to Chinese such as *koro* (a sudden extreme worry that one's sexual organs will recede into the body and ultimately cause death) are discussed. Although some may view the *CCDM* as extremely relativist, many mental health professionals who work with predominantly Chinese patients believe its strengths outweigh any weaknesses that exist.

Health-Seeking Behaviors and Coping

Whether or not individuals seek help for a psychological disorder depends on the extent to which they trust the mental health professional or the mental health system as a whole. Research on counselor dissimilarity, cultural mistrust and willingness to self-disclose has established that these factors influence health-seeking behaviors and premature termination rates among black clients (Carlos Poston, Craine, & Atkinson, 1991). In their paper about comfortableness with conversations about race and ethnicity in psychotherapy, Cardemil and Battle (2003) emphasize the utter importance of including important elements of cultural background (specifically race and ethnicity) in psychotherapy by default.

Even after an individual makes the decision to seek professional help, culture influences the symptoms that the patient presents. It has been suggested that cultural norms that encourage avoidance coping among Asians and Asian Americans often result in reports of physical complaints associated with stress and not emotional complaints, as the latter is viewed as unacceptable (Iwamasa, 2003).

A group's perception of an illness and cultural worldview also influences how well the individual and close relatives cope with mental illness. People from cultures in which mental illness is linked with supernatural causes (e.g., sorcerer, witchcraft, evil eye) are less likely to seek help from a mental health professional and more likely to seek help from a traditional healer or medicine man (Mateus, dos Santos, & de Jesus Mari, 2005). Similarly, James Myers, Young, Obasi, and Speight (2003) report that for many persons of African descent, "pathology in the individual is presumed to be reflective of dysfunction in the larger social group and context, and, healing would be required for the collective, as well as the individual."

The importance of cultural competence among mental health professionals is best summarized in the report on psychological treatment of ethnic minority populations presented by the Council of National Psychological Associations for the Advancement of Ethnic Minority Interests (2003). This report emphasizes that mental health professionals:

- are *aware* of and sensitive to their own racial and cultural background and biases;
- have *knowledge* about their own cultural heritage as well as that of their patients and acknowledge how they influence their perceptions; and
- actively seek to understand themselves and other cultures with a goal of developing important *skills* needed to work with specific cultural groups.

Sociocultural Influences on Mental Illness

Symptoms of mental illnesses are manifested within the background of certain cultural concepts and constructs. These include ethnicity, race, or nationality, acculturation, individualism-collectivism, ethnocentrism, power-distance, and uncertainty avoidance.

Ethnicity, Race, and Nationality

Ethnicity, race, and nationality are often used interchangeably in our society. It is common to hear someone describing an individual's behavior, values, or beliefs by saying "he is African" or "she is Asian." These descriptions may be factual since the individual identifies with a country within those continents. However, after close interactions with the person you may find that they prefer a more specific description, such as Indian or Ghanaian. Furthermore, it may be even more important to them to identify with a specific ethnic or tribal group (e.g., Gujarati for the Indian, Ashanti for the Ghanaian, and Dina (Navajo) for a First Nations person). Interestingly these generalized descriptions are commonly made by people in the western world, but it is very rare to hear westerners describe themselves as Europeans or North Americans. Regardless of our assumptions, it is imperative to inquire about how an individual or a group views themselves.

Although we tend to use these terms loosely, the first, obvious, descriptive impression to us is race or skin color. The term race is used in two ways – biological and sociocultural. Biological definitions of race tend to focus on people sharing physical and genetic qualities such as skin color, hair texture, and eye color, which have resulted in historical classifications of Caucasoid (white), Mongoloid (Asian), and Negroid (Black). However, the biological classifications of race have been challenged (Relethford, 2002; Smedley & Smedley, 2005), and some authors have argued that race is used as an easy way out of a complex situation (Atkinson, 2004). The sociocultural definition of race is related to geographic migration of different groups and also for the purpose of identity formation. Mio writes that the sociocultural concept of race refers to:

> the perspective that characteristics, values, and behaviors that have been associated with groups of different physical characteristics serve the social purpose of providing a way for outsiders to view another group and for members of a group to perceive themselves.
>
> (Mio, Barker-Hackett, & Tumambing, 2006, p. 9)

In other words we continue to use race as a classification because it helps us describe people, regardless of the fact that these descriptions have been artificially constructed. The current consensus based on existing evidence is that racial groups are not genetically discrete, reliably measured, or scientifically meaningful although the labels have many social consequences as regards to how people treat one another (Eberhardt, 2005; Smedley & Smedley, 2005; Sternberg, Grigorenko, & Kidd, 2005).

Ethnicity and nationality are other ways of viewing an individual. An ethnic group refers to a group of people with common ancestry, who often have similar physical and cultural attributes, such as language, physical features, rituals and norms. Nationality on the other hand refers to a political community, which typically shares common origin or descent. Although it is easier to assume aspects of a person's background based on their race, it is imperative that mental health professionals be more cautious and conduct a thorough interview of the individual, as racial categorizations do not necessarily provide salient background information. For instance, based on the US Federal classifications of racial and ethnic minority groups, people from the Dominican Republic may identify their ethnicity as Hispanic or Latino and their race as black. A true understanding of a person, then, requires that professionals go beyond obvious categorizations to a much deeper level of inquiry and meaningfulness.

Acculturation

Our world is becoming more and more global because of rapid increases in traveling and migration for different reasons. Increased migration rates have made acculturation a crucial topic to be considered. Acculturation is a transition in which an individual gradually accommodates and eventually takes on some of the values and beliefs of a new culture. Berry (1992) described acculturation as a process of "culture shedding and culture learning," that involves intentionally or unintentionally losing selected cultural values or behaviors with the passage of time, while adopting new values and behaviors from the new group. Generally, acculturation depends on how open the host culture is to interact, and also how willing the immigrant group is to adopt the norms and values of the host group (Berry, 2001): A kind of mixing of the original and new cultures in a way that maximizes the individual's transition into the new culture.

Being acculturated may mean different things to different people and there have been many approaches to studying acculturation (Padilla, 1980). Roland (1990), who has studied and compared various cultures, sees the acculturation process as primarily entailing the adoption of one culture at the expense of the other. In contrast, Berry, Trimble, and Olmedo (1986) define four models of acculturation. Berry (1970) described four different forms of acculturation based on the extent to which an individual has preference for his or her own culture and the extent to which he or she prefers the values and norms of the new culture. They are integration, assimilation, separation, and marginalization. Integration is when the individual (or immigrant) is willing to adopt behaviors and adapt to the host culture, while also maintaining their own cultural norms and values – some form of a balance between the two. This is different from separation, in which the individual focuses almost exclusively on adopting the cultural norms of the host group (or country) and basically disregards their own cultural heritage. Assimilation is more or less the opposite of separation. With assimilation, the person puts most of their efforts toward maintaining their own cultural heritage, and very little effort toward adopting the norms of the host group. Last, marginalization refers to an individual who neither adopts their own cultural heritage, nor that of the host or dominant group. Marginalization is the least preferred type of acculturation and has been associated with diverse adjustment challenges, some of which will be further explored later in this book. Figure 1.1 summarizes the basic process involved in acculturation and how the four different forms of acculturation come about.

Berry (1998) argues that acculturation does not necessarily result in serious psychological challenges. In summarizing his views he identified three levels at which acculturation could influence an individual's mental health. The first level involves letting go of behaviors that are not helpful in adapting to the new culture, while learning new behaviors and skills that are useful for the new culture. This level of acculturation involves mild to moderate conflict. The second level of acculturation involves moderate to significant conflict. This level of conflict occurs when the process of learning new skills and unlearning old skills becomes more of a challenge and results in acculturative stress. The final level is associated with severe conflict and psychological disorders. It represents a situation in which the changes involved in acculturation are overwhelming and beyond the individual's ability to cope (see Berry, 1997 for review). Degree of

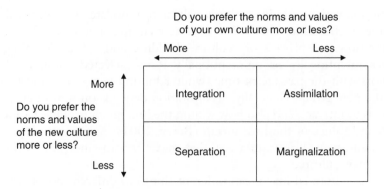

Figure 1.1   Depiction of different types of acculturation based on Berry's conceptualization (Berry, 1970)

acculturation and one's sense of identity are therefore crucial to accurate assessment, diagnosis, and treatment outcome.

Attending to acculturation and ethnic identity takes us beyond the basic cultural differences in mental health. For example, African Americans have been found to have higher rates of mental disorders as compared to European Americans and Mexican Americans but these findings vary with acculturation level (Robins, Locke, & Regier, 1991; Ying, 1995). In many cases, greater acculturation is associated with better mental health (e.g., Landrine & Klonoff, 1996) although this is not the case for all ethnic groups or with physical health. Higher acculturated Mexican Americans, for example, have been found to be more depressed than recent immigrants with lower acculturation scores (Vega, Kolody, Aguilar-Gaxiola, Alderete, Catalano, & Caraveo-Anduaga, 1998).

Individualism and Collectivism

It has been argued that psychotherapy is a product of western culture and thus, counselors tend to emphasize individualism and promotion of the self, as opposed to collectivism and promotion of the group (Dwairy & van Sickle, 1996). Individualism refers to a person's general affinity towards independence, self-reliance, and competitiveness while collectivism refers to a preference for the group, our need to fit into the group, and increased concern for harmony within the group. Hofstede (1983) originally presented individualism and collectivism as two opposing views, with individualism emphasizing independence and collectivism emphasizing interdependence. A review of studies suggests that portrayal of either cultural construct depends on the situation as well as the national background of the individual (Triandis, 1995).

Triandis (1995, 2001) has further identified two levels each of individualism and collectivism, namely, horizontal individualism – HI; vertical individualism – VI; horizontal collectivism – HC; and vertical collectivism – VC (Triandis &

Table 1.1 Self-statements portraying Triandis' different types of individualism/collectivism

	Individualism	Collectivism
Vertical (hierarchy)	Vertical individualism "I want to do better than everyone else"	Vertical collectivism "I want my in-group to do better than all other groups"
Horizontal (equality)	Horizontal individualism "I want to do as well as everyone else"	Horizontal collectivism "I want my group to do as well as the other groups"

Source: Berry (1970).

Gelfand, 1998). HI pertains to a desire to be distinct, but not necessarily better than one's group and VI applies to a desire to be distinct and better than the group (connoting competitiveness). On the other hand, HC refers to an individual who emphasizes interdependence or the willingness to share common goals with others group, while VC describes an individual who places his or her group's goals over their personal goals. The differences between the four levels of individualism/collectivism are shown in Table 1.1.

Individualism and collectivism influence how individuals perceive and respond to mental illness. Heinrichs, Rapee, Alden, et al. (2006) asked respondents from eight different countries (Australia, Canada, Germany, Japan, Korea, the Netherlands, Spain, and the USA) to evaluate the extent to which an actor's behavior was socially acceptable. Participants from collectivistic countries were more accepting of socially reserved and withdrawn behaviors than were those from individualistic countries. Furthermore, on a personal level, those from collectivistic countries reported higher levels of social anxiety and related symptoms than their counterparts from individualistic countries. Their results suggest that people who had experienced significant levels of social anxiety were also more accepting of social withdrawal. These findings have implications for counseling and psychotherapy, especially when the therapist and client have different cultural perspectives.

In their argument against directly applying western psychotherapy in Arabic societies, Dwairy and Van Sickle (1996) explain that "individuals [in Arabic societies] live in a symbiotic relationship with their families, seeing themselves as extensions of a collective core identity ... individualism will be viewed as deviant and will face condemnation." The authors further identify ways in which western psychotherapy may be at odds with core values in many Arabic societies and pose as barriers in psychotherapy, which could be easily misinterpreted by the therapist. These include low levels of self-disclosure, avoidance of self-exploration, differences in emotional expressivity, and differences in conception of time (see Dwairy & Van Sickle, 1996 for review). Similar conditions and experiences may exist in other collectivist cultures in Africa, Asia, and South America (Sue & Sue, 1990).

Ethnocentrism

Therapists and counselors have been encouraged to consider their clients' cultural background more seriously. However, it is equally important that they are aware of their own stereotypes and biases. Some studies have demonstrated that stereotyping and wrong diagnoses are mostly due to cultural misinterpretations (Cheetham & Griffiths, 1981). A common way in which stereotyping occurs in interactions between mental health professionals and individuals seeking help is ethnocentrism. This refers to the assumption that an individual or his/her group is superior to other individuals or group. Simply put, it reflects an attitude of "us-better–them worse" (Berry et al., 1992). Typically ethnocentrism occurs because we are likely to perceive our norms and expectations as the basis or standard for judging others. Anyone reflecting on the vignette presented in the preface probably has his or her views about what the normal process of bereavement should be, based on their own experiences, expectations, and justifiable reasons. But is our way necessarily the right way (even if there is scientific research to support it)?

Ethnocentrism is often difficult to identify, especially when it comes from the dominant cultural group. Take the example of arranged marriages in certain cultures; is it fair to assume that the couple may not have a happy marriage? Are passion, romance, and love at first sight, crucial to the conceptualization of marriage? Or do successful marriages hinge more on practical factors like companionship and economic sustenance? Responses to these questions may vary, but unless a person's history and cultural background is considered, it is unfair, presumptuous, and may even be unhealthy psychologically to judge their views or behaviors. Part of being a good scientist-practitioner is being open to experience and systematically investigating a behavior before making judgment. As mentioned earlier, the new emphasis on cultural influences adopted in the *DSM–IV–TR* may help decrease levels of ethnocentrism and other cultural biases.

Power Distance

Power distance is "the extent to which the less powerful persons in a society accept inequality in power and consider it as normal" (Hofstede, 1986, p. 307). Although inequality in power exists in every society, each one differs in the extent to which the inequality is accepted or at least tolerated. Hofstede (1980) studied employees of a multinational corporation spanning over 40 countries and noted that societies with small power distance scores believed in equal rights for all, power should be based on formal position, and that the use of power had to be legitimate (among others). The other end, were societies with large power distance scores such as Malaysia and Panama. They believed that the powerful have privileges, power is based on family, friends, and the use of force, and that whoever holds the power is right.

Power distance may have implications for prevalence rates, health seeking behaviors and treatment. Rudmin and colleagues (2003) analyzed data from 33 nations, over a 20-year period and reported, among other findings, that power distance was a negative correlate of national suicide rates. That is, overall, nations with high power-distance levels had lower suicide rates. However, they noted that this was not the case for the young women in their sample. The authors attempted to explain the results for young women by hypothesizing that whereas the inflexibility observed in high power-distance societies may offer a sense of security and success for most people, it could have an adverse effect for women in societies that do not value gender equality. Findings such as these buttress the importance of cultural constructs for psychological well-being.

Another way in which power distance could influence mental health is in intervention methods. People in high power-distance societies have been found to sanction a norm of submissiveness to superiors and preference for leaders to make decisions for them (Hofstede, 1980). In essence this cultural construct is related to social class and privilege. The latter may have implications for psychotherapy, where clients may view the therapist as the superior and hence expect to merely follow his or her directions without necessarily involving them in the decision-making.

Uncertainty Avoidance

Uncertainty avoidance is "the extent to which people within a culture are made nervous by situations which they perceive as unstructured, unclear, or unpredictable, situations which they therefore try to avoid by maintaining strict codes of behavior and a belief in absolute truths" (Hofstede, 1986, p. 308). Hofstede (1980) found Denmark, Jamaica, and Singapore to have low uncertainty avoidance scores, while Greece, Guatemala, and Portugal were on the high end. In general, he noted that the nations on the high end of uncertainty avoidance were more active, aggressive, emotional, and intolerant than those on the low end of the scale.

Uncertainty avoidance has been found to predict differences in levels of subjective well-being across nations. Nations with low scores have been found to have high scores for subjective well-being (Arrindell, Hatzichristou, Wensink, et al., 1997). In another study involving 11 countries (Australia, East Germany, Great Britain, Greece, Guatemala, Hungary, Italy, Japan, Spain, Sweden, and Venezuela), Arrindell, Eisemann, Oei, et al. (2003) found a significant relationship between scores on uncertainty avoidance and phobic anxiety. They reported that high uncertainty avoidance scores predicted high national scores and national levels on fears of bodily illness/death, sexual and aggressive scenes, and harmless animals.

Diverse Perspectives on Cultural Influences on Mental Health

A final point of consideration is to provide a framework for which to understand how culture influences behavior and mental health. In considering a framework for sociocultural influences on mental health, let's first review some of the approaches that have been presented over the years. These include the sociobiological, ecocultural, and biopsychosocial perspectives.

The *sociobiological* approach emphasizes how biological and evolutionary factors influence human behavior and culture. The notion of a sociobiological view suggests that culture is not static, but instead changes with time for the benefit and survival of the society. The *ecocultural* approach focuses on the link between culture and ecology. According to proponents of this perspective, our environment influences or shapes our behavior and beliefs, our behavior in turn and influences our environment. The third viewpoint, the *biopsychosocial* approach, holds that biological, psychological, and social factors combine to influence behavior. In other words, this approach culture's influence on mental health stems from an interaction of biological, cognitive, and affective factors in our social interactions (Mio, Barker-Hackett, & Tumambing, 2006). Although the utility of taking a biopsychosocial approach has already paid dividends, there is still a need to better incorporate research on diverse cultural backgrounds. The fact is that it is really not enough of a "socio" focus in the "biopsychosocial" approach (Keefe, Smith, Buffington, Gibson, Studts, & Caldwell, 2002). Indeed what we do and why we do it is shaped by a variety of factors, and our well-being is no exception. A *biopsychocultural* approach (Gurung, 2006) might provide clinical psychology with stronger direction for it not only incorporates the social nature of our interactions, but explicitly acknowledges the role that culture plays in our lives.

Another perspective that has become increasingly important in our postmodern world with much migration and resettlement is *multiculturalism*. It literally means many cultural views. It is a view that emphasizes importance, equality, and acceptance for all cultural groups within a society, supported by a strong desire to increase awareness about all groups to the benefit of the society as a whole (see Mio et al., 2006 for review).

Discussions in this chapter thus far point to the importance of culture in conceptualization of psychological illnesses. As summarized by Draguns (1997), "the most general implication for working counselors is an attitudinal one. It behooves them to be aware of and open to the cultural factors in their clients' experience, expectations, and self presentation." This book will clearly illuminate these cultural factors. Our approach is one that represents an integration of main themes from the approaches described earlier. It is the biopsychocultural approach, which stresses that cross-cultural differences and similarities in behaviors and processes are influenced by a combination of biological, psychological, social, and cultural factors. The biopsychocultural model is not new. It is a model that flows naturally from the biopsychosocial perspective and has been used quite extensively in the forensic sciences (Silva, Leong, Dasson, Ferrari, Weinstock, & Yamamoto, 1998) and also in consideration of multicultural models of training in psychiatry and other medical fields (Lu, Nang, Gaw, & Lin, 2002). It is also closely related to the views of the psychosociocultural approach applied extensively in the area of multicultural psychology (Gloria & Ho, 2003; Gloria & Rodriguez, 2000). As you will see in the following chapters, adopting this approach is crucial because it is comprehensive and considers intercultural and intracultural variables that directly and indirectly influence behavior.

References

American Psychiatric Association (2000). *Diagnostic and statistical manual of mental disorders – text revision (DSM–IV–TR)*. Washington, DC: Author.

Arrindell, W. A. (2003). Cultural abnormal psychology. *Behavior Research and Therapy*, *41*, 749–753.

Arrindell, W. A., Eisemann, M., Oei, T. P. S., et al. (2003). Phobic anxiety in 11 nations: Part II. Hofstede's dimensions of national cultures predict national-level variations. *Personality and Individual Differences*, *37*(3), 627–643.

Arrindell, W. A., Hatzichristou, C., Wensink, J., et al. (1997). Dimensions of national culture as predictors of cross-national differences in subjective well-being. *Personality and Individual Differences*, *23*(1), 37–53.

Atkinson, D. R. (2004). *Counseling American minorities* (6th ed.). Boston: McGraw-Hill.

Berry, J. W. (1970). Marginality, stress and identification in an acculturating aboriginal community. *Journal of Cross-Cultural Psychology*, *1*, 239–252.

Berry, J. W. (1992). Acculturation and adaptation in a new society. *International Migration*, *30*, 69–85.

Berry, J. W. (1995). Culture and ethnic factors in health. In R. West (Ed.), *Cambridge Handbook of Psychology, Health and Medicine* (pp. 84–96). New York: Cambridge University Press.

Berry, J. W. (1998). Acculturation and health: Theory and practice. In S. S. Kazarin & D. R. Evans (Eds.), *Cultural clinical psychology: Theory, research, and practice*. New York: Oxford University Press.

Berry, J. W. (2001) A psychology of immigration. *Journal of Social Issues*, *7*(3), 615–631.

Berry, J. W., Trimble, J. E., Olmedo, E. L. (1986). Assessment of acculturation. In W. J. Lonner & J. W. Berry (Eds.), *Field methods in cross-cultural research* (pp. 291–324). Thousand Oaks, CA: Sage.

Cardemil, E. V., & Battle, C. L. (2003). Guess who's coming to therapy? Getting comfortable with conversations about race and ethnicity in psychotherapy. *Professional Psychology: Research and Practice*, *34*(3), 278–286.

Carlos Poston, W. S., Craine, M., & Atkinson, D. R. (1991). Counselor dissimilarity confrontation, client cultural mistrust, and willingness to self disclose. *Journal of Multicultural Counseling & Development*, *19*(2), 65–73.

Castillo, R. J. (1997). *Culture and mental illness*. Pacific Grove, CA: ITP.

Cheetham, R. W. S., & Griffiths, J. A. (1981). Errors in the diagnosis of schizophrenia in Black and Indian patients. *South African Medical Journal*, *59*, 71–75.

Chen, Y. F. (2002). Chinese classification of mental disorders (CCMD-3): Towards integration in international classification. *Psychopathology*, *35*(2–3), 421–431.

Council of National Psychological Associations for the Advancement of Ethnic Minority Interests (2003). *Psychological treatment of ethnic minority populations*. Washington, DC: Association of Black Psychologists.

Draguns, J. G. (1990). Applications of cross-cultural psychology in the field of mental health. In R. W. Brislin (Ed.), *Applied cross-cultural psychology*. Newbury Park, CA: Sage.

Draguns, J. G. (1997). Abnormal behavior patterns across culture: Implication for counseling and psychotherapy. *International Journal of Intercultural Relations, 21*(2), 213–248.

Dwairy, M., & van Sickle, T. (1996). Western psychotherapy in traditional Arabic societies. *Clinical Psychology Review, 16*(3), 231–249.

Eberhardt, J. L. (2005). Imaging race. *American Psychologist, 60*, 181–190.

Gloria, A. M., & Ho, T. A. (2003). Environmental, social and psychological experiences of Asian American undergraduates: Examining issues of academic persistence. *Journal of Counseling and Development, 81*, 93–105.

Gloria, A. M., & Rodriguez, E. R. (2000). Counseling Latino university students: Psychosociocultural issues for consideration. *Journal of Counseling and Development, 78*, 145–154.

Gurung, R. (2006). *Health psychology: A cultural approach*. San Francisco: Wadsworth Publishing.

Heinrichs, N., Rapee, R. M., Alden, L. A., et al. (2006). Cultural differences in perceived social norms and social anxiety. *Behavior Research and Therapy, 44*, 1187–1197.

Hofstede, G. (1980). *Culture's consequences*. Beverly Hills, CA: Sage.

Hofstede, G. (1983). National cultures revisited. *Behavior Science Research, 18*, 285–305.

Hofstede, G. (1984). National cultures and corporate cultures. In L. A. Samovar & R. E. Porter (Eds.), *Communication between cultures*. Belmont, CA: Wadsworth.

Hofstede, G. (1986). Cultural differences in teaching and learning. *International Journal of Intercultural Relations, 10*, 301–320.

Iwamasa, G. Y. (2003). Recommendations for the treatment of Asian-American/Pacific Islander populations (Chapter 2). *Psychological treatment of ethnic minority populations, Council of National Psychological Associations for the Advancement of Ethnic Minority Interests*, Washington, DC: Association of Black Psychologists.

James Myers, L., Young, A., Obasi, E., & Speight, S. (2003). Recommendations for the psychological treatment of persons of African descent (Chapter 3). *Psychological treatment of ethnic minority populations, Council of National Psychological Associations for the Advancement of Ethnic Minority Interests*, Washington, DC: Association of Black Psychologists.

Keefe, F., Smith, S., Buffington, A., Gibson, J., Studts, J. L., & Caldwell, D. S. (2002). Recent advances and future directions in the biopsychosocial assessment and treatment of arthritis. *Journal of Consulting and Clinical Psychology, 70*(3), 640–655.

Landrine, H., & Klonoff, E. A. (1996). The schedule of racist events: A measure of racial discrimination and a study of its negative physical and mental health consequences. *Journal of Black Psychology, 22*(2), 144–168.

Linton, R. (1945). *The cultural background of personalities*. New York: Appleton-Century Crofts.

Lu, F. G., Nang, D., Gaw, A., & Lin, K. M. (2002). A psychiatric residency curriculum about Asian-American issues. *Academic Psychiatry, 26*(4), 225–236.

Mateus, M. D., dos Santos, J. Q., de Jesus Mari, J. (2005). Popular conceptions of schizophrenia in Cape Verde, Africa. *Revista Brasileira de Psiquiatria, 27*(2) 101–107.

Mio, J. S., Barker-Hackett, L., & Tumambing, J. (2006). *Multicultural psychology: Understanding our diverse communities*. Boston, MA: McGraw Hill Companies, Inc.

Padilla, A. M. (1980). Notes on the history of Hispanic psychology. *Hispanic Journal of Behavioral Sciences, 2*(2), 109–128.

Relethford, J. H. (2002). Apportionment of global human genetic diversity based craniometrics and skin color. *American Journal of Physical Anthropology, 118,* 393–398.

Robins, L. N., Locke, B. Z., & Regier, D. A. (1991). An overview of psychiatric disorders in American. In L. N. Robins & D. A. Regier (Eds.), *Psychiatric disorders in America.* New York: The Free Press.

Roland, A. (1990). *In search of self in India and Japan: Towards a cross-cultural psychology.* Princeton, NJ: Princeton University Press.

Rudmin, F. W., Ferrada-Noli, M., & Skolbekken, J. (2003). Questions of culture, age, and gender in the epidemiology of suicide. *Scandinavian Journal of Psychology, 44,* 373–381.

Sam, D. L., & Moreira, V. (2002). The mutual embeddedness of culture and mental illness. In W. J. Lonner, D. L. Dinnel, S. A. Hayes, & D. N. Sattler (Eds.), *Online readings in psychology and culture* (Unit 9, Chapter 1), Center for Cross-Cultural Research, Western Washington University, Bellingham, Washington, USA.

Silva, J. A., Leong, G. B., Dasson, A., Ferrari, N. M., Weinstock, R., & Yamamoto, J. (1998). A comprehensive typology for the biopsychosociocultural evaluation of child-killing behaviors. *Journal of Forensic Sciences, 43*(6), 112–118.

Smedley, A., & Smedley, B. D. (2005). Race as biology is fiction, racism as a social problem is real: Anthropological and historical perspectives on the social construction of race. *American Psychologist, 60,* 16–26.

Sternberg, R. J., Grigorenko, E. L., & Kidd, K. K. (2005). Intelligence, race, and genetics. *American Psychologist, 60,* 46–59.

Sue, D. W., & Sue D. (1990). *Counseling the culturally different: Theory and practice* (2nd ed.). New York: John Wiley & Sons, Inc.

Triandis, H. C. (1995). *Individualism and collectivism.* Boulder, CO: Westview.

Triandis, H. C. (1996). The psychological measurement of cultural syndromes. *American Psychologist, 51*(4), 407–415.

Triandis, H. C. (2001). Individualism-collectivism and personality. *Journal of Personality,* 69, 907–924

Triandis, H. C., & Gelfand, M. J. (1998). Converging measurements of the horizontal and vertical individualism and collectivism. *Journal of Personality and Social Personality, 74,* 118–128.

Tyler, E. B. (1974). *Primitive culture: Researches into the development of mythology, philosophy, religion, art, and custom.* New York: Gordon Press. (First published in 1871.)

UNESCO (2002). Universal Declaration on Cultural Diversity. (www.unesco.org/confgen/press_rel/021101_clt_diversity.shtml). Retrieved November 29, 2006.

U.S. Department of Health and Human Services (1999). *Mental health: A report of the Surgeon General.* Rockville, MD: Author.

Vega, W. A., Kolody, B., Aguilar-Gaxiola, S., Alderete, E., Catalano, R., & Caraveo-Anduaga, J. (1998). Lifetime prevalence of *DSM–III–R* psychiatric disorders among urban and rural Mexican-Americans in California. *Archives of General Psychiatry, 55,* 771–778.

World Health Organization (1992). *The ICD-10 classification of mental and behavioral disorders: Clinical descriptions and diagnostic guideline,* Geneva, Switzerland: Author.

Ying, Y. (1995). Cultural orientation and psychological well-being in Chinese Americans. *American Journal of Community Psychology, 23*(6), 893–911.

2

Culture and Mental Health Assessment

Bonnie A. Green

Mental health is a complex topic, even in the absence of cultural differences. To capture that complexity in the form of a measure is even more daunting indeed. The purpose of a mental health measure is to separate normal from abnormal and to assist in determining the extent that mental health care is needed. This chapter provides a review of the challenges faced in measuring mental health within the context of culture. First I provide you with some examples of the challenges and successes psychologists have in assessing mental health while also taking into account culture. However, given the diversity of both mental health topics and measures, along with the diversity of the influence of culture on each of these areas, it would be impossible to cover all critical nuances of this complex landscape. As such, the second section of the chapter is devoted toward some basic though crucial components regarding measurement that need be taken into account before evaluating the validity and culturally sensitivity of a particular mental health assessment.

The idea that a measure of mental health, like an assessment of narcissistic personality disorder behavior or drug abuse, would consistently diagnose one cultural group one way while another a different way, even when there are few differences in the prevalence of such conditions, is not pleasant to think about. Yet many examples abound. For example, when comparing the performance on the Million Clinical Multiaxial Inventory (MCMI) between African-American and White males matched for psychiatric diagnosis Choca, Shanley, Peterson, and VanDenberg (1990) found that 45 of the 175 items on the MCMI did not seem to be measuring the same thing for each of these groups. Moreover, this difference in performance on individual items translated into differential diagnoses of the participants across cultural lines even though the participants were matched for psychiatric diagnosis. African-American males were more likely to be diagnosed with narcissistic and antisocial personality disorder, psychotic delusions, and substance addiction compared to the White participants. Given the selection procedure for the participants, the stark difference in scores and possible diagnosis suggests that this measure may be capturing something different in one culture than in the other. Such differentiations are problematic, as mental health help and progress in research requires accurate assessment.

While some mental health issues cross cultural boundaries (e.g., narcissism and antisocial behavior), others are culturally bound, only being seen within a particular culture. Once such illness is S'eizisman, a mental health condition brought on by strong emotions like rage, anger, sadness, and occasional extreme happiness. As described by Nicolas, DeSilva, Grey, and Gonzalez-Eastep (2006), S'eizisman is only seen in Haitian populations and is accompanied by paralysis that could last hours or days. Blood is believed to rush to the head, resulting in loss of vision, headache, increased blood pressure, stroke, heart attack, and even death. If a pregnant woman is believed to be afflicted with S'eizisman, her developing child is believed to be destined to miscarriage or be permanently harmed. Moreover, nursing mothers who become afflicted with S'eizisman are believed to pass on contaminated breast milk to their offspring.

Haitians tend to alter their behavior to help minimize the likelihood of S'eizisman, including encouraging people to be still following a traumatic experience and providing stressed people with herbal tea and other home remedies believed to keep one from acquiring S'eizisman. Measuring a culturally bound condition like S'eizisman takes on particular challenges. However, simply attempting to assess this mental health condition as a type of anxiety or stress induced disorder will isolate the behaviors and treatments deemed beneficial from their cultural context (Nicolas, DeSilva, Grey, & Gonzalez-Eastep, 2006).

Even though it is challenging, finding or developing a culturally appropriate mental health measures is possible. One such example is a large study designed by Alegria and her colleagues (Alegria et al., 2004a, 2004b). The purpose of the study was to translate a series of mental health measures from English into Asian and Latino languages in order to determine the prevalence of mental health disorders in Asian and Latino populations. In the process of the National Latino and Asian American Study (NLAAS), researchers discovered that by making use of both qualitative measures, like focus groups, and quantitative measures they could emphasize three key components assuring quality measures: cultural relevance, equivalence, and generalizability.

A measure that is to be used cross-culturally should be culturally relevant for each group with which it will be used; that is, it should make sense and be in a form that is comfortable to the person being assessed. The measure should also be culturally equivalent in that the assessment tool should be capturing the same information regardless of the language in which it has been translated or the cultural group for which it is being used. Lastly, the measure should produce results that can be generalized beyond the immediate testing session in that it provides use for diagnosing or predicting future mental health. In making these adjustments in translating measures from English to Spanish and Asian languages, Algeria and her colleagues (2004a, 2004b) did not keep the measures identical, though the construct that they were measuring was the same. Questions were taken out or added to the measure depending on the language in which it was translated to assure the cultural relevance, equivalence and generalizability of the measures. Moreover, at times, multiple Spanish words were used to assure that proper information was conveyed whether a person was speaking Cuban Spanish, Mexican Spanish, or Puerto Rican Spanish. It is this combination of focusing on the purpose of the measure combined with flexibility within the realm of culture and language that results in a measure being designed for cross-cultural use.

Though there is no such thing as a perfect psychological assessment, by understanding the various variables that shape mental health, the universal component, along with the cultural influence, we can arrive at a measure that will be useful. Being aware of measurement will aid your ability to be cross-culturally competent (Allen, 2007).

The Science of Measurement

Psychometrics, the science of measuring psychological phenomenon came out of a philosophical belief in the existence of an "absolute truth," a theoretical orientation called absolutionism. After all, why attempt to measure something that isn't true? By understanding the root of psychometrics, one can further see that from an absolutionistic perspective, culture is not critical (Sam & Moreira, 2002). It is not that absolutionism purports culture has no impact on the mental health constructs to be measured, but an absolute truth would be culturally neutral, as it would be seen in every culture, and not influenced by local customs or norms. As such, an absolutionism perspective shares the idea of cultural neutral influences as found in the etic paradigm.

The etic perspective lends itself to formalized assessment because assessment is precisely all that etic thinking is, a way for scientists to capture what is going on. From an etic perspective, the researcher is the one who establishes the unit of measure, looking for the absolute truth, through an external view (Pike, 1967). Etic analysis results in precise, logical, comprehensive, replicable, falsifiable, and observer independent information (Lett, 1996). For example psychologists believe that in a stressful situation everyone, regardless of their culture, will experience a stress response. Stress elicits a stress response and this is seen cross-culturally. As such, this would correspond with an etic paradigm and absolutionism, and is, as such, measurable as one measure should work regardless of the person being measured. However, there are cultural influences as to what constitutes a stressor as well as how a person is going to behave in the midst of a stress response.

This lends credence to those who believe understanding cannot be taken out of culture; the only true path to scientific understanding is through the emic perspective, where everything is relative based on the culture being studied (Pike, 1967). The emic philosophy is a way of looking at cultural experiences that are regarded as meaningful and appropriate by members of the culture under study. Validation of this information is based on consensus within the culture (Lett, 1996).

Yet, the emic approach lacks the strength of the etic approach. It is because of the strengths and weaknesses of these two perspectives, that Berry (1989) proposed that, in order to understand psychological phenomenon like mental health, the best of both perspectives needed to be integrated.

Building upon this idea of the absolute truth, one can see why measures of mental health constructs, such as anxiety, attempt to get at the truth of those constructs. That truth should be the same regardless of who is measuring it, who is being measured, and why anxiety is being measured. Yet, there are differences in who is measuring, who is being measured, and why something is being measured, and some of these differences are influenced by culture. As such, it should come as little surprise then that the field of psychometrics has lagged in the arena of multiculturalism, in attempting to capture cultural differences, as the focus has been in the truth of the construct, void of culture. Since mental health can only be interpreted in the context of culture (Sánchez-Johnsen & Cuéllar, 2004), the use of psychological assessments needs to come away from an absolutionistic view and toward a multicultural view. A multicultural view, according to Sam and Moreira (2002), is the belief that to understand mental health, one must understand both the universal components, or the etic, as well as the influence of culture, or the emic, on mental health.

Now that we have a basic background regarding psychonomics, its history and some of the challenges we have attempted to measure mental health within the context of culture, we need to look more closely at some key issues in psychometrics: Test construction, measurement error, translations, test administration, and interpretation.

In search of behavioral phenotypes that are etic, or universal to all cultural, Frank et al. (2005) were able to develop a measure for agoraphobia that, through appropriate translation, can capture agoraphobia in multiple cultures (US and Italy). The process of designing their measure is one that started with understanding the construct. By understanding the physiological symptoms of agoraphobia, it became possible to devise an appropriate, cross-cultural measure.

Next, knowledge of the population for which the measure is to be used must be obtained. People who know the population from within can be helpful with the construction of items in the measure. Vogt, King, and King (2004) found that most researchers developing assessment instruments failed to make use of the members of the population being tested during the construction phase of the measure. This is unfortunate because they demonstrated that by speaking with people of the target population regarding the measure being designed, the usefulness of each item on the measure was improved. In their study, Vogt, King, and King (2004) spoke directly to veterans who experienced war. The veterans were involved during the developmental stage of test construction for a measure that was designed to assess war-related stress. They further applied focus groups involving the sample of the population for which the measure was intended. During the focus groups, participants aided in the development of test items based on their personal understanding of the construct or condition being assessed. Since the strength of the overall measure rests with the strength of the individual item, involving people from within a given culture to assist in item design aids in the overall quality of the measure.

The third area of attention with regard to test construction rests on our understanding of the interaction between the construct and culture. One critical area of interaction is that of social desirability. Culture influences what is desirable and what is not. Designing measures that are not influenced by social desirability is a problem psychometricians are currently studying (e.g., Holmes & Hughes, 2007). To date, there is no published account regarding the best method of designing a measure free from social desirability. With any measure that involves self-report, you have the implicit or unconscious component of the construct and the influence of social desirability, which is driven in large part by a person's culture. These come together to form the explicit or conscious report that is provided to the psychologist (Holmes & Hughes, 2007). It is important to be aware of any social desirability influences of a culture on a construct, prior to attempting to measure it. As more is learned in this area of psychometrics, benefit will be translated to the field of cultural psychology. Until that point, awareness is your best tool.

Humanists insist, "It's all about the love!" Though true for humanists, for psychometricians, "It's all about the truth!" When we measure human behavior and mental processes, we are attempting to assess the truth. That is, we are attempting to measure the true level of the measured construct, which is surrounded by a vast sea of error. Though there are many causes of error, it is measurement error that is of greatest concern in this chapter. Measurement error is anything that is being measured that is not the construct you intend to measure. Measurement error is a problem in research, but it can be disastrous for individuals, as "measures" have become the gatekeepers to the future for many people. A test that fails to properly diagnose a person with depression will result in a person being left untreated with the consequences that follows. A person who is following their own cultural norm can be diagnosed as abnormal, and hence as having a mental illness if given a measure that fails to account for those cultural norms. Thus, measurement error could have grave consequences.

Measurement error can either be unsystematic error, that is error that is random, or it can be systematic error, that is error that is consistent in the same direction for the same types of participants. Classical test theory assumes that the error we speak of is unsystematic, that is it is random. The assumptions of classical test theory are true; all that needs to be done to get an idea of the true level of the measured construct, assuming a nondeveloping organism, is for a person to be subjected to a test multiple times, and to find the average of all the performances. The average score will be fairly representative of the truth.

If the measurement error that is masking the true level of the measured construct is indeed unsystematic for everyone, there would be little reason for a chapter such as this one, as in the case of a test of depression there would be the true level of depression and random error. Sometimes people's scores would overestimate their level of depression and other times it would underestimate it and issues like culture would be inconsequential, as culture is not random. Unfortunately, not all error is random. Sometimes, when a measure sets out to capture a construct it picks up something else, error that is systematic. Culture can be one of those things picked up with a measure. Think back to the Million Clinical Multiaxial Inventory (MCMI) that was more likely to diagnose African-American males with narcissism, antisocial personality disorder, drug and alcohol abuse, and psychotic delusions even though they were psychiatrically matched to the White male participants in the study. Clearly, the measure had systematic error, in that African-American and White males had different outcomes on the measure.

Validity is an indication of how well a measure is in capturing the truth. Typically, validity is divided into three different classifications. *Content validity* occurs when each item or piece of an assessment is capturing what it is supposed to be capturing. In the test construction section of this chapter, the benefit of cultural focus groups for determining the item selection or content validity was discussed. *Construct validity* occurs when the assessment is capturing the construct of interest. Below a more detailed explanation of how to evaluate construct validity is discussed. *Criterion validity* occurs when an assessment captures the underlying criterion. With most mental health measures, this criterion comes from the *DSM–IV–TR* (2000). As one would expect, the clearer the definition of the criterion, the better the criterion validity of a measure. Included in the criterion could be culturally specific criterion; as such, the more one understands the culture and the construct, the more likely a measure is to have criterion validity. Focus groups certainly could also assist in the establishment of this validity.

One tool that is receiving a lot of use in validating construct validity and cultural equivalence of a measure designed in one culture and used with another is that of factor analysis. Factor analysis is a statistical tool that psychometricians use to identify the underlying constructs of a measure. So, for example, Furukawa et al. (2005) used the Hamilton Rating Scale for Depression with 5185 individuals diagnosed with major depression in Japan, Europe, and North America. From this, he uncovered that the Hamilton Rating Scale was measuring five different constructs of depression: anhedonia/retardation, guilt/agitation, bodily symptoms, insomnia, and appetite. By separating each cultural group and looking for systematic differences in the constructs, Furukawa et al. was able to evaluate construct validity while demonstrating cultural equivalence. In addition to the use of factor analysis, to assure construct validity one must be vigilant to actively search for signs of cultural influence that could function as systematic error.

Schmitt and Allik (2005) followed a similar format in assessing Rosenberg's Self-esteem scale in 53 different nations. With use of factor analytic type statistics, they were able to identify that this measure had construct validity, cross-culturally. Schmitt and Allik went beyond this statistical application as well, and applied a technique which is more commonly used in experimental psychology to assess content validity. They looked for the presence of hypothesized statistical relationships cross-culturally and found that reported self-esteem levels were associated with whether respondents resided in a collectivistic or an individualistic culture, with people from the latter culture more apt to openly express signs of positive self-esteem. Thus, Schmitt and Allik found a core structure of self-esteem that transcended culture as well as an expected cultural difference in self-esteem based on collectivistic and individualistic cultural influences.

Test bias is a psychometric issue, one that empirically evaluates the presence of systematic error in the test when administered as directed. Test bias should not be confused with test fairness. Test fairness is a social value based on the consequence that interpreting a measure may have on a particular portion of the population (Gregory, 2007). As the importance of testing (e.g., Callet, 2005) becomes more evident, the issue of test fairness becomes more critical. Issues of test fairness were originally raised by Arvey (1972) in that test items could be differentially familiar based on the culture in which one resides. Yet he concluded in his summary of an attempt to devise a culturally fair test, that no measure can be free of culture.

Reliability is another method of determining if a measure is capturing what it is intending. Reliability does this by assuming that all that is consistent and systematic is the construct, while all that is unsystematic is error. However, culture brings systematic changes to constructs. Reliability calculations mistakenly pick up the systematic difference due to culture as the construct being measured. This will provide a false indication that the measure is accurate, given that you have a measure that is capturing two different things: the construct and culture. It is often advisable to use validity measures and not reliability measures as an indication of the quality of a measure.

A great deal of information has been listed regarding psychometric properties and procedures to assure a quality measure. To summarize:

1. To design a quality measure, one must:
    (a) understand the construct being measured;
    (b) know the population to be measured;
    (c) recognize the interaction between the construct and culture (e.g., the influence of social desirability on valid measures.)
2. Measurement error can be systematic or unsystematic.
3. Validity is a way of determining if a measure is satisfying its intended purpose. We discussed three types.
    (a) Content validity is how well each individual item is measuring what it is intended to be measuring.
        • Use of cultural focus groups during the design of test items will help in assuring content validity.

   (b) Construct validity is how well the measure is capturing the construct.

- The better we understand the construct, the better the construct validity.
- Use of factor analysis will assist in evaluation and assuring construct validity.
- Looking for hypothesized relationships to demonstrate that the measure is capturing the construct will help with construct validity.

   (c) Criterion related validity is the evaluation of specific attributes that contribute to the overall construct.

- The more clearly defined the criterion, the better the validity.
- Again, make use of cultural focus groups to identify criterion that may be culturally bound.

4. It is possible that a test can be culturally valid, but lacking in fairness, in that the weight and consequence of a measure may disproportionately hurt one cultural population over another.
5. Culture can become systematic error in a measure.
6. Reliability is only a good indication of minimized measurement error when you know that there is no possibility of systematic error in a measure.
7. Given culture can be a systematic error and reliability can give a false sense of validity by capturing that systematic error, it is never a good idea to rely upon reliability measures as an indication of a quality measure.

Challenges in Translating Measures

Often, when speaking of measures being used cross-culturally, concerns regarding translating measures become apparent. Parsing a part language and culture can be a tricky business. Different cultures think about language differently, impacting how a measure could be communicated to each other. For example, Italians used more adjectives and fewer verbs to describe others, while the reverse was seen in Japanese participants (Maass, Karasawa, Politi, & Suga, 2006). This pattern of language was also seen between Australian and American speakers, using adjectives to describe people, while Koreans used verbs (Kashima, Kashima, Kim, & Gelfand, 2006). This one example highlights the challenges in translating a measure, in that simple translation, word by word, will not assure a culturally equivalent measure as different cultures think about language differently, particularly in regard to thinking about humankind. As such, for many years, people (e.g., Geisinger, 1994) have been calling upon psychologists to assure that measurement instruments are not merely translated but also verified to be communicating and assessing what it is intended to be doing.

Translating a measure from one language into another does not guarantee that the measure is valid. The Child Behavior Checklist (CBCL) has been translated into over 60 languages. In looking at the quality of the CBCL and its ability to accurately diagnose adolescent syndromes, Weiss, Weiss, Suwanlert, and Chaiyasit (2006) found that using American-based syndromes and translating measures into Thai does not result in the measure accurately capturing the syndromes seen in Thai adolescence. Moreover, they found evidence for what they call the syndromal sensitivity model, which asserts that a combination of rewards and punishments that differ cross-culturally can result in certain mental health issues being seen in one culture and not in another. As such, particular caution should be taken with measures that were designed and validated in one culture and language, then translated into another. Verify that the change in the instrument went beyond a mere language translation. Verify that construct validity is reevaluated with the translated measure. Also verify that a new normative sample is used and that this sample is representative of the population for which the translated measure is intended (Geisinger, 1994).

According to Canino and Guarnaccia (1997) building upon the recommendation of others (e.g., Geisinger, 1994), it is important to take into account five key components with translation to assure validity. Firstly, one should assure that the semantic aspect of the measure is equivalent across languages. The meaning of each word, phrase, and question should contain the same semantic information; it should convey the same meaning. The technical method of assessing the individual should also be appropriate for the culture. So, for example in a study that looked at Mini-mental State performance of older African Americans, it was discovered that the less formal education this population had, the more likely they were to be falsely identified as having dementia (Strickland, Longobardi, Alperson, & Andre, 2005). Prior experience to test taking, for this measure, increases performance. There could be cultural differences in the amount of formalized testing a person is exposed to. Issues like this need to be evaluated cross-culturally. The last three components that Canino and Guarnaccia feel need to be included when translating a measure from one language to another align with critical areas of validity: content, criterion, and conceptual. Specifically, one must validate the measure in each culture for which it is intended. As such, the content, or each individual item, should be relevant and measuring the same information regardless of culture. Though what is classified as abnormal may differ from one culture to the next, the criterion for establishing when a person passes from "normal" to "abnormal" must be appropriate for the culture. Lastly, the conceptual, or the underlying theoretical construct, should be what is being measured.

Critical components to be kept in mind when translating a measure:

- Language and culture are strongly intertwined, and yet are not equivalent.
- Simple word for word translation will not assure a quality measure
- Assure there is semantic equivalence between versions

- Make sure the assessment technique is culturally appropriate
- Validate the measure for each translation

The Art and Science of Test Administration and Interpretation

It is incumbent upon all test administrators to select properly validated measures. To do so, you should be aware of the purpose of the measure along with the methods with which it was validated. There are times when you will see measures validated off older versions of the measure. The assumption is, the older version was capturing the construct of interest, as such, if the newer version is also capturing the construct of interest it is highly correlated with the older version. However, let us suppose that the older measure possessed systematic bias toward a particular culture, the newer measure will most likely continue with the same bias. As such, not all forms of validating a measure are equally likely to yield a measure free from a systematic error due to cultural differences. You should also only select measures that have been normed recently and include an appropriate norm group encompassing the culture of interest.

Even the best designed, translated, and validated measure can become a problem if it is poorly administered. A quality measure mandates quality administration. It is critical that tests be administered as they have been designed. Tests are normed and as such interpreted under those conditions (Gregory, 2007). Proper administration of tests are critical to assure cultural fairness of a measure. Even slight changes in the directions can change the construct that is being measured, decreasing content validity (Ployhard & Ehrhart, 2003).

Even with best intentions, problems can arise in test administration. One such problem is when the biases or beliefs of the test administrator alter the performance of the test taker. This is called, interpersonal expectancy effect. Interpersonal expectancy effect was unintentionally discovered by Rosenthal (discussed in Rosenthal, 1994) while he was working on his dissertation. He discovered that because of the way he treated his subjects, they behaved as he had expected them to. The participants' performance was an artifact of how Rosenthal treated them during the study. He quickly realized he had stumbled upon an interesting human phenomenon of interpersonal expectancy effect, where the belief of one person alters how he/she interacts with another, which elicits from that person the very behavior the first person was expecting to see. So, if Jon enters into a situation with Marc, expecting Marc to be irrational, Jon may treat Marc irrationally, causing Marc to behave irrationally. Clearly, when dealing with the assessment of mental health, the beliefs of the person administering the test should not be the reason why an individual is classified as possessing a mental illness or not, yet, with interpersonal expectancy effect, this is a real possibility. Thus, there is a need for mental health professionals to openly and readily assess their own biases.

The first guideline of the American Psychological Association's multicultural guidelines for psychologists (APA, 2002) states that "Psychologists are encouraged to recognized that, as cultural beings, they may hold attitudes and beliefs that can detrimentally influence their perceptions of and interactions with individuals who are ethnically and racially different from themselves" (p. 17). The best way to minimize assessors' bias is to be as fully aware as you can be of your own thoughts regarding differences in people. Also, assuring implementing all assessments in the prescribed fashion will help minimize any bias. However, it is crucial that mental health professionals acknowledge that they may not be aware of their own personal biases. Not all beliefs are explicit attitudes, attitudes of which you are consciously aware. A study on the presence of implicit attitudes, attitudes of which are not award, regarding White and Black race revealed that as we go from six years of age into adulthood, we possess fewer negative explicit attitudes toward someone of another race (Baron & Banaji, 2006). Our implicit negative attitudes, however, do not diminish with age. That is, though we may no longer be consciously aware of having negative attitudes regarding other races, we still may have negative attitudes towards another race and simply not be aware of our attitudes.

Cultural differences tend to be more pronounced in studies that compare implicit attitudes cross-culturally and less pronounced when explicit attitudes are compared cross-culturally (Heine & Norenzayan, 2006). As such, measures that capture implicit components of mental processes, that is thoughts, feelings, memories, attitudes, and the like, that are not available to consciousness, will be critical in this next stage of research in cultural psychology.

Ultimately, we want to avoid artifacts from test administration. Proper test administration is critical as any deviation from the prescribed method of assessment is adding to the error of the measure, decreasing validity. Yet, even when attempting to provide informal feedback to a person being assessed, their behavior can be altered impacting their performance on the assessment. As an example, when female Japanese college students were provided with contrived feedback regarding their performance on a personality assessment, women who were told they scored as extrovert behaved in an extroverted fashion and later characterized the false feedback of them being extroverts as an accurate assessment (Sakamoto, Miura, Sakamoto, & Mori, 2000).

Once a test is administered, the results must also be interpreted. It is important that all responses be interpreted within the context of culture. This is particularly true for children as they can be more impacted by their culture (Canino & Guarnaccia, 1997) given their limited experience with other cultures. This includes the possibility of people responding a particular way due to their culture, where their responses are not fully reflecting their beliefs, but are reflecting an aspect of their culture. This is termed, response bias or response style. One such bias is the moderacy response style which is a tendency for an individual or a group of people from one culture to give responses that lean toward the center of a scale, compared to other cultures. For example, Chen, Lee, and Stevenson (1995) conducted a study that revealed that people from collectivistic cultures, like Japan and China, are more apt to respond using the midpoint options. So, for example, if a client is asked to answer a question like, "I am receiving enough sleep," with the responses being either strongly agree, agree, somewhat agree, somewhat disagree, disagree, or strongly disagree, people from collectivistic cultures would be more likely to use the answers somewhat agree or somewhat disagree, whereas people from individualistic cultures are more likely to answer with strongly agree or strongly disagree. Awareness of possible response biases could assist in the interpretation of a measure.

The interpretation of Likert scale questions needs to be carefully evaluated for a possible reference-group effect that occurs when members from different cultural groups use a different reference point in which to make judgments on self-report questions (Heine, Lehman, Peng, & Greenholtz, 2002; Peng, Nisbet, & Wong, 1997). In other words, Sri Lankans would compare themselves to Sri Lankans while Cherokee would compare themselves to Cherokee.

Even the implicit attitude of the test taker can have an adverse effect. When thinking about cultural differences in performance, one attitude that could decrease the validity of a measure, increasing the bias, is that of stereotype threat (Wicherts, Dolan, & Hessen, 2005). A stereotype threat is a belief a person holds with regard to others' stereotypical thinking of him/her. If their behavior coincides with the negative stereotypical belief held by others, they may feel others are viewing them stereotypically which can lead to feelings of self-consciousness and anxiety, thus interfering with test performance (Osborne, 2007). Wicherts, Dolan, and Hessen did find that if a test taker is experiencing a stereotype threat, the measure will not be a valid one and will, instead, include a bias from the stereotype threat. The phenomenon of stereotype threat is even more observable in high performing minority test takers. There are some ways to counteract stereotype threat: individual awareness on the part of the test taking and test provider, affirmation provided to the test taker by the test provider, and the increase of exposure to others in the stereotype group.

To summarize, the important points regarding test administration and interpretation are:

1. Proper test selection is key, keeping in mind the following:
   - purpose of the measure;
   - population for which the measure was design and normed;
   - recentness of norming the measure;
   - test construction and/or translation that involves members of the culture of interest;
   - appropriate validation that is culturally inclusive.
2. Always follow the prescribed directions in administering the measure, as alterations in the standardization will decrease the validity of the measure.
3. Be aware of your own cultural biases and behavior, recognizing:
   - Not all biases are available to consciousness (explicit attitudes). Implicit biases (not available to consciousness) can be present and tend to be both stronger and longer lasting than explicit biases.

- Your personal biases can impact the person you are measuring. This is called interpersonal expectancy effect.
- Even subtle, informal feedback can change the behavior and beliefs of a person being assessed.

4. Recognize that cultural differences can result in how a person responds to a measure as is seen in the moderacy response style, where people from collectivistic cultures are more likely to respond using midpoint choices while people from individualistic cultures are more likely to respond using extreme choices.
5. When asked to compare oneself to others, there is a natural tendency for people to select, as their reference group, others from their own culture. This is referred to as a reference group effect.
6. Stereotype threat, a belief that a person holds with regard to others stereotypical thinking of him/her, can result in increased anxiety and a change in behavior.

In Closing

Measuring anything as complex as mental health, particularly in the context of cultural differences, will present a host of challenges. However, given the importance of accurate assessment, failure is not an option. With careful consideration regarding mental health constructs, cultural influence, and the interaction each has on the other, coupled with a strong understanding of psychometric principles, we can have better measures, creating increased understanding of mental health within the context of culture.

REFERENCES

Alegria, M., Takeuchi, D., Canino, G., et al. (2004a). Considering context, place and culture: The National Latino and Asian American Study. *International Journal of Methods in Psychiatric Research, 13*, 208–220.

Algeria, M., Vila, D., Woo, M., et al. (2004b). Cultural relevance and equivalence in the NLAAS instrument: Integrating etic and emic in the development of cross-cultural measures for a psychiatric epidemiology and service study of Latinos. *International Journal of Methods in Psychiatric Research, 13*, 270–288.

Allen, J. (2007). A multicultural assessment supervision model to guide research and practice. *Professional Psychology: Research and Practice, 38*, 248–258.

American Psychological Association (2002). Guidelines on multicultural education, training, research, practice, and organizational change for psychologists. http://www.apa.org/pi/multiculturalguidelines.pdf

Arvey, R. D. (1972). Some comments on culture fair test. *Personnel Psychology, 25*, 433–448.

Baron, A. S., & Banaji, M. R. (2006). The development of implicit attitudes: Evidence of race evaluation from age 6 and 10 and adulthood. *Psychological Science, 17*, 53–58.

Berry, J. W. (1989). Imposed etics-emics-derived etics: The operationalization of a compelling idea *International Journal of Psychology, 24,* 721–735.

Canino, G., & Guarnaccia, P. (1997). Methological challenges in the assessment of Hispanic children and adolescents. *Applied Developmental Science, 1,* 124–134.

Claes, R., Beheydt, C., & Lemmens, B. (2005). Unidimensionality of abbreviated proactive personality scale across culture. *Applied Psychology: An International Review, 54,* 476–489.

Callet, V. J. (2005). High-stakes testing: Does the California high school exit exam measure up? *Language Assessment Quarterly, 2,* 289–307.

Chen, C., Lee, S., & Stevenson, H. W. (1995). Response style and cross cultural comparison among East Asians and North American students. *Psychological Science, 6,* 170–175.

Choca, J. P., Shanley, L. A., Peterson, C. A., & Van Denberg, E. (1990). Racial bias and the MCMI. *Journal of Personality Assessment, 54,* 479–90.

DSM–IV–TR (2000). *Diagnostic and statistical manual of mental health disorders* (4th ed., text revision). Washington, DC: American Psychiatric Association.

Frank, E., Shear, M. K., Rucci, P., et al. (2005). Cross cultural validity of the structured clinical interview for panic-agoraphobic spectrum. *Social Psychiatry and Psychiatric Epidemiology, 40,* 283–290.

Furukawa, T. A., Streiner, D. L., Azuma, H., et al. (2005) Cross-cultural equivalence in depression assessment: Japan-Europe-North American study. *Acta Psychiatrica Scandanavica, 112,* 279–285.

Geisinger, K. F. (1994). Cross-cultural normative assessment: Translation and adaptation issues influencing the normative interpretation of assessment instruments. *Psychological Assessment, 6,* 304–312.

Gregory, R. J. (2007). *Psychological testing: History, principles, and application* (5th ed.). Boston: Allyn & Bacon.

Heine, S. J., Lehman, D. R., Peng, K., & Greenholtz, J. (2002). What's wrong with cross cultural comparisons of subjective Likert scales?: The reference group effect. *Journal of Personality and Social Psychology, 82,* 903–918.

Heine, S. J., & Norenzayan, A. (2006). Toward a psychological science for a cultural species. *Perspectives on Psychological Science, 1,* 251–269.

Holmes, J., & Hughes, L. (2007). The reactivity of explicit racial attitude measures: An examination of scale transparency. *Eastern Psychological Association Conference,* March 22–26, 2007, Philadelphia, PA.

Kashima, Y., Kashima, E. S., Kim, U., & Gelfand, M. (2006). Describing the social world: How is a person, a group, and a relationship described in the East and West? *Journal of Experimental Social Psychology, 42,* 388–396.

Lett, J. (1996). Emic/etic distinctions. In D. Levineson & M. Ember (Eds.), *Encyclopedia of cultural anthropology* (pp. 382–383). New York: Henry Holt Co.

Maass, A., Karasawa, M., Politi, F., & Suga, S. (2006). Do verbs and adjectives play different roles in different cultures? A cross-linguistic analysis of person representation. *Journal of Personality and Social Psychology, 90,* 734–750.

Malcarne, V. L., Chavira, D. A., Fernandez, S., & Liu, P. J. (2006). The scale of ethnic experience: Development and psychometric properties. *Journal of Personality Assessment, 86,* 150–161.

Nicolas, G., DeSilva, A. M., Grey, K. S., & Gonzales-Eastep, D. (2006). Using a multicultural lens to understand illnesses among Haitians living in America. *Professional Psychology: Research and Practice, 37,* 702–707.

Norenzayan, A., & Heine, S. J. (2005). Psychological universals: What are they and how can we know? *Psychological Bulletin, 131,* 763–784.

Osborne, J. W. (2007). Linking stereotype threat and anxiety. *Educational Psychology, 27,* 135–154.

Peng, K., Nisbett, R. E., & Wong, N. Y. C. (1997). Validity problems comparing values across cultures and possible solutions. *Psychological Methods, 2,* 329–344.

Pike, K. L. (1967). *Language in relation to a unified theory of the structure of human behavior* (2nd ed.). Hague: Mourton De Gruyter.

Ployhart, R. E., & Ehrhart, M. G. (2003). Be careful what you ask for: Effects of response instruction on construct validity of situational judgment tests. *International Journal of Selection and Assessment, 11 (1),* 1–16.

Rosenthal, R. (1994). Interpersonal expectancy effect: A 30 year perspective. *Current Direction of Psychological Science, 3,* 176–179.

Sakamoto, A., Miura, S. Sakamoto, K., & Mori, T. (2000). Popular psychological tests and self-fulfilling prophecy: An experiment of Japanese female undergraduate students. *Asian Journal of Social Psychology, 3,* 107–124.

Sam, D. L., & Moreira, V. (2002). The mutual embeddedness of culture and mental illness. In W. J. Lonner, D. L. Dinnel, S. A. Hayes, & D. N. Sattler (Eds.), *Online readings in psychology and culture.* Western Washington University, Department of Psychology, Center for Cross-Cultural Research. Website: *www.wwu.edu/~culture*

Sánchez-Johnsen, L. A. P., & Cuéllar, I. (2004). Culturally competent assessment and evaluation. In C. Negy (Ed.), *Cross-cultural psychotherapy.* Reno, NV: Bent Tree Press.

Schmitt, D. P., & Allik, J. (2005) Simultaneous administration of the Rosenberg Self-esteem Scale in 53 nations: Exploring the universal and cultural-specific features of global self esteem. *Journal of Personality and Social Psychology, 89,* 623–642.

Strickland, T. L., Longobardi, P. G., Alperson, B. L., & Andre, K. (2005). Mini-mental state and cognistat performance in an older adult African American sample. *Clinical Neuropsychologist, 19,* 87–98.

Tilfors, M. Why do some individuals develop social phobias? A review with emphasis on neurobiological influences. *Nordic Journal of Psychiatry, 58,* 367–376.

Vogt, D. S., King, D. W, & King, L. A. (2004). Focus groups in psychological assessment: Enhancing content validity by consulting members of the target population. *Psychological Assessment, 16,* 231–243.

Weiss, J. R., Weiss, B., Suwanlert, S., & Chaiyasit, W. (2006). Culture and youth psychopathology: Testing the syndromal sensitivity model in Thai and American adolescents. *Journal of Counseling and Clinical Psychology, 74,* 1098–1107.

Wicherts, J. M., Dolan, C. V., & Hessen, D. J. (2005). Sterotype threat and group differences in test performance: A question of measurement invariance. *Journal of Personality and Social Psychology, 89,* 696–716.

3

Stress and Mental Health

Regan A. R. Gurung and
Angela Roethel-Wendorf

Stress is a term that everyone uses freely and that we all seem to understand naturally. It is also one of the twenty-first century's most potent health hazards. A thorough understanding of the nature of stress helps provide a better understanding of both physical and psychological health and is particularly helpful in the understanding of the etiology of mental illness. Stress can play a role both in the development of a disorder and in the recovery from it. Given that many mental disorders have physiological concomitants, the stress experience may interact with and exacerbate the mental illness. In this vein, the factor that has not received enough attention is the role played by culture. Culture influences both the appraisal and experience of stress. It is therefore no surprise that the interaction of stress and culture can play a major role in mental health. In this chapter we will first provide a description of the phenomenon of stress with a look at key contributing factors, measurement issues, and major types and theories of stress. Next we will review the literature on cultural differences in stress, highlighting how this can influence mental health.

What is Stress?

Stress can be defined in many different ways (see Gurung, 2006 for a review). Many early definitions of stress rely heavily on biological activity. Cannon (1929) viewed stress as the biological mobilization of the body for action, involving sympathetic activation and endocrine activity. Selye (1956) similarly saw stress as the activation of a host of physiological systems. Later theorists added more psychological components to the process of stress (e.g., Lazarus, 1966). Although these different definitions have all been well supported, the easiest way to define stress and one that allows for subjective differences and allows for physiological and psychological components is: stress is the upsetting of homeostasis (Cannon, 1929) or a state of balance within one's body.

Main Theories of Stress

Cannon's Fight or Flight Theory

Walter Cannon applied the concept of homeostasis to the study of human interactions with the environment (Cannon, 1914). Specifically, he studied how stressors affect the sympathetic nervous system (SNS). His basic idea is when under stress SNS activation increases circulation, respiration, and metabolism, all factors that fuel your body to ready it either to fight the stressor or flee. The SNS also turns off certain systems in response to stress. The SNS down regulates (turns off) the digestive system and the reproductive system in times of stress. The SNS in turn activates the adrenal glands that secrete epinephrine and norepinephrine (the catecholamines). This fight-or-flight system has eight clear-cut effects (Guyton, 1977). Blood pressure, blood flow to large muscles, total energy consumption, blood glucose concentration, energy release in the muscles, muscular strength, mental activity, and the rate of blood coagulation all increase.

Taylor et al.'s Tend-and-Befriend theory

Shelley Taylor and colleagues (Taylor, Klein, Lewis, Gruenewald, Gurung, & Updegraff, 2000; Taylor, Lewis, Gruenewald, Gurung, Updegraff, & Klein, 2002) suggested that women tend-and-befriend in addition to fighting or fleeing. Diverse findings in the stress literature just do not fit with the fight-or-flight model. The fight or flight model assumes that men and women faced the same challenges in our evolutionary history. However, this was not true. Females have always been primary caregivers of infants due to their greater investment in giving birth (a minimum investment of nine months for women versus minutes for men). Men have easily been able to fight or flee, but women often had to look after infants. If women fought and lost they would leave their infant defenseless. If women ran they would either have to leave their infant behind or the weight of the infant would surely slow them down and lead to capture. Instead, Taylor et al. (2000) argued that women developed additional stress responses aimed to protect, calm, and quiet the child, to remove it from harm's way (i.e., tending), and to marshal resources to help. Essentially, women create social networks to provide resources and protection for themselves and their infants (i.e., befriending). The tend-and-befriend response, thus, provides more reasonable stress responses for females than the basic fight or flight theory. This new theory builds on the brain's attachment/caregiving system, which counteracts the metabolic activity associated with the traditional fight-or-flight stress response – increased heart rate, blood pressure and cortisol levels – and leads to nurturing and affiliative behavior.

Existing evidence from research with nonhuman animals, neuroendocrine studies, and human-based social psychology supports this new theory. Neuroendocrine research shows that although women show the same immediate hormonal and sympathetic nervous system response to acute stress, other factors intervene to make fight-or-flight less likely in females. In terms of the fight response, while male aggression appears to be driven by hormones such as testosterone, female aggression is not. In fact, a major female hormone, oxytocin, actually counteracts the effects of stress chemicals such as cortisol and the catecholamines. Oxytocin inhibits flight and enhances relaxation, reduces fearfulness and decreases the other stress responses typical to the fight-or-flight response. Supporting the role of oxytocin in befriending, blocking oxytocin in women actually makes them spend less time with their friends (Jamner, Alberts, Leigh, & Klein, 1998).

Tending is observed in animal studies when rat pups are removed from their nest for brief periods – a stressful situation for pups and mothers – and then returned. The mothers immediately move to soothe their pups by licking, grooming, and nursing them (Meaney, 2001). Similar behaviors are seen in sheep (Kendrick et al., 1997) and monkeys (Martel et al., 1993). In humans, breastfeeding mothers are found to be calmer (Uvnäs-Moberg, 1996), and touch have been shown to soothe both the mother and infant (Field, 1996). In clear support of the theory (and relating to the discussion of work stress in the chapter by Eshun & Kelley – Chapter 4, this volume) Repetti and Wood (1997) showed on the one hand, that after a stressful day on the job, men want to be left alone and often fight with their spouses and kids. Women, on the other hand, actually tended when stressed, spending more time with their kids and having more physical contact with them.

Seyle's General Adaptation Syndrome

Hans Seyle (1956) exposed rats to a variety of stressors such as extreme heat and cold, sounds, and rain and found that in every case, the rats developed ulcers. Seyle concluded that organisms must have a general nonspecific response, a general adaptation syndrome, to a variety of stressful events. Specifically, he hypothesized that no matter what the stressor, the body would react in the same way, and theorized that these responses were driven by the hypothalamic-pituitary-adrenal (HPA) axis.

The first part of the HPA sequence of activation resembles the characteristics of SAM activation. The hypothalamus activates the pituitary gland that then activates the adrenal gland. The difference in Seyle's theory is that it is a different part of the adrenal gland, the cortex, which gets activated. The cortex is the outer part of the adrenal gland (the medulla in SAM activation is the inner part) and secretes a class of hormones called corticosteroids. The major hormone in this class is cortisol (hydrocortisone). Cortisol generates energy to deal with the stressor.

Seyle argued that organisms have a general way of responding to all stressors, which he called a General Adaptation Syndrome (GAS). When faced with a stressor, whether a wild animal, a threatening mugger, or intense cold, the body first goes into a state of alarm. HPA activation takes place and the body attempts to cope with the stressor during a period of resistance. If the stressor persists for too long, the body breaks down in a state of exhaustion. Many acute or short-term stressors can be successfully dealt with in the resistance stage. Chronic or long-term stressors drive us to exhaustion. Chronic stressors can exert the true physiological and psychological damage on human bodies.

Lazarus' Cognitive Appraisal Model

Richard Lazarus (1966) devised the first psychological model of stress. Lazarus saw stress as the imbalance between the demands placed on the individual and that individual's resources to cope. He argued that the experience of stress differed significantly across individuals depending on how they interpreted the event and the outcome of a specific sequence of thinking patterns called appraisals.

All of us are faced with demands. According to Lazarus, these demands are just *events* until *we deem them* to be stressful. The main cognitive process at work here is that of making *appraisals*. Lazarus suggested that we make two major types of appraisals when we face any potentially stressful event. During primary appraisals, we ascertain whether the event positive, is negative, or neutral, and if negative, if it is harmful, threatening, or challenging. A harm (or harm-loss) appraisal is made when we expect to lose or actually lose something of great personal significance. For example, when we break up a close relationship we lose a confidant. The event can involve the loss of psychological aspects like support from the ex-partner or love of a parent who is dying, harm to one's self-esteem with the loss of a job, or even physical harm and loss like the diagnosis of a terminal illness. Threat appraisals are made when we believe the event will be extremely demanding and will put ourselves at risk for damage. If you think that your bad performance on an upcoming project can severely ruin your reputation or that taking part in a certain race will hurt your body, you are seeing the project or race as a threat. Challenge appraisals occur in situations when we believe that we can grow from dealing with the event and may even look at the positive ways that we can benefit from an event. For example, you can view an exam as harmful to your self-esteem and a threat if you expect to do badly or as a challenge to your intelligence and how much you have studied. A primary appraisal can be heavily influenced by the stake we have in the outcome of the event (Lazarus, 1991).

After we make a primary appraisal, we assess whether or not we have the necessary resources to cope with the event. During secondary appraisal we essentially determine whether we can deal with the event and how we can cope. We may think about the social support we have, who can help us, and what exactly can be done. We are asking ourselves the question, "Do I have what it takes to cope?" The answer is critical. If our answer is no and we appraise the event as harmful and threatening and determine that we do not have the resources to cope, then we appraise the event as a stressor. If we appraise the event as a challenge and feel we have the resources to deal with it, the event remains just that, an event. All along this process there is often cognitive reappraisal taking place where we can change how we view the situation.

The Role of Culture

Given the central role of appraisal to the process of stress, anything that influences your appraisals correspondingly can influence how much stress you experience. One major influence on appraisals is culture. Different cultural groups have different expectations for various aspects of life and these different expectations can make a low-threat event to one cultural group be a high-threat event to another group. Culture also influences the experience of stress. For example, everyone in the United States is not treated the same way. Therefore, members of some cultural groups may experience more stress than others (Contrada et al., 2000).

Together with age and gender cultural differences, some of the most critical differences in the experience of stress are due to race and ethnicity. It may be stressful for a White European American to live in a predominantly African-American neighborhood or for an African American to live in a predominantly White European American neighborhood. The United States of America has made many advances since the segregated days of the sixties, but we still have a long way to go. Prejudice and stereotyping often rear their ugly heads in our society. Many minority groups experience high levels of stress because of their ethnicity, race, or religious beliefs. Many cities in America are enclaves for certain ethnic groups that may make outsiders feel unwelcome. For example, driving through a Chinatown in New York, Toronto, or San Francisco and not being Chinese, or strolling through little Havana in Miami and not being Cuban, or through little Italy in Boston and not being Italian, can be stressful to many. Of course, a large part of the stress may be in the mind of the perceiver, but real or not, a perception of stress is bad enough for our bodies.

Cultural differences in appraisal and in exposure to situations have led to the formulation of multicultural models of the stress process. Hobfoll (1989) points our attention to how the appraisal process can be biased by a range of conscious and nonconscious processes, such as cultural and familial norms. If your family has raised you to fear a certain group, pulling you out of the path of an approaching person of color, you are going to be conditioned to fear persons of that group. Discrimination and prejudice have important consequences for the mental health of minority individuals and will be dealt with in more detail shortly.

Slavin, Rainer, McCreary, and Gowda (1991) expanded Lazarus's (Lazarus & Folkman, 1984) cognitive-appraisal model of stress to include a number of culture-specific dimensions. Slavin et al. (1991) argue that the occurrence of potentially stressful events can vary based on minority status, discrimination, or specific cultural customs. Furthermore, the primary appraisal of the occurring event can be biased by how the culture interprets the event. Similarly, the secondary appraisal, coping efforts, and final outcomes can be modified by the culture of the individual. For example, some cultural groups (e.g., Mexican and African Americans) have closer family ties and more active social support networks that could influence secondary appraisals. These cultural differences can even be seen at the level of the family (influenced by but not necessarily completely due to race or ethnicity). Some family cultural environments, based on the way the parents raise their kids, can be a lot more stressful than others. Families where both the parents are always fighting or where low socio-economic levels lead to hardships can be stressful for families (Repetti, Taylor, & Seeman, 2002). Many other factors contribute to the appraisals of events (such as the duration of the event, whether it is positive or negative, and how controllable it is) but a full discussion of these factors are beyond the scope of this chapter.

Consequences of Stress

Stress can have direct physiological effects on the body (e.g., suppression of the immune system and neuronal damage), direct cognitive and behavioral effects (e.g., distraction and memory loss), and secondary effects by exacer-bating illnesses, making them worse and delaying recovery (see Dougall & Baum, 2002).

Most of the early major theories of stress (e.g., Selye and Cannon) paid a lot of attention to the physiological changes in the body that accompany the experience of stress. There is a good reason for that. A lot happens in our body when we get stressed. For example, the sympathetic nervous system has connections all over the body (nerves project all over the body from the brain and spinal cord) from sweat gland to muscles and hair follicles, all of which are stimulated to some extent during stress. We have also discussed the two main systems that are activated: the hypothalamic-pituitary-adrenal (HPA) releasing corticosteroids and the sympathetic-adrenomedullary (SAM) releas-ing norepinephrine and epinephrine. From a practical standpoint the activa-tion of these systems is important and critical. They prepare our bodies to deal with the stressor. A problem arises when we experience stress for a long time. Chronic, long-term stressors cause wear and tear on body systems lead-ing to tissue damage and irregular responding. How long is too long? The answer to that question depends on the individual. Let us not forget that the potentially stressful event can be acute or chronic, a person's appraisal and awareness of the stressor can be acute or chronic, and the actual mental and physiological consequences can be acute or chronic (Baum, O'Keefe, & Davidson, 1990).

Chronic stress can lead to other physiological consequences. Some people develop heart problems or loss of an appetite. Others have sexual problems (e.g., men are unable to have or maintain an erection), develop skin problems (e.g., rashes) or nervous ticks (e.g., uncontrollable jerky movements or winking). Chronic stress is a problem for many people and can be either objective (living in a noisy neighborhood), or subjective (overworking week after week and month after month). Going beyond physiology, stress makes us act, feel, and think differently. Paying bills on time, remembering appointments, taking medicines, watering plants or caring for a pet can all be negatively influenced (Baba, Jamal, & Tourigny, 1998; McNally, 1997). Obviously, the quality of work and the nature of interactions with friends and colleagues can also suffer. In some cases, people may not be able to sleep and may experience changes in their eating and drinking behavior (Conway, Vickers, Weid, & Rahe, 1981; Mellman, 1997).

Stress and Psychopathology: The Diathesis-Stress Model

The relationship between stress and psychopathology has been well documented in children and adolescents (see Compas et al., 2001; Lewinsohn, Joiner, & Rohde, 2001) and adults (Hammen, 2003; Mazure, 1998; Segrin, 1999). Yet, not everyone who experiences stressful life events and chronic stress develops psychological disorders.

To explain this, one of the main frameworks in which the etiology of psychopathology is described is through the diathesis-stress model. This multidimensional model, first described in the context of schizophrenia (Bleuler, 1963; Rosenthal, 1970) involves a relationship between vulnerable predispositions (diathesis) and stress as contributors to the development of psychopathology. The theory posits that stress may serve as an activator of the diathesis, leading to the development and manifestation of psychopathology (Monroe & Simons, 1991). Individuals with a diathesis who are exposed to significant stress may be more likely to develop mental disorders than individuals who do not have similar predispositions (Monroe & Simons, 1991).

Both social and biological sources of stress have been proposed to activate the diathesis (Walker & Diforio, 1997) and the diathesis-stress model has most commonly been used to discuss the development of schizophrenia as well as the affective disorders, such as the depressive disorders, bipolar disorder, and anxiety disorders.

For example, in depression, studies suggest an interaction between a diathesis of cognitive distortions and stressful life events (Robins & Block, 1989). Other studies have found that poor self-concept (Hammen, 1988) and problematic coping strategies such as rumination (Nolen-Hoeksema, 1987) may also comprise the cognitive diathesis for depression. Stressful life events have also been associated with bipolar disorder, shown to precede the onset of manic episodes and influence the course of treatment of this disorder (Johnson & Roberts, 1995). A trait or temperament diathesis of "negative affectivity" has been described in the development of anxiety disorders (see Zinbarg & Barlow, 1996).

Stress activates the diathesis in certain individuals who possess this diathesis, and the result may be the development of an anxiety disorder.

For individuals suffering from a mental disorder, the occurrence of stressful life events may act to further sensitize the individual to subsequent stressful life events and may initiate future episodes or relapse of the mental disorder, as seen with major depressive disorder (Harkness, Bruce, & Lumley, 2006; Mazure, 1998; Monroe & Harkness, 2005; Post, 1992) and schizophrenia (Ventura, Nuechterlein, Lukoff, & Hardesty, 1989).

Culture as a Critical Stressor

Culture may act as a stressor in the diathesis-stress model of psychopathology, activating certain vulnerabilities and predispositions which may lead to the emergence of psychopathology. In a study comparing differences in psychological distress, social stress, and resources in a sample of culturally diverse adolescents, Hispanic and Asian Americans reported higher levels of social stress, were more likely to experience psychological distress, and had lower scores on resources in the context of family, coping, self-esteem, and socioeconomic status than European Americans. Furthermore, compared to European Americans, Hispanic and African Americans had an increased likelihood of experiencing social stress (Choi, Meininger, & Roberts, 2006).

The interaction between physical and mental stressors and mental health issues are clearly seen in studies of specific ethnic groups such as American Indians. American Indians have a high risk of developing mental health disorders and have higher numbers of this population in need of mental health services (Harris, Edlund, & Larson, 2005; Nelson, McCoy, Stetter, & Vanderwagen, 1992). Two major studies document the magnitude of this problem. Data from the National Health Interview Survey indicated that American Indians were significantly more likely to report experiencing recent "serious psychological distress" and feelings of helplessness compared to all other ethnic groups surveyed (Barnes, Adams, & Powell-Griner, 2005). Data from the Behavioral Risk Factor Surveillance System (BRFSS) regarding health-related quality of life show that during the years 2000–2004, American Indians had experienced the greatest mean number of mentally unhealthy days per month (4.8), and experienced the greatest percentage of frequent mental distress, defined as 14 or more unhealthy days in a month (15.1 percent) compared to all the other ethnic groups in the nationwide sample (Centers for Disease Control and Prevention, 2005). As a general survey of the mental health prevalence in American Indian populations living on or near a reservation in the Northern Plains and the Southwest area of the United States, Beals et al. (2005) found that diagnoses of alcohol dependence, posttraumatic stress disorder, and depression were the most prevalent *DSM–IV* diagnoses. American Indians in both tribes had a higher prevalence of PTSD, higher prevalence of substance abuse, and lower prevalence of depression, as compared to a nationally representative survey documenting the prevalence of mental health disorders.

Perceived Discrimination

One of the biggest cultural chronic stressors that has serious implications for the development and treatment of mental illness is perceived discrimination. The current emphasis of research in race-based discrimination spans disciplines such as sociology, psychology, and neuroscience. For example, Mays, Cochran, and Barnes (2007) describe and review current perspectives in a comprehensive approach for understanding the mediating and moderating variables in the relationship between race-based discrimination and health disparities. Specifically, these perspectives are social spaces and environments, family environments and development, and physiological approaches. In a nationally representative study of discrimination viewed in the context of "major discrimination" and "day-to-day perceived discrimination," it was found that for all races, "major discrimination" was significantly correlated with psychological distress and major depression, while "day-to-day perceived discrimination" was significantly associated with the development of emotional problems and mental disorders such as psychological distress, depression, and generalized anxiety disorder (Kessler et al., 1999).

The link between perceived discrimination and depression is most common and has been found in a number of ethnic groups (Moradi & Risco, 2006). In a study examining the relationship between perceived discrimination and depression and moderating variables of coping, acculturation, and ethnic social support in a sample of Korean immigrants living in Canada, Noh & Kaspar (2003) found a significant association between perceived discrimination and depression. The data also indicate that the use of problem-focused coping moderated the impact of perceived discrimination such that frequent problem-focused coping in the context of personal confrontation was associated with fewer depressive symptoms. Conversely, the use of emotion-focused coping was associated with more depressive symptoms. However, the utilization of ethnic social support moderated the relationship between perceived discrimination, emotion-focused coping, and depressive symptoms. Individuals who used emotion-focused coping frequently and had more ethnic social support had fewer depressive symptoms, as compared to others who had less ethnic social support and more depressive symptoms (Noh et al., 1999; Noh & Kaspar, 2003).

A significant association between perceived discrimination and depressive symptoms was also seen in a sample of Mexican immigrants and US-born individuals of Mexican descent in California. Mexican immigrants who were highly acculturated were the most likely to have experienced perceived discrimination, followed by less acculturated immigrants, and US-born individuals of Mexican descent who were the least likely to have experienced perceived discrimination (Finch, Kolody, & Vega, 2000). Perceived discrimination was also associated with depressive symptoms in a sample of American Indians in the upper Midwest (Whitbeck et al., 2002). However, involvement in traditional practices such as participation in traditional activities such as powwows and knowledge and use of tribal languages (reflecting measures of cultural identification) decreased the association between discrimination and depression (Whitbeck et al., 2002).

There is some evidence that the effects of discrimination stress can have a stronger effect on men. Utsey, Payne, Jackson, and Jones (2002) found gender differences in the relationships among race-related stress, quality of life, and life satisfaction in a sample of elderly African Americans. Males in this sample had significantly higher scores than females for race-related stress in the context of institutional racism and collective racism. Data also indicated a significant relationship between institutional racism as a predictor of quality of life and life satisfaction; higher ratings of race-related stress attributed to institutional racism predicted a lower rating of quality of life and life satisfaction.

Perceived discrimination has also been studied in the relationship with mental health service utilization. Spencer and Chen (2004) found that discrimination played a role in informal help-seeking in a population of Chinese Americans. Sources of informal services for emotional problems could be considered as primarily help from friends and relatives (ethnic social support) or from traditional practitioners or physicians. In this study, subjects who reported experiencing language-based discrimination (i.e., poor treatment due to language barriers) were more likely to use informal support services for emotional problems. Additionally, there were significant gender differences. Females in the sample were more likely than males to seek informal services and help.

The negative effects of discrimination go beyond the ethnic and racial aspects of culture. Individuals in sexual minority groups may be at increased risk for suffering from mental disorders. Studies have shown that there is a higher prevalence of mental health disorders among lesbian, gay, and bisexual populations. Explanations for the increased prevalence may include sources of minority stress such as prejudice, stigmatization, and discrimination (see Meyer, 2003). A study by Diaz et al. (2001) found that social discrimination was a strong predictor of mental health symptoms and psychological stress in a sample of gay and bisexual men in three large US cities. Furthermore, social isolation and low-self-esteem were two sources of stress identified which may be viewed in the context of stemming from social discrimination.

Other stressors can compromise mental health such as socioeconomic status. A study by Rosen et al. (2003) examined the prevalence of psychiatric disorders and substance abuse in a sample of Caucasian and African-American single mothers and found that being white and on welfare increased the risk of developing mental health problems. Very often low SES participants live in high-crime neighborhoods which can also be a source of stress as it contributes to mental health outcomes. Neighborhoods that have areas of concentrated poverty, disorder, and low cohesion may be associated to negative mental health outcomes and increased risky behaviors (for review, see Sampson, Morenoff, & Gannon-Rowley, 2002).

Coping and Culture

Although culture brings its own unique set of problems to accentuate stress and accordingly mental illness, culture also has its strengths. It is also important to consider variation in coping methods and strategies when individuals are dealing with stress. Coping styles vary across cultures; in fact culture can be a factor that influences, or mediates, specific coping styles and strategies (see Chun, Moos, & Cronkite, 2006; Gurung, 2006). Terms such as individualistic and collectivistic are often used to describe the general orientation of other cultures, and can also be extended to describe the individuals' coping styles in these cultures. For example, many East Asian cultures are collectivistic, which emphasizes interdependence on others in many roles and functions, while the orientation of the United States and European countries is individualistic, which emphasizes independence and reliance on the self (Markus & Kitayama, 1991; Oyserman, Coon, & Kemmelmeier, 2002). These cultural orientations, in turn, may influence how individuals in these cultures cope with stress (Chun, Moos, & Cronkite, 2006; Yeh & Inose, 2002). Specific coping methods within the collectivistic orientation included individualistic coping (coping alone through participation in solitary activities), seeking social support from family, members of their ethnic groups, or individuals who had gone through similar loss, forbearance (emotion-based coping), religiosity, and traditional healing practices. Coping strategies typically associated with individualistic cultures are approach-based, while avoidance-based coping strategies are often associated with collectivistic cultures (Chun, Moos, & Cronkite, 2006). In an example of these styles, Yeh, Inman, Kim, & Okubo (2006) found that in a sample of Asian-American families who had lost a family member in the September 11th attacks, the subjects used collectivistic coping methods to deal with the stress caused by their losses.

Ethnic Identity

One of the major mediators of the stress-mental health relationship is ethnic identity. Dubow, Pargament, Boxer, and Tarakeshwar (2000) found that ethnic identity was positively correlated with ethnic-related stressors and coping strategies in Jewish adolescents. That is, the Jewish adolescents in the study reported experiencing stressors related to religious and social practices, yet they were able to rely on coping strategies and resources unique to their ethnic group for better outcomes. In another example, Mossakowski (2003) assessed the relationship of perceived discrimination, ethnic identity, and mental health outcomes in a sample of Filipino Americans. Higher ratings of ethnic identity were associated with low rates of depression and depressive symptoms. Conversely, Gamst et al. (2002) found that in a sample of Latinos, individuals who had low levels of ethnic identity were more likely to have poorer mental health outcomes, as assessed by declining global assessment of functioning (GAF) scores during a three-month period of community mental health treatment.

Mental health outcomes may be better for immigrants to the United States, as opposed to people from the same cultural group born in the United States. For example, Landale, Oropesa, Llanes, and Gorman (1999) found that Puerto Rican immigrant women, compared to Puerto Rican women born in the United States, reported fewer stressful life events and fewer adverse health behaviors during pregnancy. Similarly, Vega et al. (2004) compared 12-month prevalence rates of mood, anxiety, and substance use disorders of Mexican American immigrants and US-born citizens of Mexican descent, finding that the prevalence rates of these disorders were significantly less in the immigrant population than in the US-born population. Another study on the same ethnic group found Mexican Americans to have better mental health ratings than Mexican citizens and non-Hispanic whites, while Mexican citizens reported higher ratings of physical health than Mexican Americans and non-Hispanic whites (Farley et al., 2005).

Being an immigrant can sometimes make things worse. For example, for immigrants the rates of psychiatric disorders may increase with duration of time living in the United States. While Vega et al. (2004) found lower rates of mood, anxiety, and substance use disorders in Mexican American immigrants, results also indicated that immigrants who had lived in the USA for 13 years or less had 12-month prevalence rates of 9.2 percent, increasing to 18.4 percent for residents residing for greater than 13 years, as compared to US-born Mexican Americans with prevalence rates of 27.4 percent for any psychiatric disorder within the past 12 months.

Other studies have looked at the impact of generational status on rates of mental health disorders for immigrants to the United States. Williams et al. (2006) found that in a sample of black Caribbean immigrants and African Americans, ethnicity, gender, and generational status variables influenced the risk of 12 month prevalence of psychiatric disorders. For instance, Caribbean black women had lower rates of psychiatric disorders than African-American women, while Caribbean black men had higher rates of psychiatric disorders than African-American men in the past 12 months. Furthermore, the prevalence of psychiatric disorders varied by generational status, such that third-generation immigrants had the highest rates of psychiatric disorders, while first-generation immigrants had the lowest rates of psychiatric disorders in the past 12 months.

Social Support

Another major stress buffer is social support, another area where some ethnic groups fare better than others. The term, social support, has been principally defined as either available or perceived support, or alternatively as received or enacted support (see Dunkel-Schetter, Gurung, Lobel, & Wadhwa, 2001). Mexican-American families tend to live in close units with extensive bonds to other family units and the extended family serving as the primary source of support (Chilman, 1993). Similarly, the family is the most important source of support to African Americans (Cauce, Felner, & Primavera, 1982; Miller, 1992). In a direct test of ethnic differences in social support, Sagrestano, Feldman, Killingsworth-Rini, Woo, and Dunkel-Schetter (1999) analyzed data from two multiethnic prospective studies of 246 and 504 African-American, Latina, and non-Hispanic White pregnant women, and found strong ethnic differences in support from family and friends. Multivariate analyses of ethnic differences controlling for sociodemographic variables showed that African-American women reported receiving the most support from family followed by Latinas and White women. However, White women reported more family members in their social networks than did Latinas. Furthermore, Latinas reported higher quality interactions with family.

More recently, findings from three studies by Taylor et al. (2004) indicate that Asians and Asian Americans were less likely to rely on social support for coping with stress than European Americans. Additionally, the data indicate that these cultural differences in seeking social support may be due to concerns with violating relationship norms. In the collectivist (or interdependent) Asian cultures, the emphasis is to maintain group harmony and cohesion, putting the needs of others before the self. Therefore, relying on others for social support was seen as disrupting this balance (Taylor et al., 2004).

Stress and Treatment Seeking

Individuals in racial and ethnic minority groups may be less likely to seek treatment for mental health problems than non-Hispanic whites. For instance, Wang et al. (2005) found that the odds of seeking treatment were greatest for non-Hispanic whites, followed by Hispanics, African Americans, and "Other." Other factors that significantly increased the likelihood of mental health services utilization involve age, marital status, and income. For example, being less than 60 years of age, being previously married, and not having a low average family income increased the odds of seeking treatment (Wang et al., 2005).

In a study assessing mental health care attitudes and provider services among older Caucasian and African-American adults, Dupree, Watson, & Schneider (2005) found that individuals in both groups preferred seeking advice from a family member, clergy member, or family doctor than a mental health care provider. Furthermore, Caucasians preferred seeking service from mental health professionals, while African Americans preferred seeking service from clergy or family doctors. In another study with a sample of Vietnamese Americans, factors that increased help seeking for mental health problems included an individual's greater willingness to disclose, greater preference for professional resources than family and community services, and higher ratings of mental health concerns than ratings of other relevant personal issues (Nguyen & Anderson, 2005).

The stigma of mental illness may be a significant stressor for minorities; research evaluating stigmatizing attitudes has found that mental illness may be viewed similar to, or even more negatively by members of racial and ethnic groups than by non-Hispanic whites (U.S. Department of Health and Human Services, 2001).

In a study examining differences in attitudes and utilization of mental health services by race and ethnicity, African Americans evaluated mental health service use more positively than whites prior to treatment, but held more negative attitudes than whites following treatment. Additionally, African Americans were less likely than whites to seek help for mental health problems despite the more positive attitudes initially held toward these services (Diala et al., 2000).

Conclusions

Culture shapes beliefs about health and illness and provides the context by which an individual evaluates his or her situation and decides whether he or she is stressed or not. Culture furthermore can accentuate the experience of stress and is an important moderator of the stress and coping process. Different cultural groups experience different stressors by virtue of how they appraise stress and by how they are treated (e.g., low SES individuals experience higher stress levels). Different cultural models of stress exist to incorporate such factors and mental health providers would do well to be familiar with culture-specific stressors as well as cultural differences in the experience and expression of stress, especially as these differences influence the recognition, reporting, and treatment of mental health problems.

REFERENCES

Baba, V. V., Jamal, M., & Tourigny, L. (1998). Work and mental health: A decade in Canadian research. *Canadian Psychology, 39*, 94–107.

Barnes, P. M., Adams, P. F., & Powell-Griner, E. (2005). Health characteristics of the American Indian and Alaskan Native adult population: United States, 1999–2003. *Centers for Disease Control and Prevention.* Advance Data No. 356.

Baum, A., O'Keefe, M. K., & Davidson, L. M. (1990). Acute stressors and chronic response: The case of traumatic stress. *Journal of Applied Social Psychology, 20*, 1643–1654.

Beals, J., Novins,Whitesell, N. R., Spicer, P., Mitchell, C. M., & Manson, S. M. (2005) Prevalence of mental disorders and utilization of mental health services in two American Indian reservation populations, *American Journal of Psychiatry, 162*: 1723–1732.

Bleuler, M. (1963). Conception of schizophrenia within the last fifty years and today. *Proceedings of the Royal Society of Medicine, 56*, 945–952.

Cannon, W. B. (1914). The interrelations of emotions as suggested by recent physiological researches. *American Journal of Physiology, 25*, 256–282.

Cannon, W. B. (1929). *Bodily changes in pain, hunger, fear and rage.* Oxford, England: Appleton.

Cauce, A. M., Felner, R. D., & Primavera, J. (1982). Social support in high-risk adolescents: Structural components and adaptive impact. *American Journal of Community Psychology, 10*(4), 417–428.

Chilman, C. S. (1993). Hispanic families in the United States. In H. P. McAdoo (Ed.), *Family ethnicity: Strength in diversity.* Newbury Park, CA: Sage Publications.

Choi, H., Meininger, J. C., & Roberts, R. E. (2006). Ethnic differences in adolescents' mental distress, social stress, and resources. *Adolescence, 41*, 263–283.

Chun, C. A., Moos, R. H., & Cronkite, R. C. (2006). Culture: A fundamental context for the stress and coping paradigm. In P. T. P. Wong & L. C. J. Wong (Eds.), *Handbook of multicultural perspectives on stress and coping.* New York: Springer.

Compas, B. E., Connor-Smith, J. K., Saltzman, H., Thomsen, A. H., & Wadsworth, M. E. (2001). Coping with stress during childhood and adolescence: Problems, progress, and potential in theory and research. *Psychological Bulletin, 127*, 87–127.

Contrada, R. J., Ashmore, R. D., Gary, M. L., et al. (2000). Ethnicity-related sources of stress and their effects on well-being. *Current Directions in Psychological Science, 9*(4), 136–139.

Conway, T. L., Vickers, R. R., Weid, H. W., & Rahe, R. (1981). Occupational stress and variation in cigarette, coffee, and alcohol consumption. *Journal of Health and Social Behavior, 22*, 155–165.

Coyne, J. C., & Downey, G. (1991). Social factors and psychopathology: Stress, social support, and coping processes. *Annual Reviews of Psychology, 42*, 401–425.

Diala, C., Muntaner, C., Walrah, C., Nickerson, K. J., LaVeist, T. A., & Leaf, P. J. (2000). Racial differences in attitudes toward professional mental health care and the use of services. *American Journal of Orthopsychiatry, 70*, 455–464.

Diaz, R. M., Ayala, G., Bein, E., Henne, J., & Marin, B. V. (2001). The impact of homophobia, poverty, and racism on the mental health of gay and bisexual Latino men: Findings from 3 US cities. *American Journal of Public Health, 91*, 927–932.

Dougall, A. L., & Baum, A. (2002). Stress, health, and illness. In A. Baum, T. A. Revenson, & J. E. Singer (Eds.), *Handbook of health psychology* (pp. 321–338). Mahwah, NJ: Lawrence Erlbaum Associates.

Dubow, E. F., Pargament, K. I., Boxer, P., & Tarakeshwar, N. (2000). Initial investigation of Jewish early adolescents' ethnic identity, stress, and coping. *Journal of Early Adolescence, 20*, 418–441.

Dunkel-Schetter, C., Gurung, R. A. R., Lobel, M., & Wadhwa, P. (2001). Psychosocial processes in pregnancy: Stress as a central organizing concept. In A. Baum, J. Singer, & T. Revenson (Eds.), *Handbook of health psychology* (pp. 321–356). New York: Wiley.

Dupree, L. W., Watson, M. A., & Schneider, M. G. (2005). Preferences for mental health care: A comparison of older African Americans and older Caucasians. *Journal of Applied Gerontology, 24*, 196–210.

Farley, T., Galves, G., Miriam-Dickinson, L., & Perez, M. J. (2005). Stress, coping, and health: A comparison of Mexican immigrants, Mexican-Americans, and non-Hispanic whites. *Journal of Immigrant Health, 7*, 213–220.

Field, T. M. (1996). Touch therapies for pain management and stress reduction. In R. J. Resnick & R. H. Rozensky (Eds.), *Health psychology through the life span: Practice and research opportunities* (pp. 313–321). Washington, DC: American Psychological Association.

Finch, B. K., Kolody, B., & Vega, W. A. (2000). Perceived discrimination and depression among Mexican-origin adults in California, *Journal of Health and Social Behavior, 41,* 295–313.

Gamst, G., Dana, R. H., Der-Karabetian, A., Aragon, M., Arellano, L. M., & Kramer, T. (2002). Effects of Latino acculturation and ethnic identity on mental health outcomes. *Hispanic Journal of Behavioral Sciences, 24,* 479–504.

Gurung, R. A. R. (2006). *Health psychology: A cultural approach.* San Francisco: Wadsworth.

Guyton, A. C. (1977). *Basic human physiology: Normal function and mechanisms of disease.* Philadelphia: Saunders.

Hammen, C. (1988). Self cognitions, stressful events, and the prediction of depression in children of depressed mothers. *Journal of Abnormal Child Psychology, 16,* 347–360.

Hammen, C. (2003). Interpersonal stress and depression in women. *Journal of Affective Disorders, 74,* 49–57.

Harkness, K. L., Bruce, A. E., & Lumley, M. N. (2006). The role of childhood abuse and neglect in the sensitization to stressful life events in adolescent depression. *Journal of Abnormal Psychology, 115,* 730–741.

Harris, K. M, Edlund, M. J., & Larson, S. (2005) Racial and ethnic differences in the mental health problems and use of mental health care, *Medical Care, 43,* 775–784.

Hobfoll, S. E. (1989). Conservation of resources. *American Psychologist, 44,* 513–524.

Jamner, L. D., Alberts, J., Leigh, H., & Klein, L. C. (1998). Affiliative need and endogenous opioids. Paper presented at the annual meetings of the Society of Behavioral Medicine, New Orleans, LA.

Johnson, S. L., & Roberts, J. E. (1995). Life events and bipolar disorder: Implications from biological theories. *Psychological Bulletin, 117,* 434–449.

Kendrick, K. M., Da Costa, A. P., Broad, K. D., et al. (1997). Neural control of maternal behavior and olfactory recognition of offspring. *Brain Research Bulletin, 44,* 383–395.

Kessler, R. C., Mickelson, K. D., & Williams, D. R. (1999). The prevalence, distribution, and mental health correlates of perceived discrimination in the United States. *Journal of Health and Social Behavior, 40,* 208–230.

Landale, N. S., Oropesa, N. S., Llanes, D., & Gorman, B. K. (1999). Does Americanization have adverse effects on health?: Stress, health habits, and infant health outcomes among Puerto Ricans. *Social Forces, 78,* 613–641.

Lazarus, R. S. (1966). *Psychological stress and the coping process.* New York: McGraw-Hill.

Lazarus, R. S. (1991). Progress on a cognitive-motivational-relational theory of emotion. *American Psychologist, 46*(8), 819–834.

Lazarus, R. S., & Folkman, S. (1984). *Stress, appraisal, and coping.* New York: Springer.

Lewinsohn, P. M., Joiner, T. E., & Rohde, P. (2001). Evaluation of cognitive diathesis-stress models in predicting major depressive disorder in adolescents. *Journal of Abnormal Psychology, 110,* 203–215.

McNally, R. J. (1997). Implicit and explicit memory for trauma-related information in PTSD. In R. Yehuda & A. C. McFarlane (Eds.), *Psychobiology of posttraumatic stress disorder: Annals of the New York Academy of Sciences* (Vol. 821, pp. 219–224). New York: New York Academy of Sciences.

Markus, H. R., & Kitayama, S. (1991). Culture and the self: Implications for cognition, emotion, and motivation. *Psychological Review, 98,* 224–253.

Martel, F. L., Nevison, C. M., Rayment, F. D., Simpson, M. J. A., & Keverne, E. B. (1993). Opioid receptor blockade reduces maternal affect and social grooming in rhesus monkeys. *Psychoneuroimmunology, 18,* 307–321.

Mays, V. M., Cochran, S. D., & Barnes, N. W. (2007). Race, race-based discrimination, and health outcomes among African Americans. *Annual Reviews of Psychology, 58,* 201–225.

Mazure, C. M. (1998). Life stressors as risk factors in depression. *Clinical Psychology: Science and Practice, 5,* 291–313.

Meaney, M. J. (2001). Maternal care, gene expression, and the transmission of individual differences in stress reactivity across generations. *Annual Review of Neuroscience, 24,* 1161–1192.

Meaney, M. J., Diorio, J., Francis, D., et al. (1996). Early environmental regulation of forebrain glucocorticoid receptor gene expression: Implications for adrenocortical response to stress. *Developmental Neuroscience, 18,* 49–72.

Mellman, T. A. (1997). Psychobiology of sleep disturbances in posttraumatic stress disorder. In R. Yehuda & A. C. McFarlane (Eds.), *Psychobiology of posttraumatic stress disorder. Annals of the New York Academy of Sciences* (vol. 821, pp. 142–149). New York: New York Academy of Sciences.

Meyer, I. H. (2003). Prejudice, social stress, and mental health in lesbian, gay, and bisexual populations: Conceptual issues and research evidence, *Psychological Bulletin, 129,* 674–697.

Miller, M. C. (1992). Winnicott unbound: The fiction of Philip Roth and the sharing of potential space. *International Review of Psycho-Analysis, 19*(4), 445–456.

Monroe, S. M., & Harkness, K. L. (2005). Life stress, the "kindling" hypothesis, and the recurrence of depression: Considerations from a life stress perspective. *Psychological Review, 112,* 417–445.

Monroe, S. M., & Simons, A. D. (1991). Diathesis-stress theories in the context of life stress research: Implications for the depressive disorders, *Psychological Bulletin, 110,* 406–425.

Moradi, B., & Risco, C. (2006). Perceived discrimination experiences and mental health of Latina/o American persons. *Journal of Counseling Psychology, 53,* 411–421.

Mossakowski, K. N. (2003). Coping with perceived discrimination: Does ethnic identify protect mental health? *Journal of Health and Social Behavior, 44,* 318–331.

Nelson, S., McCoy, G., Stetter, M., & Vanderwagen, W. C. (1992). An overview of mental health services for American Indians and Alaska Natives in the 1990's. *Hospital & Community Psychiatry, 43:* 257–261.

Nguyen, Q. C. X., & Anderson, L. P. (2005). Vietnamese Americans' attitudes toward seeking mental health services: Relation to cultural variables. *Journal of Community Psychology, 33,* 213–221.

Noh, S., Beiser, M., Kaspar, V., Hou, F., & Rummens, J. (1999). Perceived racial discrimination, depression, and coping: A study of Southeast Asian refugees in Canada. *Journal of Health and Social Behavior, 40,* 193–207.

Noh, S., & Kaspar, B. (2003). Perceived discrimination and depression: Moderating effects of coping, acculturation, and ethnic support. *American Journal of Public Health, 93,* 232–238.

Nolen-Hoeksema, S. (1987). Sex differences in unipolar depression: Evidence and theory. *Psychological Bulletin, 10,* 259–282.

Oyserman, D., Coon, H. M., & Kemmelmeier, M. (2002). Rethinking individualism and collectivism: Evaluation of theoretical assumptions and meta-analyses. *Psychological Bulletin, 128,* 3–72.

Post, R. M. (1992). Transduction of psychosocial stress into the neurobiology of recurrent affective disorder. *American Journal of Psychiatry, 149*, 999–1010.

Repetti, R. L., Taylor, S. E., & Seeman, T. E. (2002). Risky families: Family social environment and the mental and physical health of offspring. *Psychological Bulletin, 128*(2), 330–366.

Repetti, R. L., & Wood, J. (1997). Effects of daily stress at work on mothers' interactions with preschoolers. *Journal of Family Psychology, 11*, 90–108.

Robins, C. J., & Block, P. (1989). Cognitive theories of depression viewed from a diathesis-stress perspective: Evaluations of the models of Beck and of Abramson, Seligman, and Teasdale. *Cognitive Therapy and Research, 13*, 297–313.

Rosenthal, D. (1970). *Genetic theory and abnormal behavior.* New York: McGraw-Hill.

Rosen, D., Spencer, M. S., Tolman, R. M., Williams, D. R., & Jackson, J. S. (2003). Psychiatric disorders and substance dependence among unmarried low-income mothers. *Health and Social Work, 28*, 157–165.

Sagrestano, L. M., Feldman, P., Killingsworth-Rini, C., Woo, G., Dunkel-Schetter, C. (1999). Ethnicity and social support during pregnancy. *American Journal of Community Psychology, 27*, 869–898.

Sampson, R. J., Morenoff, J. D., & Gannon-Rowley, T. (2002). Assessing "neighborhood effects": Social processes and new directions in research. *Annual Review of Sociology, 28*, 443–478.

Segrin, C. (1999). Social skills, stressful life events, and the development of psychosocial problems. *Journal of Social and Clinical Psychology, 19*, 14–34.

Seyle, H. (1956). *The stress of life.* New York: McGraw-Hill.

Slavin, L. A., Rainer, K. L., McCreary, M. L., & Gowda, K. K. (1991). Toward a multicultural model of the stress process. *Journal of Counseling & Development. Special Multiculturalism as a Fourth Force in Counseling, 70*, 156–163.

Spencer, M. S., & Chen, J. (2004). Effect of discrimination on mental health service utilization among Chinese Americans. *American Journal of Public Health, 94*, 809–814.

Taylor, S. E., Klein, L. C., Lewis, B., Gruenewald, T., Gurung, R. A. R., & Updegraff, J. (2000). The female stress response: Tend and befriend not fight or flight. *Psychological Review, 107*, 411–429.

Taylor, S. E., Lewis, B., Gruenwald, T., Gurung, R. A. R., Updegraff, J. & Klein, L. C. (2002). Sex differences in biobehavioral responses to threat: Reply to Geary and Flinn. *Psychological Review, 109*, 751–753.

Taylor, S. E., Sherman, D. K., Kim, H. S., Jarcho, J., Takagi, K., & Dunagan, M. S. (2004). Culture and social support: Who seeks it and why? *Journal of Personality and Social Psychology, 87*, 354–362.

U.S. Department of Health and Human Services. (2001). *Mental health: Culture, race, and ethnicity – a supplement to mental health: A report of the Surgeon General.* Rockville, MD: U.S. Department of Health and Human Services, Substance Abuse and Mental Health Services Administration, Center for Mental Health Services.

Utsey, S. O., Payne, Y. A., Jackson, E. S., & Jones, A. M. (2002). Race-related stress, quality of life indicators, and life satisfaction among elderly African Americans. *Cultural Diversity and Ethnic Minority Psychology, 8*, 224–233.

Uvnäs-Moberg, K. (1996). Neuroendocrinology of the mother–child interaction. *Trends in Endocrinology and Metabolism, 7*, 126–131.

Vega, W. A., Sribney, W. M., Aguilar-Gaxiola, S., & Kolody, B. (2004). 12-month prevalence of *DSM–III–R* psychiatric disorders among Mexican Americans: Nativity, social assimilation, and age determinants. *Journal of Nervous & Mental Disease, 192,* 532–541.

Ventura, J., Nuechterlein, K. H., Lukoff, D., & Hardesty, J. P. (1989). A prospective study of stressful life events and schizophrenic relapse. *Journal of Abnormal Psychology, 4,* 407–411.

Walker, E. F., & Diforio, D. (1997). Schizophrenia: A neural diathesis-stress model. *Psychological Review, 104,* 667–685.

Wang, P. S., Lane, M., Olfson, M., Pincus, H. A., Wells, K. B., & Kessler, R. C. (2005). Twelve month use of mental health services in the United States, *Archives of General Psychiatry, 62,* 629–640.

Whitbeck, L. B., McMorris, B. J., Hoyt, D. R., Stubben, J. D., & LaFramboise, T. (2002). Perceived discrimination, traditional practices, and depressive symptoms among American Indians in the Upper Midwest. *Journal of Health and Social Behavior, 43,* 400–418.

Williams, D. R., Haile, R., Gonzalez, H. M., Neighbors, H., Baser, R., & Jackson, J. S. (2006). The mental health of black Caribbean immigrants: Results from the National Survey of American Life. *American Journal of Public Health, 97,* 52–59.

Yeh, C. J., Inman, A. G., Kim, A. B., & Okubo, Y. (2006). Asian American families' collectivistic coping strategies in response to 9/11. *Cultural Diversity and Ethnic Minority Psychology, 12,* 134–148.

Yeh, C. J., & Inose, M. (2002). Difficulties and coping strategies of Chinese, Japanese, and Korean immigrant students. *Adolescence, 37,* 69–82.

Zinbarg, R.E., & Barlow, D. H. (1996). Structure of anxiety and the anxiety disorders: A hierarchical model. *Journal of Abnormal Psychology, 105,* 181–193.

4

Managing Job Stress: Cross-Cultural Variations in Adjustment

Joseph P. Eshun, Jr. and Kevin J. Kelley

Increased globalization and international diversity in the corporate arena have resulted in the need to understand how job or occupational stress affects diverse employees. The World Health Organization (2006) reports that worker stress is increasingly becoming a universal concern, prevalent and persistent not only in the industrialized economies of Europe and North America but also in the rapidly developing economies and emerging markets of China, Taiwan, and Korea, among others.

Research findings confirm a negative relationship between occupational stress and mental health or psychological well-being (Tang et al., 2006). Other studies have emphasized the important role of culture in understanding all aspects of occupational stress, including identification, appraisal, coping and adaptation to stress (Sawang, Oei, & Goh, 2006). Given that the typical full-time employee spends one-third to one-half of their day at work, it is crucial that researchers and practitioners understand the unique dynamics of the workplace and its influence on individuals.

Our chapter addresses how culture influences the link between occupational stress and mental health problems, specifically, adjustment disorders. We begin with prevalence rates as well as the costs of occupational stress across a diversity of nations. Next, we define *DSM–IV–TR* classification of adjustment disorders. These introductory sections are followed by a review of the influence of culture on occupational stress in diverse groups. The chapter ends with a discussion of cultural sensitivity in developing and implementing coping strategies and treatment interventions at the individual and organizational levels.

Prevalence Rates and Costs of Occupational Stress Across Nations

According to National Institute for Occupational Safety and Health, 40 percent of American workers reported that their job was very or extremely stressful;

25 percent viewed their jobs as the number one stressor in their lives; 75 percent of employees believed that workers have more on-the-job stress than a generation ago; 29 percent of workers felt quite a bit or extremely stressed at work; and 26 percent of workers said they were "often or very often burned out or stressed by their work" (NIOSH, 2006).

Job stress is not only prevalent and persistent in the western world. Reports from nonwestern nations demonstrate similar or higher rates. For instance, Dewa et al. (2004) found that the 63 percent of Japanese workers reported work-related stress, reflecting a 10 percent increase over the past 15 years. This sharply contrasts with the lowest levels of work-related stress, reported as 8 percent for men and 7 percent for women, for Taiwanese workers (Cheng et al., 2001). In general, work-related stress has been reported in many other nations including the Netherlands (van der Klink & van Dijk, 2003), Hong Kong (Tang et al., 2006), Nigeria (Oloyade, 2006), Trinidad and Tobago (Addae & Wang, 2006). It is noteworthy mentioning that the availability and accessibility of stress-related studies in North America and Europe is in sharp contrast to the limited studies of work-related stress in Africa and the Caribbean.

It is an established fact that work-related stress comes with economic, social, and health consequences. For example, according to the World Health Organization (WHO, 2001) occupational stress has a huge economic and social impact in direct costs (e.g., medical treatments and compensation) and indirect costs (e.g., low morale, accidents, absenteeism, staff turnover, and low productivity). WHO further reports that work-related mental health problems accounted for 10.5 percent of total disability adjusted life years (DALYS) in 1990 and is expected to increase to 15 percent by 2020. Similarly, the International Labor Organization (ILO) estimates that approximately 20 percent of adults have a mental health problem and about 3–4 percent of the gross national product (GNP) in many developed countries goes towards working days lost (ILO, 2000).

These prevalence rates of occupational stress emphasize the need to identify and adequately manage work-related stress and ultimately minimize the economic costs and consequences.

The United States is arguably the most culturally diverse country in the world. Yet, the many cultural groups that comprise America are not evenly represented across employment sectors. Racial and cultural subgroups tend to be over-represented in occupations that are lower paying, with fewer employment benefits, and that often involve more dangerous work under more stressful working conditions. Thus, in the United States, there is a link between highly stressful work settings and race or culture.

There is also a well-established link between socioeconomic status (SES) and multiple health variables that cuts across national boundaries (Alder & Ostrove, 1999; House, 2002). The higher one's SES, the better one's current health and health prospects (Marmot, Ryff, Bumpass, Shipley, & Marks, 1997); although this relationship is even more pronounced at lower SES levels (Backlund, Sorlie, & Johnson, 1996; Ecob & Smith, 1999). Three important variables contribute to the inverse relationship between SES and health outcomes. Individuals with less education (lower SES) tend to exercise less frequently, have higher body-mass indexes (BMI), and are more likely to smoke cigarettes.

The question arises as to whether or not job characteristics mediate the relationship between SES and health above and beyond the contributions of exercise, BMI, and smoking. Brand, Warren, Carayon, & Hoonakker (2006) set out to answer that question with regard to overall health status, cardiovascular and musculoskeletal health problems and depression. These authors wrote: "In general, we find that physical and psychosocial job characteristics account for some or all of these remaining associations. That is, job characteristics play an important role in mediating the relationship between SES and these health outcomes" (p. 247). Although incidences of stress, burnout, and adjustment disorders were not specifically addressed in this study, one can safely say that if more severe health consequences can be attributed to job characteristics, than less severe health consequences such as stress, burnout, adjustment problems can as well.

To summarize, individuals with lower SES tend to be over-represented among racial and cultural subgroups (especially in the United States) who are also over-represented in employment sectors involving more stressful and dangerous job characteristics. Lower SES generally, and stressful and dangerous job characteristics specifically, are associated with lowered health outcomes. Thus, especially in the United States, the relationship between stress, burnout, adjustment problems, and other health-related concerns are especially salient for individuals from racial and cultural subgroups (i.e., individuals who are non-Caucasian and non-European in origin).

Definition of Adjustment Disorder

Work-related stress may result in burnout and ultimately adjustment disorders, and exert immense cost to many countries. For instance, it is estimated that approximately one-half of mental health-related employee disability in the Netherlands is due to individuals suffering from adjustment disorders (van der Klink & van Dijk, 2003). While stress has been implicated in mood and anxiety disorders (Folkman & Lazarus, 1986), job stress, either an acute episode frequently repeated, or chronic job stress, tends to produce negative psychological effects along a continuum ranging from irritation to burnout, all the way to the development of an adjustment disorder. Whereas other causes of adjustment disorder such as life changes (e.g., death of a loved one, divorce, illness, interpersonal problems, etc.) are important, job stress is often taken for granted as a salient factor in the treatment of adjustment disorder.

We focus on job-related stress as a precursor to adjustment difficulties in this chapter because of the enormous amount of time individuals spend at work and the fact that job-related stress is of increasing concern globally (WHO, 2006).

The *DSM–IV–TR* (APA, 2000) states that "the essential feature of an adjust-ment disorder is a psychological response to an identifiable stressor or stressors that results in the development of clinically significant emotional or behavioral symptoms" (p. 679). In order for an individual to meet the criteria for a diag-nosis of adjustment disorder, the symptoms experienced must be in excess of what would be expected given the nature of the stressor or cause a significant impairment in occupational or social functioning; and they must develop within three months of the onset of the stress. Six specific subtypes of adjustment disorder have been identified and all are related, causally, to stress.

1. Adjustment disorder can occur with depressed mood, indicating that the stressor is causally linked to the onset of depressive symptoms. Note, the depressive symptoms are similar to those found in a mood disorder such as a major depressive episode; but tend to be less severe and rarely include suicidal ideation.
2. Adjustment disorder occurs with anxiety as its primary symptom. This anxiety typically consists of nervousness or worry and would not include panic attacks, for example.
3. Adjustment disorder consists of a combination of both mood and anxi-ety symptoms.
4. Adjustment disorder occurs with a disturbance in behavior. For this subtype, the predominant symptoms include behavior that violates the rights of others or significant age-appropriate social norms, such as van-dalism, reckless driving, aggressive fighting, etc.
5. Adjustment disorder occurs as a combination of the preceding four types: mood, anxiety, and behavioral symptoms predominate.
6. This category of adjustment disorder is reserved for symptomatic mani-festations of adjustment difficulties that do not meet any of the above categories. Such symptoms might include physical complaints, social withdrawal, or work inhibition.

Although not an accepted diagnostic category, burnout is a state of serious emotional exhaustion, often associated with emotional distancing, loneliness, and decreased sense of personal accomplishment (Bauer, Hafner, Kachele, Wirsching, & Dahlbender, 2003; Starrin, Larsson, & Styrborn, 1990). This psychological condition could be seen in employees who may not necessarily meet diagnostic criteria for an adjustment disorder.

Defining Stress and Occupational Stress

Lazarus (1966) referred to stress as a feeling or condition in which a person's perceived response demand exceeds the personal and social resources at the person's disposal. As discussed in greater detail in the previous chapter (see Chapter 3) stress is typically connected with and encountered in difficult situations. It arises when there is the perception of an unfavorable or undesirable situation, produced by a variety of events or occurrences. In general, stress entails an individual's interpretation of a stressor within a given cultural context.

Occupational stress or job stress is "an individual's reactions to work environment characteristics that appear physically and emotionally threatening to the individual" (Jamal, 2005, p. 130). Jamal further explains that job stress reflects a poor fit between an employee's abilities either because of excessive demands being made or the individual does not feel well prepared to deal with the challenges associated with the demands.

Overall, work-related stress has been attributed to several factors including personal factors, management style, employer–employee relationship and working patterns (Berg et al., 2005; Linzer et al., 2002; Tennant, 2001). These factors could ultimately result in or lead to an adjustment disorder if there is an imbalance between an employee's expectations/job requirements and his or her ability to address the demands of the job (Weyers et al., 2006).

Typically, researchers identify internal and external sources of occupational stress. Internal sources include conflicts within oneself while external sources often come from the physical and social environment. In applying these concepts at the organizational level, Hobfoll (1998) explained that internal sources are job-related stressors than come directly from conflicts within the organization. External sources often come from the lager society. The crucial point is that both internal and external sources of occupational stress are highly influenced by the cultural context within which they occur.

While job-related stress seems to exist in all cultures (Glazer & Beehr, 2005; Lu, Chen, Hsu, Li, Wu, & Shih, 1994; Peterson et al., 1995), what is experienced as stressful as well as the individual's subjective experience or reactions to stress appears to vary by culture (Liu, Spector, & Shi, 2007; Veenhoven, 1993).

How Culture Shapes Perception of Stress

Culture influences occupational stress in all aspects. The way we identify a stressor, how we evaluate it, and ultimately how we deal with it will depend on our own cultural values. In other words, the best way to address occupational stress is to understand the underlying cultural values and principles to which a given society adheres (Peterson & Wilson, 2004). Let us look at the United States as an example. In his assessment of the American culture in the 1800s, de Tocqueville (1835/2000) noted that Americans are in a constant state of stress. This constant state of stress stems from a Judeo-Christian cultural belief that hard work is associated with prosperity. Although his observations were over two centuries ago, American culture has not changed much. There continues to be increased competition and pressure to perform better.

Similarly, in their work on exploring the cultural underpinnings of work stress, Peterson and Wilson (2004) argued that primary American values such as individualism, self-interest, time consciousness, and a link between work and wealth determine the level of stress experienced on the job. They describe a collective American subconscious statement as "If I work harder, I can succeed, and it will be proof that I am a good person" (p. 94). This belief system or value may lead individuals to work excessively while experiencing a sense of dissatisfaction, a sure pathway to occupational stress.

Also, the American value of individualism and autonomy as well as cultural belief of equality may result in conflicts with management when they emphasize their higher rank. Adhering to these values also means that when individuals do not have control over decision-making, as is often the case in the work environment, it is not only a stressor, but is in fact a cultural threat. This condition may be different for cultures that are more collectivistic and accepting of power distance such as China.

Many variables have been identified around which cultures may vary. Examples of culture-based variables include power distance, masculinity/femininity, and time orientation (Hofstede, 2001). While a full exploration of these issues is beyond the scope of this chapter (see Chapter 1 for a fuller discussion), an illustrative example will clarify this important issue. One important factor around which culture varies which has implications for work stress is individualism/collectivism (Hofstede, 2001). Liu, Spector, and Shi (2007) examined job stress in American and Chinese cultures using a comparable sample of employees (faculty and staff at all levels) from similar-type universities. These researchers highlighted three important variables that distinguish these two cultures from each other: (1) individualism versus collectivism; (2) Confucianism; and (3) economic resources. Specifically, American culture is typically identified as individualistic in its orientation while Chinese culture is typically identified as collectivist in orientation. Chinese culture also differs from American culture in regards to two Confucian concepts: saving face (Fang, 2003) and forbearance (Hwang, 1997). Saving face refers to the strong avoidance of a sense of shame or anything that might bring shame to oneself or one's family. Forbearance refers to the tendency to maintain strong control over one's emotions especially for the purpose of maintaining positive relationships when under stressful conditions. The third variable in Liu, Spector, and Shi's (2007) study highlights the tremendous difference between American and China in terms of the economic resources available in each country. Specifically, the authors state that "American employees possess more resources at work than their Chinese counterparts" (p. 211).

In addition to these three important variables, Liu, Spector, and Shi (2007) point out that each culture is composed of one or more generations of workers who themselves vary in important ways within the cultural variables already described. Current American culture is dominated by the Baby Boom Generation and the Generation Xers. China's workforce is currently dominated by the Consolidation generation, the Cultural Revolution generation, and the Social Reform generation. The differences between these generations represent cohort effects characterized by the specific geopolitical and historical facts evident at the time each generation was growing up.

Differences in job stress between these two countries reported by Liu, Spector, and Shi (2007) were evident in both quantitative and qualitative measures. Specific quantitative differences in sources of job stress were found in the areas of job autonomy (Americans reported more), perception of organizational constraint (Americans reported more), job satisfaction (Americans are more satisfied), physical health problems (Chinese reported more), and turnover intention (Americans reported more).

Specific qualitative differences in sources of job stress were found in the areas of lack of job control (Americans reported more), nature of the type of conflicts experienced – direct versus indirect conflict (Americans reported more direct conflict), incidents related to job evaluations (Chinese reported more), and Chinese workers complained more about conditions of employment and lack of job training compared to Americans.

The effects of job stress on employees in each country also differed in several areas. American employees reported more anger and frustration while Chinese employees reported more anxiety and helplessness. Furthermore, American employees reported more tiredness while Chinese employees reported having more sleep problems and being tired. American employees reported more stomach problems while Chinese employees reported more sleep problems and feeling hot (probably due to the lack of air conditioning, reflecting a difference in economic resources between the two countries).

The Liu, Spector, and Shi (2007) data clearly illustrate the important role culture plays in the individual workers' experience of what is considered stressful at work and in how that individual experiences that stress (the stress reactions or responses). Thus, cultural issues are crucial to understanding the relationship between work and stress.

Cross-Cultural Investigations of Job Stress and Psychological Adjustment

Comparative analyses of how culture serves as a background for understanding occupational stress have been demonstrated in many nations. Most studies made comparisons between western and nonwestern nations based on reported differences in cultural constructs like individualism/collectivism and power distance. For example, Schaubroeck, Lam, and Xie (2000) examined the extent to which cultural differences in self-concepts influence how employees cope with demands among a sample of bank tellers from the USA and Hong Kong. They reported a significant interaction between self-efficacy, job demands, job control, and psychological health in both cultures. However, the type of efficacy (i.e., group-oriented vs. self-oriented) differed across cultures. Other cross-cultural studies have confirmed the important role of job-stress in mental health, job performance, and job satisfaction (for a review, see Glazer & Beehr, 2005).

There is evidence that the link between job-stress and psychological well-being may vary across cultures. In a cross-cultural comparative study of Iranian and American managers, Spector et al. (2002) reported that although there was a positive correlation between job stress and absences among Iranian managers, it was not the case for American mangers. Jamal (1999) also found cross-cultural differences in the relationship between job stress and psychological health in a study of Canadian and Pakistani professors. Specifically he found that whereas the correlation between job stress, satisfaction with pay and satisfaction with coworkers was negative for Pakistani professors, it was not for Canadians. More recently, Jamal (2005) examined the role of job stress and Type A behavior (specifically time pressure and hard driving/competitiveness) in employees developing burnout, health problems, and job dissatisfaction among a sample of Canadians and Chinese. Similar to previous studies, both job stress and Type A behaviors were significantly related to burnout, health problems and turnover motivation in both countries. Further analyses indicated that whereas time pressure and hard driving/competitiveness were associated with job satisfaction and organizational commitment in the Canadian sample, it was only significantly related to job satisfaction (not organizational commitment) in the Chinese sample.

In concluding this section, we note that when organizational goals and expectations are at odds with those of individual employees, there is a sense of frustration, job dissatisfaction, lack of motivation and a desire to leave the work environment. These negative feelings have been associated with poor mental health and therefore need to be addressed in a timely manner within a given cultural context.

Cultural Sensitivity in Developing and Implementing Coping Strategies and Treatment Interventions at the Individual and Organizational Levels

As mentioned earlier in this chapter, job stress occurs every day, everywhere, and in the lives of all people from diverse cultures. This means that it is crucial for counselors and psychologists to detect the early signs of the negative impact of and immense costs associated with job stress as early as feasible, to help reduce the likelihood of employees/clients developing adjustment disorders and other mental health problems. Any indication of an imbalance between an individual's perceptions of his or her job requirements/expectations and that of their personal cultural norms and expectations is a concern that needs to be seriously considered in developing intervention plans.

Tang and colleagues (2006) discuss the importance of early detection of stress symptoms as an initial step towards reducing the likelihood that employees will experience mental health challenges. They emphasize how physical, cognitive, emotional, and behavioral signs at the individual employee level are often associated with organizational level problems. For instance physical complaints of headaches and fatigue may be associated with feeling tense and increased suspiciousness and ultimately increase level of disputes, work-related complaints, and absenteeism. The authors also write that interventions for the negative psychological effects of occupational stress entail three steps listed below:

1. Identifying the Problem and Source of the Stress

This step involves isolating and identifying internal and external factors that may be contributing to individual and organizational level stress responses listed in Table 4.1. It is imperative that employers and counseling professionals engage in extensive interviewing and fact finding to help uncover causes of occupational stress within a given cultural context even if the employee seems to be downplaying it. For instance, ethnic minority employees may experience stressors related to racial discrimination, which is less likely with employees from the majority group. Similarly, in line with de Tocqueville's observations and Peterson and Wilson's analysis of American values, it is likely that within a global organization, an American employee's perceptions and appraisal of job-related stress will be different from that of another employee from Sri Lanka because of cultural differences.

Empirical studies support the importance of culture in identifying the source of the problem. In a cross-cultural comparative study of stress appraisal, Sawang, Oei, and Goh (2006) found that Australians and Singaporeans were more likely to appraise work demands as stressful that their Sri Lankan counterparts. Further exploration of employees' perceptions of control of stressors indicated that Australians believed they had the most control over their job stress, followed by Singaporeans, and Sri Lankans had the least.

2. Deciding What Needs to be Changed

Once the specific problem of occupational stress has been identified, the next obvious question is to decide on what needs to be done. Commonsense suggests that the best way to deal with stress is to eliminate the source or stressor. However, this is not always feasible in the work environment, particularly those that are deadline-oriented, high-paced, and time-sensitive, such as postal and package delivery services, law enforcement, and medical/health services. Many organizations rely on psychologists and other mental health experts to conduct stress management workshops as a way of educating employees about controlling or relieving the impact of job stress. In cases where job stress has already had adverse psychological effects on individuals (e.g., adjustment and affective disorders), a referral to an appropriate mental health professional or employee assistance program is indicated.

3. Taking Action

To take action means intervention at the appropriate level. Tang et al. (2006) identify three levels of intervention, which are based on DeFrank and Cooper's (1987) model. These are interventions at the individual, individual-organizational interface, and the organizational levels.

(a)   *Individual-level intervention*

Intervention at the individual level involves employing cognitive and behavioral skills to alleviate the negative effects of job stress. These include cognitive restructuring, problem-solving skills, assertiveness training, relaxation training, meditation, and behavior modification. It is recommended that psychologists and other counseling professional adopt the Dutch guidelines for managing adjustment disorders in occupational health summarized in Table 4.1 (van der Klink & van Dijk, 2003).

Appropriate cultural sensitivity when developing appropriate individual-level interventions is crucial because of significant cross-cultural differences in coping

Table 4.1   Tasks to be accomplished in the phases of recovery and the schedule for the evaluation and its criteria

Recovery phase	Tasks to be accomplished	Evaluation time	Criteria for advancement or change-over
1. Crisis and understanding	Rest, insight and acceptance	I. End of phase 1	I. The patient has a rationale for the situation or accepts one and has a problem-oriented attitude: preoccupation in thinking shifts from consequences such as symptoms to causes such as problems and stressors.
2. Insight	Defining the problem and making an inventory of stressors	II. Halfway through phase 2 III. End of phase 2	II. The patient has a problem-solving attitude and is open to the suggestion to make an inventory of possible solutions III. The patient has an application-oriented attitude and is open to the suggestions to apply strategies and to build up demanding activities
3. Rehabilitation	Working out strategies, rehabilitation	IV. End of phase 3	IV. Roles that have been dropped during the crisis are (at least partially) resumed

Source: Van der Klink & van Dijk (2003), p. 484.

strategies. While the Dutch guidelines were found to be valid for most of the population, the schedule for recovery was shorter for the Dutch Caribbean group and needed to be modified.

Modification may also be necessary depending on the group's preferred coping strategies. Tweed, White, and Lehman (2004) reported that Japanese and Asian Canadian groups were more likely to cope by accepting responsibility, accepting the problem, waiting things out, and using self-control strategies than European Canadians, who were more likely to cope by confronting other people. They attributed the differences in coping strategies to collectivism, high power-distance, and the influence of Budhism and Taoism among the Asian groups. Other studies confirm the role of culture in coping strategies (Scherer et al. 2000).

(b) *Individual–organizational interface intervention*
Intervention at this level calls for a balance between work and nonwork activities. Individual–organizational interface interventions are often handled by human behavior consultants in collaboration with leaders within the organization. Tang et al. (2006) discuss the importance of empowering employees to be participants in decision-making by establishing committees and feedback systems within the organization. Another important aspect of this level of intervention is to maintain a healthy balance between work and leisure time, by encouraging use of vacation times, organization-sponsored retreats, and days off. These have been found to decrease the occurrence of burnout.

(c) *Organizational-level intervention*
The organizational-level of intervention requires modifications in the work environment. This type of intervention could be viewed as more of a preventative measure than a cure. These interventions include modifications such as flexible work schedules and teleworking. Because teleworking is gaining more attention at a global level, we will expand on its effects on job stress in this section.

Telecommuting or telework is a method that has the potential to relieve job stress and work–family conflict because it offers employees the opportunity to perform some or all of their job duties from a location other than the work site. In the past 20 years, rates of telework penetration have risen steadily as technological improvements have advanced. The World at Work organization recently released a report indicating that by the end of 2006 the number of Americans working remotely at least one day per month reached 28.7 million (World at Work, 2007). The organization estimates that by the year 2010, the number of Americans working remotely at least one day per month will hit 100 million. In Europe, telework penetration rates vary widely. Gareis (2002) reported that the Netherlands and the Scandinavian countries have rates comparable to the United States, and lead all European nations in employee use of teleworking opportunities. France, Italy, and Spain are below the average of all European nations and Germany is far below the average, with Portugal having the lowest rates of telework among all European Union nations.

In contrast to the data from the United States and Europe, Asian countries have been slow to adopt telework (Prystay, 1999). Prystay (1999) reported that less than 1 percent of Asian companies allow telework and most of those are US firms. Perez, Sánchez, and Carnicer (2002) argue that cultural issues in Asian countries place a preference on workers' physical presence at an office, making telework less likely to be adopted. Similarly, Raghuram, London, and Larsen (2001) studied the relationship between the use of flexible employment practices (including telework) and cultural variations across 14 European countries. They found that the differences among nations in the use of flexible employment practices were explained by cultural differences; specifically, cultural differences along the dimension of femininity explained differences in utilization of telework. Other studies have confirmed the importance of cultural variables in determining use of this organizational-level intervention (Peters & den Dulk, 2003).

Another form of organizational level intervention in minimizing the negative impact of job stress is communication. Open communication has an overall positive impact of job satisfaction and an individual's perception of control (see Tang et al., 2006 for review). Explaining the rationale behind one company merging with another or why there is a sudden deadline for completing a project goes a long way to help the individual make appropriate cognitive and emotional adjustments and places them in the right frame of thought to work.

Conclusions and Suggestions for Practice and Research

In this chapter, we explored how culture influences appraisal and coping with job stress. There are many factors in the cultural environment that counseling professionals and business consultants need to be aware of in dealing with clients with adjustment disorders especially those who receive referrals from employee health programs. These include:

1. conflicts between cultural norms in the general society and work environment;
2. influence of personal and cultural constructs such as collectivism/individualism and power-distance;
3. challenges of uncertainty or lack of stability at the workplace – corporate downsizing, mergers and acquisitions, hostile takeovers, layoffs, etc.;
4. decision-making and communications styles;
5. juggling – women in the workforce;
6. spillover effect;
7. middle managers – addressing condition of learned helplessness and powerlessness;
8. actors discussed seem like everyday occurrences but have serious impact over the business – WHO resources – rates of mental illness and suicide

REFERENCES

Addae, H. M., & Wang, X. (2006). Stress at work: Linear and curvilinear effects of psychological, job, and organization-related factors: An exploratory study of Trinadad and Tobago. *International Journal of Stress Management, 13*(4), 476–493.

Alder, N. E., & Ostrove, J. M. (1999). Socioeconomic status and health: What we know and what we don't. In N. E. Adler, M. G. Marmot, B. S. McEwen, & Stewart, J. (Eds.), *Socioeconomic status and health in industrialized nations*, vol 896. Annals of the New York Academy of Sciences, pp. 96–115.

American Psychiatric Association (2000). *Diagnostic and statistical manual of mental disorders*, 4th ed., Text Revision. Washington, DC: American Psychiatric Association.

Aust, B., & Ducki, A. (2004). Comprehensive health promotion interventions at the workplace: Experiences with health circles in Germany. *Journal of Occupational Health Psychology, 9*, 258–270.

Backlund, E., Sorlie, P. D., & Johnson, N. J. (1996). The shape of the relationship between income and mortality in the United States: Evidence from the National Longitudinal Mortality Study. *Annals of Epidemiology, 6*, 12–20.

Bauer, J., Hafner, S., Kachele, H., Wirsching, M., & Dahlbender, R. (2003). Burnout und wiedergewinnung seelischer gesundheit am arbeitsplatz./The burnout syndrome and restoring mental health at the work place. *Psychotherapie Psychosomatik Medizinische Psychologie, 53*, 213–222.

Berg, A. M., Hem, E., Lau, B., Haseth, K., & Ekeberg, O. (2005). Stress in the Norwegian police service. *Occupational Medicine, 55*, 113–120.

Brand, J. E., Warren, J. R., Carayon, P., & Hoonakker, P. (2007). Do job characteristics mediate the relationship between SES and health? Evidence from sibling models. *Social Science Research, 36*, 222–253.

Cheng, Y., Guo, Y., & Yeh, W.Y. (2001). A national survey of psychosocial job stressors and their implications for health among working people in Taiwan. *International Archives of Occupational and Environmental Health, 74*, 495–504.

Cohen, S., Doyle, W. J., Turner, R., Alper, C. M., & Skoner, D. P. (2003). Sociability and susceptibility to the common cold. *Psychological Science, 14*, 389–395.

DeFrank, R. S., & Cooper, C. L. (1987). Worksites stress management interventions: Their effectiveness and conceptualization. *Journal of Managerial Psychology, 2*, 4–10.

Department of Health, United Kingdom (2001). *Making it happen: A guide to delivering mental health promotion*. London: Department of Health.

de Tocqueville, A. (2000). *Democracy in America*. In H. C. Mansfield & D. Winthrop (Eds. and Trans.). Chicago: University of Chicago Press (original work published 1835).

Dewa. C., Lesage, A., Goering, P., & Caveen, M. (2004). Nature and prevalence of mental illness in the workplace. *Healthcare Papers, 5*(2), 12–25.

Ecob, R., & Smith, G. D. (1999). Income and health: What is the nature of the relationship? *Social Science and Medicine, 48*, 693–705.

Fang, T. (2003). A critique of Hofstede's fifth national culture dimension. *International Journal of Cross Cultural Management, 3*, 347–368.

Folkman, S., & Lazarus, R. S. (1986). Stress processes and depressive symptomatology. *Journal of Abnormal Psychology, 95*, 107–113.

Gareis, K. (2002). The intensity of telework in 2002 in the EU, Switzerland and the USA. *Annual International Telework Forum Congress in Badajoz, Spain (September 3–5, 2002)*. Obtained from http://www.sibis-eu.org/publications/articles.htm on 7-16-2007.

Glazer, S., & Beehr, T. A. (2005). Consistency of implications of three role stressors across four countries. *Journal of Organizational Behavior, 26*, 467–487.

Hobfoll, S. E. (1998). *Stress, culture and community: The psychology and philosophy of stress.* New York: Plenum.

Hofstede, G. (2001). *Culture's consequences. comparing values, behaviors, institutions, and organizations across nations* (2nd ed.). Thousand Oaks, CA: Sage.

House, J. H. (2002). Understanding social factors and inequalities in health: 20th century progress and 21st century prospects. *Journal of Health and Social Behavior, 43*, 125–142.

Hwang, K. K. (1997). Guanxi and Mientze: Conflict resolution in Chinese society. *Intercultural Communication Studies, 7*, 17–42.

International Labour Organization (2000). *Mental health in the work place.* Geneva: Author.

Jamal, M. (1999). Job stress and employee well being: A cross-cultural empirical study. *Stress Medicine, 15*, 153–158.

Jamal, M. (2005). Short communication: Personnel and organizational outcomes related to job stress and Type-A behavior: A study of Canadian and Chinese employees. *Stress and Health, 21*, 129–137.

Lazarus, R. S. (1966). *Psychological stress and the coping process.* New York: McGraw-Hill.

Linzer, M., Gerrity, M., Douglas, J. A., McMurray, J. E., Williams, E. S., & Konrad, T. R. (2002). Physician stress: Results from the physician worklife study. *Stress and Health, 18*, 37–42.

Liu, C., Spector, P. E., & Shi, L. (2007). Cross-national job stress: A quantitative and qualitative study. *Journal of Occupational Behavior, 28*, 209–239.

Lu, L., Chen, Y. C., Hsu, C. H., Li, C. H., Wu, H. L., & Shih, J. B. (1994). *Occupational stress and its correlates.* Taipai: IOSH.

McLeroy, K. R., Green, L. W., Mullen, K. D., & Foshee, V. (1984). Assessing the effects of health promotion in worksites: A review of the stress program evaluations. *Health Education Quarterly, 11*, 379–401.

Maes, S., Verhoeven, C., Kittel, F., & Scholten, H. (1998). Effects of a Dutch work-site wellness-health program: The Bravantia project. *American Journal of Public Health, 88*, 1037–1041.

Marmot, M. G., Ryff, C. D., Bumpass, L. L., Shipley, M., & Marks, N. (1997). Social inequalities in health: Next questions and converging evidence. *Social Science and Medicine, 44*, 901–910.

National Institute for Occupational Safety and Health (2006). *Work, stress, and health 2006: Making a difference in the workplace.* www.cdc.gov/niosh/ohp.html (retrieved July 17, 2007).

Oloyade, D. O. (2006). Impact of work-induced stress on perceived workers' productivity in banking industry in Lagos. *Ife Psychologia, 14*(1), 15–25.

Penedo, F. J., & Dahn, J. R. (2005). Exercise and well-being: A review of mental and physical health benefits associated with physical activity. *Current Opinion in Psychiatry, 18*, 189–193.

Perez, M. P., Sánchez, A. M., & Carnicer, M. P. L. (2002). The organizational implications of human resources managers' perception of teleworking. *Personnel Review, 32,* 733–755.

Peters, P., & den Dulk, L. (2003). Cross cultural differences in managers' support for home-based telework: A theoretical elaboration. *Cross Cultural Management, 3,* 329–346.

Peterson, J. F., Smith, P. B., Akande, A., et al. (1995). Role conflict, ambiguity, and overload: A 21-nation study. *Academy of Management Journal, 38,* 429–452.

Peterson, M., & Wilson, J. F. (2004). Work stress in America. *International Journal of Stress Management, 11*(2), 91–113.

Prystay, C. (1999). Why Asia won't telecommute, *Asian Wall Street Journal,* 15 October, p. 3.

Raghuram, S., London, M., & Larsen, H. H. (2001). Flexible employment practices in Europe: Country versus culture. *International Journal of Human Resources Management, 12,* 738–753.

Sawang, S., Oei, T. P. S., & Goh, Y. W. (2006). Are country and culture values interchangeable? A case example using occupational stress and coping. *International Journal of Cross Cultural Management, 6*(2), 205–218.

Schaubroeck, J., Lam, S. S. K., & Xie, J. L. (2000). Collective efficacy versus self efficacy in coping responses to stressors and control: A cross-cultural study. *Journal of Applied Psychology, 85*(4), 512–525.

Scherer, R. F., Hwang, C., Yan, W., & Li, J. (2000). The dimensionality of coping among Chinese health care workers. *Journal of Social Psychology, 140*(3), 317–327.

Shephard, R. J. (1996). Worksite fitness and exercise programs: A review of methodology and health impact. *American Journal of Health Promotion, 10,* 436–452.

Spector, P. E., Cooper, C. L., & Aguilar-Vafaie, M. E. (2002). A comparative study of perceived job stressor sources and job strain in American and Iranian managers. *Applied Psychology: An International Review, 51,* 446–457.

Starrin, B., Larsson, G., & Styrborn, S. (1990). A review and critique of psychological approaches to the burn-out phenomenon. *Scandinavian Journal of Caring Sciences, 4,* 83–91.

Tang, A. S. Y, Lee, K. Y., Leung, R. W. M., Tsang, C. Y., Ho, M. L., & Choy, R. Y. L. (2006). Work-related stress: Its implication and management. *Journal of Psychology in Chinese Societies, 7*(1), 103–129.

Tennant, C. (2001). Work-related stress and depressive disorders. *Journal of Psychosomatic Research, 51,* 697–704.

Tweed, R. G., White, K., & Lehman, D. R. (2004). Culture, stress, and coping: Internally- and externally-targeted control strategies of European Canadians, east Asian Canadians, and Japanese. *Journal of Cross-Cultural Psychology, 35*(6), 652–668.

van der Klink, J. J. L., & van Dijk, F. J. H. (2003). Dutch practice guidelines for managing adjustment disorders in occupational and primary healthcare. *Scandinavian Journal of Work and Environmental Health, 29*(6), 478–487.

Veenhoven, R. (1993). *Happiness in Nations: Subjective appreciation of life in 56 Nations 1946–1992.* Rotterdam: Erasmus University Rotterdam.

Weyers, S., Peter, R., Bogild, H., Jeppesen, H. J., & Siegrist, J. (2006). Psychosocial work stress is associated with poor self-rated health in Danish nurses: A test of the effort-reward imbalance model. *Scandinavian Journal of Caring Sciences, 20*, 26–34.

World at Work (2007). Telework trending upward – Survey says. The Telework Advisory Group for World at Work. Obtained from http://workingfromanywhere.org/news/pr020707.html on July 10, 2007.

World Health Organization (2001). *The World Health Report 2001: Mental health: New understanding, new hope*. Geneva: World Health Organization.

World Health Organization (2006). *Preventing suicide: A resource at work. Department of Mental Health and Brain Disorders*. Geneva: World Health Organization.

5

Chronic Pain: Cultural Sensitivity to Pain

Jyh-Hann Chang

Along with the common cold and upper respiratory problems, pain complaints are one of the top three reasons why individuals visit physicians (Davidhizars & Giger, 2004). The definition of pain has changed over the years and current research has generated greater support for the recognition of the subjectivity of pain and how this subjectivity varies by culture. This is especially important as healthcare practitioners are faced with diverse populations who may express the symptoms of pain differently (Galanti, 2004; Gurung, 2006). This chapter provides an in-depth review of how pain is described and experienced, and how the treatment of the same varies by culture.

Pain is an integration of sensory and experiential processes. At the most basic level, *pain* can be referred to as *nociception*, the activation of specialized nerve fibers that signal the occurrence of tissue damage. Nociception is often accompanied by cognitive, behavioral, and affective states (Gurung, 2006). Pain can also be purely emotional in nature, without nociception, and is often described as *suffering*. Pain is a phenomenon that clearly exemplifies how important taking a biopsychosocial approach can be. Whereas pain can have direct biological causes, the experience of pain is strongly influenced by psychological and cultural factors. The World Health Organization (WHO) and the International Association for the Study of Pain (IASP) have defined pain as "sensation of unpleasant feeling indicating potential or actual damage to some body structure felt all over, or throughout the body." (WHO, 2007). The previous statement highlights the importance of treating pain as a perception and not just as an objective sensation. It involves sensitivity to chemical changes in the tissues and then the interpretation that such changes are harmful. This perception is realistic to the individual, whether or not harm has actually occurred or has the potential of occurring. Cognition is involved in the formulation of this perception. There are emotional consequences, and behavioral responses to the cognitive and emotional aspects of pain. Tissue damage or pain can be acute (short-term) or chronic (long-term).

Pain can be subdivided into two categories: acute and chronic (Dalton, 1989; Hiscock & Kadawatage, 1999; Lebovits, Florence, Bathina, Hunko, Fox, &

Bramble, 1997). Chronic pain is defined as pain that lasts longer than three months. Some experts have identified it as lasting longer than six months. Traditionally, it is more difficult to identify the root cause of chronic pain than acute pain; at times it is difficult to identify any bodily injury. Because of the complexity of the pain process, many theories and research describe the process.

Schemas Used to Describe the Complexity of Pain

Doleys, Murray, Klapow, and Coleton (1998) first described the complexity of chronic pain through four categories (a) organic pathology, (b) muscular deviation and dysfunctions, (c) mechanical deformities and abnormalities, and (d) behavioral and psychological factors. In 2000, Doleys condensed the four categories to three. They are: central-neuropathic, musculoskeletal-mechanical, and behavioral-psychological. *Central-neuropathic* is an alteration or change in the peripheral or central parts of the nervous system. *Musculoskeletal-mechanical* is a deformation due to lack of decommissioning, instability, or musculoskeletal difficulties. The *behavioral-psychological* category includes psychological states such as depression, anxiety, and somatic foreign pain disorder.

In addition to these three domains, a fourth category with an enormous influence on the perception of pain is *social-cultural*. The importance of culture and a person's social environment incorporates the most current conceptualization of chronic pain. Different ethnic and racial groups perceive, react, and adjust to pain differently (Rollman, 1998). For instance, Woodrow, Friedman, Siegelaub, and Collen (1972) assessed pressure pain tolerance in over 40,000 subjects, and African Americans showed significantly lower tolerances than Caucasian-Americans. Walsh, Schoenfeld, Ramamurthy, and Hoffman (1989) reported higher cold pressure pain tolerance in non-Hispanic European-Americans compared to a combined group of Hispanics and African–Americans. More recently, a study by McCracken (2001) compared adjustment to chronic pain of African Americans and European-Americans seeking treatment for chronic pain. The groups did not differ with regard to age, sex, education, chronicity of pain, pain location, work status, previous surgeries, medical diagnosis, medication, wage replacement, or involvement in litigation. However, the African-American group reported higher pain severity, more avoidance of activity, more fearful thinking, more physical symptoms, and greater physical and psychosocial disability. These results show that African Americans and European-Americans with chronic pain experience pain differently (McCracken, 2001), with the possibility that cultural influences on pain may underlie these differences.

Cultural Influences on Pain

There is an interrelationship between culture, health, and illness (Gurung, 2006). As described in the first chapter in this book, culture is defined as the values, beliefs, norms, rules of behavior, and lifestyle practices of a particular group of people that are learned and shared, and guide decisions and actions in a patterned manner (Leininger, 2001). Specific patterns of behavior or personality traits are greatly influenced by culture. Therefore, culture may dictate the level of pain perception.

A recent review of literature has shown that clinical and laboratory pain research indicates that a variety of cultural groups, including Italians, Japanese, Nepalese, African Americans, Native Americans, and European-Americans, differ considerably in their responses to an expression of pain (Edwards & Fillingim, 1999; Sheffield, Biles, Orom, Maixner, David and Sheps, 2000). Edwards and Fillingim (1999), in a study of healthy young adults, found that African Americans and non-Hispanic European Americans did not differ in their thermal pain threshold or ratings of thermal pain intensity. However, African Americans had lower thermal pain tolerances and subjectively rated thermal stimuli as more unpleasant. Using a similar design, a study by Sheffield et al. (2000), confirmed Edwards and Fillingim's study. Further review of the literature described the variations as shown in Table 5.1.

Table 5.1 Some examples of cultural variations in response to pain

Native Americans
May believe pain is due to taboo violation (Sobralske, 1985)
May regard pain as a way of life (Weber, 1996)
Family members may know patient has pain (Kramer et al., 1996)
Patients may say they just do not feel right (Kramer et al., 1996)
May use silence (Ondeck, 2003; Purnell & Paulanka, 2003)
Stoic endurance and emotional control (Muñoz & Luckmann, 2005; Ondeck, 2003)
Tolerate high level of pain (Galloway et al., 1999; Muñoz & Luckmann, 2005)
Seek relief when physically disabled (Stiller et al., 2003)

Mexican Americans
Nonverbal communication of pain (Douglas et al., 1989)
Wincing, groaning, grimacing (Calvillo & Flaskerud, 1991)
Try to work through pain (Villarruel, 1992)
Pain is God's will (Villarruel, 1992)
May regard pain as way of life (Villarruel & Ortiz de Montellano, 1992)
Exhibit inner control and self-endurance (Castro et al., 1994; Kosko & Flaskerud,1987)
Pain accepted as life obligation (Villarruel, 1995)
Tend not to complain of pain, stoic (de Paula, 1996)
May exhibit anxiety (Zoucha, 1998)
Mexican-Americans exhibit anxiety, nonverbal communications of pain (Zoucha, 1998)
Withstanding adversity, a cultural value (Stasiak, 2001)
Seek help if activities of daily living/work affected (Sobralske, 1985; Villarruel, 1992)
Ability to withstand pain, sign of manhood (Gravely, 2001; Klessing, 1992; Sobralske, 1985)

(cont'd)

Table 5.1   *(cont'd)*

Arab Americans
Expressive (Ondeck, 2003)
May tend to emphasize and exaggerate pain (Reizian & Meleis, 1986)
Suffering shows courage and faith (Reizian & Meleis, 1987)
May repeat message for emphasis (Reizian & Meleis, 1987)
May be more expressive around family members (Meleis, 1996)
Response may not reflect reality of pain (Meleis, 1996)
May fear pain (Meleis, 1996)
Pain helps cleanse soul (Meleis, 1996)
May be seen as punishment to redeem sins (Meleis, 1996)
May use analogies or metaphors (Reizian & Meleis, 1987)

Elders
Pain is useless, optimistic and confident of skilled professionals (Zborowski, 1969)
Association of chronic painful conditions and psychiatric morbidity (Blay et al., 2007)

Irish-American
Wanted to be left alone, proud of being able to tolerate pain, less concern of the
sensation of the pain, than the future implication (Zborowski, 1969)

Jewish
Terrific and unbearable-interpreted as to elicit offers of sympathy and help
(Zborowski 1969)

Italian-Americans
Crying, complaining, and using nonverbal gestures to express pain (Zborowski 1969)

Cultural Meaning of Pain

A person's cultural background provides a strong foundation to understand
how he or she expresses his or her pain symptoms in a given situation. Pain
symptoms have different meanings for different cultures, thus, understanding
and/or being sensitive to the meaning and expression of pain in different cultures can facilitate a health care worker's comprehension of the current pain
symptoms. Sensitivity to other cultures is an important part of understanding
the pain process. However, it is also important for the health care worker to
understand his or her own personal values and attitudes towards pain. When
others express pain in ways that are dissimilar from your own personal behavioral expressions, there may be a tendency to think that others are abnormal. This
discrepancy between patient and healthcare provider may be significant enough
to alter treatment options, even subtle cultural and individual differences,
particularly in nonverbal, spoken and written language between health care
providers and patients impact care (Weissman et al., 2004).

   Culture underlies the affective and cognitive components of pain. According
to Zborowski (1952) pain is learned through culturally transmitted values.
In his study, he noted that the differences in pain response between cultures
lessened with the length of time following immigration to the United States.

This time factor in a specific location appears to influence acculturation. The first model of pain based on cultural perception and ethnicity was Bates (1987) ethnicity and pain: Biocultural model. Bates (1987) integrated gate control theory with social learning theory. He stated that behaviors and responses to pain were influenced by culture. The meanings, attitudes, expectations, and emotional expressions of pain are learned through observations of cultural reactions and behaviors of others. This modeling of others' behavior is greatest when comparing sex differences in pain responses. Most would agree that there are cultural differences between sexes within most social societies. There is an enormous body of literature that demonstrates that women have significantly lower pain thresholds and tolerance levels than men and rate equally intense stimuli as more painful (Edwards et al., 1999; Ellermeier & Westphal, 1995; Fillingim et al., 1999; Lautenbacher & Rollman, 1993; Maixner & Humphrey, 1993; Riley III et al., 1998; Rollman et al., 1997, 2000; Rollman & Harris, 1987).

Clinicians and researchers should pay attention to both the influences of the physiological or mechanical domains but also the domain of culture and its influence on behaviors during their assessment, diagnosis, and treatment.

Assessment of Pain

It is difficult to assess how culture impacts pain sensitivity. Different cultural groups have variations in pain responses. Pain threshold is the point when the sensation of pain is perceived physically and acknowledged as painful. Clinicians should be aware of differences in sensitivity and tolerance across cultures. The current literature has indicated that there are racial differences in sensitivity. In a study comparing African Americans with European Americans, it has been suggested that enhanced pain sensitivity on the part of African Americans might partially explain the observed ethnic differences in the reported frequency and severity of clinical pain (Edwards & Fillingim, 1999).

Pain sensitivity has been detected in individuals as young as two months old (Rosmus, Johnston, Chan-Yip & Yang, 2000). In their study, Rosmus and colleagues compared the behavioral pain responses of two-month-old Canadian-born Chinese babies receiving a routine immunization to those of non-Chinese infants in similar situations. Two groups of 26 infants were obtained from a pediatric clinic held by a Chinese pediatrician and a suburban pediatric practice of a large Canadian city. Facial expression using the Neonatal Facial Coding System (Grunau, 1987) and crying using the Fast Fourier Transform were measured during 30 seconds following the insertion of the needle. Acculturation in Chinese mothers, circadian rhythm, gender, height and weight in infants were assessed. Multivariate analysis of variance revealed significant differences in pain response between these two groups with the Chinese babies showing greater response. No significant effect of circadian rhythm or gender was identified. These results (Rosmus et al., 2000) suggest the presence of differences in acute pain response in relation to culture and exhibited as early as two months of age.

In addition to racial differences in pain sensitivity there are cultural differences in tolerance levels (Hughes, 2005). Individuals vary in pain tolerance defined as the maximum level of pain one is willing to endure. Zatzick and Dimsdale (1976) identified three relevant studies, each of which reported increased pain tolerance among whites relative to African Americans. However, due to the classification based on skin color, one must be cautious in interpreting the results of the studies. It is worth mentioning that several studies report no significant differences. For example, Meehan et al. (1952) studied pain threshold with the Alaskan Indian, Inuit, and United States Air Force, Merkskey and Spear (1964) assessed pain threshold and tolerance with Caucasian and African-Asian male medical students, and Lambert, Libman, and Poser (1960) studied baseline pain tolerance values for Jewish and Protestant women. None of these studied found significant difference between groups.

Measures of Pain

McGill Pain Questionnaire

Traditionally, pain measurements are generally verbal, such as the McGill Pain Questionnaire (MPQ) which asks subjects to indicate which of a large number of adjectives describe their pain. The MPQ has been translated into a number of foreign languages (Arabic, Chinese, Flemish, Finnish, French, German, Italian, Japanese, Norwegian, Polish, Slovak, and Spanish; Melzack & Katz, 1992; Naughton & Wiklund, 1993), but most often it has been used to assess one culture at a time in one setting rather than across several cultures. The MPQ (Melzak, 1975) has been used widely to measure the level of pain characteristics and its associated clinical conditions (Dubuisson & Melzack, 1976; Graham, Bond, Gerkovich, & Cook, 1980). The questionnaire was constructed based on Melzack and Torgerson's (1971) original methodology, which involved having native speakers generate words and descriptors and classifying them into appropriate groupings (Harrison, 1988).

Questionnaires are reliable tools for cross-cultural assessment of pain. They can be revised in one of two ways for use with other languages (see related problems discussed in Chapter 2, this volume). One can directly translate the measure into another language (and back translate for validity) or one could use Melzack and Torgerson's process of developing the questionnaire described previously while keeping the specific culture in mind. Through these processes, two different versions of the same questionnaire can be generated. For example, in an Italian version of the MPQ, two sets of researchers adopted different approaches and developed essentially different questionnaires. The dictionary translation version replicates the English MPQ (Maiani & Sanavio, 1985). For the reconstructed version, the major classes of sensory, evaluative and affective were retained, added to the evaluative group. In the sensory class, several subclasses were eliminated, one was added, and another was subdivided.

The "punishment" subclass was renamed "negative emotional impact" to reflect the fact that in Italian, as in Finnish (Ketovuori & Pontinen, 1981), the concept of "punishing" such pain is not an appropriate category.

Graphic Rating Scales

GRSs are a "visual, numerical, and descriptive indicators, which asks the subject to focus successively on the worst pain he or she had experienced in the preceding 24 h, 7 days, and 2 months. The GRS consisted of printed 10 cm lines, above which appeared the numbers 1 through 5 evenly spaced along the line, and below which appeared the words "no pain," "slight pain," "moderate pain," "very bad pain," and "pain as bad as can be," positioned to correspond closely with the numbers. Subjects received instructions to circle the number which most closely corresponded to their worst pain over the specified period. For use with patients who may not speak or understand English, the numbers may be replaced by different cartoons of faces with difference emotions. The position corresponding to no pain or a 1 is a smiling face whereas the position corresponding to the worst pain is a frowning face (Gurung, 2006). This measure is also used with patients from different cultural backgrounds with simple instructions printed in different languages beneath it (McGrath et al., 2001).

Many scientists have studied the interconnections between ethnicity, attitudes, and behaviors related to health and illness. In a study by Greenwald (1991), researchers gathered data on patients on several different forms of cancer; lung, pancreas, prostate, and uterine cervix. A significant proportion of individuals with each malignancy evidenced serious pain problems. Samples of patients with the above malignancies in King and Pierce Counties, Washington, were obtained from the Cancer Surveillance System (CSS), a population-based tumor registry maintained by the Fred Hutchinson Cancer Research Center in Seattle. The study reported here was restricted to recently diagnosed, primary malignancies and to individuals older than 20 years and younger than 80 years, whose names were entered into the CSS registry during an 18 month data collection period between 1980 and 1981. This study found no relationship between ethnicity and scores on the indices most readily interpretable as reflecting pain as a purely sensory experience. Relations between ethnicity and pain measured by the GRS or the MPQ Sensory subscale were not statistically significant, but multiple regression analysis indicated statistically significant relations between several ethnic categories and pain expressed in emotional terms, as measured by the MPQ Affective subscale (Greenwald, 1991). This shows that not only are objective questionnaires important, it is also important to understand the communication or interpretation of a language in the culture describing pain within the assessment process.

Researchers and practitioners are paying an increasing amount of attention to pain in older people (Herr & Mobily, 1993). Bird (2003) identified a number of tools including the visual analogue scale (VAS), the verbal rating scale (VRS), numeric rating scale (NRS), faces pain scale, the McGill pain questionnaire (MPQ) (Melzack, 1975), and the Wong-Baker faces scale (Wong & Baker, 1988).The ideal scale for use with older populations is yet to be found, but most of the available scales have some degree of use with this patient group. Rutledge and Donaldson (1998) suggest that careful instruction is needed when using pain measurement tools with older people and that presentation should be sensitive to each patient's needs.

Culture and the Language of Pain

Efficient communication is made through a common language. The common language gives us the ability to describe specific values, knowledge and perception. Because pain is an experiential process, language is pertinent in describing the pain. Different cultures emphasize pain based on their cultural perspective. Fabrega and Tyma (1976a) write that in English, there are several basic terms-pain, sore, ache, sting, tenderness, throbbing, and hurt. However, in Thai, more than a dozen distinct basic pain terms are commonly used (Diller, 1980). In contrast, the Japanese language has a single blanket term for pain, which can be qualified by optional descriptors (Fabrega & Tyma, 1976b). The differences can be qualitative or quantitative. For instance, a Thai individual, using one of the basic pain terms, may convey information about the location or cause of pain (Diller, 1980). Zborowski (1969) recorded pain descriptors and noticed that how detached and "clinical" patients typically were in discussing their pain seemed to vary across ethnic groups.

Behavioral Responses

Aside from limitations in linguistic descriptors of pain, it is a well-established fact that diverse groups express their pain differently. For example, Italian patients are mainly concerned with the immediacy and the actual pain experience in a given situation. The concerns of patients of Jewish origin focus mainly upon the symptomatic meaning of pain and upon the significance of pain in relation to health, welfare and, ultimately, the welfare of their families (Zborowski, 1969). Italian patients express their discomfort caused by pain by displacing their behaviors and complaints upon their immediate situation such as occupation, economic situation etc.; Jewish patients express primarily their worries and anxieties as to the extent to which the pain indicates a threat to their health (Zborowski, 1969). These somewhat stereotypical response styles may not generalize to all members of the ethnic group. In fact, although Zborowski (1969) provided important insights into cultural differences in pain, caution is needed in using his findings as all his conclusions came from staff reports at one single hospital, the New York Veterans Administration hospital.

Behavioral expression of pain also depends on what is considered acceptable or appropriate for a given culture. A relatively recent study by Nayak, Shiflett, Eshun, and Levine (2000) supported the concept that a belief in appropriate behaviors will dictate overt expression of those behaviors. Nayak et al. (2000) compared beliefs about appropriate pain response among college students in India and the United States. Their results demonstrate that the sample of students in India believe that the overt expression of pain is significantly less acceptable than do a comparable group in the United States. Likewise, consistent with these normative beliefs, students in India exhibited higher pain tolerance than students in the United States (Nayak et al., 2000).

The response to pain is influenced by culture and may determine how a patient seeks care. Health care professionals have to rely on verbal descriptions and behavioral responses in making assessment and treatment decisions. As a result, disparities in pain management might occur because patients from different cultural groups express pain differently and/or physicians interpret these expressions differently based on their own cultural background. Zola (1996), compared physicians' assessments of the pain complaints (when no organic basis for pain could be identified) among female Italian and Irish patients. He found that significantly more Italian patients were diagnosed as having psychiatric problems, even when there was no independent evidence to confirm such problems. Streltzer and Wade (1981) investigated differences in postoperative pain management among a group of Caucasian, Chinese, Japanese, Filipino, and Hawaiian patients undergoing elective cholecystectomy. They found that the Hawaiian and Caucasian patients received significantly more medication than the other groups. Similarly, Pilowsky and Bond (1969) reported a study by which female patients were more likely than male patients to be provided with analgesics. Awareness of the different manner in which diverse cultural groups and genders with the way they communicate their pain may enhance the quality of medical care by making health care providers sensitive to these possible biases.

Diagnosis of Pain

Pain symptoms can be associated with many disorders and diseases. The *International Classification of Disease (ICD)* and *The Diagnostic and Statistical Manual of Mental Disorders (DSM–IV–TR)* attempt to classify diseases and disorders efficiently; promoting accurate communications between professionals. *ICD-10* was endorsed by the 43rd World Health Assembly in May 1990 and came into use in World Health Organization (WHO) Member States as from 1994. The *ICD* has become the international standard diagnostic classification for all general epidemiological and many health management purposes. These include the analysis of the general health situation of population groups and monitoring of the incidence and prevalence of diseases and other health problems in relation to other variables such as the characteristics and circumstances of the individuals affected.

The Diagnostic and Statistical Manual of Mental Disorders (DSM)

DSM is the standard classification of mental disorders used by mental health professionals in the United States. These diagnostic codes are derived from the coding system used by all health care professionals in the United States, known as the *ICD-10*. It is intended to be applicable in a wide array of contexts and used by clinicians and researchers of many different orientations (e.g., biological, psychodynamic, cognitive, behavioral, interpersonal, family/systems). The following diagnostic feature involves a pain component.

The *DSM–IV* states that the main component of Pain Disorder is pain and it is the focus of the clinical presentation. The pain causes significant distress or impairment in social, occupation, or other areas of functioning. The subtype "Pain Disorders Associated with Psychological Factors (307.8)" is used when psychological factors are judged to have a major role in the severity, exacerbation, or maintenance of the pain. General medical condition either plays no role or minimal role in the onset or maintenance of the pain. The main diagnostic criteria for pain disorder are pain self-report; it is crucial that practitioners are culturally competent and aware of generalized modes of responses as well as unique presentation styles.

Pain Treatments

The differences in attitudes, values, perception, and behaviors on chronic pain can be quite daunting for healthcare professionals. These differences may have enormous implications for the treatment process. Inadequacies in pain treatment persist in a wide array of settings and across the acute, chronic, and terminal conditions (Gurege, Von Korff, Simon, & Gater, 1998). Nonwhite patients across all ages are significantly more likely to be under treated for pain regardless of type of pain (achieved, cancer, postoperative, chronic nonmalignant, and the life) and in a wide variety of settings (Green, Anderson, Baker, et al., 2003). Treatment, assessment and diagnosis can be a daunting process because of the diversity in describing the pain process. A few studies have demonstrated discrepancies in treatment in the areas of medication and end-of-life.

Biological differences between diverse racial groups results in differences in treatment. This potential biological difference may impact medical regimens. A recent study by Chen, Kurz, Pasanen, Faselis, et al., 2005) indicated that European-Americans were more likely to be treated with opioids than African Americans and more likely to receive physical therapy. There were no significant racial differences in the use of Nonsteroidal anti-inflammatory drugs (NSAIDs), pain specialists, or other specialty providers. This discrepancy is also prevalent in end-of-life treatments.

Little is known about pain management for chronic medical illnesses within the setting of outpatient End of Life Center (EOLC), about pain reporting among older patients of different ethnicities, or about the potential influence of patient immigration status on pain treatment (Rabow, Petersen, Schanche, Dibble, & Mcphee, 2003). In order to assess whether there are ethnic differences in pain reporting or pain management in the outpatient setting among older patients with serious illnesses, Rabow et al. (2003) examined the reporting of pain and its treatment among a cohort of patients representing multiple ethnicities and countries of origins, with either terminal illness, end-stage heart disease, or end stage cultural groups and deficiencies in end-of-life care (EOLC). Results suggest that there are discrepancies in pain management at the end of life for outpatients of diverse ethnicities for both chronic and terminal illness. Pain management was especially poor for people of color (Rabow, 2005).

Models for Culturally Sensitive Treatment of Pain

Several models have been postulated to represent culturally sensitive treatment of pain. Three models, Rollman et al.'s (2004) Biopsychosocial Model, Davidhizars and Giger's (2004) Culturally Appropriate Assessment and Management Model, and Weissman et al.'s (2004) Cultural Aspects of Pain Management will be presented below.

A biopsychosocial perspective by Rollman and colleagues (2004) recognizes that a large number of factors influence individual and group differences in behavior. He postulated that biological influences must account for some of the differences between individuals and that most differences that do exist are almost certainly based upon psychological and social characteristics. Implications for future treatments of pain in patients of diverse culture should consider a model that incorporates some of the following differences in pain responsiveness (Rollman et al., 2004). Individuals will differ with respect to:

1. *monitoring* – the extent to which they pay attention to internal bodily events;
2. *symptom attribution* – the extent to which they consider bodily events as indicative of a dysfunction rather than a normal biological process;
3. *coping mechanisms* – the manner in which individuals deal with negative events, including their dependence on other individuals (such as health care providers) and agents (such as analgesics) rather than internal psychological processes;
4. *somatization* – the extent to which negative psychological events and cognitions contribute to increased reports of physical discomfort.

Davidhizars and Giger (2004), after reviewing the literature on the care of clients from diverse cultures who are in pain, developed the following strategies for the treatment of pain. The strategies that he developed can assist in culturally appropriate assessment and management of pain:

1. Utilize assessment tools to assist in measuring pain. Davidhizars and Giger (2004) has suggested using several inventories. The Brief Pain Inventory (BPI) shows a high degree of reliability and validity in countries outside the United States (Cleeland et al., 1994; Cleeland et al., 1997). The Numerical Rating Scale (NRS) has been translated into multiple languages and can be easily administered to very sick patients (McCaffrey & Pasero, 1999). The Visual Analog Scale (VAS), horizontal and vertical lines with word anchors for which an individual places a mark.
2. Appreciate variations in affective response to pain. Be sensitive to variations in communication styles. Cultural responses to pain can be divided into two categories: Stoic or emotive. Stoic is less expressive; emotive is more likely to verbalize expressions.
3. Be sensitive to variations in communication styles and aware of nonverbal communication.
4. Recognize that communication of pain may not be acceptable within a culture. For members of some cultures, requesting help may be a sign of disrespect or shame.
5. Appreciate that the meaning of pain varies between cultures. Interpretation of pain can vary; for example Catholics may seek religious and spiritual powers in coping with pain.
6. Utilize knowledge of biological variations; Salerno (1995) stated that there are subtle differences in drug metabolism, dosing requirements, therapeutic responses, and side effects in racial and ethnic groups.
7. Develop personal awareness of values and beliefs which may affect responses to pain. Health-care providers' personal orientation to pain may influence pain treatment (Davidhizars & Giger, 2004).

Weissman et al. (2002), continuing the emphasis on cultural values, also indicated the importance of the interaction or communication between health care professionals and patients. They write that to be culturally competent, one must:

1. be aware of your own cultural and family values;
2. be aware of your personal biases and assumptions about people with different values than yours;
3. be aware and accept cultural differences between yourself and individual patients;
4. be capable of understanding the dynamics of the difference;
5. be able to adapt to diversity;
6. listen with empathy to the patient's perception of their pain;
7. explain your perception of the pain problem;
8. acknowledge the differences and similarities in perceptions;
9. recommend treatment; and
10. negotiate agreement.

In addition questions that staff can use to help assess cultural differences include:

1. What do you call your pain? Do you have a name for it?
2. What do you think caused your [pain]? Why do you think it started when it did?
3. What does your [pain] do to you? How does it work?
4. How severe is your pain? Will it have a long or short course?
5. What are the most important results you hope to receive from the treatment?
6. What are the main problems your [pain] has caused you?
7. What do you fear most about your [pain]?

Conclusions

The literature reviewed indicates that significant discrepancies exist in health care (Schneider, 2002). There is strong evidence in the pain literature that racial and ethnic minority patients may receive inadequate pain assessment and treatment (Cleeland, Gonin, Baez, Loehrer, Kishan & Pandya, 1994; Cleeland et al. 1997) even at the community level whereby pharmacies in predominantly nonwhite neighborhoods of New York City do not stock sufficient medications to treat patients with severe pain adequately (Morrison, Wallenstein, Natale, Senzel, & Huang, 2000).

Researchers have postulated several reasons for the discrepancies. For example, ethnic differences in patient–physician communication, decision-making, and advance directives (McCracken, Matthews, Tang, & Cuba, 2001; Morrison, Zayas, Mulvihill, Baskin, & Meier, 1998); utilization of palliative care services and local pharmacy availability of prescribed opioids (Morrison, Wallenstein, Natale, Senzel, & Huang, 2000). However, Green, Anderson et al. (2003) stated that there is a complex relationship between pain and ethnicity. Each of the areas that likely contribute to these differences: pain perception, assessment, and treatment with regard to patient, clinician, and healthcare system perspectives. Further research, using psycholinguistic, social learning, ethological and cognitive perspectives will help to develop insights on understanding differences in what people consider to be painful and how they respond. Patient's beliefs and preferences which are developed by their culture is the most common potential source for the disparities in health care. Professionals inadequately understand these health-care disparities.

REFERENCES

Bates, M. S. (1987). Ethnicity and pain: A biocultural model. *Social Science and Medicine, 24*(1), 47–50.
Bates, M. S. (1996). *Biocultural dimensions of chronic pain*. Albany: State University of New York Press.
Bates, M. S., Rankin-Bates, M. S., Edwards, W. T., & Anderson, K. O. (1993). Ethnocultural influences on variation in chronic pain perception. *Pain 52*: 101–112.

Berlin, E. A., & Fowkes, W. C. (1983). A teaching framework for cross-cultural health care: Application in family practice. *Western Journal of Medicine, 139*(6), 934–938.

Bird, J. (2003). Selection of pain measurement tools. *Nursing Standard, 18*(13), 33–39.

Berlin, E. A., & Fowkes, W. C. (1983). A teaching framework for cross-cultural health care: Application in family practice. *Western Journal of Medicine, 139*(6), 934–938.

Blay, S. L., Andreoli, S. B., Dewey, M., & Gastal, F. b. L. (2007). Co-occurrence of chronic physical pain and psychiatric morbidity in a community sample of older people. *International Journal of Geriatric Psychiatry, 22*(9), 902–908.

Callister, L. C. (2003). Cultural influences on pain perceptions and behaviors. *Home Health Care Management & Practice, 15*(3), 207–211.

Calvillo, E. R., & Flaskerud, J. H. (1991). Review of literature on culture and pain of adults with focus on Mexican-Americans. *J Transcult Nurs, 2*(2), 16–23.

Castro, O., Brambilla, D. J., Thorington, B., Reindorf, C. A., Scott, R. B., Gillette, P. et al. (1994). The acute chest syndrome in sickle cell disease: Incidence and risk factors. The Cooperative Study of Sickle Cell Disease. *Blood, 84*(2), 643–649.

Chen, I., Kurz, J., Pasanen, M., et al. (2005). Racial differences in opioid use for chronic nonmalignant pain. *Journal of Internal Medicine, 20*, 593–598.

Cleeland, C. S., Gonin, R., Baez, L., Loehrer, P. Kishan, J., & Pandya, K. J. (1994). Pain and its treatment in outpatients with metastatic cancer. *The New England Journal of Medicine, 330*(9), 592–596.

Cleeland, C. S., Gonin, R., Baez, L., Loehrer, P., & Pandya, K. J. (1997). Pain and treatment of pain in minority patients with cancer. The eastern cooperative oncology group. *Annals of Internal Medicine, 127*(9), 813–816.

Dalton, J. (1989). Nurses' perceptions of their pain assessment skills, pain management practices and attitudes towards pain. *Oncology Nursing Forum, 16*, 225–231.

Davidhizars, R., & Giger, J. N. (2004). A review of the literature on the care of clients in pain who are culturally diverse. *International Nursing Review, 51*(1), 47–55.

Dalton, J. (1989). Nurses' perceptions of their pain assessment skills, pain management practices and attitudes towards pain. *Oncology Nursing Forum, 16*, 225–231.

de Paula, M. A. (1996). [Performance of stoma therapy in the process of rehabilitation of ostomy patients]. *Rev Bras Enferm, 49*(1), 17–22.

Diller, A. (1980). Pain. *Pain, 9*(1), 9–26.

Doleys, D. M., Murray, J. B., Klapow, J. C., & Coleton, M. L. (1998). *The management of pain.* New York: Churchill Livingstone.

Douglas, M. J., Ross, P. L., & Olsen, E. C. (1989). A simple device for improving patient comfort. *Can J Anaesth, 36*(1), 101.

Dubuisson, D., & Melzack, R. (1976). Classification of clinical pain descriptions by multiple group discriminant analysis. *Experimental Neurology, 51*(2), 480–487.

Edwards, R. R., Doleys, D. M., Fillingim, R. B., & Lowery, D. (2001). Ethnic differences in pain tolerance: Clinical implications in a chronic pain population. *Psychosomatic Medicine, 63*, 316–323.

Edwards, R. R., & Fillingim, R. (1999). Ethnic differences in thermal pain responses. *Psychosomatic Medicine, 61*, 346–354.

Ellermeier, W., & Westphal, W. (1995) Gender differences in pain ratings and pupil reactions to painful pressure stimuli. *Pain, 61*(3), 435–439.

Fabrega, H., & Tyma, S. (1976a). Culture, language and the shaping of illness. *Journal Psychosomatic Research, 20*, 323–337.

Fabrega, H., & Tyma, S. (1976b). Language and cultural influences in the description of pain. *British Journal of Medical Psychology, 47*, 349–371.

Fillingim, R. B., Maddux, V., & Shackelford, J. A. (1999). Sex differences in heat pain thresholds as a function of assessment method and rate of rise. *Somatosens Mot Res, 16*(1), 57–62.

Galanti, G. (2004). *Caring for patients from different cultures: Case studies from American hospitals.* Philadelphia: University of Pennsylvania Press.

Galloway, A., Wright, J., Murphy, O., & Dickinson, G. (1999). Sensitivity testing of Pseudomonas aeruginosa to ciprofloxacin: Comparison of the modified Stokes' method with MIC results obtained by the Etest. *J Antimicrob Chemother, 43*(2), 314–315.

Garrett, D. (1996). Differences in end-of-life decision making among black and white ambulatory cancer patients. *Journal General Internal Medicine, 11,* 651–656.

Graham, C., Bond, S. S., Gerkovich, M. M., & Cook, M. R. (1980). Use of the McGill pain questionnaire in the assessment of cancer pain: Replicability and consistency. *Pain, 8,* 377–387.

Gravely, S. (2001). When your patient speaks Spanish – and you don't. *RN, 64*(5), 65–67.

Green, C. R, Anderson, K. O., Baker, T. A, et al. (2003). The unequal burden of pain: Confronting racial and ethnic disparities in pain. *Pain Medicine, 4,* 277–294.

Green, C. R., Baker, T., & Washington, T. (2003). Health care attitudes and utilization in chronic pain patients: A comparison of African and Caucasian Americans. *Pain, 4*(2), 97.

Greenwald, H. P. (1991) Inter-ethnic differences in pain perception. *Pain, 44,* 157–162.

Grunau, R. V. (1987). Pain expression in neonates: Facial action and cry. *Pain, 28*(3), 395–410.

Gureje, O., Von Korff, M., Simon, G. E., & Gater, R. (1998). Persistent pain and well being: A World Health Organization study in primary care. *Journal of the American Medical Association, 280,* 147–151.

Gurung, R. A. R. (2006). *Health psychology: A cultural approach.* San Francisco, CA: Wadsworth.

Harrison, A. (1988). Arabic pain words. *Pain, 32*(2), 239–250.

Herr, K., & Mobily, P. (1993). Comparison of selected pain tools for use with the elderly. *Applied Nursing Research, 6*(1), 39–46.

Hill, L., & Sánchez-Ayendez, M. (1997). The effects of the cultural context of health care on treatment of and response to chronic pain and illness. *Social Science and Medicine, 45*(9), 1433–1447.

Hiscock, M., & Kadawatage, G. (1999). Comparative study of the attitudes of nurses and patients from two different cultures towards pain. *Journal of Orthopedic Nursing, 3,* 146–151.

Hughes R. A. (2005). A critical review of dimensions-specific measure health-related quality of life in cross-cultural research. Multidisciplinary Consensus Group, *Archives of Neurology, 62*(8), 1194–1198.

Ketovuori, H., & Pontinen, P. J. (1981). A pain vocabulary in Finnish: The Finnish Pain Questionnaire, *Pain, 11,* 274–253.

Kleinman, A. K., Eisenberg, L., & Good, B. (1978). Culture illness and care: Clinical lessons from anthropologic and cross-cultural research. *Ann Int Med., 88,* 251–258.

Klessing, J. (1992). Cross-cultural medicine: A decade later. *Western Journal of Medicine, 157*(3), 316–322.

Kosko, D. A., & Flaskerud, J. H. (1987). Mexican American, nurse practitioner, and lay control group beliefs about cause and treatment of chest pain. *Nurs Res, 36*(4), 226–231.

Kramer, J., Owczarek, V., & Bickert, U. (1996). [Lumbar epidural injections in orthopedic pain therapy. Standards–guidelines–current techniques–results]. *Z Orthop Ihre Grenzgeb, 134*(3), 12–17.

Laborde, E. B., & Texidor, M. S. (1996). Knowledge and attitudes toward chronic pain management among home health care nurses. *Home Health Care Management and Practice, 9,* 73–77.

Lambert, W. E., Libman, E., & Poser, E. G. (1960). The effect of increased salience of a membership group on pain tolerance. *Journal of Personality, 28,* 350–357.

Lautenbacher, S., & Rollman, G. B. (1993). Sex differences in responsiveness to painful and non-painful stimuli are dependent upon the stimulation method. *Pain, 53*(3), 255–264.

Lebovits, A., Florence, I., Bathina, R., Hunko, V., Fox, M., & Bramble, C. (1997). Pain knowledge and attitudes of healthcare providers: Practice characteristic differences. *Clinical Journal of Pain, 13,* 237–243.

Leininger, M. M. (2001). Current issues in using anthropology in nursing education and services. *Western Journal of Nursing Research, 23*(8), 795–806; discussion 807–711.

McCaffery, M., & Pasero, C. (1999). How can we improve the way we perform our pain assessments to meet the needs of patients from diverse cultures? *Am J Nurs, 99*(8), 18. in, *9*(1), 16–25.

McCracken, L. M. (2001). Predicting complains of impaired cognitive function in patients with chronic pain. *Journal of Pain and Symptom Management, 21*(5), 392–396.

McCracken L. M., Matthews, A. K., Tang, T. S,, & Cuba S. L. A. (2001). Comparison of blacks and whites seeking treatment for chronic pain. *Clinical Journal of Pain, 17,* 249–255.

McGrath, P., Vun, M., & McLeod, L. (2001). Needs and experiences of non-English-speaking hospice patients and families in an English-speaking country. *Am J Hosp Palliat Care, 18*(5), 305–312.

MacLaren, J. E., Gross, R. T., Sperry, J. A., & Boggess, J. T. (2006) Impact of opioid use on outcomes of functional restoration. *The Clinical Journal of Pain, 22*(4), 392–398.

Maiani, G., & Sanavio, E. (1985). Semantics of pain in Italy: The Italian version of the McGill pain questionnaire, *Pain, 22*(4), 399–405.

Maixner, W., & Humphrey, C. (1993). Gender differences in pain and cardiovascular responses to forearm ischemia. *Clinical Journal of Pain, 9*(1), 16–25.

Mattick, W. L., Meehan, D. J., & Haberlin, J. P. (1952). Squamous-cell carcinoma of the floor of the mouth. *Surgery, 31*(4), 575–582.

Meehan, J. P. (1959). The measurement of verbal responses to experimentally induced changes in emotional states: I. The arousal of fear. *Journal of Psychological Studies, 11,* 1–6.

Meleis, A. I. (1996). Culturally competent scholarship: Substance and rigor. *ANS Adv Nurs Sci, 19*(2), 1–16.

Melzack, R. (1975). The McGill Pain Questionnaire: Major properties and scoring methods. *Pain, 1*(3), 277–299.

Melzack, R., Katz, J., & Coderre, T. J. (1992). Methods of postoperative pain control. *Cah Anesthesiol, 40*(5), 309–315.

Melzack, R., & Torgerson, W. S. (1971). On the language of pain. *Anesthesiology, 34,* 50–59.

Merkskey, H., & Spear, F. G. (1964). The reliability of the pressure algometer. *British Journal of Social & Clinical Psychology, 3,* 130–136.

Morrison, R. S., Wallenstein, S., Natale, D. K., Senzel, R. S., & Huang, L. L. (2000). "We don't carry that": Failure of pharmacies in predominantly nonwhite neighborhoods to stock opioid analgesics. *New England Journal of Medicine, 342,* 1023–1026.

Morrison, R. S., Zayas, L. H., Mulvihill, M., Baskin, S. A., & Meier, D. E. (1998). Barriers to completion of health care proxies: An examination of ethnic differences. *Archives of Internal Medicine, 158,* 2493–2497.

Muñoz, C., & Luckmann, J. (2005). Transcultural communication in nursing (2nd ed.). Clifton, NY: Delmar Learning.

Naughton, M. J., & Wiklund, I. (1993). A critical review of dimension-specific measures of health-related quality of life in cross-cultural research. *Journal of Quality of Life Research, 2*(6).

Nayak, S., Shiflett, S. C., Eshun, S., & Levine, F. M. (2000). Culture and gender effects in pain beliefs and the prediction of pain tolerance. *Cross-Cultural Research, 34*(2), 135–151.

Ondeck, D. M. (2003). Impact of culture on pain. *Home Health Care Management & Practice, 15*(3), 255–257.

Pilowsky, I., & Bond, M. R. (1969). Pain and its management in malignant disease elucidation of staff-patient transactions. *Journal of Psychosomatic Medicine, 31,* 400–404.

Porter, C. P., & Villarruel, A. M. (1993). Nursing research with African American and Hispanic people: Guidelines for action. *Nurs Outlook, 41*(2), 59–67.

Purnell, L. D., & Paulanka, B. J. (2003). *Transcultural health care: A culturally competent approach* (2nd ed.). Philadelphia: F.A. Davis.

Rabow, M. W. (2005) Ethnic differences in pain among outpatients with terminal and end-stage chronic illness. *Pain Medicine, 6*(3), 235–241.

Rabow, M. W., Petersen, J. J., Schanche, K., Dibble, S. L., & Mcphee, S. J. (2003). The comprehensive care team: A description of a controlled trial of care at the beginning of the end of life. *Journal of Palliative Medicine, 6,* 489–499.

Reizian, A., & Meleis, A. I. (1986). Arab-Americans' perceptions of and responses to pain. *Crit Care Nurse, 6*(6), 30–37.

Reizian, A., & Meleis, A. I. (1987). Symptoms reported by Arab-American patients on the Cornell Medical Index (CMI). *West J Nurs Res, 9*(3), 368–384.

Riley, J. L., 3rd, Robinson, M. E., Wise, E. A., Myers, C. D., & Fillingim, R. B. (1998). Sex differences in the perception of noxious experimental stimuli: A meta-analysis. *Pain, 74*(2–3), 181–187.

Rollman, B. L., Mead, L. A., Wang, N. Y., & Klag, M. J. (1997). Medical specialty and the incidence of divorce. *N Engl J Med, 336*(11), 800–803.

Rollman, G. B. (1998). Culture and pain. In S. S. Kazarian & D. R. Evans (Ed.), *Cultural clinical psychology: Theory, research, and practice* (pp. 267–86). New York: Oxford University Press.

Rollman, G. B., Abdel-Shaheed, J., Gillespie, J. M., & Jones, K. S. (2004). Does past pain influence current pain: Biological and psychosocial models of sex differences. *Eur J Pain, 8*(5), 427–433.

Rollman, G. B., & Gillespie, J. M. (2000). The role of psychosocial factors in temporomandibular disorders. *Curr Rev Pain, 4*(1), 71–81.

Rollman, G. B., & Harris, G. (1987). The detectability, discriminability, and perceived magnitude of painful electrical shock. *Percept Psychophys, 42*(3), 257–268.

Rosmus, C., Johnston, C. C., Chan-Yip, A., & Yang, F. (2000). Pain response in Chinese and non-Chinese Canadian Infants: Is there a difference. *Social Science Medicine, 51*(2), 175–184.

Rutledge, D., & Donaldson, N. (1998). Pain assessment and documentation: Overview and application in adults. *Journal of Clinical Innovations, 1*(5), 1–37. Retrieved November 12, 2002, from https://www.cinahl.com/cgibin/ojcishowdoc3.cgi?index.html.

Salerno, E. (1995). Race, culture, and medications. *Journal of Emergency Nursing, 21*(6), 560–562.

Schneider, E. C., Zaslavsky, A. M., & Epstein, A. M. (2002). Racial disparities in the quality of care for enrollees in medicare managed care. *JAMA, 287*(10), 1288–1294.

Sheffield, D., Biles, L. P., Orom, H., Maixner, W., David, S., & Sheps, D. S. (2000). Race and sex difference in cutaneous pain perception. *Psychosomatic Medicine, 62*, 517–523.

Sobralske, M. C. (1985). Perceptions of health: Navajo Indians. *Top Clin Nurs, 7*(3), 32–39.

Streltzer, J., & Wade, T. C. (1981). The influence of cultural group on the undertreatment of postoperative pain. *Psychosom Med, 43*(5), 397–403.

Stasiak, M. (2001). The effect of early specific feeding on food conditioning in cats. *Dev Psychobiol, 39*(3), 207–215.

Stein, U., Klessing, K., & Chatterjee, S. S. (1991). Losigamone. *Epilepsy Res Suppl, 3*, 129–133.

Stiller, C. O., Taylor, B. K., Linderoth, B., et al. (2003). Microdialysis in pain research. *Adv Drug Deliv Rev, 55*(8), 1065–1079.

Streltzer, J., & Wade, T. C. (1981). The influence of cultural group on the undertreatment of postoperative pain. *Psychosom Med, 43*(5), 397–403.

Villarruel, A. M. (1995). Mexican-American cultural meanings, expressions, self-care and dependent-care actions associated with experiences of pain. *Res Nurs Health, 18*(5), 427–436.

Villarruel, A. M., & Ortiz de Montellano, B. (1992). Culture and pain: A Mesoamerican perspective. *ANS Adv Nurs Sci, 15*(1), 21–32.

Walsh, N. E., Schoenfeld, L., Ramamurthy, S., & Hoffman, J. (1989). Normative model for cold pressor test. *American Journal of Physical Medicine and Rehabilatation, 68*, 6–11.

Weber, S. E. (1996). Cultural aspects of pain in childbearing women. *J Obstet Gynecol Neonatal Nurs, 25*(1), 67–72.

Weissman, D. (2003) Medical oncology and palliative care: The intersection of end-of-life care. *Journal of Palliative Medicine, 6*(6), 859–861.

Weissman, D. E., Gordon, D., & Bidar-Sielaff, S. (2004). Cultural aspects of pain management. *Journal of Palliaitive Medicine, 7*(5), 715–716.

Wong, D., & Baker, C. (1988). Pain in children: Comparison of assessment scales. *Pediatric Nurse, 14*(1), 9–17.

Woodrow, K. M., Friedman, G. D., Siegelaub, A. B., & Collen, M. F. (1972). Pain tolerance: Differences according to age, sex, and race. *Psychosomatic Medicine, 34*, 548–556.

World Health Organization (2007). Sensory functions and pain. Retrieved January 5, 2008, from http://www.who.int/classifications/icf/site/onlinebrowser/icf.cfm?parentlevel=4&childlevel=5&itemslevel=5&ourdimension=b&ourchapter=2&ourblock=4&our2nd=80&our3rd=0&our4th=0.

Zatzick, D. F., & Dimsdale, J. (1990). Cultural variations in response to painful stimuli. *Psychosomatic Medicine, 52*, 544–557.

Zborowski, M. (1952). Cultural components in responses to pain. *Journal of Social Issues, 8*, 16–39.

Zborowski, M. (1969). *People in pain.* San Francisco, CA: Jossey Boss.

Zola, I. K. (1996). Culture and symptoms: An analysis of patients' presenting complaints. *American Sociological Review, 31*, 615–630.

Zoucha, R. D. (1998). The experiences of Mexican Americans receiving professional nursing care: An ethnonursing study. *J Transcult Nurs, 9*(2), 34–44.

6

Placing the Soul Back into Psychology: Religion in the Psychotherapy Process

Paul E. Priester, Shiva Khalili,
and Jose E. Luvathingal

Religion plays an especially important role in the interplay of culture and mental health and it is important to merge the growing information on religion and mental health with that on culture and mental health (Loewenthal, 2007). In contrast to many other chapters in this book that hightlight ethnic, racial, and geographic differences, this chapter focuses on a major example of culture: Religion. This chapter will explore the integration of religion in the psychotherapy process from a variety of perspectives. This topic allows for an examination of the role that culture plays in guiding psychological theory, practice, and research. First, we present a brief overview of the relationship between religion and the history and philosophy of science. Next, we review the research on the role that religion plays in mental health. We then explore the interrelation of culture, mental health, and religion, and explore what researchers have discovered regarding the impact of the inclusion of religion as a variable in the psychotherapy process. Finally, we offer suggestions to practicing clinicians regarding the use of religion in a clinical setting.

A Brief History of Religion in the Science of Psychology

Religions have contributed to the development of ideas about human behavior and mental problems by offering specific theories of personality, causes of mental illness, and how people recover from mental illness. Similarly, the scientific paradigms have had different perspectives on the existence of God and the role that religious belief and practice have in fostering or curing mental illness.

Prehistoric Era up to Medieval Age

During prehistoric times most early theories about the causes and treatments for abnormal behavior and emotional problems were focused on supernatural causes. Ointments, massage, diet, drugs, exorcism, and extraction of foreign spirits were believed to cure the disorders.

Hippocrates (fifth century BC) rejected the idea of supernatural causes and believed that brain pathology was the source of the mental problems. Some Greek and Roman philosophers (such as Plato and Aristotle) highlighted the role of rationality in human beings, which contributed to the idea that the way we think can also be the cause of our mental problems (Dryden & Mytton, 1999). The models developed by Plato and Aristotle provided a framework for Jewish, Christian, and Muslim scholars (such as Thomas Aquinas and Ibn Sina) to offer their theistic theories of persons within their philosophies.

Throughout the medieval age, Renaissance, and until the eighteenth century the Christian worldview formed the scientific paradigm in the western countries as the Islamic worldview formed a scientific paradigm in the Islamic countries. This means that a consistent system of knowledge or hierarchy of sciences was based upon a theistic worldview presented at the religious institutions and universities of the time (Russell, 2000). Mental disorders and illnesses, their causes and their treatments, were usually seen as connected to concepts of God and angels; Satan and demons; good and evil. The theistic presumptions (divine doctrines) were mixed with traditional or personal nontheological and often superstitious ideas and were held sacred alongside with the basic doctrines. Superstitions, rather than original religious teachings dominated the societies' confrontations with the mentally ill.

The sociopolitical changes in the western countries in the eighteenth and nineteenth century, together with the appearance of the philosophies of the Enlightenment – Reductionism, Materialism, and Naturalism – and the interpretations of Darwin's evolution theory, led to a gradual replacement of the metaphysical theological presumptions of the knowledge system with a naturalistic worldview, declaring that there is no need for the concepts of God, soul, demons, angels and other supernatural themes in the system of sciences, as everything (including mental illness and all psychological processes) have *natural* causes and origins.

Religion and the Psychological Theories of the Past Century

Beside the attempts to find physical causes for all mental disorders, there has been considerable interest in finding psychological causes. Modern psychology and psychotherapy in the past century grew from a naturalistic worldview using a physicalist theory of person. Despite having similar worldviews, the sociocultural contexts and personal experiences of the founders of schools of psychotherapy led to different theories in this field. Each had different basic concepts, definitions of psychological health and deviation, therapy techniques, and explanations for the origin and the meaning of religion or/and religious experience.

Biological model   One approach sees religion and religious experience as arising from a biological base caused by biological agents (Churchland, 2002; Trotter,

1919). For example, mystical experiences may be interpreted as being caused by a form of frontal lobe epilepsy. Alternatively, they may be attributed to neuro-chemical imbalances such as those that cause schizophrenics to hear voices.

Psychodynamic models   This view assumed unconscious (projection) processes are the real determinants of religious motivation (Fromm, 1950; Paloutzian, 1996): The different types of psychodynamic theories explain religion in terms of wish-fulfilling illusion, substitute for father figure (Freud, 1927, 1930; Fuller, 1994; Scharfenberg, 1973); religiosity as an archetypal occurring in the person (Frankl, 1959; Fuller, 1994; Jung, 1963); religion as a relation to a mother figure (Rizzuto, 1979); religion as an illusive intermediate space between inner and outside reality (Winnicott, 1993), and religion as the result of projection processes in the recent object-relation and attachment theories (Murken, 1998).

Behaviorist model   Religion in this view is a reality-inconsistent learned behav-ior. The behaviorists usually describe religion as being in polar opposition to science (Skinner, 1971; Wulff, 1997). Behaviorists may describe religious behavior as being created by rewards that are in the environment. For example, an individual may gain social standing by regularly attending religious services. On the other hand, the environment may reward avoiding certain behaviors proscribed by religious doctrine. If an individual follows the Ten Command-ments, he or she is less likely to be arrested or have distress in his or her personal relationships.

Cognitive model   Most of the theorists of cognitive psychology explain reli-gion as cognitive schemata in terms of an (irrational) organized cognitive struc-ture based upon earlier experiences (Ellis, 1965; McCallister, 1995; Paloutzian, 1996). Some of these adherents (e.g, Ellis) view the belief in a Divine Being as being a de facto irrational belief; the subsequent goal of psychotherapy may be to challenge this belief and replace it with "healthier," rational beliefs.

The humanistic-existential model   In the humanistic view, religion is a byprod-uct or projection of the active and conscious role of person in giving form to his life and the importance of the values in this process (Fuller, 1994). Humanism explicitly rejects the existence of a Sovereign God. Since there is no God, the responsibility for improving the lot of humans in this plain of exist-ence falls on the shoulders of humans alone.

The vast majority of existential theorists view the embracing of a Supreme Being as an attempt to avoid healthy anxiety by denying the ultimate reality of our existence. According to the existentialist school of thought, there are four ultimate truths: 1. This life is a solitary journey; we are alone. 2. There is no inherent meaning to life. 3. We are all going to die. 4. We are "condemned to freedom." This means that given that there is no inherent meaning to life, it is our personal responsibility to create meaning (May & Yalom, 2005). It is clear in these explicitly stated assumptions about the human condition, that the orientation is atheistic.

Frankl (2006) according to his existentialist view was probably one of the very few who pointed at religion and God as a truth in itself as well as to the person's responsibility before a transcendent God ("Du Gott"). According to Frankl, if you pursue ultimate meaning, you will inevitably end in affirming the existence of the Divine. The distinction is subtle but important between Frankl and the other existentialists. With Frankl, you have a responsibility to God to find meaning. With the other existentialists, since there is no God, you have the responsibility to yourself to create meaning in a meaningless world.

The sociocultural model   Religion and religious behavior are formed and shaped just like all other behavior by the family context and the sociocultural factors. These factors lead to the assumption of the religious groups norms by the person. (Batson, Schoenrade, & Ventis, 1993). In this model, religious behavior is a part of the cultural heritage of the individual in a cultural context. Religious beliefs and practices have no ultimate truth value, but are merely customs passed down from one generation to another.

Current Thoughts and Theories

Near the end of the twentieth century a host of social, political, and economic events brought into question the validity of the naturalistic scientific system and its morality and value system. New discoveries of the natural sciences (such as Big Bang Cosmology), and the changes in western philosophy (moving from modernism towards postmodernism) questioned the materialist mechanistic worldview of the Enlightenment and its presumptions (Russell, 2000). The philosophy of science has shown that a science and a scientific method that is absolutely neutral and absolutely empirical does not exist. The presumptions of the researcher influence every element of research. This is critical when we study human behavior and especially mental health. These definitions may vary from time to time and culture to culture. One of the main factors influencing the definitions of what is mentally normal or mentally ill seems to be the *underlying theory of person* either held by the majority of people and/or by the power institutions of the time. Science (including philosophy) and religion have both shaped the worldview and the theory of person of populations throughout the history of human being in a complex relationship with the power and political institutions and within their sociocultural context.

The general situation of a naturalistic-oriented system of science, and of psychology and psychotherapy in particular, together with the role of changing political and sociocultural factors have contributed to a very unclear resolution of the role of religion in mental health treatment. Not only are some basic definitions in the field not clear but the revisions and changes of its basic tools of diagnosis such as *DSM* versions seem to be more a result of the political view and sociocultural changes in western countries, rather than new scientific psychological theories offered to and accepted by the scientific community (e.g., both homosexuality and religiousness moved out of the disorders classification in recent *DSM* versions).

The professional field of psychology has undergone a revolution in the manner in which it views culture, realizing that the old model of psychology was anchored in a specific worldview that rewards certain groups (middle-class European Americans) by identifying their behaviors and beliefs as normative; while pathologizing other groups' beliefs and behaviors as being deviant or deficient. We find ourselves in a professional game of chicken (in which two individuals are in a face off and one must defer to avoid mutual self-destruction). On one side is the awareness that our psychological models have been developed out of a philosophical tradition that does not allow, due to its presuppositions, the healthy existence of God. On the other hand is the ethical mandate that we view behavior in a culturally relativistic manner; that we show respect and deference to the worldview of people who believe in such a God. Psychology has not itself resolved this standoff, but we can nevertheless explore the psychological research related to the role of religion in mental health, cultural variations in the role of religion in the helping process and suggestions for clinicians who attempt to address religious issues in the psychotherapy process.

Mental Health and Religion

The association between religion and mental health has received a mixed response from theorists. Early on, theories proposed by psychologists reflected a polarization. Ellis (1965) claimed that religion was detrimental to psychological functioning. He even went to the extent of suggesting that devout religiosity was equivalent to emotional disturbance (Ellis, 1989). Jung (1933) and Allport (1950), on the other hand, saw religion as a source of meaning and stability. argued that religion can be both a source of stress as well as a security from stress, just as it can be a means of gaining social acceptance through conformity or a means of growth and fulfillment.

Past reviews and meta-analyses of research on the correlation between religion and mental health have also shown mixed results: positive correlation, negative correlation, and absence of correlation (Loewenthal, 2007). As per the analysis of these reviews and meta-analyses by Hackney and Sanders (2003), religion, over all, had a beneficial relation to mental health (Bergin, 1983 & 1991; Payne, Bergin, Bielema, & Jenkins, 1991; Gartner, Larson, & Allen, 1991; Koenig & Larson, 2001; Larson et al., 1992; Loewenthal, 2007). Donahue (1985) found that extrinsic religious orientation was associated with negative characteristics such as prejudice and fear of death. Payne et al. (1991) did not find evidence for a connection between religiosity and the prevention of major clinical mental health disorders. Gartner, Larson, and Allen (1991) found that the correlation that exists between anxiety, sexual disorders, psychosis, prejudice, self-esteem, and intelligence, and religion, was, at best, only ambiguous. Similarly, high religious commitment was associated with specific symptoms of psychopathology (Kyriacou, 2006). Larson et al. (1992) reported that 12 percent of the studies they reviewed had only a neutral relationship between religious commitment and mental health.

Despite these mixed findings, research results suggesting religion is negatively correlated to depression, anxiety and negative effects of multiple stressors cannot be ignored. A review of published literature on religion and depression from 1996 to 2006 found that those who were religious had a lower incidence of depressive symptoms/depression. This study also found that being religious might increase the speed of recovery from depressive disorder. This protective effect was less clear cut for psychotic depression (Dein, 2006). Lonczak, Clifasefi, and Marlatt (2006) found that being raised with formal religion was predictive of decreased depressive symptoms and reduced hostility. Paying attention to the measures used is important: Using the Oxford Happiness Inventory religiosity was associated with happiness. Such a correlation was not found when using the Depression-Happiness Scale (Lewis & Cruise, 2006).

The association between religion and negative effects is mostly constant across cultures. A study among African-American young adults showed that intrinsic religiosity reduced distress and depression (Lesniak, Rudman, & Rector, 2006). Watlington and Murphy (2006) reported that those African-American women who had greater religious involvement reported fewer depressive symptoms and posttraumatic stress symptoms in the aftermath of domestic violence. A national survey reported that belief in life after death reduced anxiety, depression, obsessive compulsion, paranoia, phobia, and somatization (Flannelly, Koenig & Ellison, 2006).

A large number of cross-cultural studies have yielded following results:

- Among college students, religiosity was correlated to life satisfaction (Gauthier, Christopher, & Walter, 2006).
- In England, church attendance was shown to offer significant protection against suicide (Kay & Francis, 2006).
- Among Kuwaiti adolescents, religiosity was positively associated with happiness and mental health and negatively associated to depression and anxiety (Abdel-Khalek, 2007).
- Among Chinese and Korean American elderly between the ages of 69 and 72, religious support was associated with decreased depression and increased life satisfaction (Lee, 2007).
- A cross-cultural study among the Yoruba, the Bengladeshis and White British found that coping methods for depression included practice of religion (Lavender et al., 2006).
- Among women in a South African town, engagement in formal religion buffered the aggregate effects of multiple stressors including effects of stressful work and experience of racism on physical health. Prayer buffered the effects of work stress on physical health and reduced the deleterious effects of work stress and racism on depressive symptomatology (Copeland-Linder, 2006).

- Aspects of religion and spirituality were found to be positively correlated to self-efficacy in career decision, career values, and job satisfaction (Duffy, 2006).
- Individuals with schizophrenia and schizoaffective disorder perceived religious coping to be significantly more helpful for recovery than those diagnosed with depressive disorders (Reger & Rogers, 2002).
- Patients recovering from schizophrenia mentioned God and religion as part of their survival experience (Humberstone, 2002).
- Organizational religiosity was inversely related to somatization and obsessive compulsiveness, and nonorganizational religiosity was inversely related to interpersonal sensitivity (Lesniak, Rudman, & Rector, 2006).
- Lonczak, Clifasefi, and Marlatt (2006) found that religious pleading had a significant association with increased somatization.
- In individuals aged between 65 and 100, frequent church attendance was associated with a reduced prevalence of depression in women, but increased prevalence in men (Norton et al., 2006).

For all of the different studies that show how religion is beneficial in general for mental health and in coping with particular mental illnesses, there are a few studies showing the negative effects of religion in reducing negative affects and decreasing psychiatric symptoms associated with psychopathology. Among a high risk group of pregnant women addicted to various substances undergoing treatment in a residential treatment facility negative religious coping was associated with greater PTSD symptoms, greater depressive symptoms, and greater syndromal depression after controlling for background demographic and addiction variables. Other aspects of religiousness, including positive coping and involvement with organized religion, were not associated with mental health outcomes. These results suggest that negative aspects of religiousness, particularly religious struggle, merit greater attention from clinicians and investigators (Conners, 2006).

The discrepancy in research findings regarding the association between religion and psychopathology could be attributed to the kind of religiosity that is practiced and the way it is practiced. Allport and Ross (1967) called the kind of religiosity that brings health to mind *intrinsic* and called the type of religiosity that reduces mental health *extrinsic*. The extrinsically religious person uses religion as a means of security or status, whereas the intrinsically religious person internalizes beliefs and lives by them regardless of social pressure.

Hackney and Sanders (2003) found an overall pattern where institutional religiosity produced the weakest and the only negative correlation to mental health. Religion defined as ideology produced stronger correlations and religion defined as personal devotion produced the strongest correlation. Religion defined as institutional participation was negatively correlated to lowering anxiety and depression. The authors reasoned that such differing links between various aspects of religiosity and mental health was the result of the fact that institutional participation focused on the least existentially relevant aspects of religion while personal devotion produced the greatest existential satisfaction. Between these two ends of the continuum came religion as ideology. The authors found that when researchers operationally defined religiosity and mental health in an internal, identified manner, the correlation between these two constructs were stronger (Hackney & Sanders, 2003).

A national survey in England that explored the connection between mental health and religion found that lack of religious belief was associated with a higher prevalence of common mental disorders, but only in people who reported having a spiritual view of life (King, Weich, & Nazroo, 2006). Yet another study (Dezutter, Soenens, & Hutsebaut, 2006) found that religious orientations and social cognitive approaches to religion, and not religious involvement, were related to well-being and distress. Literal approaches to religion were negatively related to well-being and positively to distress; intrinsic religiosity predicted higher well-being; and extrinsic religiosity predicted lower well-being.

Discrepancy in the correlations between religion and mental health could also be due to lack of uniform definitions of mental health and religiosity. Analysis by Hackney and Sanders (2003) of 34 studies found that different types and strengths of correlations between religiosity and mental health were associated with diverse definitions of religiosity and mental health utilized by psychologists. Research suggested the need for more refined measurements that could accommodate such distinctions (Kirkpatrick, 1989). Ellison (1998) found that researchers have generally used various measures of mental attributes such as personality variables, psychological well-being (e.g., life satisfaction), distress, symptom counts (e.g., depression, anxiety), and clinical or simulated diagnoses of various psychiatric disorders (e.g., major depressive episode). The hypothesis that the kind of scale used to measure mental health can affect the correlation between religiosity and mental health was not refuted by Lewis and Cruise (2006) in their recent study.

There are a host of potential moderator variables that can impact the religion-mental health relationship. A study about religious coping styles in relation to recovery from serious mental illnesses such as schizophrenia, schizoaffective disorder, bipolar disorder, major depression, substance abuse, and personality disorders found that the style of religious coping moderated the impact of religion on recovery. Collaborative approaches to religious coping involve looking at problem-solving as a joint responsibility of God and the individual. Deferring coping style implies placing all responsibility of problem-solving on God passively waiting for solutions from God. In the pleading coping style, the individual petitions for God's miraculous interventions to bring about personally desirable outcomes. The self-directing approach emphasizes the individual's personal responsibility and active role in problem-solving and excludes God from the process. The results of the study indicated that the collaborative approach was characterized by greater involvement in recovery enhancing activities leading to increased empowerment and recovery. The deferring style was associated with improved quality of life. The self-directing and pleading styles were linked with less positive psychosocial outcomes (Yangarber-Hicks, 2004).

In conclusion, a cautious generalization that religious beliefs and practices are associated with positive mental health across cultures can be made. This relationship is not uniform and some studies have found religious belief and practices to be associated with negative mental health. One must be cautious in using the broad term religion. Researchers have benefited from breaking this vast concept into meaningful sub groups such as extrinsic versus intrinsic religiosity and different styles of religious coping. It must be noted that this line of research is also plagued with scales that would be considered mediocre at best, in terms of acceptable psychometric properties.

The Interrelationship between Religion, Culture, and Psychotherapy

An Anthropological View of the Psychotherapy Process

Frank and Frank (1991) provided a creative, fresh perspective on the process of psychotherapy. In considering psychotherapy he embraced a transtheoretical, anthropological perspective on how people change. According to Frank, each culture contextually defines which behaviors are "healthy" and which are "unhealthy" or abnormal. An individual who is engaging in behaviors categorized by the culture as "abnormal" will feel social alienation and decreased morale. This individual, the "patient," will eventually seek help from a culturally sanctioned "healer." This identified healer then engages in a ritualized attempt to decrease the suffering from the patient. The patient, having participated in this socially endorsed ritual, feels an increase in morale, less alienated from his or her peers, and hopefully decreases the proscribed behaviors which lead to the referral to the healer.

This creative approach to understanding how people change was critical in that it emphasized that the cultural content in which we live establishes through mutual consensus what behaviors or thoughts are acceptable and which need to be changed. We explore two examples of the different ways in which cultures define "unhealthy" behavior, who the healer is, and the ritualized process that takes place to increase the morale and decrease the social alienation of the patient.

Hallucinogens: Salvation or Damnation?

The use of hallucinogens or psychedelic psychoactive substances, present an excellent example of a behavior that has been attributed different meanings by different cultures. In the European American, western culture of the United States, the use of psychedelic substances is for recreational purposes by members of specific subcultures (e.g., hippies; punks; goths) and is criminalized. These drugs (such as LSD) are seen as having no therapeutic value and are a high risk for abuse. The main argument against the recreational use of psychedelics is that they can cause psychological damage to users. There is no religious component to this proscription; it is merely a public health concern.

Psychedelic drugs are viewed so negatively, that it is exceedingly difficult for bona fide psychological and psychiatric researchers to get permission to use them in research. This is odd in that other drugs in the same classification (e.g., marijuana) have much fewer federal restrictions on research uses.

A European American who suffers legal trouble or social alienation for psychedelic use may follow the socially sanctioned ritual of entering substance abuse treatment. Here the healer, the substance abuse counselor, provides support to the patient. If the patient is in the substance abuse range of drug use, according to the *DSM*, the clinician may implement a harm reduction approach in which psycho-educational interventions are geared towards the patient learning how to decrease the negative impact of the drug use on his or her life.

If the patient is in the substance dependence range of classification according to the *DSM*, it is likely that the clinical goal will be abstinence from all mind-altering chemicals. Traditionally, a twelve-step approach is used, during which the patient is convinced that he or she is powerless over the substance and needs assistance from a self-defined Higher Power to overcome this powerlessness and to maintain abstinence. The twelve-step approach can best be described as a spiritual rather than a religious approach, as it focuses solely on an individual's relationship with a self-defined Divine Being, rather than using an institutionalized approach that focuses on specific doctrinal beliefs or behaviors mandated by a specific religion or sect. In receiving this treatment, the patient feels an increase in morale from this treatment and attempts to modify his or her behavior so as to fit into the cultural norms of the larger reference group which has the political and economic power. If the individual is in the substance dependence range of clinical classification, and he or she embraces the twelve-step approach and subsequent abstinence, a person of faith would describe the agent of change as divine intervention from a Higher Power upon which the patient has developed a healthy reliance.

A cultural group that has a different meaning attributed to psychedelics is a Native American tribe: the Navajo (Dine). In traditional religious rituals, the Navajo make use of psychedelics, which are referred to as entheogens in this context. Etheogens are plant sources of psychedelic psychoactive substances. The Navajo use the peyote cactus that has high levels of natural occurring mescaline. The peyote, or divine cactus, is used for several therapeutic purposes. First, it is used as a means of bringing about a mystical experience, in which the Divine Being(s) directly communicate to the individual. Alternatively, it is used as a treatment for alcoholism (Calabrese, 2007). In this application, the patient has been engaging in behavior that is viewed as being unacceptable by the larger culture (i.e., drinking alcohol) and is feeling subsequently alienated from his or her peers due to this behavior. The patient seeks a culturally identified "healer," in this case a Medicine Man. The Medicine Man and the patient engage in a culturally sanctioned ritual; fasting and prayer followed by the Medicine Man administering the peyote to the patient. The patient gains insight and assistance in the form of direct divine intervention as the result of the administration of the peyote. The patient feels an increase in morale, a decreasing sense of alienation and the problematic behavior decreases. This decrease would be described by psychologists as resulting from insight from the ritual and the interpersonal support form the Medicine Man. People of faith may describe the change in the problematic behavior as resulting from assistance and intervention from a Supreme Being.

A cultural context that attributes a different religious meaning to the use of psychedelics is Shi'a Islam. In the Islamic worldview, the use of all intoxicants (*sukara*) is prohibited. The Qu'ran explicitly forbids such use, especially alcohol. It is seen as being a morally debasing influence on the individual. Alcohol, especially, is seen as being the handiwork of Satan and is used by Satan to lead an individual away from prayer and holiness. Alcohol is the most stigmatized mind-altering substance, given its specific mention in the Qu'ran, but psychedelics are also seen as being a particularly pernicious mind-altering substance. When comparing the use of heroin to psychedelics, most Islamic theologians, while decrying the use of either, will single out psychedelics as being the more dangerous of the two. Shi'ite experts claim that when using psychedelics, the individual's soul is at great risk as being vulnerable. When under the influence of such drugs, the individual is experiencing spiritual realms with which they are ill equipped to deal and it is their very soul that is in danger.

The culturally sanctioned process that the Muslim individual may undergo to overcome feelings of social alienation due to engaging in the proscribed behavior may be slightly different when compared to the previous two examples. The individual will seek assistance from the ultimate "Healer": Allah. He or she may fast extra days beyond Ramadan, engage in extra prayers, or make a spiritual pilgrimage (*haj*) to Mecca. There has also been the recent development of mental health counseling and the successful introduction of twelve step meetings into parts of the Middle East (Priester, 2008; Priester & Jana-Masri, 2006). In this case, we are seeing new forms of rituals being introduced into the culture that can be used in addition to the traditional rituals of fasting, prayer, and pilgrimage. The degree to which Middle Eastern culture embraces the new approaches of counseling and twelve-step groups will predict whether it becomes a socially sanctioned new healing process.

In this example of hallucinogens, we see how three different cultures identify what abnormal behavior is (i.e., who is unhealthy); who is the healer responsible for assisting the patient; and what is the socially sanctioned ritual that is used to decrease the alienation and suffering of the patient. In the Unites States, alcohol use is celebrated and the use of psychedelics is criminalized and seen as having little value. In the Navajo nation, alcohol use is seen as the poisoning agent and psychedelics are the antidote. In Shi'ia Islam, both alcohol and psychedelics are seen as being unhealthy and morally corrupting influences on the individual and the society. It is interesting to note that across all three cultures, religion or spirituality plays a critical role in the culturally endorsed treatment approach.

Epilepsy: A Condition to be Controlled, Exorcized, or Celebrated?

According to Western culture, epilepsy is a common neurological disorder marked by intermittent seizures. During the seizures, the individual may appear normal but be unresponsive to communication or may lose consciousness and engage in spastic, rhythmic muscle contractions. In western culture, the proper, culturally sanctioned treatment is the use of prescription medication that limits the occurrence of seizures. In severe cases, surgery may be suggested. Epilepsy provides another interesting case study of how cultures conceptualize mental illness and germane religious realities.

The Hmong have a dramatically different understanding of epilepsy. The Hmong are an immigrant group from the Laotian mountains who came to the United States after serving as allies to the United States during the Vietnam conflict. Upon the defeat of the United States in Vietnam, the Hmong were placed in refugee camps and eventually some were allowed to migrate to the United States. There is a religious divide in the Hmong community, with the majority converting to Christianity and a minority carrying on their traditional pantheistic, shamanic religion. Traditionally, the Hmong see the epileptic seizure as a temporary possession by an evil spirit. Having survived this encounter with another metaphysical reality, the individual is seen as having magical powers and capable of becoming a shaman, who is a healer and respected leader in the traditional community. Epilepsy is seen as having a supernatural origin. Although acutely negative, the long-term consequence of having survived these seizures is seen as being highly positive. An excellent exploration o the conflict that the traditional Hmong worldview can have with the western medical model is presented in the book, *The Spirit Catches You and You Fall Down* (Fadiman, 1997).

Muslims have developed a sophisticated, multifaceted approach to understanding the etiology and differentially treating epilepsy. Sunni Muslims conceptualize epileptic seizures as coming either from medical or meta-physical origins. There is an elaborate, sophisticated process for differentially diagnosing the cause of the seizures. The diagnostic process for *jinn* possession is to visit a sheik, a socially recognized healer and expert on Islam. The sheik reads specific passages from the Qu'ran and closely observes the individual to differentiate between wholesale possession, marked by seizure activity and requiring a formal exorcism; temporary visitation by the jinn, marked by twitching fingers and requiring the incantation specific prayers or drinking a glass of water into which a Qu'ranic verse has been placed; or physiologically induced seizures, which is marked by no response to the readings. *Jinn* are supernatural creatures that attempt to meddle in the affairs of humans. There are positive and negative *jinn*. In the case of possession, an individual has come under the influence of a negative *jinn*. The socially sanctioned treatment is exorcism by an exorcist. If the afflicted individual does not respond to the Qu'ranic reading with a seizure, the cause is seen to be physiological and the patient is referred to a physician for medical treatment (Al-Ashqar & Zarabozo, 1998). Shiite scholars view the attribution of epilepsy to the influence of *jinn* and this approach to treatment as being an example of a purely cultural, as opposed to religious phenomenon.

In the two examples of psychedelic drug use and epilepsy, we see the various ways in which culture and religion intermix to provide us with cognitive maps of normality and mental illness. We have also seen that each culture provides its own socially sanctioned version of the healing process, oftentimes including religious components in the treatment of the perceived illness. It is interesting to note that in the western cultural context, mainstream psychologists, until recently, have neglected to include such a religious component in the healing process. This undoubtedly is due to the historical context discussed at the beginning of this chapter in which psychology, as ensconced in the materialistic, reductivistic scientific paradigm, inherently pathologizes the existence of God and the role that such a God could play in the healing process. The role of healer also varies from one cultural context to another.

Research on the Impact of Integrating Religion into Psychotherapy

There are a myriad of ways in which religion can be integrated into the clinical practice of psychotherapy. One distinction that is made is between implicit and explicit approaches to such an integration. In the implicit approach, the focus is on the clinician's values. An example of this could be that a psychologist who is a Christian might bring his or her value of agape (a nonsexual version of compassionate love) into the session. The clinician's own embracing of this value could lead him or her to show more compassion toward the clients with which they are working.

Explicit approaches to the integration of religion and psychotherapy include religion as an active force in the helping process. This section of the chapter will explore research on several forms of such an integration. First, an overview of the literature related to counselor preference for religious clinicians will be offered. Then, we will examine three separate examples of clinical research that compares secular versions of a form of psychotherapy or clinical practice to similar explicitly religious forms. These three areas are: cognitive-behavioral therapy, eating disorder treatment, and meditation.

Client Preferences

There is a considerable amount of research that explores the impact of pretherapy information about the clinician on client perceptions. In a typical study, written material about a mock counselor is given to the research participants. The participants read this material and then rate the clinician or their anticipated counseling experience with this clinician. Half of the participants would be given a description that identifies the clinician as being religious. The other half receives information that describes the counselor as being secular. This style of research is described as an analogue research method.

As with the research on the relationship between religion and mental health, there are many studies in this line of research that find contradictory results. Still, a few cautious summary statements are warranted. It seems that degree of religiosity is a significant potential moderator. Highly religious Jews, Mormons, Protestants, and Roman Catholics typically prefer clinicians with similar religious values (Worthington, Kurusu, McCullough, & Sandage, 1996). Individuals in western culture with low levels of religiosity do not differ in their preferences for a Christian versus non-Christian clinician (Keating & Fretz, 1990). Christians rate all counselors, regardless of being identified as religious or not more favorably than do agnostic participants (Godwin & Crouch, 1989). The content of what may be disclosed by the client can be altered by the explicit religious identification of the clinician. For individuals with low to moderate levels of religiosity, the participants disclose less intimate material to explicitly identified religious counselors, when compared to disclosures to counselors who are not explicitly identified as religious. On the other hand highly religious Christian participants chose more intimate topics to disclose to the religiously identified clinician (Wyatt & Johnson, 1990).

Methodological limitations   There are numerous methodological flaws in some of the research that addresses this topic. The most common criticism is that the artificial nature of analogue research (i.e., reading a written description of a clinician) limits the generalizability of the findings to the real world of psychotherapy. Another external validity-related concern is that some but not all of these studies use undergraduate students as participants. Once again, the concern is that findings associated with undergraduate students may not generalize to what one would find with actual psychotherapy clients. In addition, some of the studies fail to stand up to acceptable standards of analogue research. For example Lewis and Epperson (1991) had undergraduate students read a newspaper advertisement for a counseling clinic that is described as either being feminist or Christian in its orientation. Finally, virtually all of the studies have been carried out in the United States with Christians and Jews being the only religious groups under consideration. Some promising new work is beginning to be carried out in the Middle East with Muslims, but it has yet to make its appearance in the scientific literature (Priester, 2006).

Explicit integration of religion into extant models of psychotherapy   The next area of research related to the integration of religion into psychotherapy addresses the comparison of clinical efficacy of treatment approaches that have an explicitly religious component with similar but secular models. A good example of an additive model is newer iterations of Ellis's Rational Emotive Behavioral Therapy (REBT). It is an interesting example, as Albert Ellis represented psychology's traditional antagonism towards religious belief. Rational Emotive Behavioral Therapy maintains that unhealthy behaviors and negative emotions are caused by irrational beliefs. Thus, if you are unhappy or engaging in harmful behaviors, it is evidence that you are operating under the assumption of irrational beliefs.

In REBT, the clinician works with the client to uncover irrational beliefs that govern their life. Once uncovered, the irrational beliefs are tested, rejected, and replaced with rational beliefs. The replacement of the irrational beliefs with healthier, rational beliefs ameliorates negative emotional and behavioral consequences (Ellis, 1989). Ellis summarized the traditional secular psychological perspective wonderfully when he posited that belief in God is itself an irrational belief. The proof of this lies in the fact that so many wars and acts of violence have occurred related to religions (i.e., the existence of negative behaviors, religious wars, flows from an irrational belief, that there is a God). According to Ellis, the clinician should help clients replace the irrational belief in God with a healthier, rational one; that God does not exist; there are no absolute truths; so I can not use the claim of an ultimate truth to justify hurting another. On a more personal level, practitioners of REBT work to ease shame and guilt that oftentimes stems from behavior being in conflict with religious doctrine. Ellis uses the term "the JEHOVIAN SHOULD" to label irrational beliefs that result in feeling of shame or guilt.

It is ironic that Christian counselors use REBT as a psychological model upon which to add religion as an important cultural variable to assist in the change process. Examples of explicitly Christian REBT can be found in Nielsen (2001). In the religious version of REBT, the process is identical, but the way that irrational beliefs are identified is wholly different. For example, a negative behavior could be engaging in extramarital sexual activity. The harmful emotional states related to this behavior could be shame and guilt. In this situation, the Christian counselor may help the client uncover the irrational belief, "It is acceptable to engage in this behavior as so many other people do it." The rational belief that could serve as replacement could be, "It is important to honor my marriage vows and as a Christian I will do so." Alternatively, the irrational belief could be, "I have sinned and am unacceptable to God." This could be replaced with, "I am a sinner and that is why I need God. God loves me as a sinner." As you can see, the process remains the same. It is the operational definition of irrational and rational which differ, with them now being based on religious doctrine and helping the individual aligns their behavior to conform with religiously prescribed comportment.

There has been some highly interesting research comparing the treatment efficacy of this Christian version of REBT. In one study, Propst, Ostrom, Watkins, Dean, and Mashburn (1992) exposed clients to one of three treatment protocols: nonreligious cognitive behavioral therapy (NRBCT); religious cognitive behavior therapy (RCBT); tradition pastoral counseling treatment (PCT). The participants in these three treatment modalities were then compared to a wait list control group. At the end of the treatment period, RCBT reduced depression when compared to the wait list control group, while NRCBT and PCT did not.

Other studies offer tentative support for the assertion that a religious version of cognitive behavioral therapy was more efficacious when compared to a secular, traditional version of the treatment modality. Some researchers found this advantage only to be marginal (Johnson, 1993). Once again, degree of religiosity of the clients is seen as a potential moderator variable, with individuals with relatively higher levels of religiosity responding more favorably to the religious version of the treatment (McCullough, 1999).

Eating disorder treatment   One shining example of a tightly designed and well executed outcome study was completed by Richards, Berrett, Hardman, and Eggett (2006). This research project compared eating disorder treatment with a spiritual component to a traditional secular version of eating disorder treatment. Inpatient clients were randomly assigned to one of the two conditions. Outcome data was gathered on a weekly basis and at the completion of the treatment period. Clients receiving the spiritual version of the treatment modality improved significantly more quickly during the first four weeks of treatment. At the conclusion of treatment, the individuals receiving the spiritual version of treatment scored lower on psychological disturbance, scored lower on eating disorder symptoms and higher on spiritual well-being, when compared to the control, secular treatment modality.

Meditation   The practice of mediation offers fertile ground for exploring the religious versus secular forms of treatment intervention. There is little controversy over whether meditation is beneficial. Research indicates that the practice of meditation has many positive psychological and physiological benefits (Alexander, Rainforth, & Gelderloos, 1991; Astin, 1997). The controversy related to the research and practice behind meditation is what exactly are the active ingredients? Benson and Klipper (2000) maintain that it is the physiological action of relaxing the body muscles that causes the benefits of meditation. They coined the term, "the Relaxation Response" in describing the process. Other researchers (Dillbeck & Orme-Johnson, 1987) maintain that it is the spiritual component of meditative practice rather than the mere physiological response that brings about the positive results.

Wachholtz and Pargament (2005) tested this question in a well-designed clinical trial. They randomly assigned undergraduate college students to one of three conditions: relaxation, secular meditation, and spiritual meditation. There were no significant differences between the members of the groups based on demographic and preliminary assessment data. All three groups were trained according to a similar protocol to learn how to relax their muscles (i.e., the Relaxation Response). The secular meditation group was also given a list of four positive statements from which to choose one statement upon which to reflect: "I am joyful," "I am happy," "I am content," or "I am good." The spiritual meditation group was instructed to use one of four phrases that best fitted their spiritual system: "God is peace," "God is joy," "God is love," "God is good." All participants were instructed to practice their respective meditation technique for 20 minutes a day for a two-week period. After two weeks, the participants were tested. The spiritual meditation group had greater decreases in anxiety, more positive mood, spiritual health, and spiritual experiences than did the other two groups. The spiritual meditation group also tolerated pain almost twice as long as the other two groups, as measured by timing how long an individual could keep his or her hand in a bowl of ice water.

Although this is only one study, it suggests that there may be additional benefits to practicing a spiritual form of meditation as opposed to a secular version. This is not to say that the Relaxation Response (i.e., secular meditation) does not bring about positive results, but that even greater results can be obtained from a spiritual form of meditative practice.

Suggestions for Addressing Religious or Spiritual Issues in Psychotherapy

Finally, we offer some suggestions to guide clinical work as it relates to addressing religious issues in the psychotherapy process. These are only meant as an introduction to these concepts and future reading in a more elaborate and thorough manner is recommended (see Richards & Bergin, 2005):

1. *Do not pathologize.*
The profession has a long tradition and history of pathologizing the religious beliefs of individuals. This can be especially difficult when the client that you are treating comes from a dramatically different religious background than your own. When we encounter an individual who is so different, particularly along religious dimensions, the automatic response is to focus on differences and your perceptions of the relative weakness of the other's position in comparison to your own views.

A good practice is to do two things when interacting with a client from a different religious perspective than your own. First seek to identify the positive aspects of the religion. How has the religious beliefs helped the individual in their journey through life? It is helpful to identify similarities that exist between your beliefs and the clients. This helps you form a bond with the client and can potentially reduce negative stereotyping on your part. It is not necessary, and possibly contraindicated that you share these insights regarding similarity with your client. The intent is to help you maintain a positive frame of reference when viewing the client.

2. *Learn about your client's religion.*
Make a specific exerted effort to understand what meaning if any, religion has in your client's life. One way to do this is through a religious history. Start with the client's childhood. Potential questions could include:

- What was your experience of religion as a child?
- What aspects of your parents' religion did you like and/or dislike?
- Did you go through any major religious changes in your life? Any conversion experiences? Any changes in denomination?

- What religious beliefs bring you the most comfort?
- What religious practices bring you the most comfort or feelings of support?
- At what point in your life did you feel closest to your God(s)?
- At what point in your life did you feel most distant from God?

This religious history can be taken at intake or at any point during the course of treatment. It will help you understand the role that religious beliefs and behaviors play in the client's life.

3. *Use religious leaders as resources.*

A client's faith community is a rich source of natural support. Engaging the clergy or religious leaders of your client can allow you to build a bridge between the psychotherapy and this natural support network. Clergy can help educate you about the specific details about your client's faith, especially if you are unfamiliar with the specific denomination, religion, or sect. Even if you are familiar with the particular faith, engaging the clergy as a partner in meeting the needs of the client is a powerful clinical move. It can help get the client to "buy into" the counseling process.

A word of caution is warranted here. It is imperative that you engage the client's religious leader, only with explicit (and legally required written) authorization of the client. It could be that the client is seeking psychological services as they are ashamed of a behavior and do not want their faith community to know about it. Alternatively, it could be that the client is considering leaving that particular faith community and joining another. By engaging the clergy in an overly eager manner, you may seem to be aligning yourself with this religious authority, rather than with the client. If you do not know much about the faith community of the client, it is fine to contact clergy to gain knowledge and information about the faith, rather than the specific clients issues. For example, if you have a client who is a Muslim, you may contact the local mosque and ask the Mullah questions that you may have about Islam. It is critical that if you are doing so, that you do not break the confidentiality of the client in these information-seeking activities. Sometimes, it is best to call a different mosque, synagogue, temple or church than the one that your client attends.

4. *Do not recommend novel religious interventions to a client who does not share your particular beliefs.*

One has to be extremely careful when suggesting interventions with an explicitly religious component to clients. This is particularly true in the situation where you do not belong to the same faith community as the client. You may be transgressing a religious norm and have no awareness of it. For example, if you are providing psychotherapy to a member of the Church of Jesus Christ of the Latter Day Saints (i.e., Mormons). You may consider yourself to be culturally responsive in suggesting that the client join you in prayer at the beginning of the session. Not being of the same group, you would have no idea that in the Latter Day Saints' belief system, only clergy may lead an individual in prayer. In your attempt to be culturally responsive, you may be actively usurping the authority of the client's clergy (Richards & Bergin, 2005).

When suggesting religiously oriented interventions, it is always best to help the client return to religious behaviors that he or she has used in the past. Refer back to the religious history that you completed with the client. What behaviors were they engaging in the past when they felt close to God and were doing well in life? Now as a clinician, you can coach the client in bringing back these adaptive behaviors. When trying to decide whether an intervention is culturally appropriate, once again, the clergy are an excellent source of information and support to your clinical activity.

5. *Do not proselytize.*
Therapists aim to meet the needs of the client and function from within the clients' worldview. It would be professionally unethical to use the psychotherapy setting as a forum from which to convert clients to your religious beliefs. Of course, there are some exceptions. For example, if you are working as a substance abuse counselor and are a recovering addict who practices the twelve-step program of recovery, it may well be within the clinical goals of treatment to assist the client in adopting the beliefs of the twelve-step program and working through any obstacles that you have in adopting these beliefs. This is the exception. When one comes from a religious perspective that values an evangelical approach to converting others, it can be tempting to offer your beliefs to the client. This can only be done if a client has specifically sought out Christian counseling and, by entering the explicitly Christian setting, he or she is expecting such an approach.

6. *Learn about religions and faiths.*
In our culturally diverse world, there is a wonderful range of religious expression. Commit to being a lifelong learner who seeks knowledge about other groups. Attend a religious ceremony of a different group. Participate in interfaith discussion groups that occur in many communities. Seek out friendships with individuals who have a different faith than your own. It is good to remember that as you do these activities, maintain an attitude of positive curiosity and seek to identify similarities rather than differences.

Conclusion

This chapter has attempted to provide a wide-ranging discussion of religion as a cultural variable in mental illness and especially psychotherapy. We have explored the topic from the broader perspective, placing attempts to integrate religion and psychology within a historical context of the dialogue between religion and science, to the practical level of the individual clinician attempting to address such issues when sitting across from a client. For too long, religion has been pathologized or worse yet, neglected by psychologists. Religion is one of the critical guiding forces upon which many individuals' worldviews are based. In psychotherapy, clinicians must work from within the worldview of the client (APA, 2002) and wrestle with how to do so in the case of religion.

Research on the relationship between religious beliefs and practices and mental health is often contradictory and laced with methodological causes for concern. Similarly, the research on the impact of integrating religion into psychotherapy is, at times, ill defined, and suffers from equally disturbing methodological flaws. Attempts to offer suggestions on how to address such issues in psychotherapy can be so broad as to sound like platitudes and can raise more questions than answers. In describing the interrelationships between religion, culture, and psychotherapy, the line between which aspects are strictly cultural versus which aspects are strictly religious is blurred. What can one do? The final words of the Buddha seem appropriate when considering whether the psychological study of religion is even possible or should be pursued, "Strive on with diligence!"

REFERENCES

Abdel-Khalek, A. M. (2007). Religiosity, happiness, health, and psychopathology in a probability sample of Muslim adolescents. *Mental Health Religion and Culture, 10,* 571–583.

Al-Ashqar, U. S., & Zarabozo, J. A. (1998). *The world of jinn and devils.* Boulder, CO: Al-Basheer Publications & Translations.

Alexander, C. N., Rainforth, M. V., & Gelderloos, P. (1991). Transcendental meditation, self-actualization, and psychological health: A conceptual overview and statistical meta-analysis. *Journal of Social Behavior and Personality, 6,* 189–248.

Allport, G. W. (1950). *The individual and his religion: A psychological interpretation.* New York: Macmillan.

Allport, G. W., & Ross, J. M. (1967). Personal religious orientation and prejudice. *Journal of Personality and Social Psychology, 5,* 432–443.

American Psychological Association (2002). Ethical principles of psychologists and code of conduct. *American Psychologist, 57,* 1060–1073.

Astin, J. (1997). Stress reduction through mindfullness meditation: Effects on psychological symptomatology, sense of control, and spiritual experiences. *Psychotherapy and Psychosomatics, 66,* 97–106.

Batson, C. D., Schoenrade, P., Ventis, W. L. (1993). *Religion and the individual: A social-psychological perspective.* New York: Oxford University Press.

Benson, H., & Klipper, M. Z. (2000). *The relaxation response.* New York: HarperCollins.

Bergin, A. E. (1983). Religiosity and mental health: A critical reevaluation and meta-analysis. *Professional Psychology: Research and Practice, 14,* 170–184.

Bergin, A. E. (1991). Values and religious issues in psychotherapy and mental health. *American Psychologist, 46,* 394–403.

Calabrese, J. D. (2007). The therapeutic use of peyote in the Native American Church. In M. J. Winkelman & T. B. Roberts (Eds.), *Psychedelic medicine: New evidence for hallucinogens as treatments.* Westport, CT: Praeger/Greenwood.

Churchland, P. S. (2002). *Brain-wise: Studies in neurophilosophy.* Cambridge, MA: MIT Press.

Conners, N. A., Whiteside-Mansell, L., & Sherman, A. C. (2006). Dimensions of religious involvement and mental health outcomes among alcohol- and drug-dependent women. *Alcoholism Treatment Quarterly, 24,* 89–108.

Copeland-Linder, N. (2006). Stress among black women in a South African township: The protective role of religion. *Journal of Community Psychology, 34,* 577–599.

Dein, S. (2006) Religion, spirituality and depression: Implications for research and treatment. *Primary Care & Community Psychiatry, 11,* 67–72.

Dezutter, J., Soenens, B., & Hutsebaut, D. (2006) Religiosity and mental health: A further exploration of the relative importance of religious behaviors vs. religious attitudes. *Personality and Individual Differences, 40,* 807–818.

Dillbeck, M. C., & Orme-Johnson, D. W. (1987). Physiological differences between transcendental meditation and rest. *American Psychologist, 42,* 880–881.

Donahue, M. J. (1985). Intrinsic and extrinsic religiousness: Review and meta-analysis. *Journal of Personality and Social Psychology, 48*(2), 400–419.

Dryden, W., & Mytton, J. (1999) *Four approaches to counseling and psychotherapy.* Florence, KY: Taylor & Frances/Routledge.

Duffy, R. (2006). Spirituality, religion, and career development: Current status and future directions. *The Career Development Quarterly, 55,* 52–63.

Ellis, A. (1965). The psychotherapist's case against religion. Paper presented at a meeting of the Humanist Society. New York.

Ellis, A. (1989). Rational–emotive therapy. In R. J. Corsini & D. Wedding (Eds.), *Current psychotherapies.* (4th ed., pp. 197–238). Itasca, IL: Peacock.

Ellison, C. G. (1998). Introduction to symposium: Religion, health, and well-being. *Journal for the Scientific Study of Religion, 37,* 692–694.

Fadiman, A. (1997). *The spirit catches you and you fall down.* New York: Farrar, Straus & Giroux.

Flannelly, K., Koenig, H., & Ellison, C. (2006). Belief in life after death and mental health: Findings from a national survey. *Journal of Nervous and Mental Disease, 194,* 524–529.

Frank, J. D., & Frank, J. B. (1991). *Persuasion and healing: A comparative study of psychotherapy.* Baltimore, MD: Johns Hopkins University Press.

Frankl, V. (1959). The spiritual dimension in existential analysis and logotherapy. *Journal of Individual Psychology, 15,* 1959. 157–165.

Frankl, V. (2006). *Man's search for meaning.* Boston: Beacon Press.

Freud, S. (1927). *Totem and taboo.* Oxford, UK: New Republic.

Freud, S. (1930). *Le mot d'esprit et ses rapports avec l'inconscient.* Oxford, UK: Gallimard.

Fromm, E. (1950). *Psychoanalysis and religion.* New Haven, CT: Yale University Press.

Fuller, A. R. (1994). *Psychology and religion: Eight points of view* (3rd ed.). Lanham, MD: Littlefield Adams Quality Paperbacks.

Gartner, J., Larson, D., & Allen, G. (1991). Religious commitment and mental health: A review of the empirical literature. *Journal of Psychology and Theology, 19,* 6–25.

Gauthier, K., Christopher, A., & Walter, M. (2006). Religiosity, religious doubt, and the need for cognition: Their interactive relationship with life satisfaction. *Journal of Happiness Studies, 7,* 139–154.

Godwin, T. C., & Crouch, J. G. (1989). Subjects' religious orientation, counselor's orientation and skill, and expectations for counseling. *Journal of Psychology and Theology, 17,* 284–292.

Hackney, C. H., & Sanders, G. S. (2003). Religiosity and mental health: A meta-analysis of recent studies. *Journal for the Scientific Study of Religion, 42,* 43–55.

Humberstone, V. (2002). The experiences of people with schizophrenia living in supported accommodation: A qualitative study using grounded theory methodology. *Australian and New Zealand Journal of Psychiatry, 36*, 367–372.

Johnson, W. B. (1993). Christian rational-emotive therapy: A treatment protocol. *Journal of Psychology and Christianity, 12*(3), 254–261.

Jung, C. G. (1933). *Modern man in search of a soul.* New York: Harcourt Brace Jovanovich.

Jung, C. G. (1963). *Essays on a science of mythology.* Oxford, UK: Harper & Row.

Keating, A. M., & Fretz, B. R. (1990). Christians' anticipations about counselors in response to counselor descriptions. *Journal of Counseling Psychology, 37*, 293–296.

Kay, W., & Francis, L. (2006). Suicidal ideation among young people in the UK: Church-going as an inhibitory influence? *Mental Health, Religion & Culture, 9*, 127–140.

King, M., Weich, S., & Nazroo, J. (2006). Religion, mental health and ethnicity: A national survey of England. *Journal of Mental Health, 15*, 153–162.

Kirkpatrick, L. A. (1989). A psychometric analysis of the Allport–Ross and Feagin measure of intrinsic–extrinsic religious orientation. In M. L. Lynn & D. O. Moberg (Eds.), *Research in the social and scientific study of religion* (Vol. 1, pp. 1–31). Greenwich, CT: JAI Press.

Koenig, H. G., & Larson, D. B. (2001). Religion and mental health: Evidence for an association. *International Review of Psychiatry 13*, 67–78.

Kyriacou, B. (2006). Exploring the role of religious commitment in psychopathology. *Dissertation Abstracts International: Section B: The Sciences and Engineering, 67*, 1705.

Larson, D., Sherill, K., Lyons, J., et al. (1992). Associations between dimensions of religious commitment and mental health reported in the *American Journal of Psychiatry* and the *Archives of General Psychiatry*, 1978–1989. *American Journal of Psychiatry 149*, 557–559.

Lavender, H., Khondoker, A. H., & Jones, R. (2006). Understandings of depression: An interview study of Yoruba, Bangladeshi and White British people. *Family Practice, 23*, 651–658.

Lee, E. O. (2007). Religion and spirituality as predictors of well-being among Chinese American and Korean American older adults. *Journal of Religion, Spirituality & Aging, 19*, 77–100.

Lesniak, K., Rudman, W., & Rector, M. (2006). Psychological distress, stressful life events, and religiosity in younger African American adults. *Mental Health, Religion & Culture, 9*, 15–28.

Lewis, C., & Cruise, S. (2006). Religion and happiness: Consensus, contradictions, comments and concerns. *Mental Health, Religion & Culture, 9*, 213–225.

Lewis, K. N., & Epperson, D. L. (1991). Values, pretherapy information and informed consent in Christian counseling. *Journal of Psychology and Christianity, 10*(2) 113–131.

Loewenthal, K. (2007). *Religion, culture, and mental health.* New York: Cambridge University Press.

Lonczak, H., Clifasefi, S., & Marlatt, G. (2006). Religious coping and psychological functioning in a correctional population. *Mental Health, Religion & Culture, 9*, 171–192.

McCallister, B. J. (1995). Cognitive theory and religious experience. In R. W. Hood, Jr. (Ed.), *Handbook of religious experience* (pp. 312–352). Birmingham, AL: Religious Education Press.

McCullough, M. E. (1999). Research on religion-accommodative counseling: Review and meta-analysis. *Journal of Counseling Psychology, 46,* 92–98.

May, R., & Yalom, I. (2005). Existential psychotherapy. In Corsini, R. J. & Wedding, D. (Eds.), *Current psychotherapies* (pp. 269–298). Belmont, CA: Thomson, Brooks/Cole.

Murken, S. (1998). Hilft die Gottesbeziehung bei der Lebensbewältigung? Eine beziehungstheoretische Analyse. In E. Nestler and C. Henning (Eds.), *Religion und Religiosität zwischen Theologie und Psychologie. Bad Boller Beiträge zur Religionspsychologie* (pp. 205–236). Frankfurt, Germany: Lang.

Nielsen, S. L. (2001). Accommodating religion and integrating religious material during rational emotive behaviour therapy. *Cognitive and Behavioral Practice, 8,* 34–39.

Norton, M. C., Skoog, I., Franklin, L. M. et al. (2006). Gender differences in the association between religious involvement and depression: The Cache County (Utah) study. *Journals of Gerontology: Series B: Psychological Sciences and Social Sciences, 61B,* 129–136.

Paloutzian, R. F. (1996). *Invitation to the psychology of religion.* Needham Heights, MA: Allyn & Bacon.

Payne, I., Bergin, A., Bielema, K., & Jenkins, P. (1991). Review of religion and mental health: Prevention and the enhancement of psychosocial functioning. *Prevention in Human Services 9,* 11–40.

Priester, P. E. (2006, April). The impact of the explicit integration of Islam into counseling on perceptions of counselor social influences. Paper presented at the First International Congress on the Dialogue between Religion and Science, Tehran, Iran.

Priester, P. E. (2008). Mental health counseling in the Islamic Republic of Iran: A marriage of religion, science and practice. *Counseling and Values, 52,* 253–264.

Priester, P. E., & Jana-Masri, A. (August, 2006). Is the 12 step addiction model culturally appropriate for Muslims? Paper presented at American Psychological Association conference, New Orleans, LA.

Propst, L. R., Ostrom, R., Watkins, P., Dean, T., & Mashburn, D. (1992). Comparative efficacy of religious and nonreligious cognitive-behavioral therapy for the treatment of clinical depression in religious individuals. *Journal of Consulting and Clinical Psychology, 60,* 94–103.

Reger, G. M., & Rogers, S. A. (2002). Diagnostic differences in religious coping among individuals with persistent mental illness. *Journal of Psychology and Christianity, 21,* 341–348.

Richards, P. S., & Bergin, A. E. (2005). *Spiritual strategy for counseling and psychotherapy* (2nd Edition). Washington, DC: American Psychological Association.

Richards, P. S., Berrett, M. E., Hardman, R. K., & Eggett, D. L. (2006). Comparative efficacy of spirituality cognitive, and emotional support groups for treating eating disorder inpatients. *Eating Disorders, 14,* 401–415.

Rizzuto, A. M. (1988). The father and the child's representation of God: A developmental approach. In S. H. Cath, A. R. Gurwitt & J. Munder (Eds.), *Father and child: Developmental and clinical perspectives* (pp. 357–381). Cambridge, MA: Basil Blackwell.

Russell, R. J. (2000). *Theology and science: Current issues and future directions.* Retrieved October 11, 2003, from www.ctns.org/russell_article.html

Scharfenberg, J. (1973). Narcissism, identity, and religion. *Psyche: Zeitschrift für Psychoanalyse und ihre Anwendungen, 27*(10), 949–966.

Skinner, B. F. (1971). *Beyond freedom and dignity*. New York, NY: Knopf/Random House.

Spilka, B., & Werme, P. H. (1971). Religion and mental disorder: A research perspective. In M. Strommen (Ed.), *Research on religious development: A comprehensive handbook* (pp. 161–181). New York: Hawthorn.

Trotter, W. (1919). *Instincts of the herd in peace and war* (4th edn). New York: Macmillan.

Wachholtz, A. B., & Pargament, K. I. (2005). Is spirituality a critical ingredient of meditation? Comparing the effects of spiritual meditation, secular meditation, and relaxation on spiritual, psychological, cardiac, and pain outcomes. *Journal of Behavioral Medicine, 28*(4), 369–384.

Watlington, C., & Murphy, C. (2006). The roles of religion and spirituality among African American survivors of domestic violence. *Journal of Clinical Psychology, 62*, 837–857.

Winnicott, D. W. (1993). Transitional objects and transitional phenomena: A study of the first not-me possession. In G. H. Pollock (Ed.), *Pivotal papers on identification* (pp. 139–157). Madison, CT, US: International Universities Press.

Worthington, E. L., Kurusu, T. A., McCullough, M. E., & Sandage, S. J. (1996) Empirical outcomes on religion and psychotherapeutic processes and outcomes: A 10 year review and research prospectus. *Psychological Bulletin, 119*(3), 448–487.

Wulff, D. M. (1997). *Psychology of religion: Classical and contemporary* (2nd edn). Chichester, UK: John Wiley & Sons, Ltd.

Wyatt, S. C., & Johnson, R. W. (1990). The influence of counselors' religious values on client perceptions of the counselor. *Journal of Psychology and Theology, 18*, 158–165.

Yangarber-Hicks, N. (2004). Religious coping styles and recovery from serious mental illnesses. *Journal of Psychology and Theology, 32*, 305–317.

7

Psychotherapy in a Culturally Diverse World

Laura R. Johnson, Gilberte Bastien,
and Michael J. Hirschel

Worldwide, increases in population growth and mobility have resulted in a society that is increasingly multicultural in nature. Forced and voluntary migration, economic globalization and technological advances have resulted in new opportunities and demands related to cross-cultural interactions. With trends in population growth and mobility expected to continue, mental health practitioners will increasingly serve clients from diverse geographical, language and cultural backgrounds (Global Commission on International Migration, 2005; Population Resource Center, 2005). Over the last few decades, the United States has also witnessed a tremendous shift in terms of cultural, racial, ethnic, and religious diversity.

Given the huge demographic changes occurring worldwide, it is no longer acceptable for psychologists to operate from Eurocentric assumptions. The discrepancy between the cultural context from which modern psychology was constructed and the culturally diverse contexts in which it is being applied presents an ethical dilemma for conscientious psychologists (Pedersen, 1997). This dilemma calls us to question the generalizability of our approaches to therapy and also for a more culturally sensitive application of theory in various practice contexts.

In this chapter, we provide an overview of key issues to consider when providing counseling and therapy in the context of cultural differences. We begin with a discussion of cultural competence and its deliberate cultivation via the development of cultural awareness, knowledge and skills. Next, we describe the *DSM–IV* cultural formulation as a tool for understanding and working with culture in therapy. The cultural formulation also gives us an opportunity to highlight some important cultural constructs to consider when conceptualizing cases, such as identity, explanatory models, and relational issues. In the second half of the chapter we discuss steps to providing culturally responsive treatment, including reducing treatment barriers, improving communication, building relationships, and planning and carrying out effective treatments.

Culturally Competent Psychotherapy

Despite the changing demographic and cultural landscape worldwide, mainstream psychological theories and practices and the make-up of professionals within the field remain far from reflective of a diverse, multicultural population. A clear implication of the under-representation of minorities among mental health professionals is that now more than ever, clinicians will work with clients who are from a cultural, ethnic, language, geographic, and religious backgrounds different from their own. Even when the clinician and the client are from similar cultural backgrounds, there will invariably be some degree of cultural difference. As such, all therapy is considered cross-cultural, at least to an extent (Pedersen, 1991).

When cross-cultural interactions are not approached appropriately, clients are more likely to be misdiagnosed, receive inappropriate treatment, give up on treatment, and receive fewer benefits than their European American counterparts (Kurasaki, Sue, Chun, & Gee, 2000; Sue, Zane, & Young, 1994). Ethnic, cultural and other minority groups may view mental health services and institutions as inaccessible, unaffordable, culturally insensitive or otherwise inappropriate. Many have had personal negative experiences, such as experiences of racism or discrimination in similar institutions (e.g., health or educational), while others are wary based on collective histories and shared memories of oppression, genocide, enslavement, servitude, segregation, forced sterilization and unethical research practices. It is not surprising that many ethnic minorities have developed a certain level of mistrust for social service institutions. While this is often called a functional or healthy paranoia, this cultural mistrust also impacts help-seeking behavior. It is well known that many ethnic minority populations tend to avoid seeking professional psychological treatment. Many that seek psychological help do so as a last resort, when symptoms may have escalated. Often, those seeking professional help receive services of different quality and type, and health and mental health disparities have been well documented for ethnic and cultural minority groups (U.S. Department of Health and Human Services, 2001). Thus, the increase in opportunities for cross-cultural interaction comes with an increased responsibility for clinicians to cultivate the cultural competence necessary to better meet the needs of our increasingly diverse, multicultural society.

Cultural Competence

Cultural competence is a developmental process that requires psychologists and other mental health practitioners to value diversity, and be able to effectively meet the needs of clients in the context of cultural differences (APA, 2003). Cultural competence evolves over time and enhances major areas of professional activity such as research, teaching, and practice. The importance of developing cultural competence cannot be adequately stressed. The potential consequences of failing to educate oneself about the issues surrounding treatment of the culturally different can range from misdiagnosis to the use of inappropriate or ineffective interventions. On the other-hand, the benefits of cultural competence include:

- clinician flexibility in roles and treatments;
- ability to adapt to a changing patient population;
- increased success interacting with people of different cultural back-grounds;
- increased patient satisfaction and treatment adherence; and
- reduced mental health disparities (National Center for Cultural Compe-tence, 2007).

Cultural competence requires that clinicians be (1) aware of cultural values, assumptions, and biases – cultural awareness; (2) knowledgeable of a client's worldview – cultural knowledge; and (3) develop specific interventions and strategies that are appropriate for use with members of different cultural groups – cultural skills (Mio, Barker-Hackett, & Tumambing, 2006). Cultural compe-tence has been operationalized in terms of awareness, knowledge, and skills (Sue, Arredondo & McDavis, 1992). The following section provides a detailed description of these essential components as applicable to the practice of psychotherapy.

Cultural Awareness

A major prerequisite of providing culturally competent treatment is that clinicians must be aware of the unique cultural context from which they are operating. Without this personal consciousness, clinicians cannot provide appropriate treatment in different cultural contexts. Cultural influences such as gender, ethnicity, religion, age, or socioeconomic status can greatly influence a clinician's worldview, as well as their attitudes towards and beliefs about psychopathology and therapy. As a result, clinicians should periodically con-duct cultural self-assessments to evaluate the potential impact of these factors on treatment (APA, 2003). Other important factors to consider in assessing personal awareness include worldview, values, assumptions, stereotypes, expec-tations, privileges, communication style, as well as theoretical orientation and approach to treatment (Smith, 2004a). Recommended methods for facilitating personal awareness among psychologists include: participation in cultural activities, travel, and interacting with diverse others, such as through forming a multicultural discussion group. Deliberate self-reflection, discussion, and journaling can aid the process of examining one's own cultural heritage and the messages one receives about others (Hong, Garcia, & Soriano, 2000; Martin & Nakayama, 2005). Doctoral students of the first author of this chapter, for example, interviewed international students and facilitated an intentional student support group. Following this, they wrote about and discussed their experiences. In the process, students identified their lack of knowledge about other countries and cultures (e.g., "I knew *nothing* about Moldova.") and about international students in general. They became very aware of their lack of knowledge of the other educational systems and also conscious of differences in communication and fundamental cultural values.

Beyond the personal level of awareness just described, clinicians must be cognizant of the cultural context of the field itself. Modern psychology emerged from a predominantly western and individualistic worldview (Marsella & Yamada, 2000), quite unlike the majority of the world's population which is nonwestern and has a more collectivist or sociocentric worldview (traditionally). Lack of sufficient representation of various cultural groups in professional circles, lack of cultural content in the training curriculum for psychologists, and our shortcomings in meeting the psychological needs of ethnic minorities are just a few indicators of the cultural encapsulation of psychology as it is practiced in the US (Kazarian & Evans, 1998). Psychologists cannot afford to deny the cultural encapsulation of the theoretical foundations that drive professional activity in psychology. Clinicians must be prepared to critically examine and address the manifestations of the western and individualistic roots of the field. As illustrated in Table 7.1, values that are rooted in Eastern perspectives or in collectivist cultures have the potential to impact psychotherapeutic content and processes in markedly different ways than a western or individualistic outlook (Hays, 2001; Johnson & Sandhu, 2007b; Sandhu & Rigney, 1995; Triandis, 1995; Tseng, 2003).

According to the Health Resources and Services Administration (HRSA, 2005) of the Bureau of Primary Health Care, it is crucial that cultural awareness as well as other components of cultural competence be monitored and assessed to determine the efficacy of cultural competence training. It is critical that such assessments employ a comprehensive approach that includes both qualitative as well as quantitative methods and that evaluations encompass changes on the individual, group, and organizational levels (Pedersen, 2000). In their report on the guidelines for assessing cultural and linguistic competence, the HRSA provided recommendations to facilitate assessment of three key components of cultural competency training: (1) education (e.g., program curriculum, student learning, student use of skills taught); (2) clinical skills (i.e., actual application of skills and knowledge in practice settings); and (3) organizational evaluations (Bureau of Primary Health Care, Health Resources and Services Administration, 2007).

While such guidelines provide an approach for assessing the effectiveness of cultural competence training from the perspective of mental health professionals and organizations, they fail to address the efficacy of cultural competence training from the perspective of patients, families, and communities. There is currently a dearth of empirical research delineating the effect of culturally competent practices on mental health outcome. Barriers to these types of empirical investigations include the need for a clear definition of cultural competence, lack of consistent models or theoretical frameworks to guide such research, as

Table 7.1 Influences of individualism and collectivism on psychotherapy

Possible influence on psychotherapy	Individualistic world views (e.g. Australia, North America, Western Europe, including mainstream Western psychotherapy)	Collectivist world views (e.g. Africa, Asia, Eastern Europe, Latin America, including ethnic minority groups in USA)
Therapeutic relationship	• Collaborative relationship with therapist • Expectation of therapist anonymity	• Expectation for therapeutic relationship varies • May expect "expert" advice and authority from therapist or collaboration • May expect personal relationship with therapist
Communication	• Direct and low context communication • Direct expression of feeling • Psychological expression of symptoms	• Indirect and high context communication • Expression of feelings may be restrained or exaggerated • Symptoms may be expressed somatically or spiritually
Treatment process	• Self expression; Talk about problems • Psychological relief • Self-improvement • Analytic thinking, relative values	• Self control • Get advice or concrete help • Social and emotional support • Family involvement • Holistic thinking, absolute values
Focus of treatment	• Focus on internal processes (thoughts, feelings) • Problems in the individual	• Focus on social relations and social roles • Holistic focus (person-environment interaction)
Goals of treatment	• Goals focused on self (individual needs and goals prioritized) • Self-actualization; self-understanding; Self-fulfillment • Active adjustment; reduce psychological symptoms; Behavior change; • Learn new skills	• Goals of group (e.g. family) are more important • Happiness obtained through pleasing others; Approval from others; conforming to others • Passive acceptance (of social roles or of problems in life); Patience • Spiritual healing; Community or social action

well as a number of challenges associated with collection and analysis of data on race, ethnicity, and culture (Goode, Dunne, & Bronheim, 2006). What little work that has been done on the health outcomes of cultural competence is promising (e.g., the Health Resources and Services Administration indicates improved diagnoses, increased patient support for treatment plans, reduced delays in health care seeking, enhanced patient-practitioner communication and increased patient satisfaction, HRSA, 2005). However, a great deal of work remains to be done in moving these efforts beyond the preliminary phases.

Cultural Knowledge

In addition to developing awareness, it is necessary that psychologists work to acquire cultural knowledge that is both general (i.e., applicable across cultural groups) and culture-specific. General cultural knowledge refers to an understanding of the nature of culture and its influence on all aspects of life. Clinicians must strive to understand the complex, interactive, and dynamic process in which culture influences individuals, systems, and organizations. General cultural knowledge also includes a familiarity with multicultural theories as well as the significance of cross-cultural concepts such as acculturation, racial identity, worldview, etc.

Concomitantly, clinicians must acquire specific cultural knowledge relevant to the individual clients with which they work. This requires an effort to educate oneself about various forms of human diversity, including racial, religious, gender, sexual orientation, etc. This knowledge can be acquired by reading relevant literature, enlisting a cultural consultant, watching films and documentaries, and through practical experience with specific culture groups. The American Psychological Association's (APA) public interest directorate has made available via the Internet an annotated bibliography of references related to different groups. In addition, different divisions of the APA have produced guidelines for providers of services to different ethnic and cultural groups (e.g., *Guidelines for Psychotherapy with Lesbian, Gay and Bisexual Clients* (http://www.apa.org/pi/lgbc/publications/guidelines.html)).

Using a cultural consultant or cultural broker can also be useful for obtaining general cultural information, such as group norms, values, stigmas and so on. They may also be useful for quickly accessing necessary and specific information relevant to a particular case. Cultural consultants may be professional interpreters (some are trained to provide this dual role), professionals in mental health or related field with expertise and experience with the culture, or community or religious leaders or other lay members of the culture who serve as a cultural ambassador (Johnson & Sandhu, 2007b). Through these activities, clinicians can obtain pertinent information about cultural norms, sociopolitical history of a particular group, communication styles, as well as information about perceptions of mental health within a particular population (Gong-Guy, Cravens, & Patterson, 1991; Hong et al., 2000; Singh, McKay, & Singh, 1999; Vasques & Javier, 1991).

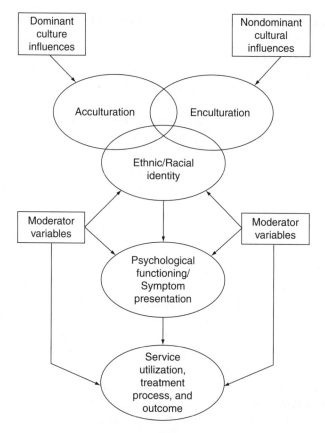

Figure 7.1 Impact of culture on psychological symptoms, help-seeking, and treatment
Source: Aponte & Johnson (2000); reprinted with permission from Allyn & Bacon

It is also important to consider the potential influence of cultural factors on assessment and treatment of psychological conditions. For instance, culture often shapes beliefs and attitudes about pathology, explanations of illnesses, expectations of treatment, as well as the quality of the therapeutic relationship. In addition to cultural differences in explanations for illnesses, certain psychological illnesses present differently across culture groups and may vary in terms of symptom meaning and severity. Figure 7.1 illustrates how key cultural factors (including ethnic identity, acculturation, and dominant and nondominant cultural influences) may impact the entire treatment pathway, from symptom recognition and meanings to help-seeking behaviors, treatment processes and treatment outcomes.

Depression is a good example of this phenomenon. Although depression is thought to be a universal phenomenon across cultures, there are significant ethnic and cultural differences in the types of symptoms endorsed, and in beliefs about how depression should be responded to. Around the world many cultures, including ethnic minorities in the US, tend to present with more somatic symptoms than their White counterparts (Kleinman, 1980; Ng et al., 2006). Some cultures may view depression as "problems of living" or hardships that must be endured rather than treated. Beliefs that depression is indicative of spiritual, social or cultural problems are also common and these beliefs may have implications for beliefs about the type of treatment needed and goals for treatment (Kleinman, 1980).

Although clinicians cannot realistically expect to learn all there is to know about every cultural group, they should acknowledge the limits of their cultural knowledge and commit to ongoing efforts to learn about different cultures. Beyond personal efforts, clinicians must advocate for institutionalization of cultural knowledge by utilizing policies, values, structures, and service (APA, 2003; Hage, 2005).

Cultural Skills

Finally, clinicians cannot offer culturally competent treatments without cultivating therapeutic skills that facilitate consideration of cultural factors in treatment. To this end, clinicians must actively engage in self-reflection; apply multicultural theory and research; access literature and cultural consultants; and be flexible and open to modifying the treatment process to address cultural issues, such as incorporating cultural resources into treatment. Clinicians must also anticipate and plan for communication difficulties and learn how to adapt their communication and relational style. Specific skills which clinicians can work on to facilitate the provision of culturally competent treatment include: building rapport with clients, intercultural communication, conducting culturally sensitive assessments, making accurate diagnoses, and developing culturally congruent and effective treatment plans (APA, 2003; Hong et al., 2000). Specific strategies and examples are discussed in the Steps Toward Treatment section of the chapter.

Guidelines for Culturally Competent Practice in Psychology

In 2002, the American Psychological Association approved the development and implementation of a set of guidelines that would guide clinicians' efforts to increase cultural competence in research, training, practice, and organizational policy (APA, 2003). The "Guidelines on Multicultural Education, Training, Research, Practice, and Organizational Change for Psychologists" proposes six guiding principles, which are briefly summarized below:

1. Psychologists must be aware of the potential influence of their cultural context on interactions with and treatment of culturally different clients.
2. Psychologists have a responsibility to acquire knowledge and an understanding of various cultural groups (especially those of their clients).
3. As it relates to psychological education, psychologists must incorporate multicultural constructs into teaching.

4. Psychologists must be committed to conducting culturally sensitive psychological research to contribute to the growing knowledge in the field about diverse groups of people.
5. Psychologists must strive to apply culturally appropriate skills in working with clients in clinical as well as other applied settings.
6. Finally (and perhaps most importantly), psychologists must push for organizational reform and policy changes that reflect a growing sensitivity to cultural issues in the field. This guideline highlights the expectation that psychologists be agents of change in protecting clients from the potentially detrimental affects of prejudice and discrimination.

Cultural Formulation

A number of diagnostic manuals have been developed to facilitate classification and diagnosis of psychological disorders over the years. These include resources such as the *International Classification of Diseases* (*ICD*, current version is *ICD-10*) or the *Chinese Classification of Diseases. The Diagnostic and Statistical Manual of Mental Disorders* (*DSM*, current version is *DSM–IV–TR*) is the most commonly used diagnostic manual in the US. Although some clinicians ascribe to the belief that the criteria described in the *DSM* are universally applicable and appropriate, it is clear that this work is a reflection of the western cultural context from which it emerged. Given the widespread use of the *DSM* in the field, clinicians must take cultural factors into consideration to ensure effective use of this tool in different cultural contexts. In response to challenges against the utility of the *DSM* with minority populations, the APA approved a few changes to reflect sensitivity to cultural issues. One such change was the addition of the Cultural Formulation.

Although it is little known, and probably more rarely used due to its location in Appendix I, The *DSM–IV* Outline for Cultural Formulation is a helpful tool for systematically assessing a client's cultural context and its potential impact on the course and process of treatment. Constructing the cultural formulation asks the therapist to obtain information regarding the client's cultural background, culture-specific attitudes, as well as beliefs regarding psychological ailments and treatment. It also assesses cultural differences between the patients and clinician that may affect the therapeutic relationship. The Cultural Formulation should be completed in conjunction with the multiaxial diagnostic assessment to ensure consideration of cultural factors that may influence framing of symptoms and/or dysfunction based on the *DSM* axes (Hays, 2001). The information obtained through a Cultural Formulation is organized into five major categories.

1. Cultural Identity of the Client

As individuals grow and evolve, they often begin to ask questions such as "Who am I?", "What do I value?", "What career path will I take?", or "How do I fit into the overall society?" The answer to these and similar identity questions are enmeshed in the cultural context(s) in which we have been immersed. The development of a cultural identity is believed to result from continuous assessment of the members of one's own cultural group as well as members of other cultural groups. This leads to the development of a pattern of behaviors, values, and beliefs that are considered to be common among members of a particular culture groups and distinguishes them from other cultural groups (Aponte & Johnson, 2000; Tseng, 2003). Examples of some models of cultural identity are included in Table 7.2. The People of Color (POC) Identity Model (Helms, 1995) is described here.

The POC Identity Model is comprised of five stages or "statuses", each of which describes an individual's appraisal of his/her own race as well as the race of others (Helms, 1995). Individuals in the *conformity* status tend to view their race as inferior due to biological or other insufficiencies. The *dissonance* status is characterized by general confusion about racism and questioning of validity of racial hierarchies. Next, is the status of *immersion-emersion*, in which the individual values his/her own culture while rejecting the cultural norms of the dominant group. This status is often accompanied by feeling of rage and distrust toward Whites. Finally, in the status of *internalization/integrative awareness*, the individual begins to embrace a more balanced appreciation for people and works towards judging people on an individual basis rather than generalizing stereotypes to all members of a particular racial group. Information processing strategies (IPS) describe the approach with which individuals tend to cope with racial experiences at each stage. The IPSs typically employed in the first four statuses include selective attention, hyper-vigilance, and dichotomous thinking.

Enculturation A client's cultural identity is, in large part, due to their enculturation experiences. Enculturation describes the process through which one is socialized into their cultural, ethnic, or social group (Aponte & Johnson, 2000). Thus enculturation is a part of psychological development and growth that varies from culture to culture. This is an ongoing process that can be facilitated directly or indirectly through teaching, modeling, and reinforcing specific behaviors. The agents that often facilitate this socialization include parents, other relatives, peers, teachers, and/or institutions. Environmental influences such as the media also play a role in the enculturation process. This cultural socialization begins at birth and takes a passive form until an individual becomes an adolescent, at which point he/she is able to evaluate and make decisions regarding cultural values which he/she might or might not hold dear. Ideally, enculturation produces an awareness of, pride in, and connectedness to one's culture of origin (Phinney, 1990). Furthermore, individuals who successfully progress through this process obtain the cultural competencies necessary to function effectively within their culture group (Aponte & Johnson, 2000). However, enculturation can be problematic when the cultural values from an individual's culture of origin differ significantly from the cultural norms of the dominant culture group. This can result in identity confusion or even clinical problems such as depression or anxiety.

Table 7.2 A selection of identity development models

Models	Population	Description	Authors
Black racial identity development (BRID)	African Americans	The BRID model describes a process in which African Americans can overcome internalized racism by establishing a sense of belonging to the African American 'group culture' followed by the encouragement of objective and neutral relations to Whites.	Cross, 1971, 1995; Helms, 1990
White racial identity development (WRID)	White Americans	The WRID model describes a process in which Whites recognize the realities of racism and abandon a sense of entitlement thereby developing a new, non-racist identity.	Helms, 1990, 1995
White racial consciousness		This model analyzes changes in racial attitudes and characteristics when describing the identity process. The model classifies unachieved (avoidant, dependent, dissonant) and achieved White racial consciousness (dominative, conflictive, reactive, integrative) types and through assessment is able to indicate the person's identity type. These models share many comparisons and similarities in terms of theory, concept, and measures used.	Rowe, Bennett, Atkinson, 1994
Minority identity development (MID)	Racial/Ethnic minorities	These models, largely derived from (BRID), describe similar processes of overcoming internalized racism and racism toward other racial/ethnic groups.	Atkinson, Morten, Sue, 1998
Person of color identity development (PCID)	Racial/Ethnic minorities	The models focus on developing a sense of belonging to a personal cultural group, relating objectively to Whites, and developing an integrated identity combined with social action.	Helms, 1995

(cont'd)

Table 7.2 (*cont'd*)

Models	Population	Description	Authors
Latin identity development	Latinos/as		Ruiz, 1990
Asian American identity development	Asian Americans		Kitano, 1999
Bicultural identity development	Internationally adopted persons	This model explains the process of birth culture recognition. It is meant to instill a sense of belonging to a preferred culture while relating objectively to both the birth and adopted cultures.	Friedlander, 1999, et al. 2000
Homosexual identity development	Gay, bisexual, lesbian persons	(Cass) The model is a tool used to recognize thoughts and behaviors as homosexual and ultimately develop feelings of acceptance and tolerance through stages. The model aims to develop a sense of belonging to the Gay/Lesbian subculture followed by objective relations to Heterosexuals. (D'Augelli) This version of the model describes identity formation as processes in which the person must renounce a Heterosexual identity in order to fully develop a personal and social Gay/Lesbian one. Once a level of intimacy is reached he/she can comfortably accept the Gay/Lesbian community.	Cass, 1979; D'Augelli, 1994
Biracial development	Biracial/ multiethnic persons	This model describes a process to facilitate identity acceptance by first identifying with the racial background of the parent of choice, followed by identification by with other groups. The goal is to develop a sense of belonging to a different cultural group and ultimately adopt a symbolic race or ethnicity.	Poston, 1990; Root, 1990, 1996

Acculturation Acculturation is a process through which cultural patterns (e.g., values, beliefs, behaviors) change as a result of sustained contact between individuals from different cultures (Berry, 1997; Berry & Kim, 1988). Unlike enculturation, acculturation occurs as a result of contact with a culture group other than the culture of origin. Acculturation can describe changes at the individual level as well as the group level. According to Berry's acculturation model, the two underlying issues for acculturating individuals are decisions about maintaining their connection with their original culture as well as continuing to have acculturative contact with other cultures (Rudmin & Ahmadzadeh, 2001). Decisions regarding these two basic issues form the basis for four basic acculturation strategies: assimilation, separation, integration, and marginalization. It is important to point out that these modes are not always "chosen" by the acculturating individual. For example, some may wish to assimilate, but not be fully allowed to do so by the dominant society; others may wish to remain separated, but may be forced to assimilate. Consider, for example the case of American Indian children who, up until the 1940s, were routinely removed from their native homes and reservations and sent to boarding schools where they were forbidden from speaking their native language and otherwise pressured to shed their American Indian cultural identity (Trafzer, Keller, & Sisquoc, 2006).

The psychological outcomes of acculturation can include behavioral shifts or adjustments to beliefs and behaviors to adapt to the new cultural context. Another possible outcome of the acculturation process is referred to as *acculturative stress*. Acculturative stress refers to mild to moderate difficulties adjusting to the demands of a new cultural situation. Major difficulties adapting to a new culture can result in more severe psychological problems. Specific examples of possible manifestations of acculturative stress include somatic complaints, perceived discrimination, family conflicts, depression, anxiety, identity confusion, and increased risk for suicide among immigrant populations (Berry, 1997, 1998; Berry, Kim, Minde, & Mok, 1987; Hovey, 2000; Hovey & King, 1996).

2. Cultural Explanations of the Problem

In treating clients from different culture groups, it is important that clinicians take into consideration clients' understandings of their problems (APA, 2003). Clients often come into therapy with culturally defined labels and causal explanations for their illness. For example, a client who defines himself/herself as deeply religious and spiritual may view psychological illness as stemming from spiritual conflicts. Others still may rely on natural explanations of mental ailments based on the assumption that human behavior and health, like all other activities, are governed by principles of nature. In other cultures, the condition of the physical body is believed to play a key role in mental health. That is, psychological illnesses are believed to be a result of unfavorable conditions within the body (Tseng, 2003). These culturally embedded conceptualizations of illness are examples of Explanatory Models (EMs) (Kleinman, 1980). EMs serve as the framework from which symptom meanings, onset, probable course of illness, severity, and level of impairment can be understood. Explorations of a clients' EMs often yields important information about their fears regarding the illness, the problems it has caused, as well as their attitudes toward and expectations of treatment (Chrisman & Johnson, 1996; Kleinman, 1980). Thus, understanding the EMs of culturally different clients provides clinicians with a better understanding of the client's illness experience, treatment choices, use of mental health services, as well as treatment outcomes (Kleinman, 1980; Pelto & Pelto, 1996; Weiss & Kleinman, 1988).

3. Cultural and Psychosocial Factors

In order to facilitate as thorough an understanding of the cultural context of behavior and client functioning as possible, psychosocial factors must be taken into consideration in treatment. Factors such as poverty and violence often play just as much (if not more) of a role in the development of psychopathology as biological and/or cognitive factors. This is especially true in working with clients of different cultural backgrounds because culture may influence an individual's interpretations of and reaction to social stressors in ways that clinicians may not have considered.

It is well documented in the multicultural literature that members of unique populations such as immigrants, migrants, and refugees are often particularly vulnerable to psychological distress due to significant differences in cultural norms, values, and discrepancies between the expectations of their culture of origin and the new culture (Berry, 1997; Hovey & Magana, 2000; Vega, Warheit, & Palacio, 1985). Many experience a great deal of stress as a result of separation from family, language difficulties, experiences of discrimination, shift in social status, lack of financial and social resources, and the like. Migrant workers, for example, are often plagued by health issues because they rarely seek treatment when they are ill due to fear of being deported, lack of insurance, as well as reluctance to miss work and risk being fired (Vega, Warheit, & Palacio, 1985). Furthermore, members of this population are often paranoid and suspicious of authority figures because of their undocumented status. Refugee children and adults also suffer unique concerns related to past traumas, camp experiences, displacement, dependence, and the loss of family, friends, country and culture (Bemack & Chung, 2000). The potentially detrimental effect of the aforementioned stressors on the mental health of these individuals is further exacerbated by the stress associated with the acculturation process.

These examples illustrate the importance of taking psychosocial factors into consideration in working with clients from a different culture. The potential consequences of failing to address these issues in treatment are far too great for clinicians to risk such negligence. By giving careful consideration to these environmental factors, clinicians can greatly improve the effectiveness of the services they provide to individuals from these groups (Mio et al., 2006).

4. Cultural Elements of the Relationship

This component of the cultural formulation deals with the quality of the clinician–client relationship. The therapeutic relationship is an essential aspect of psychological treatment, as it generally requires face-to-face interactions between the parties involved. The quality of the therapeutic relationship has been found to be a powerful marker of the quality of treatment and outcome, and thus can be considered a therapeutic tool in and of itself (Asay & Lambert, 1999). In the absence of a strong therapeutic relationship, it is at the very least extremely difficult to render effective psychological services. The implications of the quality of this relationship are even greater in the context of cross-cultural interactions. As such, the potential influence of the different cultural qualities that both the client and clinician bring into the therapeutic relationship must be given special consideration in every phase of the treatment process.

These cultural differences may include differences in cultural background, social status, religious affiliation, etc., which may impact the clinician's credibility with the client (Okazaki, 2000). Differences in communication styles can also greatly influence the course of treatment (Sue & Sue, 2003). For instance, a clinician may interpret a client's minimal or complete lack of direct eye contact as indicative of low self-esteem, when in fact this may be more attributable to cultural norms regarding appropriateness of direct eye contact. Beyond a mere recognition of cultural differences, clinicians must develop a plan and be open to making necessary adjustments to address potential problems associated with these differences in treatment (Hays, 2001). Specific strategies for achieving this end will be outlined later in the chapter.

5. Overall Cultural Assessment for Diagnosis and Care

The formulation of a case conceptualization is generally guided by a therapist's theoretical orientation as well as sociocultural factors and experiences. These influences inevitably affect clinicians' choices at every phase of the treatment process. As a result, factors that may influence diagnosis and care must be identified and addressed as clinicians move into the construction of an overall case formulation. Only in this way can cultural factors and other potential therapist biases be accounted for, ensuring that clients receive appropriate and effective services.

Clinicians committed to providing culturally competent treatment must strive to maintain a systemic perspective in their approach to treatment. Staying grounded in one's theoretical orientation can be helpful in this regard. As previously mentioned, the *DSM–IV* Outline for Cultural Formulation is a useful tool that can facilitate this perspective. One suggestion for effectively incorporating the cultural formulation in treatment was proposed by Hays (2001). She recommends the addition of a 6th axis to the multiaxial diagnostic formulation. Under this axis, the clinician can delineate elements of a client's culture (e.g., age, disability, religious affiliation, social economic status, sexual orientation, ethnicity, etc.) that are believed to be particularly salient influence on functioning. Hays recommends that this axis be completed first, followed by Axis IV (which addresses psychosocial and environmental stressors). Next, the 3rd axis (concerning medical conditions) should be completed. The information contained under these axes will provide a broader framework from which decisions can be made regarding Axis I & II diagnoses.

Steps Toward Treatment

One of the main purposes of the cultural formulation and conceptualization is to assess the role that an individual's culture might play on both the reasons for therapy referral and on the therapeutic process itself (Sánchez-Johnsen & Cuéllar, 2004; see also Chapter 9 this volume). Having obtained this information, it is the job of the therapist, using the help of the client, to determine how cultural variables might play a role in therapy. Culturally competent therapists should research cultural norms to obtain a sense of what they might expect from their clients, and how they might best adapt to client needs and expectations. However, hypotheses based on group-level cultural norms should be carefully and critically examined in each case, at the individual level. Therapists should not assume that clients will match group-level cultural norms and characteristics, as these norms are merely averages and not hard-set rules. Due to the complex and dynamic intermix of cultural factors, planning for therapy must always be an idiographic process tailored to each client and context.

Treatment Barriers

Psychotherapists should consider how different barriers to therapy might impact the treatment process. Three types of cultural treatment barriers which can create problems with therapy are those related to culture, economic class, and language (Sue & Sue, 2003). Cultural barriers refer to differences in thinking and behaving patterns between the client and therapist due to dissimilar backgrounds and contexts. They are easily overlooked as they are ingrained in oneself and are not often thought about. Examples include cultural differences in levels of individualism versus collectivism, in manners of communication, and in ideas about the distinction and separation of mental and physical health. Economic class barriers refer to issues surrounding the cost, availability, and accessibility of appropriate treatment. Language barriers refer to spoken language difficulties, such as not speaking the same language, using a different vernacular or dialect of the same language, or having an accent (Sue & Sue, 2003).

While these barriers make the therapeutic process more difficult, they do not render it impossible. Therapists should identify the complications specific to each client and do what they can to overcome the hurdles. For instance, for the economic and accessibility issues, psychologists might want to consider options such as sliding fee scales and meeting clients in more convenient locations including where the clients live. Community-based approaches and systems-level interventions may also be helpful (Aponte & Bracco, 2000).

Pre-therapy, which refers to the process of orienting the client to therapy, may be needed when clients are unfamiliar with the treatment setting (Sue, 2006). Pre-therapy activities might include extra time for building rapport, and more detail and attention in explaining technical aspects such as scheduling and confidentiality, role clarification, and expectations. The overall aim of pre-therapy is to help the client become comfortable with the therapy process. The "workings of therapy" are explained and client concerns are alleviated as much as possible with the therapist accommodating client desires where appropriate and possible. Cultural barriers may also be addressed at this stage.

Relationship Building

Research has consistently highlighted the value and need of establishing a good working relationship with clients and has further suggested that the therapist–client relationship may be particularly important with culturally diverse and minority clients in cross-cultural interactions (Asay & Lambert, 1999; Pedersen, 2004a). However, the question of how best to develop that working relationship and what it might look like is a question of culture and cultural differences in and of itself. Most research in this area has focused on mainstream, western culture clients and techniques that might not be applicable or desirable for some minorities and nonwestern culture clients (Hays, 2001). To be effective working with cultural minorities, psychologists will need to be able to readily adapt their relational style and treatment approach in a culturally appropriate manner.

For example, showing proper respect is a major concern in many minority cultures (Hays, 2001) and is normally similar in nonwestern cultures. Figuring out how to best address a client helps illustrate this example. It has been suggested that the best way to address clients is to begin with a more formal style, particularly with older clients, and then to inquire how clients would like to be referred to early on in therapy (Hays, 2001). Illustrating a potential conflict, U.S. dominant style pushes for using the first name of a client, while many therapists also expect their clients to call them by their first name. The aim of this is not to be disrespectful, but usually to minimize the status difference, help the client feel more relaxed and comfortable, or emphasize the collaborative nature of the relationship. However, many cultures might find this casualness disrespectful. Therapists referring to themselves as "doctor" might be expected by clients from cultures which emphasize hierarchy. Using a more casual or even a collaborative style might detract from the therapist's creditability in the eyes of the client (Tseng, 2003).

In building a relationship with a client, it is crucial that the therapist intentionally examine his or her own biases. A failure to identify biases may result in communication, diagnosis, and treatment decisions that are based on unchecked assumptions, negative stereotypes, and defensive reactions. For example, therapists may overestimate the importance of race as a critical factor in explanations for problems, while failing to consider economic, environmental, or cultural issues (Paniagua, 2005). For instance, IQ scores tend to be lower on average for most ethnic minorities compared to Whites, and incidence of schizophrenia tends to be higher for African Americans and those of Hispanic descent compared to other groups, but when other variables are added to the analysis such as socioeconomical status and amount of schooling, the racial divisions disappear. Problems of over-diagnosing as well as under-diagnosing clients occur based on assumptions of the relationship between cultural membership and specific disorders (Paniagua, 2005). Nobody is immune to prejudice. All therapists and all clients, regardless of cultural affiliation, might hold biases or feel discrimination against them (Negy, 2004).

Communication

In therapy, communication is of the utmost importance. After all, therapists and clients must be able to understand each other in order for therapeutic goals to be reached. Cultural factors can hinder communication in therapy due to differences in spoken languages, differences in language abilities, differences in styles of communication, and even subtle differences in accents, or the use of expressions and idioms.

Style of communication refers to both the verbal and nonverbal parts of communication extending past the message itself and can include pitch, intonation, eye contact level, facial expressions, as well as many other aspects (Sue & Sue, 2003). The variability of communication styles both within groups and across groups is wide, often resulting in confusion and misunderstanding. For example, handshake strength can communicate drastically different messages. In mainstream U.S. culture a weak handshake might depict a lack of being self-secure whereas in American Indian cultures it is more of the norm and a stronger handshake might be taken as hostile (Hays, 2001). Another nonverbal consideration centers on personal space. In some cultures, such as those in Latin America, communication distances tend to be much smaller than those of the United States; American therapists might feel uncomfortable being close to clients and move away, which in turn could subtract from the quality of the relationship (Sue & Sue, 2003). In Japan, it is common to repeat "yes" in a conversation merely to indicate that the listener is paying attention and not necessarily that he/she agrees with what is being said, which can lead to misunderstandings (Tseng, 2003). A "yes" could also represent a face saving attempt if a client feels that a "no" will be disappointing or bring shame or embarrassment to the therapist, the client or both. These examples highlight the need for therapists not to rush towards interpretation and also point out the possible utility of explaining to clients that some culturally based confusion might occur during treatment.

One of the largest cultural contrasts regarding communication is between direct and indirect styles. While mainstream U.S. culture stresses a more direct style (i.e., people say exactly what they mean), many cultures prefer a non-direct manner and view being direct as disrespectful. Another common difference between cultures is whether they rely more on high-context or more low-context communication. The degree of context refers to a group's shared knowledge base and results in a reduced amount of explicit, direct verbal effort to make a point. In high-context communication, it is not what is said that is important, but who says it, in what style, and at what time (Sue & Sue, 2003).

When the language barrier is large, or even if it is not so large but the client would be more comfortable in a different language, a referral should be made to a therapist who can communicate in the preferred language. When that is not an option, using an interpreter is advised. Interpreters ideally should share cultural characteristics with the client, should have some professional instruction in the area of psychology, and should not be related to the client (Paniagua, 2005). Other important considerations in using interpreters include: training of both the interpreter and the therapists; negotiating gender issues (matching may be important in some cultures); cultural, ethnic, and religious backgrounds and related conflicts; and issues related to confidentiality in small ethnic communities. In Middle Eastern cultures for example, gender matching is especially important as it is considered inappropriate to discuss certain topics while in the presence of members of the opposite sex. Therapists should keep in mind other important differences, such as religious, political, ethnic or tribal that may impact treatment. For example, while working in a refugee clinic, the first author of this chapter found that careful attention was given to matching among Bosnian and Serbian patients and interpreters.

Assessment and Treatment

Another type of communication difficulty arises when therapists and their clients have different ways of thinking about referring issues. Clients will often have their own idea about the origin and maintaining factors for their problems, and very often these ideas will sharply contrast the beliefs of the therapist (Kleinman, 1980). For instance, in many Asian and African cultures spiritual causes are suggested to be the origin of mental problems and therefore, spiritual solutions are sought (Chiu & Lee, 2004). In fact, ethnic minorities in the US and most cultural groups around the world hold spiritual or somatic conceptualizations of their mental health problems and help seeking. It is important that therapists ask clients to share their ideas and attempt to integrate the client's language, problem conceptualization, and treatment expectations into treatment as much as possible. Clients often need to feel that they have some control over what is being worked on and that they are being heard. As such, it is very possible for clients to select goals which might not correspond with the ideas of the therapist. Therapists are encouraged toward flexibility in their approach, and should, in each case, consider how to develop a treatment plan that is culturally and personally acceptable to the client.

Treatment Planning

The modality of therapy should ideally be decided with the help of the client. Options include individual therapy, group therapy, and family therapy, as well as community-based services and systems-level interventions. Some clients might prefer to include members of their family, or even their church in therapy, and therapists should remain open to those ideas. With family involvement there are more sources of information about the presenting problem, and improvements could have a greater likelihood of being sustained. Conversely, neglecting to work with family members may result in a lack of support for treatment and poor patient adherence. When working with diverse clients, the definition of family should be flexible and potentially extended to include distant relatives as well as close friends and religious figures, as these significant persons can all play an important role in the therapeutic process (Paniagua, 2005).

Group therapy approaches can often be a good option for minority clients. Group therapy provides an opportunity to network with people from one's own or different cultures, practice skills, and share common concerns. Groups are often suggested for working with culturally related problems, such as acculturation and identity-related concerns, and other situations in which the aims of treatment include normalization of the experience and increased client social support. However, groups can also be problematic. There is a potential for multicultural groups to mimic intercultural conflicts of the larger society. In addition, there is also the heightened potential for a lack of anonymity due to individuals' minority status. Cultural concerns, beliefs, taboos, and stigmas may further inhibit the sharing of personal information with a group of people of different (or similar) genders or backgrounds (Hays, 2001).

Not only does the format of therapy need to be matched to the clients' needs, but the style may need to be adjusted as well. Just as there is no one format of therapy that is practiced for mainstream culture clients, there is not a single version that will work for each member of a minority cultural group. From client to client, there will be more within group cultural variability than between, resulting from a complex interplay of personality characteristics, life experiences, identity salience, and contextual factors. However, research has shown that some ethnic minorities prefer therapies that are directive in nature and have an active, solution focused role for the client (Sue & Sue, 2003). Approaches that are holistic and that pay attention to contextual issues, such as financial hardships, health problems, problems in the environment and in living, also have broad multicultural appeal.

Treatment Approaches

Adapting Mainstream Treatments

Most therapists working with diverse clients will likely use treatment techniques that have shown success in mainstream culture. Unfortunately, there are relatively few studies examining the effectiveness and appropriateness of these empirically supported treatments for diverse populations. More outcome research in this area would definitely be helpful in assisting clinicians to figure out the best course of action. While *some* of these treatments may be effective with *some* minority cultural group members, others will likely need an adapted approach to treatment. Treatment adaptations might include altering the language of the treatment, including a family component, or adding and integrating cultural material to the treatment, such as cultural resources, values, or healing practices (Griner & Smith, 2006).

As an example of an adapted treatment, Hays (2001) recommends analyzing for a cultural perspective in every element when using multimodal therapy. Specifically when examining client behavior she suggests thinking about how it is influenced by culture, and when examining client cognitions she suggests thinking about cultural norms for beliefs and principles. Another example of an adaptation is using rational emotive behavior therapy with devoutly Christian clients, and challenging their thoughts with verses from the Bible (Johnson & Ridley, 1992).

Another approach to treatment adaptation involves employing creative and expressive techniques, such as music, art and play that do not require verbal communication (Hays, 2001). These techniques can be particularly useful when language barriers exist or when verbal communication is uncomfortable for the client. Artwork is a common form and is especially good with children as that is an activity many children engage in naturally. Other options include gardening, expressive movement, dance, drumming, singing, and storytelling. Many culture-specific treatments rely on similar healing approaches.

Culture-Specific Treatments

Based on group-level cultural norms, values, and beliefs, some specific approaches have been developed for members of particular ethnic or cultural groups. For instance, telling stories is a common practice among many American Indian groups and can provide a good method of practice for therapists (Hays, 2001). In Native American talking circles, a special object such as a stick signifies who has the right to speak. The object is then passed along the circle providing all involved an opportunity to speak their minds (Standley, 2007). As an example of how they can be useful, Becker, Affonso, and Beard (2006) effectively used talking circles in their research as a culturally sensitive means of addressing health concerns in American Indian women. A similar storytelling technique, known as Cuento therapy, has also been shown to be successful in treating Puerto Ricans and its methodology fits well into usual cultural practices (Arbona, 2004; Lee & Ramirez, 2000). These stories indirectly provide advice to the listener through their morals and help provide guidance. As music and dance tend to be a strong component of Latino culture, therapies based on both could be used as indirect methods of addressing concerns. Different types of music and dance are specifically associated with different problems, for instance salsa is associated with survival concerns and bolero with relationship issues (Paniagua, 2005). It has been suggested that dance serves as a different means of self-expression and as a way to build new relationships. Therapy using Salsa, for example has produced benefits for some individuals with emotional problems and others with low self-esteem (Salleh, 2007).

When working with African-American and other clients of African ancestry, there are a few culturally specific practices to consider. Due largely to a lengthy history of oppression, discussing the topic of race is important, as is getting a sense of the client's racial identity (Brooks, Haskins, & Kehe, 2004). An individual's racial identity may be quite complex. Consider for example different aspects of the "black racial identity" of an African-American urban youth from Detroit, a "Black Indian" from New Orleans or someone of Gullah heritage living off the South Carolina coast in the US. Some persons of African descent may benefit from and prefer treatments based on Afrocentric values, such as the Nguzo Saba (i.e., seven principles including unity, faith, purpose, collective work and responsibility, creativity, shared economics, self-determination). Afrocentric interventions that utilize a rites-of-passage developmental paradigm have been adapted from traditional African approaches and are now used in community settings to address problems of cultural and personal identity in African-American youth. These programs stress the importance of healthy male-female relationships, personal responsibility for behavior, and bringing about social change for the benefit of the collective community (Brookins, 1996; Hill, 1992). Some research indicates that if done well, these programs can be rather successful (Whaley & McQueen, 2004).

When working with clients of Japanese heritage, adapted forms of Naikan and Morita therapies could be of use. Morita therapy in its original form consists of a series of stages where at first one's activity level is severely limited and intense reflection takes place; slowly one takes on more, and the focus is on acceptance and a new outlook on life (Hedstrom, 1994). Naikan therapy involves concentration and introspection of one's life and one's relationships with others, with the goals of changing the way prior concerns were viewed and also altering problem behaviors (Tseng, 2003).

Spirituality can frequently be a useful part of therapy with members of ethnic minority groups (e.g., African Americans, Latinos, Asians) due to high group participation levels in religious and spiritual activities (Brooks, Haskins, & Kehe, 2004). Therapists should ask clients about their spiritual involvement and see if it might be an area of the clients' lives that can be effectively brought into therapy or if the client needs to be referred for religious or spiritual counseling. The first author, for example, has facilitated an Iranian client's use of the

Moslem daily prayer into a stress reduction program and Christian bible verses into cognitive-behavior therapy for a Lebanese woman suffering from panic and depression. While it is important to be comfortable talking about spirituality, therapists should keep in mind the client's priorities and not dwell on issues unless they are important to the client (Paniagua, 2005). Moreover, psychologists can and should refer clients to pastoral counselors or religious leaders if clients are asking for religious or spiritual guidance. Referrals, consultations and psychoeducation may be helpful for clients with predominately spiritual or religious presentations or problem conceptualizations.

Traditional and Indigenous Treatments

In the past, psychologists in the United States typically have not been interested in indigenous healing methods. These practices tend to be drastically different from mainstream norms and are based on belief systems that do not match most western, mainstream psychologists' beliefs. However, with high rates of immigration and increased numbers of clients from diverse cultures, psychologists are coming into more frequent contact with traditional healing beliefs and many are gaining popularity as alternative approaches in society (Koss-Chioino, 2000; Myers et al., 2005). Indigenous healing is different from mainstream culture practices in many respects, but similar in others. Specifically mainstream, western-based treatments typically have more of an individualistic focus, whereas indigenous healing tends to have a more holistic focus on the interrelationships between the person and their environment.

Many traditional approaches arise from different metaphysical views (e.g., they do not view the mind and body as separate; or the physical and supernatural or spiritual realms as distinct) and contain more spiritually related aspects. However, there are similarities as well. Psychologists and healers are both considered experts in healing (having received some type of education or training), each have a particular way of conceptualizing and treating problems, and each hope to bring some relief or improvement in functioning to the patient. Although it is difficult for many psychologists to see these similarities and to place value in traditional healing beliefs, the fact that many clients hold such ideas as central to their beings should be enough reason for therapists to take them seriously (Sue & Sue, 2003). Moreover, use of traditional healing practices and supports may serve as useful adjuncts to traditional psychotherapy approaches.

For example, Haitian immigrants who are practitioners of *voodoo* (a complex religion which combines African and Catholic beliefs) often consult voodoo specialists (e.g., *hougan, bòkò,* or *manbo*) for health problems. Additionally many Haitians who are not of the voodoo religion seek health care from a variety of indigenous healers including herbal specialists (or "leaf doctors"), granny midwives, injection specialists, and other spiritual leaders either in addition to or as a substitute for formal medical treatment. In Uganda, East Africa, traditional healers exist in 80 percent of communities. They are a varied group with a wide range of approaches, many of which are akin to western psycho-therapeutic techniques such as proving social support, conflict resolution, and behavioral strategies (Johnson & Tucker, 2007). Healers often address concerns at a family or community level and their approach frequently has a spiritual or cultural component. Prayer, herbal medications, medication bathing/purification, compresses, divining, ancestor communication or veneration, and other rituals or tasks may be a part of the treatment.

There are several recommendations for therapists to follow regarding indigenous healing (Myers et al., 2005; Sue & Sue, 2003). First, being careful not to disrespect client beliefs is important. Also, therapists should spend time learning thoroughly about the beliefs and traditional practices in clients' cultures. In addition, adopting openness to working with indigenous healers is advised. Consultation provides the advantages of working with someone who might be able to better understand and explain the problems and world of the client, gaining trust from the client that their beliefs and values are taken seriously, and adding an additional component of therapy which might assist in client goals (Sue and Sue, 2003). Following this advice might not be a simple task for therapists, but will likely lead to better treatment of their clients in a culturally competent manner.

Working with Culturally Related Problems

Acculturative Stress

As previously discussed, this concept of acculturative stress can apply to everyone who goes through acculturation whether they are immigrants, refugees, international students, or minorities within mainstream culture. Symptoms include unhappiness, irritation, nervousness, somatic discomfort, confusion over self, alcohol and drug abuse, and relationship problems (Berry & Kim, 1988; Sandhu & Asrabadi, 1998). Acculturation is an ongoing process that takes time. Nobody can move across cultures and be fully acculturated overnight. Factors that influence a client's level of acculturative stress include the length of time in the new culture, how old the client was at the time of the change, and the degree of difference between the cultures (Paniagua, 2005; Babiker et al., 1980). Amount of contact with the new culture is another factor to consider. Everyone is different and both the time it takes to acculturate and the degree of acculturation will vary by the person.

One problem with acculturative stress can occur when different members within the same family are at different levels of acculturation. This problem has been found to be fairly common for children in western cultures whose parents grew up in nonwestern cultures. Sue and Sue (2003) reported this among Asian Americans whose parents grew up in Asia. Such children struggle with the contrast of adapting to a lifestyle like their American friends while holding on to enough of their Asian roots to please their parents. At the same time the parents struggle with figuring out how best to raise their children in the situation (Sue & Sue, 2003).

As a construct, acculturation is complex and often misunderstood. In the past acculturation was viewed as unilinear, involving the process of discontinuing practices and beliefs from an old culture and adopting ones from the new culture. However, acculturation is now most often considered to be a multidimensional and directional process in which the shedding or maintenance of culture-of-origin practices and values is considered to be separate (i.e., orthogonal process) from that of second culture acquisition or rejection. This way of thinking about acculturation is more sophisticated and allows for a more complex set of acculturation strategies and outcomes, than would a unilinear process. That is, in addition to assimilation and separation, biculturalism and multiculturalism can result from retention of old culture and acquisition of the new culture, whereas marginalization from all cultures can result when people shed one, but do not adopt the new ways. Many researchers and clinicians stress the importance of bicultural competence, where people can function well in two cultures at the same time (LaFromboise, Coleman, & Gerton, 1993). Bicultural Effectiveness Training (BET) is a therapeutic strategy that can be used to build bicultural competence by increasing cognitive and behavioral flexibility (Szapocznik & Kurtines, 1993).

Issues with Cultural Identity

Acculturation plays a role in altering and shaping an individual's identity; in fact, identity modification can be considered to be a component of acculturation (Sánchez-Johnsen & Cuéllar, 2004). This idea makes sense in that as people become integrated into a new culture, they change their behaviors and ways of thinking, causing how they view themselves to change as well. Sometimes the change in identity will be a smooth process without complications. For others it could be a difficult time of questioning oneself. People might think about whether or not they like who they have become. The problem might even be that a client feels a lack of any cultural identity. Therapists can help clients explore who they are and how they feel about themselves, and can focus on helping clients to develop a meaningful cultural identity. Encouragement can be given to learn more about one's own culture through reading, attending cultural events, or other activities.

Therapists can use identity as a concept to assist in obtaining a better understanding of clients, and also in helping clients obtain a better understanding of themselves. More specifically, a deeper knowledge of a client's identity will provide insight into what has had the most impact on the client in the past. However in terms of discussing cultural influences on clients, it is advised to spend time researching these influences out of session after gaining a little understanding from the client rather than relying on the client to explain it all (Hays, 2001).

Like many other aspects, the way different people view their cultural identities varies greatly. Although originally describing biracial individuals, the ideas presented by Root (1996) can easily be extended to anyone experiencing a multicultural identity. She suggests that such people might view themselves as completely within both cultures all of the time; might switch back and forth in terms of cultural identity depending on the context; might hold a mixed cultural identity; or might hold one single cultural identity for some time (Root, 1996). All of these are acceptable ways of handling the influence of multiple cultures on an individual. It is a matter of figuring out what is best for each person and working with them to identify and resolve identity issues and conflicts as they arise.

Identity struggles also exist outside of the acculturation process. Analogous to identity concerns within mainstream society, members of minority groups may experience issues fitting in within their own cultures. Specifically, there can be much variety in the views and behaviors of members of any minority group (Sue and Sue, 2003). Even with this within group variability, those individuals who behave in a manner inconsistent with the norms for their group can have problems being accepted and feeling part of the group. As noted earlier in the chapter, identity development models have been developed for many minority groups including African Americans, Asian Americans, and Hispanic Americans. These models can help provide theoretical and practical insight into typical paths of identity growth common among group members (Sue and Sue, 2003). Therapists might be able to use these models to figure out where an individual's development might be and then use the knowledge to help clients resolve their identity concerns and advance their identity awareness. Group approaches (e.g., empowerment groups, ethnic consciousness groups) or programs that educate clients about their cultural history (including oppression and power issues), and group cultural strengths and values may be effective in addressing identity concerns. For many cultural groups, social support networks are extremely important and play a central role in identity. It can be useful for therapists to help clients identify important social supports and learn ways to benefit from social relationships. Encouraging mentoring relationships, social and recreational programs, and active community involvement or volunteer may be especially crucial for individuals from collectivist backgrounds. Not only do these approaches provide a social network, but they also have broad multicultural appeal (Aponte & Bracco, 2000).

Prejudice and Discrimination

There are many examples unfortunately highlighting that racism and discrimination remain prevalent in American society. Statistics show how racially motivated hate crime rates have increased in recent years and quotes of well-known individuals with prejudice views show that even the rich and famous are not unaffected (Sue & Sue, 2003). The tragic events of September 11th have increased racism against many minorities in the country, especially but not limited to Arabs and those of Middle Eastern descent. As a case in point, a client of one of ours of Indian heritage was accused at school of being a terrorist and having brought a bomb with him. The school took the accusation seriously and searched the child, causing much humiliation and discomfort, despite absolutely no evidence to support the claims. Presumably his darker than average skin color played a part in the manner in which he was treated.

Awareness of the reality of this prejudice and discrimination is important for therapists to have for several reasons. Firstly, it gives insight into clients' lives and the discrimination they face, providing rationale for why many clients might have a hard time trusting and opening up to therapists. Secondly, such prevalence of prejudice demands psychologists explore and work through their own biases. Only in understanding the worlds of clients and understanding and dealing with prejudices in our own worlds, can we serve effectively in therapy (Sue & Sue, 2003).

For some clients, the experience of racism or prejudice might be a commonplace experience. As such, it is important for therapists to realize that a certain amount of distrust and suspicion might be adaptable in society for these clients and should not immediately be seen as abnormal. When this issue appears to be a problem, it is advisable to discuss cultural differences with clients as that has been shown to reduce anxiety and lead to more trust and a better therapeutic relationship (Paniagua, 2005).

Also, when clients have experienced prejudice and discrimination, it might be a topic they want to pursue in therapy. If this is the case, areas that could be useful to clients include assertiveness training as well as social action involvement. In assertiveness training, clients are taught to stand up for their rights and respond in an appropriate way to situations they do not like. In terms of prejudice, this training might help clients in dealing with situations in which they are being discriminated against. Social action is when work is being done to change parts of society. Therapists might suggest that clients join groups working toward reducing prejudice in society.

Monitoring Progress and Making Mistakes

As with every client, it is extremely important to constantly monitor the success of therapy and make adjustments as necessary. The needs of clients can change with time as new issues arise. Clients may experience changes in their circumstances, in their views of things, or in their readiness to engage in treatment, address more sensitive topics, or undertake more difficult tasks. Over the course of treatment, a range of different techniques and approaches may be used, and along the way it can be expected that some techniques may not work well, lacking feasibility, relevance, and/or appropriateness. Occasionally mistakes will be made. The therapist needs to be aware of how therapy is progressing, maintaining the positive aspects, and altering as necessary to the benefit of the client. What appears to be "resistance" on the part of the client such as not showing up for sessions or not completing homework assignments indicates a need for the therapist to re-assess the situation and do something different.

With diverse populations, there is the added challenge of handling cultural differences. The chance of making mistakes is increased due to various reasons such as having different ways of viewing problems and holding stereotypical biases; therapists should work past these issues through self-analysis, the assistance of experts and references, and being mindful of their thoughts and feelings (Smith, 2004b). Blunders will occur at times, and while preventing too many is good, what is most important is recovering, correcting mistakes, and moving on (Hays, 2001; Pedersen, 2004b). Smith, Richards, Granley, and Obiakor (2004, p. 13) state it well when they say that "all helping relationships require effort, adaptation, and more than a little humility." Ongoing attendance to the therapeutic relationship, client respect, cultural knowledge, and an awareness about one's limits in helping diverse others, could enhance a therapist's ability to recover from cultural missteps in treatment.

Conclusions

This chapter has underscored some of the major concerns surrounding practicing psychotherapy in today's culturally diverse world. We began by high-lighting the importance of culture and cultural competence as an ethical imper-ative in psychotherapy. Next, we reviewed the *DSM–IV* outline for a cultural formulation as an example of cultural competence in conceptualizing cases. The outline also presented an opportunity to introduce key cultural concepts, such as cultural identity, acculturation, enculturation, and explanatory models that are useful from theoretical, conceptual and practical perspectives. Next, we discussed the process of planning treatments that are culturally appropriate. Examples of cultural competence in treatment planning included addressing treatment barriers, adapting ones' style or treatment approach, and working with problems related to culture. Different treatment approaches, such as adapting mainstream approaches and use of indigenous approaches to healing were described. We also briefly outlined some of the concerns that clients may have that are related to their cultural background, such as those related to acculturation, identity and discrimination. Lastly, we discussed the importance of monitoring the progress of therapy and the quality of the therapeutic rela-tionship, and making changes as needed.

In order to effectively meet the needs of this increasingly diverse society, psychology must acquire cultural knowledge that can be translated into changes in psychotherapy practice, as well as in other areas of mental health service delivery and in society as a whole. This effort towards cultural competence must be approached from an ethical perspective and must be guided by a genu-ine respect for the worth and dignity of all members of society.

REFERENCES

American Psychological Association (1994). *Diagnostic and statistical manual of mental disorders* (4th ed.). Washington, DC: Author.

American Psychological Association (2002). Rules and procedures: October 1,2001 [Ethics Committee Rules and Procedures]. *American Psychologist, 57,* 626–645.

American Psychological Association (2003). Multicultural guidelines: Education training, research, practice and organizational change for psychologists. *American Psychologist, 58,* 377–402.

Aponte, J. F., & Bracco, H. F. (2000). Community approaches among ethnic minorities. In J. F. Aponte & J. Wohl (Eds.), *Psychological intervention and cultural diversity* (2nd ed., pp. 131–148). Needham Heights, MA: Allyn & Bacon.

Aponte, J. F., & Johnson, L. R. (2000). The impact of culture on intervention and treatment of ethnic populations. In J. F. Aponte & J. Wohl (Eds.), *Psychological intervention and cultural diversity* (2nd ed., pp. 18–39). Needham Heights, MA: Allyn & Bacon.

Arbona, C. (2004). Counseling Puerto Ricans. In C. Negy (Ed.), *Cross cultural psychotherapy: Toward a critical understanding of diverse clients* (pp. 115–139). Reno, NV: Bent Tree Press.

Asay, T. D., & Lambert, M. J. (1999). The empirical case for the common factors in therapy: Quantitative findings. In M. A. Hubble, B. L. Duncan, & S. D. Miller (Eds.), *The heart and soul of change: What works in therapy* (pp. 23–55). Washington, DC: American Psychological Association.

Atkinson, D. R., Morten, G., & Sue, D. W. (1998). Current issues and future directions in minority group/cross-cultural counseling. In D. R. Atkinson, G. Morten, & D. W. Sue (Eds.), *Counseling American minorities: A cross-cultural perspective* (5th ed., pp. 303–359). Boston, MA: McGraw-Hill.

Babiker, I. E., Cox, J. L., & Miller, P. M. (1980). The measurement of cultural distance and its relationship to measurement to medical consultations, symptomatology, and examination performance of overseas students at Edinburgh University. *Social Psychiatry and Psychiatric Epidemiology, 15*(3), 109–116.

Becker, S. A., Affonso, D. D., & Beard, M. B. H. (2006). Talking circles: Northern Plains tribes American Indian women's views of cancer as a health issue. *Public Health Nursing, 23,* 27–36.

Bemack, F., & Chung, R. (2000). Psychological interventions with immigrants and refugees. In J. F. Aponte & J. Wohl (Eds.), *Psychological interventions and cultural diversity* (pp. 200–212). Needham Heights, MA: Allyn & Bacon.

Berry, J. W. (1997). Immigration, acculturation, and adaptation. *Applied Psychology: An International Review, 46,* 5–68.

Berry, J. W. (1998). Acculturation and health: Theory and research. In S. Kazarian & D. Evans (Eds.) *Cultural clinical psychology: Theory, research, and practice* (pp. 39–57). New York: Oxford University Press.

Berry, J. W., & Kim, U. (1988). Acculturation and mental health. In P. R. Dasen, J. W. Berry, & N. Sartorius (Eds.), *Health and cross-cultural psychology* (pp. 207–236). Newbury Park, CA: Sage.

Berry, J. W., & Kim, U., Minde, T., & Mok, D. (1987). Comparative studies of acculturative stress. *International Migration Review, 21,* 490–511.

Brookins, C. C. (1996). Promoting ethnic identity development in African American youth: The role of rites of passage. *Journal of Black Psychology, 22*, 388–417.

Brooks, L. J., Haskins, D. G., & Kehe, J. V. (2004). In T. B. Smith (Ed.), *Practicing multiculturalism* (pp. 145–166). Boston, MA: Allyn & Bacon.

Bureau of Primary Health Care, Health Resources and Services Administration. (2007) Transforming the face of health professions through cultural & linguistic competence education: The role of the HRSA Centers of Excellence. Retrieved on August 11, 2007 from http://www.hrsa.gov/culturalcompetence/curriculumguide/chapter7.htm.

Cass, V. C. (1979). Homosexual identity formation: A theoretical model. *Journal of Homosexuality, 4*, 219–235.

Chiu, E. Y., & Lee, E. (2004). Cultural frameworks in assessment and pychotherapy with Asian Americans. In C. Negy (Ed.), *Cross-cultural psychotherapy: Toward a critical understanding of diverse clients* (pp. 205–229). Reno, NV: Bent Tree Press.

Chrisman, N. J., & Johnson, T. M. (1996). Clinically applied anthropology. In C. F. Sargent & T. M. Johnson (Eds.), *Medial anthropology: Contemporary theory and method* (rev. ed., pp. 88–109). Westport, CT: Praeger Publishers.

Cross, W. E. (1971). The Negro-to-Black conversion experience. *Black World, 20*, 13–27.

Cross, W. E. (1995). The psychology of nigrescence: Revisiting the Cross model. In J. G. Ponterotto, J. M. Casas, L. A. Suzuki, & D. M. Alexander (Eds.), *Handbook of multicultural counseling* (pp. 93–122). Thousand Oaks: Sage.

D'Augelli, A. R. (1994). Identity development and sexual orientation: Toward a model of lesbian, gay, and bisexual development. In E. J. Trickett, R. J. Watts, & D. Birman (Eds.), *Human diversity: Perspectives on people in context* (pp. 312–333). San Francisco: Jossey-Bass.

Friedlander, M. L. (1999). Ethnic identity development of internationally adopted children and adolescents: Implications for family therapists. *Journal of Marital and Family Therapy, 25*, 43–60.

Friedlander, M. L., Larney, L., Skau, M., Hotaling, M., Cutting, M., & Schwam, M. (2000). Bicultural identification: Experiences of internationally adopted children and their parents. *Journal of Counseling Psychology, 47*, 1–12.

Global Commission on International Migration (2005). Migration in an interconnected world: New directions for action. Report of the Global Commission on International Migration (pp. 1–98). Retrieved November 5, 2006 from www.gcim.org/attachments/gcim-cimplete-report-2005.pdf

Gong-Guy, E., Cravens, R. B., & Patterson, T. E. (1991). Clinical issues in mental health service delivery to refugees. *American Psychologist, 46*(6), 642–648.

Goode, T. D., Dunne, M. C., & Bronheim, S. M. (2006). The evidence base for cultural and linguistic competency in health care. Retrieved August 11, 2007 from http://www.commonwealthfund.org/publications/publications_show.htm?doc_id=413821

Griner, D., & Smith, T. B. (2006). Culturally adapted mental health interventions: A meta-analytic review. *Psychotherapy: Theory, Research, Practice, Training, 43*, 531–548.

Hage, S. M. (2005). Future considerations for fostering multicultural competence in mental health and educational settings: Social justice implications. In M. G. Constantine & D. W. Sue (Eds.), *Strategies for building multicultural competence* (pp. 285–302). Hoboken, NJ: John Wiley & Sons, Inc.

Hays, P. A. (2001). *Addressing cultural complexities in practice: A framework for clinicians and counselors.* Washington, DC: American Psychological Association.

Hedstrom, L. J. (1994). Morita and Naikan therapies: American applications. *Psychotherapy: Theory, Research, Practice, Training, 31,* 154–160.

Helms, J. E. (1990). *Black and white racial identity: Theory, research, and practice.* New York: Greenwood.

Helms, J. E. (1995). An update of Helm's white and people of color racial identity models. In J. G. Ponterroto, J. M. Casas, L. A. Suzuki, & C. M. Alexander (Eds.), *Handbook of multicultural counseling* (pp. 181–198). Thousand Oaks, CA: Sage.

Hill, P. (1992). *Coming of age: African American male rites-of-passage.* Chicago: African American Images.

Hong, G. K., Garcia, M., & Soriano, M. (2000). Responding to the challenge: Preparing mental health professionals for the new millennium. In I. Cuéllar & F. A. Paniagua (Eds.), *Handbook of multicultural mental health* (pp. 455–476). San Diego, CA: Academic Press.

Hovey, J. D. (2000). Acculturative stress, depression, and suicidal ideation in Mexican immigrants. *Cultural Diversity and Ethnic Minority Psychology, 6*(2), 134–151.

Hovey, J. D., & King, C. A. (1996). Acculturative stress, depression, and suicidal ideation among immigrant and second-generation Latino adolescents. *Journal of the American Academy of Child and Adolescent Psychiatry, 35*(9), 1183–1192.

Hovey, J. D., & Magana, C. (2000). Acculturative stress, anxiety, and depression among Mexican immigrant farmworkers in the Midwest. *Journal of Immigrant Health, 2*(3), 119–131.

HRSA (2005). Cultural competence. retrieved March 19, 2005 from http:// bphc.hrsa. gov/cultural competence.

Johnson, L. R., & Sandhu, D. S. (2007a). Acculturation, isolation and adjustment issues: Intervention strategies for counselors. In H. Singaravelu (Ed.), *Handbook of counseling with international students in the United States* (pp. 13–35). American Counseling Association, VA.

Johnson, L. R., & Sandhu, D. S. (2007b). Treatment planning in a multicultural context. In M. Leach & J. Aten (Eds.), *Culture and the therapeutic process: A guide for mental health professionals,* Lawrence Erlbaum Associates.

Johnson, L. R., & Tucker, C. (2007). Cultural issues in the assessment and treatment of children. In M. Hersen & A. Gross (Eds.) *Handbook of child psychopathology.* Chichester: John Wiley & Sons, Ltd.

Johnson, W. B., & Ridley, C. R. (1992). Brief Christian and non-Christian rational-emotive therapy with depressed Christian clients: An exploratory study. *Counseling and Values, 36,* 220–229.

Kazarian, S. S., & Evans, D. R. (1998). Cultural clinical psychology. In S. Kazarian & D. Evans (Eds.), *Cultural clinical psychology: Theory, research, and practice* (pp. 3–38). New York, NY: Oxford University Press.

Kitano, H. H. L. (1999). *Race relations* (5th ed.). Upper Saddle River, NJ: Prentice Hall.

Kleinman, A. (1980). *Patients and healers in the context of culture.* Berkeley, CA: University of California Press.

Koss-Chioino, J. D. (2000). Traditional and folk approaches among ethnic minorities. In J. F. Aponte & J. Wohl (Eds.), *Psychological intervention and cultural diversity* (2nd ed., pp. 149–166). Needham Heights, MA: Allyn & Bacon.

Kurasaki, K. S., Sue, S., Chun, C., & Gee, K. (2000). Ethnic minority intervention and treatment research. In J. F. Aponte & J. Wohl (Eds.), *Psychological intervention and cultural diversity* (2nd ed., pp. 234–249). Needham Heights, MA: Allyn & Bacon.

LaFromboise, T., Coleman, H. L., & Gerton, J. (1993). Psychological impact of biculturalism: Evidence and theory. *Psychological Bulletin, 114*(3), 395–412.

Lee, R. M., & Ramirez III, R. M. (2000). The history, current status, and future of multicultural psychotherapy. In I. Cuéllar & F. A. Paniagua (Eds.), *Multicultural mental health* (pp. 279–309). San Diego, CA: Academic Press.

Marsella, A.J., & Yamada, A. M. (2000). Culture and mental health: An introduction and overview of foundations, concepts, and issues. In I. Cuéllar & F. A. Paniagua (Eds.), *Handbook of multicultural mental health* (pp. 3–24). San Diego, CA: Academic Press.

Martin, J. N., & Nakayama, T. K. (2005). *Experiencing intercultural communication* (2nd ed.). New York, NY: The McGraw-Hill Companies.

Mio, J. S., Barker-Hackett, L. B., & Tumambing, J. (2006). *Multicultural psychology: Understanding our diverse communities.* Boston: McGraw-Hill.

Myers, L. J., Ezemenari, M. O., Jefferson, M., Anderson, M., Godfrey, T., & Purnell, J. (2005). Building multicultural competence around indigenous healing practices. In M. G. Constantine & D. W. Sue (Eds.), *Strategies for building multicultural competence* (pp. 109–126). Hoboken, NJ: John Wiley & Sons.

National Center for Cultural Competence (2007). Improving quality and achieving equity: The role of cultural competence in reducing racial and ethnic disparities in health care. Retrieved on August 11, 2007 from: http://www.commonwealthfund. org/publications/publications_show.htm?doc_id=413825

Negy, C. (Ed.). (2004). *Cross-cultural psychotherapy: Toward a critical understanding of diverse clients.* Reno, NV: Bent Tree Press.

Ng, C. H., Easteal, S., Tan, S., Schweitzer, I., Ho, B. K. W., & Aziz, S. (2006). Serotonin transporter polymorphisms and clinical response to sertraline across ethnicities. *Progress in Neuro-Psychopharmacology & Biological Psychiatry, 30,* 953–957.

Okazaki, S. (2000). Assessing and treating Asian Americans: Recent advances. In I. Cuéllar & F. A. Paniagua (Eds.), *Handbook of multicultural mental health* (pp. 171–193). San Diego, CA: Academic Press.

Paniagua, F. A. (2005). *Assessing and treating culturally diverse clients: A practical guide* (3rd ed.). Thousand Oaks, CA: SAGE Publications, Inc.

Pederson, P. (1991). Multiculturalism as a generic approach to counseling. *Journal of Counseling Development: Special Issue on Multiculturalism as a Fourth Force, 70,* 6–12.

Pedersen, P. (1997). *Culture-centered counseling interventions: Striving for accuracy.* Thousand Oaks, Ca: Sage.

Pedersen, P. (2000). *A handbook for developing multicultural awareness* (3rd ed.). Alexandria, VA, US: American Counseling Association.

Pedersen, P. (2004a). *Culture-centered counseling.* APA Psychotherapy Videotape Series II, Washington, DC: American Psychological Association.

Pedersen, P. (2004b). The multicultural context of mental health. In T. B. Smith (Ed.), *Practicing multiculturalism* (pp. 17–32). Boston, MA: Allyn & Bacon.

Pelto, P. J., & Pelto, G. H. (1996). Research designs in medical anthropology. In C. F. Sargent & T. M. Johnson (Eds.), *Medical anthropology: Contemporary theory and method* (pp. 293–324). Westport, CT: Praeger.

Phinney, J. (1990). Ethnic identity in adolescents and adults: Review of research. *Psychological Bulletin, 108*(3), 499–514.

Population Resource Center (2005). Providing the demographic dimension of public policy, 2005 Annual report (pp. 1–32). Retrieved November 5, 2006 from www. prcd.org/html/annual-reports.html.

Poston, W. C. S. (1990). The Biracial Identity Development model: a needed addition. *Journal of Counseling and Development, 69*(2), 152–155.

Root, M. P. P. (1990). Resolving the "other" status: Identity development of biracial individuals. In L. Brown & M. P. P. Root (Eds.), *Diversity and complexity in feminist theory and therapy* (pp. 181–189). Newbury Park, CA: Sage.

Root, M. P. P. (1996). The multiracial experience: Racial borders as a significant frontier in race relations. In M. P. P. Root (Ed.), *The multiracial experience: Racial borders as the new frontier* (pp. xiii–xxviii). Thousand Oaks, CA: Sage.

Rowe, W., Bennett, S. K., & Atkinson, D. R. (1994). White Racial Identity Models. *The Counseling Psychologist, 22*, 129–146.

Rudmin, F. W., & Ahmadzadeh, V. (2001). Psychometric critique of acculturation psychology: The case of Iranian migrants in Norway. *Scandinavian Journal of Psychology, 42*, 41–56.

Ruiz, A. S. (1990). Ethnic identity: Crisis and resolution. *Journal of Multicultural Counseling and Development, 18*, 29–40.

Salleh, A. (2007). Salsa therapy. Retrieved July 6, 2007, from http://www.abc.net.au/health/features/salsa

Sánchez-Johnsen, L. A. & Cuéllar, I. (2004). Culturally competent assessment and evaluation. In C. Negy (Ed.), *Cross-cultural psychotherapy: Toward a critical understanding of diverse clients* (pp. 37–60). Reno, NV: Bent Tree Press.

Sandhu, D. S., & Asrabadi, B. R. (1998). An acculturative stress scale for international students: A practical approach to stress measurement. In C. P. Zalaquett & R. J. Wood (Eds.), *Evaluating stress: A book of resources, Vol. 2* (pp. 1–33). Lanam, MD: Scarecrow Press.

Sandhu, D. S., & Rigney, J. R. (1995). Culturally responsive teaching in U.S. public schools. *Kappa Delta Pi Record, 31* (4), 157–162.

Singh, N. N., McKay, J. D., & Singh, A. N. (1999). The need for cultural brokers in mental health services. *Journal of Child and Family Studies, 8*(1), 1–10.

Smith, T. B. (2004a). Awareness and identity: Foundational principles of multicultural practice. In T. B. Smith (Ed.), *Practicing multiculturalism* (pp. 35–50). Boston, MA: Allyn & Bacon.

Smith, T. B. (2004b). A contextual approach to assessment. In T. B. Smith (Ed.), *Practicing multiculturalism* (pp. 97–119). Boston, MA: Allyn & Bacon.

Smith, T. B., Richards, P. S., Granley, H. M., & Obiakor, F. (2004). Practicing multiculturalism. In T. B. Smith (Ed.), *Practicing multiculturalism* (pp. 3–16). Boston, MA: Allyn & Bacon.

Standley, L. J. (2007). American Indian talking circles. Retrieved July 6, 2007, from http://www.drstandley.com/nativeamerican_talking_circles.shtml

Sue, S. (2006). Cultural competency: From philosophy to research and practice: *Journal of Community Psychology, 43*, 237–245.

Sue, D. W., Arredondo, P., & McDavis, R. J. (1992). Multicultural competencies/standards: A pressing need. *Journal of Counseling and Development, 70*(4), 477–486.

Sue, D. W., & Sue, D. (2003). *Counseling the culturally diverse: Theory and practice* (4th ed.). New York: John Wiley & Sons.

Sue, D. W., & Sue, S. (1987). Cultural factors in the clinical assessment of Asian Americans. *Journal of Consulting & Clinical Psychology, 55*(4), 479–487.

Sue, S., Zane, N., & Young, K. (1994). Individualism-collectivism, social-network orientation, and acculturation as predictors of attitudes toward seeking professional psychological help among Chinese Americans. *Journal of Counseling Psychology, 41*(3), 280–287.

Szapocznik, J., & Kurtines, W.M. (1993). Opportunities for theory, research, and application. *Family Psychology and Cultural Diversity, 48*(4), 400–407.

Trafzer, L., Keller, J., & Sisquoc, L. (2006). *Boarding school blues: Revisiting the American Indian educational experience.* Lincoln, NE: University of Nebraska Press.

Triandis, H. (1995). *Individualism and collectivism.* Boulder, CO: Westview.

Tseng, W. (2003). *Clinician's guide to cultural psychiatry.* San Diego, CA: Academic Press.

U.S. Department of Health and Human Services (2001). *Mental health: Culture, race and ethnicity – A supplement to mental health: A report of the Surgeon General.* Rockville, MD: U.S. Department of Health and Human Services, Public Health Office, Office of the Surgeon General.

Vasquez, C., & Javier, R.A. (1991). The problem with interpreters: Communicating with Spanish speaking patients. *Hospital & Community Psychiatry, 42*(2), 163–165.

Vega, W., Warheit, G., & Palacio, R. (1985). Psychiatric symptomatology among Mexican American farm-workers. *Soc. Sci. Med., 20*(1), 39–45.

Weiss, M. G., & Kleinman, A. (1988). Depression in cross-cultural perspective: Developing a culturally informed model. In P. R. Dasen, J. W. Berry, & N. Sartorius (Eds.), *Health and cross-cultural psychology* (pp. 179–205). Newbury Park, CA: Sage.

Whaley, A. L., & McQueen, J. P. (2004). An Afrocentric program as primary prevention for african american youth: Qualitative and quantitative exploratory data. *The Journal of Primary Prevention, 25,* 253–269.

8

International Perspectives on Culture and Mental Health

P. S. D. V. Prasadarao

From times immemorial human beings across all cultures worldwide have experienced symptoms of mental illness (DHHS, 2001) and our healing traditions are as age old and diverse as humanity (Pesek, Helton, & Nair, 2006). There have been constant efforts to enhance our knowledge on how culture influences mental health and illness. There are strengths in understanding the healing approaches and traditions across cultures (Pesek et al., 2006). It is well known that an individual's perceptions, values, beliefs and emotions are formed and shaped by a wide range of factors within one's own culture (Cuéllar & Paniagua, 2000; DHHS, 2001). This chapter focuses on how mental health and illness varies by nationality and it explains some of the approaches of understanding mental health and illness from an international perspective.

From an international perspective, an extensive literature concerning the role of culture in mental illness has focused on the following aspects: (a) understanding psychiatric diagnostic categories based on cultural models (e.g., depression, somatization, postpartum depression, and anorexia nervosa); (b) the role of culture in mental health and illness in specific cultural/ethnic groups (e.g., mental health conceptualizations and belief systems in Hindus, Chinese, Muslims, indigenous peoples and aboriginal groups); (c) the role of culture and its impact on mental health issues among high risk populations (e.g., refugees, immigrants, and persons from war-struck regions); (d) the role of culture and its impact on sociocultural and sociopolitical processes, and pathological cultural processes (e.g., urbanization, globalization, modernization, and multicultural environment); and (e) the role of culture in understanding and conceptualizing nosological and classificatory systems of mental illness (e.g., *ICD, DSM,* and culture-bound syndromes) (Marsella & Yamada, 2000). Such literature provides significant insights and impetus into the understanding of cultural models of mental illness across the globe. Some of these aspects have been discussed in the preceding chapters of this book.

Mental Illness Attributions and Explanatory Models

It has been of interest to both clinicians and researchers, in the area of health in general and mental health in specific, to understand how illness is conceived by people from different cultures. These explanatory models describe how illness is understood from their own framework and how people attribute meaning to their illness (Coleman, Koffman, & Daniels, 2007). The concept of explanatory models has been studied in mental health for sometime (Aidoo and Harpham, 2001). These models focus on "cultural construction" and "specificity" of mental disorders in a given individual with specific cultural roots. It is also known that how an individual responds to his/her illness is dependent on the conceptualizations and the explanatory model unique to the individual and his/her culture (Coleman et al., 2007). For example, in India, Banerjee and Banerjee (1995) found that patients who attributed their epilepsy to supernatural causes initially consulted traditional healers, whereas those attributed to biomedical causes sought modern medical treatment. A similar pattern is evident in persons with schizophrenia (Banerjee and Roy, 1998). These international conceptualizations of mental health need to be understood in order to appreciate the illness in a proper perspective (Durie, 2004). Developing insights into these explanatory models facilitates health professionals in formulating culturally appropriate communication paradigms and diagnostic tools, and culturally sensitive intervention programmes (Coleman et al., 2007). Furthermore, comprehensive understanding of such models can have influence on the mental health policy planning and developing culturally appropriate mental health care models (Aidoo & Harpham, 2001).

Mental Health Models Across the World

Internationally mental illness has reached an alarming proportion. About 450 million people suffer from a mental or behavioural disorder throughout the world. More than 150 million persons suffer from depression at any given time and about one million people commit suicide annually. About 25 million suffer from schizophrenia, 38 million from epilepsy and more than 90 million from drug and alcohol problems. These numbers are likely to increase further due to the worsening of sociopolitical conflicts and unrest, and as the population across the globe are ageing. Such an alarming magnitude of mental illness creates enormous economic burden (WHO, 2003). According to the World Health Organization Mental Health Atlas, 2005, over 40 percent of countries in the world have no formal mental health policy. Half of all the countries in the world have less than one psychiatrist and psychiatric nurse per 100,000 population. About 37 percent of countries worldwide do not have community health care services. Forty percent of the countries worldwide are unable to provide treatment for severe mental disorders at primary care level. Furthermore,

20 percent of countries do not have basic psychotropic medicines in primary care settings (WHO, 2005). Scarcity of qualified mental health professionals is a phenomenon evident not only in the underdeveloped or developing countries, but also in the developed world. Mental health perspectives worldwide need to be understood and appraised in the backdrop of these harsh realities.

In most of the countries around the globe, mental health models are dominated by two major approaches, namely, the western evidence-based medical approach and the traditional indigenous healing approach. Traditional healing system, in general, is well established and highly accepted by people and communities, probably due to the existing consonance in explanatory models (unlike in evidence-based medicine) between people in these cultures and traditional health care providers. In such a traditional system, a wide range of practitioners provide help to affected persons and their families. For example, in Sub-Saharan Africa, four types of traditional healers provide health care, namely, (a) traditional birth attendants (TBAs), (b) faith healers, (c) diviners and spiritualists, and (d) herbalists. The TBAs focus on pregnancy related problems and offer treatment to women. Faith healers, mostly men, use religious scriptures, prayers and holy water, in their treatment approach. Diviners, mostly women, seriously ill themselves prior to becoming healers, specialize in diagnosing illness through divination. They act as medium between people and their ancestors and Gods. Spiritualists use supernatural forces in diagnosis and treatment. Herbalists, mostly men, apply herbal medicines in their healing approach (Stekelenburg, Jager, Kolk, Westen, van der Kwaak, & Wolffers, 2005).

According to the recent studies more than 85 percent of the world's population lives in 153 low-income and middle-income countries (Jacob et al., 2007). Patel (2007) reviewed research on mental disorders in adults in low- and middle-income countries (LAMIC) since 2001. Mental disorders account for 11.1 percent of the total burden of disease in these LAMIC. Unipolar depressive disorder is the single leading cause of disease burden. Mental disorders are associated with other public health issues such as maternal and child health and HIV/AIDS. Social factors, namely, poverty, low education, social exclusion, gender disadvantage, conflict and disasters contribute to the onset of mental disorders. Most of these countries have scarce mental health resources. Majority of people with mental disorders do not receive evidence-based care which contributes to chronicity, extensive suffering in people and increased costs of care (Patel, 2007). Many of these countries lack mental health policies and legislations to direct their mental health programmes and services. There have been gaps and inconsistencies in the mental health information available about these countries. Most of these countries have a shortage of qualified mental health staff, poor mental health infrastructure, and scarce financial resources (Jacob et al., 2007).

In most of these countries progress in mental health service development has been rather slow. Barriers to such a development include a shortage of qualified mental health professionals, challenges in implementing mental health care in primary-care settings, the prevailing public-health priority agenda and its effect on funding, and problems in decentralization of mental health services (Saraceno et al., 2007).

In the following section, brief geographic and sociodemographic characteristics, cultural conceptualizations and belief systems, indigenous mental health models, and prevailing mental health policies and services in a few representative countries (both low- or middle-income and high-income) are described. As it is practically not possible to cover all the countries and cultures over the globe, this chapter focuses on the following countries: India, Pakistan, Nepal, China, Malaysia, Bulgaria, Chile, New Zealand, Philippines, Thailand, Kenya, Uganda, and Zambia. What follows in this chapter is not intended to be an exhaustive analysis of the mental health issues and models in these countries, but to give the reader an overview of the above aspects within the cultural framework and explanations. Issues such as culture-bound syndromes, biological markers across cultures, mental health aspects related to migration and acculturation, and multicultural treatment approaches are out of the scope of this chapter since they deserve special attention and some of these have been discussed elsewhere in this book. Notably, the journal *International Review of Psychiatry* (2004) has devoted a special issue to mental health country profiles providing valuable information on the cultural models across various nations. Papers appeared in this journal have largely formed basis for the following section.

India

India is the second most populous country in the world with a population of 1.086 billion and equates to one-sixth of the world's population. Nearly 75 percent of India's population lives in rural areas and 36 percent lives below the poverty line. The literacy rate is 68 percent in males and 45 percent in females. The life expectancy is 61 years in males and 63 years in females (Engenderhealth, 2007a; Khandelwal et al., 2004). India is a multicultural society and people practice a wide range of religions. Approximately 83 percent of the population practice Hinduism, 13 percent Islam and 2.5 percent Christianity. Other religions practiced include Sikhism, Jainism, and Buddhism, to name a few. Thus, India is described as the country of "unity in diversity" (Khandelwal et al., 2004; Prasadarao & Sudhir, 2001).

Mental health problems in India affect approximately 10–20 per 1000 population, and approximately 10 million people suffer from serious mental illness (Weiss, Isaac, Parkar, Chowdhury, & Raguram, 2001). A meta-analysis of 13 epidemiological studies yielded an estimated prevalence rate of 5.8 percent (Reddy & Chandrashekar, 1998). Care of mentally ill persons is primarily the responsibility of the family; the family may tolerate, protect and shield or reject the mentally ill family member. The family makes important decisions concerning treatment and care of their mentally ill family member. Patients are often accompanied by their family members when they seek mental health consultation (Khandelwal et al., 2004).

An Indian Hindu Perspective

Hinduism, one of the world's oldest religions, made significant contributions to the understanding of mental health and illness in India. The roots of Indian psychology can be traced back to the religious scriptures such as Vedas, Yoga Sutras, and Bhagavad Gita. Systematic attempts have been made to understand human behaviour based on the insights gained from ancient Indian scriptures and folklore (Balodhi, 1990, 1991). There have also been attempts to understand the concept of positive mental health. In Indian psychology, personality is a composition of three basic human qualities (*gunas*), namely, *sattva* (clarity, light), *rajas* (passion, desire), and *tamas* (dullness, darkness). According to this Indian concept, human beings are endowed with a combination of these gunas from the time they were born, and it is determined by their actions in the past lives (Kakar, 1978). This is also explained in terms of the person's state of mind. The ideal state of mind is called *sattvik*, where there is equipoise and harmony among all three attributes. However, when the mind is under stress, agitated or frustrated, this equilibrium is disturbed. Such a state is called *rajasik* (equated with the sympathetic activity of the autonomic nervous system). When the mind is in a state of lethargy and gloominess, it is considered *tamasik* (corresponds to the parasympathetic activity of the autonomic nervous system) (see Antony, 2001; Juthani, 2001). Kakar (1978) explained the Hindu world view in three core concepts, namely, dharma (righteousness that determines one's own behaviour), moksha (self-realization, transcendence, salvation, and release from the worldly affairs) and karma (course of one's life in terms of fate and cycles of birth and death).

In Indian culture, mental illness is explained by a wide range of models. It is commonly believed that karma (one's actions in a past life) determines one's present life's successes, failures and illnesses. Karma is defined as "the sum of a person's actions in this and previous states of existence, viewed as affecting their future fate" (Oxford Dictionary, 10th ed., 1999, p. 772). Thus, illness is perceived as a punishment for the wrong doings in a past life. Other common explanations, especially in the rural cultures include supernatural visitation and environmental shock (Khandelwal et al., 2004).

Contributions from Ayurveda

Ayurveda, a traditional Indian holistic system of medicine developed by Charaka (Lyssenko, 2004; Sharma, 2000; Singh, 2007), formed basis for conceptualization and treatment of both physical and mental illness. Charaka described four causative factors in mental illness, namely, (a) diet (incompatible, vitiated, and unclean food); (b) disrespect to gods, elders, and teachers; (c) mental shock due to emotions such as excessive fear and joy; and (d) faulty bodily activity. Thus, Ayurveda considers a biopsychosocial approach in formulating causative factors in mental illness (Balodhi, 1999; Prasadarao & Sudhir, 2001).

Charaka while emphasizing the need for harmony between body, mind, and soul, focused on preventive, curative, and promotive aspects of mental health (Balodhi, 1987, 1999). According to Charaka, mental disorders are classified into three broad categories, namely, (a) purely psychological or emotional disorders (e.g., jealousy, fear, inferiority and grief); (b) "psychosomatic disorders" (e.g., epilepsy, obsession and hysteria); and (c) unspecified/exogenous disorders (diseases caused by the ill effects of God's anger) (Balodhi, 1999; Prasadarao & Sudhir, 2001). The psychological and unspecified abnormalities are dealt with such strategies as chanting mantras, using precious stones, participation in auspicious rites, oblations, offerings, fasting, benedictions, worshipping gods, and pilgrimage, whereas, the "psychosomatic" disorders are treated with such strategies as cleansing body, drugs, and adjuvant psychological strategies (Balodhi, 1999; Prasadarao & Sudhir, 2001). Yoga is another Indian approach that integrates various aspects of human life. Patanjali advocated an eight-step approach dealing with these aspects. These include *yama* (observance), *niyama* (discipline), *asana* (postures), *pranayama* (deep breathing exercises), *prathyahara* (withdrawal of senses), and three stages of meditation, namely, *dharana* (concentration), *dhyana* (meditation), and *samadhi* (enlightenment). Such a comprehensive holistic approach focuses on an individual's overall well-being that goes beyond a simple curative dimension (Balodhi, 1986).

In India mental illness is also attributed to the supernatural powers; certain Hindu deities are believed to guard people against evil powers. Thus, priests and religious healers play a cardinal role in providing help to persons affected with mental illness and their families (Kapur, 1975, 1979; Khandelwal et al., 2004; Raguram, Venkateswaran, Ramakrishna, & Weiss, 2002).

The Role of Traditional Healers in India

Kapur (1975, 1979) conducted studies in an Indian rural village to explore the preference for a type of healer by people and the conceptual framework of the healers. He pointed out that besides modern medical practitioners, three types of traditional healers, namely, *vaids* (healers practising indigenous system of medicine), *mantarwadis* (healers using astrology and charms for cure), and *patris* (healers who act as mediums for spirits and demons) offer treatment to physical and mental illness in rural villages of India.

The *vaids* practice Ayurveda, the traditional Indian medicine system, and they offer treatment predominantly by administering medications. These *vaids* believe that the illness is due to "an imbalance between the natural elements" brought forth by environmental factors, certain diets, uninhibited sexual indulgence, and by the influence of demons. These factors cause "excess heat, cold, bile, wind or fluid secretions," leading to the development of physical and mental illness. Mental illness (unmada) is caused by the exaggerated activity of any of the three humors and three types of madness, namely, *vatounmada* (due to wind), *pittounmada* (due to bile) and *kaphounmada* (due to water) are described. According to these *vaids*, certain food substances cause excess heat, leading to excitement whereas some others cause excess cold, contributing to the development of depression. The centre for heat in man is considered to be in the head and he loses heat through an excessive seminal discharge. The centre for heat in woman is in the vagina and the heat is lost as a consequence of childbirth. For both physical and mental illness, *vaids* provide treatment using various substances, namely, herbal medications, oils, decoctions, and by prescribing certain dietary restrictions (Kapur, 1975, 1979).

Both *mantarwadis* and *patris* also believe that illness is due to misdeeds either in the past or present life. These misdeeds are punished by Lord Shiva, by affecting an individual through spirits and demons or by influencing the malign conjunction of stars. Accordingly, the symptoms of a particular "illness" are dependent on the constellation of stars and the nature of specific demons/spirits acting on the individual. These *mantarwadis* treat by chanting mystical verses, offering a talisman (a sacred object that has special powers and brings good luck to the person who wears it on one's body), sacred threads, and by suggesting a specific penance for the individual's "misdeeds." The *patris* act as a medium for spirits and demons and they don't claim any special abilities. Since illness is conceptualized as the negative effect of these demons and spirits, interventions are conducted through "negotiations" with these demons/spirits which affected the individual. In this complex process, specific offerings are negotiated (e.g., an animal sacrifice, a feast, or offering a "house" for the demon's use) with the demon/spirit. The client is expected to obey and perform these agreed upon rituals and practices (Kapur, 1975, 1979).

Kapur (1975, 1979) found that a large majority (59 percent) consulted one or more of these healers. The selection of a specific healer was determined by the severity of illness rather than by the sociodemographic factors (i.e., age, educational level, and financial status) of the affected person. Interestingly, most people consulted both traditional healers and modern practitioners despite the clear contradictions in their operating framework.

Mental Illness and Temple Healing in India

Raguram et al. (2002) conducted a study at a south Indian temple, a popular healing place for people with severe psychiatric problems. The mentally ill patients are brought by their family members to stay in this temple. The person with psychiatric problem takes part in a wide range of daily routine rituals of the temple (e.g., cleaning and watering). During the study period, 31 people sought help and stayed at the temple. The severity of psychopathology in subjects was assessed by a psychiatrist using the Brief Psychiatric Rating Scale (BPRS; Overall and Gorham, 1962) on the first day of their stay in the temple. Subjects' impressions, caregivers' perceptions of change over the course at the temple, and their level of satisfaction were assessed. Caregivers rated satisfaction with their experience at the temple and the change they noted in their mentally ill family member. A significant reduction in scores on the BPRS was evident in these subjects at the time of their departure from temple. As rated by the family caregivers, 22 subjects "improved" and three had "total recovery." These researchers pointed out that the "help" received at this temple served as an alternative to modern psychiatric treatment for people with severe mental illness. They noted significant improvement in the symptoms in people, who received no formal psychiatric treatment, during their stay in the temple. Raguram et al. opined that the "cultural power" of residing in the temple known for its "healing potency," may have contributed to such a change in psychopathology among these subjects; improvement may also be attributed to the "supportive, non-threatening, and reassuring" environment of the temple. Raguram et al. concluded that healing temples may constitute a community resource for people with psychiatric problems in settings where they are recognized and valued. These researchers suggest that the role of such healing places in local community settings needs to be understood and acknowledged whilst making policies and planning for mental health services; they highlighted the need to consider an alliance with such indigenous resources.

Mental health has been neglected in India over the range of other health priorities (Weiss et al., 2001). There are an estimated 4000 psychiatrists in India, representing a ratio of approximately 1 psychiatrist for 250,000 people (WHO, 2005). A small proportion of trained clinical psychologists contribute to the assessment of and psychological interventions to persons with psychiatric problems (Prasadarao & Sudhir, 2001). Kapur (1975, 1979) and Raguram et al. (2002), through their seminal work, highlight the role the traditional indigenous resources may play in providing care to mentally ill persons at the community level. The National Mental Health Programme was developed in 1982 which is now known as the National Mental Health Plan (NMHP). The NMHP aims at (a) ensuring availability of and accessibility to mental health care to all; (b) the application of mental health knowledge in general health care and social development; and (c) promoting community participation in mental health service development (Ministry of Health and Family Welfare, 1982). There have been concerted efforts to increase the awareness about mental health and illness and as a result a gradual change is being noticed in the attitude of people towards mental illness. Similarly, awareness of the prevalence, of suffering and disability caused by mental disorders has increased in the recent times; this has contributed to a better response from the policy makers and efforts to develop effective mental health services. Notably, the mental health policies have recognized the importance of illness prevention and mental health promotion (Weiss et al., 2001).

Pakistan

The Islamic republic of Pakistan is one of the Southeast Asian countries, and has a population of 159.2 million (Engenderhealth, 2007g). About 70 percent of its population lives in rural areas. Pakistan is a low-income group country (see WHO, 2005). The literacy rate is as low as 60 percent in males and 21 percent in females. The life expectancy is 60 years for males and 62 years for females (Engenderhealth, 2007g). Pakistan has a high refugee population (Karim, Saeed, Rana, Mubbashar, & Jenkins, 2004). Pakistan has four major ethnic groups, namely, Punjabis, Pathans, Sindhis, and Baluchis. Islam is the principal religion in Pakistan though minorities practice other such religions as Christianity, Hinduism, and Buddhism (Karim et al., 2004).

Mumford and associates conducted a series of community based epidemiological surveys in Pakistan. These studies yielded high prevalence rates of depression ranging 12.5 percent to 53 percent (Mumford, Minhas, Akhtar, Akhtar, & Mubbashar, 2000; Mumford, Nazir, Jilani, & Baig, 1996; Mumford, Saeed, Ahmed, Latif, & Mubbashar, 1997). Similarly, studies on schizophrenia indicated prevalence rates of 8.1 percent in males and 6.1 percent in females (Karim et al., 2004).

People in Pakistan perceive mental illness as a "state of arrested or incomplete development of the mind that results in impaired intelligence and social functioning and is associated with aggressive or seriously irresponsible conduct." Mental illness is often considered to be caused by such supernatural forces as spirit possession, jinni, black magic or exaltation, or as a punishment to one's own sins. Some believe that mental illness is due to "gastrointestinal" or "hepatobiliary" dysfunctions. These beliefs and perceptions about mental illness are largely influenced by religious values. "Good" mental health which leads to "ideal conduct is considered as the best representation of man being God's agent on earth." Stigma attached to mental illness is one of the major problems in Pakistan. People tend to hide the illness from others and not to seek medical help. While dealing with mentally ill persons, people respond according to the nature of symptomatology; patients with violent behaviours or at risk of self-harm are often physically restrained (Karim et al., 2004). Some believe that mental illness is a sign that God granted a special status to their family member, and hence they don't seek medical help. There have been some changes in these perceptions due to the influence of education (Karim et al., 2004).

Traditional healers play a significant role in the management of mentally ill persons. They are the first to be consulted by mentally ill persons and their families. These healers include khalifs, gadinashins, imams, hakims, and others who practice magic and sorcery (Karim et al., 2004). Farooqi (2006) studied the nature of traditional healing consultation in 87 Muslim psychiatric patients treated at public hospitals in Pakistan. This study revealed that 55–73 percent of patients with various psychiatric disorders did seek help from one or more traditional healers. More males than females consulted traditional healers and the former had more frequent visits than the latter. The author pointed out that Islamic traditions and cultural norms practiced in Pakistan influence help seeking behaviours of psychiatric patients.

In 2000, Pakistan had 342 psychiatrists and 450 psychologists (Karim et al., 2004). There is scarcity of qualified mental health professionals (Farooqi, 2006). Pakistan's National Mental Health Programme was formulated in 1986 and the mental health legislation was enacted in 2001 (WHO, 2005). It aims at increasing resources, developing national guidelines for the care of mentally ill, enhancing human resources, integrating mental health into primary health care, and enhancing its capacity for research and medical education. The major barriers to the implementation of this programme include absence of epidemiological data, lack of training facilities, insufficient financial resources and the absence of mechanisms for integrating mental health into primary health care (Karim et al., 2004).

Nepal

Nepal has a population of 24.7 million, the majority of whom live in the rural areas. The literacy rate is 59 percent in males and 24 percent in females. The life expectancy is 59 years in males and 58 years in females (Engenderhealth, 2007f). Nepal is considered as one of the poorest countries in the world. It is constantly affected by a wide range of natural disasters including floods, landslides and failure of crops. Although Nepal is a multicultural country, Hinduism and Buddhism are the two major religions practised (Regmi, Pokhare, Ojha, Pradhan, & Chapagain, 2004).

About 14 percent of Nepalese suffer from psychiatric problems (Pradhan, 2003). Mental illness is generally considered "crazy" or "lunatic" and possession by gods is often the explanation. People in the rural areas believe that mental illness is a consequence of "bad fortune" and faith healers are frequently visited for "cure." Somatization is common in people of Nepal (Wright et al., 1989). People also believe in black magic. Religious beliefs have significant influence on the perceptions of mental illness. Stigmatization of mentally ill patients is prevalent and mentally ill persons are not generally accepted socially. Persons with mental illness are looked down upon. Mental illness is regarded as "shame," "disgrace," or "disapproval," resulting in rejection of mentally ill patients and their families. Family plays a crucial role in providing care to the mentally ill by making care decisions, and by providing financial and emotional support. Most people with mental illness consult religious healers prior to attending any mental health care facility. Traditional healers such as tantrics, lamajhankris, herbalists and palm-readers provide initial care to persons with psychiatric problems. It is not uncommon for the traditional healers to refer mentally ill persons to the modern mental health care system (Acharya, 1998; Regmi, Pokhare, Ojha, Pradhan, & Chapagain, 2004).

There is no mental health act in Nepal and the National Mental Health Policy formulated in 1997 is yet to be fully operational. In 1997, the Nepalese government adopted a National Mental Health Policy and subsequently included mental health as an element in primary health care. Mental health continues to be a low priority on the national health agenda. Currently no law exists to protect the rights of the mentally ill, though there are some legal provisions concerning the Government's responsibility towards the mentally ill persons. There are only 194 psychiatric beds for the country's total population. Nepal's mental health programme suffers from problems such as poor knowledge and awareness of mental illness in the general public and associated problems of poor drug compliance, inadequate treatment facilities, inadequacy of trained mental health personnel, stigmatization of mentally ill persons, rapidly increasing drug and alcohol problems and insufficient voluntary organizations to support mentally ill and their advocacy (Pradhan, 2003; Regmi et al., 2004).

China

The People's Republic of China is the most populous country in the world with a population of 1.3 billion in 2005, equating to one-fifth of the world's population. Every year another 12 million people are added to this magnitude. China is considered as a lower middle income group country. The literacy rate is 92 percent in males and 76 percent in females. The life expectancy is 70 years in males and 73 years in females. The major ethnic group in China is Han. Other ethnic groups include Zhuang and Man (Engenderhealth, 2007d; WHO, 2005).

With regard to prevalence rates, China has an estimated 4·25 million people with schizophrenia, with higher prevalence in women than in men (unlike most other countries) and greater in urban than in rural areas. China also has high rates of suicide with greater risk in women than in men (Phillips, Yang, Li & Li, 2004).

Parental factors seem to play a role in the onset of mental health problems. For example, Xia and Qian (2001) studied 127 adolescents (16–22 yrs) from two Chinese sub-cultures – Han and Kejia – to assess the relationship between parenting styles and self-rated mental health problems. The authors found that a high degree of psychosomatic symptoms and poor general mental health, in both genders, were associated with parental factors such as rejection and denial, high punitive tendencies, overprotection, over-involvement and poor emotional warmth and understanding.

In Chinese traditional literature there is no phrase equivalent to mental health. Words such as *fa lok* (happiness), *wor* (harmony) *sim on* (internal sense of security) and *tin yu* (relaxed) have been used in a manner that is similar to western concepts of mental health. The phrase *jing shum geen hong* is sometimes considered equivalent to the term "mental health" (Yip, 2005). The traditional Chinese mental health model is influenced by three major ancient schools of thought, namely, (a) traditional Chinese medicine (b) Confucianism, and (c) Taoism. According to traditional Chinese medicine, health is based on three major concepts, namely, *yin, yang*, and *wu xing*. *Yin* (the shade or the female) and *yang* (the sunshine or the male) are the two natural forces which create things in the universe. *Wu xing* comprises five basic elements, namely, metal, wood, water, fire, and earth. From the Chinese traditional medicine perspective, mental health is the balance of *yin* and *yang*, and the mutual equilibrium of the five elements. Thus, mental health is conceptualized as a harmony between nature and the individual. From the Confucian perspective, there are specific internal and external requirements on the part of the individual to maintain positive mental health. The internal requirements include aspects such as self-cultivation, practicing paths to achieve collective harmony and restraining from expression of intense emotions. The external requirements involve maintaining moral standards in everyday interpersonal relationships. Confucius described principles which are considered important in life including being kind, humane, and considerate towards others (*yen*), righteousness and equality (*yin*), being faithful towards the country, family and friends (*chung*), and forgiving faults and shortcomings of others (*shu*). These principles need to be practiced as per the social norms in a culture. In Taoism, mental health is considered as an ultimate peace of mind and absolute happiness in relating to the universe. One achieves such an "absolute happiness" through a state of nothingness (infinite Tao), and when one allows events such as life, death, and calamity to happen naturally (see Yip, 2005).

In China, the mental health policy was formulated in 1987; however, there is no existing mental health legislation in this country (WHO, 2005). Mental health services in China are provided by three governmental agencies, namely, the public health system (under the Ministry of Health); the civil administration system (under the Ministry of Civil Affairs); and the public security system (under the Ministry of Public Security), with a mutual cooperation amongst these three. Currently, the Mental Health Act in China is in its draft form (see Hu, Higgins, & Higgins, 2006). There is a considerable demand for mental health services; however, the professional and financial resources are meager. According to the estimates, there are at least 16 million persons with mental illness, 30 million adolescents and children with emotional or behavioral problems and three million people with epilepsy. Furthermore, the Chinese government has withdrawn funding from mental hospitals and community mental health services. Since the 1990s, hospitals and the outpatient clinics have been expected to generate 50 percent funding by themselves (see Yip, 2006). Although large cities have fairly well developed mental health infrastructure, the rural and remote areas have scarce mental health facilities. Most of the psychiatric care is provided by the general psychiatric hospitals throughout the country (see Hu et al., 2006). The family is generally responsible for providing support to the ill, in terms of seeking, providing and paying for physical and mental healthcare (Hu et al., 2006). Friends and retired workers also offer support in providing care to the ill persons (Lago, 2006).

An acute shortage of qualified mental health professionals and culturally rooted stigma towards mental illness are some of the constraints in providing mental health services in China (Hu et al., 2006). Yip (2006) reiterates that China has been experiencing difficulty in providing mental health services due to several factors such as a high demand for the mental health services with inadequate mental health resources, withdrawal of government funding, inaccessibility of services to deprived communities and remote rural areas, and "tight political control." Yip states that if these problems are not addressed, community mental health will only be "a myth rather than a reality" in China.

Malaysia

Malaysia is a tropical country in Southeast Asia with a population of 25.3 million. The average life expectancy is 69 years for males and 74 years for females (WHO, 2007b). More than 8 percent of the population lives in two major cities. Malaysia is a multicultural society with three major ethnic groups, namely, Malays (51 percent), Chinese (28 percent), and Indians (8 percent) living in harmony. The Malays predominantly follow Islamic religion, Chinese are mostly Buddhists, and the Indians largely practice the Hindu religion (Deva, 2004; Edman & Koon, 2000). These ethnic groups follow diverse cultural and religious practices, distinct dietary patterns and habits, and their own native languages (Deva, 2004).

In Malaysia and Brunei, the traditional Malay people emphasize three major aspects based on the Islamic perspective; these include things that are forbidden (*haram*), things that could be tolerated (*makruh*), and things that fall under the embrace of Islam (*halal*). Eating pork, consuming meat not slaughtered under Islamic religious rites, alcohol use, casual touching, adultery, and contact with the wet nose or hair of a dog are considered haram. Smoking and eating shellfish are considered *makruh*. Similarly, spiritual, and religious practices play a vital role in the mental health of Malay people. The symptoms of mental illness are understood to be due to (a) the loss of *semangat* (soul substance) which makes people physically weak and confused; (b) the presence of *angin* (wind) in stomach, nerves, and blood vessels, which may cause hallucinations and delusions; and (c) the possession by the Jinn (Genie), where ancestors wish to stay in the bodies of their offspring after death (Kumaraswamy, 2007).

According to the Islamic perspective, mental illness is perceived as a consequence of abandoning or neglecting Islamic values, principles, and practices. Human behaviour is considered the result of the dynamic interplay between material and nonmaterial forces and is entirely in the control of the individual's consciousness. Religious practices which could purify thoughts and actions make people closer to God, which in turn lead to the experience of positive mental health. The traditional Malays also attribute santau (black magic) to psychological problems. Santau is applied through traditional ingredients mixed in food or drinks or through Satan or Jinn for reasons such as taking revenge, envy, or gaining personal strength (Haque, 1998, 2004; Haque & Masuan, 2002; Kumaraswamy, 2007).

In view of the strong cultural beliefs, people seek guidance from traditional healers who are said to possess knowledge and skills to cure psychiatric illness by getting rid of the possessed spirits. The *bomohs* use three different types of healing processes, namely, through Quran (Islamic scripture) as a guide for diagnosis and treatment, through application of herbal and traditional medicine and by practising Malay magic (Ilmu Batin) (Kumaraswamy, 2007).

The National Mental Health Policy, which was formalized in 1998, is a guiding document for the delivery of mental health services in the country. Malaysia approximately has 160 psychiatrists and 25 clinical psychologists. The 32 general hospital mental health units offer mental health care to psychiatrically ill. However, there has been a shortage of qualified professionals such as clinical psychologists and social workers; there is a dearth of specialists in areas such as child and adolescent mental health, forensic mental health and psychiatric rehabilitation (Deva, 2004).

Bulgaria

Bulgaria is situated in South Eastern Europe and is a lower middle income group country (WHO, 2005). Bulgaria's population is 7.726 million and it is decreasing at the rate of 50,000 every year due to such factors as low fertility rates, increasing mortality and emigration. Bulgaria has a high literacy rate and 69.8 percent people live in urban areas. The population comprises of Bulgarians (85.8 percent) who practice orthodox Christianity, ethnic Turks (9.7 percent), Roma (3.4 percent) and other groups (1.1 percent). In 2004, life expectancy at birth was 72.6 years (Tomov, Mladenova, Lazarova, Sotirov, & Okoliyski, 2004; WHO, 2005; DFID, 2007).

In Bulgaria, though the general well-being is linked to wealth and a comfortable standard of living, the concept of mental well-being is much less clearly defined. It is believed that education improves intelligence and is associated with satisfaction in life. Resilience to adversity is often regarded as positive mental health. Sociocultural issues such as domestic violence and discrimination against the mentally ill are widespread in Bulgaria. There are restrictions on the human rights of mentally ill individuals. Mental illness is regarded as an irreversible condition, and it depletes mental faculties of an individual. It is considered as something "beyond help" with no useful remedy. Affected persons are considered untrustworthy and to be kept at a distance (Tomov et al., 2004). Mental illness is generally attributed to brain disorder caused by heredity, assault (physical or psychological), infections, or as a consequence to alcohol and drug use. It is also attributed to factors such as sex life, black magic or radiation. Some forms of mental illness are believed to be caused by the possession of evil forces. People regard psychosis as "intolerable anxiety and fear," "inappropriate behaviour," "confusion," and "uncontrolled aggression." When a family member is affected by mental illness, the family experiences pity, guilt, shame and anger (Tomov et al., 2004).

In Bulgaria mental illness and disability are kept within the family and when the resources are depleted, the family seeks institutional care. Medical consultation is sought only after the "alternative" approaches have been tried out

(Tomov et al., 2004). Although some community-based services such as day care centers, clubhouses, and special housing arrangements are available (NCPHP, 2007), structured community support for the mentally ill is not common in Bulgaria (Tomov et al., 2004).

In 2001 the Bulgarian government endorsed Programme for Mental Health for the Citizens of the Republic of Bulgaria, 2001–2005. This document later became the Bulgarian Mental Health Programme (Tomov et al., 2004). Following development of the National Mental Health Programme, mental health services are placed under a special category called "socially important" diseases or health problems (NCPHP, 2007).

Bulgaria still doesn't have a mental health act (WHO, 2005). In this country mental health is a part of the primary health care system. However, treatment of severe mental disorders is not commonly available at the primary care level and it is offered by mental health specialists. While offering modern medical care to mentally ill persons, general practitioners act as gate-keepers to specialist and hospital care (NCPHP, 2007; WHO, 2005).

Chile

Chile's population is 15.997 million and 85.2 percent of its people live in urban areas. Chile is a higher middle income group country. The literacy rate is 95.8 percent for males and 95.6 percent for females. Life expectancy at birth is 73.4 years for males and 80 years for females. About 70 percent of the population are Roman Catholics. The unemployment rate is 9.7 percent (Stewart, 2004; WHO, 2005). Chile has a high prevalence of mental disorders. Approximately one-third (31.5 percent) of the population has had a lifetime psychiatric disorder, and 22.2 percent have had a disorder in the past 12 months. Over 60 percent of the population is expected to have a mental disorder, but do not receive treatment (WHO, 2007c). The common problems seen in communities include domestic violence against children and women, depression, dependence on alcohol, illicit drug abuse, attention-deficit hyperactivity disorder, and anxiety disorders (Stewart, 2004). In Chile no laws exist to ensure parity between mental and physical health, promote the development of community-based treatment facilities and improve access to subsidized housing, education and sheltered work (WHO, 2007c).

Chile has two principal cultures, the Chilean and the Mapuche. In the Chilean culture psychosocial problems such as physical violence against women, alcohol abuse, marijuana abuse, cocaine sniffing, and amphetamine use to improve performance at work are frequently seen. The Chilean culture equates mental health with factors such as equilibrium, quality of life, and well-being; mental illness is often considered as "madness." Mentally ill persons are often stigmatized and discriminated against. Symptoms of mental illness tend to be recognized late. Family members generally admit persons with mental illness to psychiatric settings to restore their "equilibrium." According to the Mapuche perspective, health is dependent on the "harmony and equilibrium of the universe"; any acts that threaten this equilibrium lead to illness. Family members consider they "own" mentally ill persons, provide care within the families, with women usually taking a supportive role. Mothers generally play a significant role in supporting the mentally ill within their families (Stewart, 2004).

In rural areas, traditional healers provide treatment to persons with anxiety and depression. In urban areas treatment is provided by both traditional approaches and modern psychiatric interventions. Alternative approaches such as homeopathy and acupuncture are not uncommon. Other less commonly used care strategies include chiropractic, reflexology, massage, hydrotherapy, iridology, and floral therapy (Stewart, 2004).

Health care in Chile is provided by the public health system as well as by the private sector. Mental health care is evolved with a focus on inpatient care for persons with severe mental illness. Over the past decade, the National Mental Health Care Plan was developed to reorganize the delivery of mental health services. The National Policy on Mental Health and Psychiatry was formulated in 2000. In Chile, mental health is delivered as part of the primary health care system (WHO, 2005). Efforts have been made to encourage deinstitutionalization, increase utilization of general medical infrastructure for mental health care, and promote mental health care at the primary care level. The National Mental Health Care Plan also aims to address the growing burden of mental illness by providing services at community level (Saldivia, Vicente, Kohn, Rioseco, & Torres, 2004; WHO, 2005). Implementation of this National Mental Health Care Plan has led to the development of community based services as an alternative to the mental health services provided by the psychiatric institutions. There has been an increase in mental health care provided through primary health care settings, which has improved access to services and treatment (WHO, 2007c).

New Zealand

New Zealand has a population of 4.24 million people. Three-quarters of the population live in the north island and 85 percent live in urban areas. Twenty-nine percent of New Zealanders live in its largest city, Auckland. The New Zealanders of European origin constitute 75 percent of the population, Māori (the New Zealand indigenous people) 14.7 percent, Pacific people 6.5 percent and Asians 9 percent. Asians are the fastest-growing ethnic group, increased by around 140 percent over the past decade. In New Zealand 96.1 percent of the population speaks English and 4.5 percent speaks Māori. Sixteen percent of the people are bilingual or multilingual speakers (Pavagada & DeSouza, 2007; Statistics New Zealand, 2005). In line with other westernized countries, the population in New Zealand is ageing. As a consequence, biomedical and psychosocial aspects of older persons are increasingly becoming important (Prasadarao, 2007).

Te Tiriti O Waitangi (the treaty of Waitangi), a historical accord between the Crown and the Māori, forms the formal relationship between the major ethnic groups in New Zealand. In delivering health services, the treaty of Waitangi emphasizes concepts of biculturism and cultural safety, while incorporating the principles of "partnership, participation, protection and equity" (Durie, 1985, 1994).

Mason Durie has made significant contributions to the understanding of cultural aspects of mental health in New Zealand. From Māori cultural perspective, health is conceptualized as a holistic phenomenon. This model, called *whare tapa wha* (four cornerstones of health), comprises four significant realms of human existence, namely, *taha tinana* (physical; equates with biomedical aspects); *taha hinengaro* (emotion; equates with existential anthropological and psychosocial aspects); *taha whānau* (social; equates with the sociocultural and socioeconomic aspects); and *taha wairua* (spiritual; equates with interconnectedness and interdependence) (Durie, 1985, 1994, 2001; Rochford, 2004). Individuals with a strong sense of identity, self-esteem, personal responsibility, respect for others, economic security, knowledge of *te reo* (the Māori language), *whānau* (family) awareness, strong *whānau* (family) support, and *tikanga* (customs) are considered healthy (Rochford, 2004). Māori people attribute illness to the violation of *tapu* (supernatural influence or restriction) or the presence of *mākutu* (curses) (Durie, 2001). Psychosocial issues such as westernization and urbanization have significant influence on the traditional family concept and tribal structure, as a consequence, the traditional family support system is affected (McCreary, 1968; Sachdev, 1989).

The health system in New Zealand follows a western evidence-based model. Primary health care is largely delivered through a public-based system; the district health boards provide predominantly community-based mental health services with the objective of improving, promoting and protecting the mental health of people and communities. The Mental Health Commission was established in 1997 to implement the National Mental Health Strategy. This commission monitors the standardization of mental health care and delivery of mental health services to the community in New Zealand. Te Tahuhu – a new mental health policy has been developed to provide comprehensive integrated mental health services to people and improve mental health, 2005–2015. This policy focuses on the early access to primary health care, and prevention and promotion of mental health (Ministry of Health, 2005). Financial constraints and a shortage of qualified mental health professionals are some of the constraints that impact delivery of mental health care. Nongovernmental organizations and consumer groups play a pivotal role in the health care and have made significant contributions to the care of and support to the persons with mental illness and their families/ *whānau*. In the recent past, with immigration of people from other cultural settings, New Zealand has made a rapid transformation into a multi-cultural society. As a consequence, the issues are becoming increasingly multi-cultural from the traditional concept of biculturism. This highlights the role of cultural perspectives in mental health care (Pavagada & DeSouza, 2007).

Philippines

The Philippines is an archipelago comprising of thousands of islands, nearly 900 of which are inhabited. It is one of the most heavily populated countries in the world, with one of the highest population growth rates in Asia. The population of the Philippines is 83.7 million (Engenderhealth, 2007h). More than half of the country's population lives on the island of Luzon concentrated in the capital city Manila. Approximately 83 percent of its population are Roman Catholics and 5 percent practice Islam (Conde, 2004). Education is highly valued by the people in Philippines resulting in one of the highest literacy rates in the world. The literacy rate is 96 percent for males and 95 percent for females. The life expectancy is 67 years for males and 72 years for females (Engenderhealth, 2007h).

In 1993–1994 a population survey was conducted by the University of the Philippines. This survey reported a prevalence rate of 35 percent mental disorders. The most frequent diagnoses among adults were: anxiety (14.3 percent), panic (5.6 percent) and psychosis (4.3 percent). Amongst children and adolescents, the most prevalent psychiatric conditions were: enuresis (9.3 percent), speech and language disorders (93.9 percent), mental sub-normality (3.7 percent), adaptation reaction (2.4 percent) and neurotic disorder (1.1 percent) (Conde, 2004).

In the Philippines, religion has a strong influence on people and spirituality is recognized as a major coping mechanism. Suicide rates are relatively low since taking one's own life is considered a sin. In view of the strong spiritual practices psychosocial interventions often integrate spiritual approaches along with other psychological practices. Philippinos also believe in spirits being the cause of physical and mental illness (Conde, 2004).

The health care delivery system in Philippines primarily relies on the private sector. For several decades the mental health programme provided care in mental hospital settings. There have been efforts to provide mental health care in the university psychiatric wards and private hospitals. In 1988–1990, the National Program for Mental Health was initiated and it identified five priority areas including mental disorders, victims of violence, disasters and child abuse, street children, substance abuse and "overseas workers." It also focused on the integration of mental health services with general health care (Conde, 2004).

Thailand

Thailand is situated in Southeast Asia and has an estimated population of 64 million of which approximately 9.3 million live in Bangkok and its vicinity. Thailand has a high literacy rate of 93.8 percent. Ninety-four percent of the population is Thai-speaking Buddhists (Burnard, Naiyapatana, & Lloyd, 2006; Siriwanarangsan, Liknapichitkul & Khandelwal, 2004; United Nations Thailand, 2007). The Theravada or Hinayana Buddhism is the state religion. About five percent of the population practices Islamic religion. Other religious groups include

Taoists, Christians, Hindus, and Sikhs (United Nations Thailand, 2007). Although Thais have strong family structure, this has undergone rapid transformation due to the globalization and westernization; recently, consumerism and materialism do find their place in the Thai culture (Siriwanarangsan et al., 2004). Health determinants such as chronic hardships, low income, and cultural differences influence stress-related mental disorders. Further, it contributed to the increased consumption of alcohol and violence. There has been a significant increase in alcohol and drug abuse. Psychiatric problems among female sex workers have also risen in the recent past (Siriwanarangsan et al., 2004).

The principles of Buddhism have significant influence on the way people understand mental illness (Burnard et al., 2006). Since Thailand is predominantly a Buddhist country, its philosophy doesn't incorporate belief in spirits. However some still belief in animism, spirits, and ghosts, and they attribute mental illness to these supernatural forces (Suwanlert, 1976).

Mental health care in Thailand involves application of a combination of modern psychiatric treatments as well as traditional approaches (e.g., visiting temples for cure) (Burnard et al., 2006). Thailand has a total of 8,594 psychiatric beds at a ratio of one for every 7,553 population; the central region and Bangkok have the largest share of these beds (Siriwanarangsan et al., 2004). In the recent past there has been a considerable progress in the mental health care in Thailand due to various socioeconomic and cultural changes. There have been efforts to integrate mental health into general health care. Further, mental health resources have improved considerably. The current challenge is to ensure adequate mental health care to children, women and people with drug and alcohol problems. Thailand's Mental Health Plan was developed in 1992 as part of its seventh Health Development Plan. The goals of the mental health policy include reducing the incidence of mental illness, developing quality mental health care within the community setting, enhancing self-reliance, encouraging participation in mental health care, and developing strategies to prevent mental illness and promote mental health. There have been constant efforts to integrate mental health services into general health care. Over the years, mental health resources have improved considerably. However, the trained mental health professionals are generally concentrated in Bangkok and the Central region. Several nongovernmental organizations have made concerted efforts to improve mental health care and support persons with mental illness and their families (e.g., the Samaritans, the Foundation for the Better Life for Children, The Psychiatric Association of Thailand, the Mental Health Association of Thailand, to name a few) (Siriwanarangsan et al., 2004).

Kenya

Kenya is one of the three East-African countries with a population of approximately 32.4 million (Engenderhealth, 2007e) and 20 percent of its population lives in urban areas (Kiima, Nnenga, Okonji, & Kigamwa, 2004). Kenya's literacy rate is 89 percent for males and 76 percent for females. The life expectancy rate is 48 years for males and 53 years for females (Engenderhealth, 2007e). Kenya is a multicultural society with Christians (66 percent) and Muslims (7 percent) as the major religious groups; it comprises about 42 different tribal groups. Epidemiological studies indicate high prevalence rates of psychiatric illness ranging between 20 and 75 percent, and the patients with HIV sero-positive status are most affected by psychiatric illness (Kiima et al., 2004).

In Kenya, in line with other African countries, it is believed that mental illness is caused by supernatural powers such as gods and evil spirits; it is also believed that mental illness is an atonement for sins committed by the clan against their ancestors and is the result of bewitchment. Religion plays an influential role in the belief systems about mental illness; the Protestants believe in spiritual faith healing as a treatment of choice for mental illness. Similarly, people practising Islamic religion consult sheiks (Islamic clergy) seeking relief from psychiatric problems. Due to growing westernization these traditional beliefs are slowly changing and the younger generation tends to believe more in the modern concepts of mental illness (Kiima et al., 2004).

The Kenyan government recognized the role traditional healers play in the mental health care. Hence legislation is being formulated to regulate the practice of these traditional healers. Currently there is no formal National Mental Health Policy; The Mental Health Act of 1989 became operational in 1991 and the Government is currently formulating strategies for its implementation (Kiima et al., 2004). Kenya has formulated its National Mental Health Programme in 1996; it has adopted mental health as the ninth essential element of its primary health care provision (WHO, 2005).

Uganda

Uganda has a population of 26.7 million (Engenderhealth, 2007b) most of whom live in rural areas. Uganda has predominantly Christian population with a small proportion practicing Islamic religion.

Uganda comprises four major ethnic groups, namely, Bantus the majority ethnic community, Nilotics, Nilohamites and Hamies. There is a strong community support among these ethnic groups (Ndyanabangi et al., 2004).This country has a low literacy rate of 77 percent in males and 57 percent in females. The poverty levels are high with 35 percent of the population living below the poverty line with an unemployment rate of 31 percent. Uganda has a low life expectancy of 45.4 years for men and 46.9 years for women (Ndyanabangi et al., 2004; Engenderhealth, 2007b). Uganda is prone to natural disasters including landslides as well as severe drought. Man-made disasters such as internal displacement, cattle rustling, terrorism, war and refugee influx all impact the socioeconomic situation. Furthermore, the high prevalence of infectious diseases such as Malaria and HIV/AIDS add to the serious psychosocial problems (Ndyanabangi et al., 2004). A study conducted to assess the prevalence of mental illness in one district indicated a high prevalence rate of 30.7 percent (Kasoro et al., 2002).

In Uganda, positive mental well-being is described as a "state of physical, spiritual, social and financial health enabling participation in daily activities and contribution towards the well-being of others." Mental illness is perceived as an abnormal behaviour characterized by such symptoms as aggression, violence, and inappropriate behaviour. Mental illness is considered a punishment from ancestors as a consequence to the failure to perform funeral rites appropriately for an elderly family member. Similarly, such beliefs as bewitching and possession by the evil spirits are prevalent in these communities (Ndyanabangi et al., 2004). People also attribute mental illness to such infections as HIV/AIDS, Malaria, sexually transmitted diseases, and snakebites. Attributions to bad spirits and "extra intelligence" are not uncommon (Kasoro et al., 2002). People don't seek treatment for alcohol related problems since consumption of alcohol is viewed as a symbol of manhood and therefore not considered as a medical problem (Ndyanabangi et al., 2004).

Stigmatization of mentally ill persons is prevalent in Uganda. Problems such as discrimination, family isolation, use of derogatory/slang words are prevalent. Since people believe that mental illness should not be exposed to strangers, often persons with mental illness and their families hide or disguise the symptoms. Families hide their mentally ill family members or lock them away. Persons with mental illness do not inherit property and they are not entrusted with responsibility of religious positions such as priestship, nunhood or brotherhood. People also somatize psychiatric illness (Ndyanabangi et al., 2004).

In view of the strong belief that mental illness is caused by the influence of spirits, the mentally ill persons are ill-treated and often those with chronic illness (e.g. schizophrenia) are abandoned. The burden of providing care to the mentally ill falls on the women within families. Often nonviolent mentally ill persons are well tolerated within the community and assistance is provided to them. Ageing parents and older persons with mental illness or dementia are well looked after by their families (Ndyanabangi et al., 2004). Isolation is one of the principal methods of managing mentally ill using such strategies as tying them to a tree, locking them inside a house or in a prison (Kasoro et al., 2002).

Utilization of formal health care facilities for mental illness is generally low. Although people attach value to their mental well-being, most people discourage formal mental health services due to the belief that mental illness is caused by "curses and demons." Families initially consult traditional healers (Ndyanabangi et al., 2004). The traditional healers practice a wide range of approaches such as herbal therapy, hydrotherapy, "counselling," divination and exorcism (Mental Health Uganda, 2001; cited in Ndyanabangi et al., 2004). Approaching specialist services and seeking formal medical help is considered as an option only in certain chronic conditions or when the traditional healer is unsuccessful in alleviating symptoms (Ndyanabangi et al., 2004). Occasionally, the traditional healers refer persons with mental illness to a formal mental health care facility (Mental Health Uganda, 2001; cited in Ndyanabangi et al., 2004).

Christian "counsellors" consider mental illness as a sign of guilt or sin; churches practice faith healing and provide counselling services to the persons with mental illness and their families (Ndyanabangi et al., 2004).

The Ugandan Mental Health Programme was initiated in 1996 and provision of mental health care services is considered as one of the important services within general health care. There have been attempts to integrate mental health care into the general health services. Shortage of qualified mental health professionals is one of the problems in delivering mental health care to the community. The general health personnel provide mental health services in areas where mental health professionals are not available. Problems such as cultural beliefs which encourage stigmatization and discrimination of mentally ill persons, absence of structured legislation to regulate the services of traditional healers, absence of data concerning prevalence of mental health problems, strong negative attitude among health care workers about providing mental health care, and lack of funds in the health sector impact mental health care of people in Uganda (Ndyanabangi et al., 2004).

Zambia

Zambia has a population of 10.3 million and it is one of the most urbanized countries in sub-Saharan Africa. Zambia is a low income group country (see WHO, 2005). Zambia's principal religion is Christianity. It has high poverty level and unemployment. Zambia is affected by the man-made disasters (such as wars, gender-based violence) as well as natural disasters (unpredictable pattern of rainfall leading to drought or floods). Zambia shelters an estimated 240,000 refugees from the neighboring countries. The HIV/AIDS prevalence rates are the highest amongst all the South African countries with 20 percent among the reproductive group of 15–49 years (Mayeya, Chazulwa, Mayeya, et al., 2004).

Several socioeconomic, political, environmental, cultural and religious factors influence the mental health of people of Zambia. In Zambia mental health is largely perceived as the ability to cope with the demands of life. Mental health is also equated with "stable mind" where an individual could live in harmony with the environment and perform functions that society expects. It is believed that mentally ill persons disturb the peace of the family and community. They are believed to be involved in behaviours such as shouting for no apparent reason, talking nonsense, not talking, and restlessness, destroying property, or behaving violently. Mental illness is also believed to be a regression into childhood and persons with mental illness are perceived as dangerous to themselves and to society. Mental illness is often ridiculed with such derogatory terms as *kufunta, ukupena,* and *usilu.* Persons with mental illness are considered "invalids" since they may not contribute financially. These persons are often stigmatized, humiliated, and condemned. Mental illness is also considered as a form of spirit possession, or social punishment, and a consequence of witchcraft. Some are of the opinion that mental illness should be treated through traditional approaches and not by modern medicine. Family members usually take the mentally ill person to the traditional healer for consultation. Older people (both mentally ill and with dementia) are considered as the responsibility of the family and they are well accepted in community; family members offer care and support to these older persons (Mayeya et al., 2004).

People practising Christianity believe in prayer as a method of treatment for healing, mental illness and spirit possession. Traditional practitioners of medicine include herbalists and diviners (spiritual healers). About 70–80 percent of people with mental health problems consult the traditional practitioners for help. Zambia has about 44,000 traditional health practitioners registered under the Traditional Health Practitioners Association of Zambia. Acupuncture is also practised as a treatment modality (Mayeya et al., 2004). The National Mental Health Policy was formulated in 2004, which is still in a draft form. There currently isn't a national mental health programme in Zambia (WHO, 2005).

Concluding Comments

Mental illness is of concern to people across the globe. As has been reviewed in this chapter, different cultures and nations have their own unique explanatory systems. It is fair to say that everyone is concerned and seems to be doing the best (as far as they can tell) to alleviate the pain of mental illness. However, it is sad to note that many less developed countries do not have a formal mental health policy, and even those in developed countries who have policies are not reaping the best out of the policies. Furthermore, the differences in the way "abnormal behavior" and mental illness is conceptualized and treated around the world as reviewed here, highlight the importance of being informed about cultural differences. Nonetheless, a major recurrent theme and main factor against seeking help for mental illness is the deep stigma associated with it. There is need for more education about mental health to help reduce the stigma in a significant way.

REFERENCES

Acharya, K. (1998). Knowledge, attitude and practice of mental illness in a village population. Unpublished doctoral dissertation, Tribhuvan University, Kathmandu, Nepal.

Aidoo, M., & Harpham, T. (2001). The explanatory models of mental health amongst low-income women and health care practitioners in Lusaka, Zambia. *Health Policy and Planning, 16,* 206–213.

Antony, P. A. (2001). The concept of mind in Ayurveda. Paper presented at the National Seminar on Psychology in India: Past, Present and Future. 12th Annual Conference of NAOP, 22nd –24th October, 2001, Kollam, India.

Balodhi, J. P. (1986). Perspective of Rajayoga in its application to mental health. *NIMHANS Journal, 4,* 133–138.

Balodhi, J. P. (1987). Constituting the outlines of a philosophy of ayurveda: Mainly on mental health import. *Indian Journal of Psychiatry, 29,* 127–131.

Balodhi, J. P. (1990). Psychotherapy based on Hindu philosophy. *Journal of Personality and Clinical Studies, 6,* 51–56.

Balodhi, J. P. (1991). Holistic approach in psychiatry: Indian view. *NIMHANS Journal, 9,* 101–104.

Balodhi, J. P. (1999). Traditional Indian system of medicine as applicable to treatment of mental illness. In A. Sahni (Ed.), *Mental health care in India* (pp. 132–138). Bangalore: Indian Society of Health Administrators.

Banerjee, G., & Roy, S. (1998). Determinants of help-seeking behaviour of families of schizophrenic patients attending a teaching hospital in India: an indigenous explanatory model. *International Journal of Social Psychiatry, 44,* 199–214.

Banerjee, T., & Banerjee, G. (1995). Determinants of help-seeking behaviour in cases of epilepsy attending a teaching hospital in India: an indigenous explanatory model. *International Journal of Social Psychiatry, 41,* 217–230.

Bearon, L. B., & Koenig, H. G. (1990). Religion, cognitions and use of prayer in health and illness. *Gerontologist, 30,* 249–253.

Bernal, G., & Sáez-Santiago, E. (2006). Culturally centered psychosocial interventions. *Journal of Community Psychology, 34,* 121–132.

Burnard, P., Naiyapatana, W., & Lloyd, G. (2006). Views of mental illness and mental health care in Thailand: a report of an ethnographic study. *Journal of Psychiatric and Mental Health Nursing, 13,* 742–749.

Chatters, L. M. (2000). Religion and health: Public health research and practice. *Annu. Rev. Public Health, 21,* 335–367.

Chisholm, D., Sekar, K., Kishore Kumar, K., Saeed, K., James, S., Mubbashar, M., et al. (2000). Integration of mental health care into primary care. *British Journal of Psychiatry, 176,* 581–588.

Cochran, J. K., Beegley, L, & Bock, E. W. (1992). The influence of religious stability and homogamy on the relationship between religiosity and alcohol use among Protestants. *Journal for the Scientific Study of Religion, 32,* 441–456.

Coleman, K., Koffman, J., & Daniels, C. (2007). Why is this happening to me? Illness beliefs held by haredi Jewish breast cancer patients: an exploratory study. *Spirituality and Health International, 8,* 121–134.

Conde, B. (2004). Philippines mental health country profile. *International Review of Psychiatry, 16,* 159–166.

Cora-Bramble, D., Tielman, F., & Wright, J. (2004). Traditional practices, "folk remedies," and the Western biomedical model: Bridging the divide. *Clinical Pediatric Emergency Medicine, 5,* 102–108.

Cuéllar, I., & Paniagua F. A. (2000) (Eds). *Handbook of multicultural mental health: Assessment and treatment of diverse populations.* San Diego: Academic Press.

Department for International Development. (2007). Retrieved October, 2007, from http://www.dfidhealthrc.org/publications/Country_health/europe/Bulgaria.pdf.

Department of Health and Human Services (2001). *Mental health: Culture, race, and ethnicity – a supplement to mental health: A report of the Surgeon General.* Rockville, MD: Author.

Deva, M. P. (2004). Malaysia mental health country profile. *International Review of Psychiatry, 16*, 167–176.

Durie, M. (1985). A Māori perspective of health. *Soc. Sci. Med., 20*, 483–486.

Durie, M. (1994). *Whaiora: Māori health development.* Auckland: Oxford University Press.

Durie, M. (2001). *Māori ora: The dynamics of Māori health.* Auckland, NZ: Oxford University Press.

Durie, M. (2003). Providing health services to indigenous peoples. *British Medical Journal. Editorial. 327*, 408–409.

Durie, M. (2004). Understanding health and illness: Research at the interface between science and indigenous knowledge. *International Journal of Epidemiology, 33*, 1138–1143.

Edman, J. L., & Koon, T.Y. (2000). Mental illness beliefs in Malaysia: ethnic and intergenerational comparisons. *International Journal of Society Psychiatry, 46*, 101–109.

Engenderhealth (2007a). Retrieved October 2007, from http://www.engenderhealth. org/ia/cbc/india.html.

Engenderhealth (2007b). Retrieved October 2007, from http://www.engenderhealth. org/ia/cbc/uganda.html.

Engenderhealth (2007c). Retrieved October 2007, from http://www.engenderhealth. org/ia/cbc/ bangladesh.html.

Engenderhealth. (2007d). Retrieved October 2007, from http://www.engenderhealth. org/ia/cbc/china.html.

Engenderhealth (2007e). Retrieved October 2007, from http://www.engenderhealth. org/ia/cbc/kenya.html.

Engenderhealth (2007f). Retrieved October 2007, from http://www.engenderhealth. org/ia/cbc/nepal.html.

Engenderhealth (2007g). Retrieved October 2007, from http://www.engenderhealth. org/ia/cbc/ pakistan.html.

Engenderhealth (2007h). Retrieved October 2007, from http://www.engenderhealth. org/ia/cbc/ philippines.html.

Farooqi, Y. N. (2006). Traditional healing practices sought by Muslim Psychiatric patients in Lahore, Pakistan. *International Journal of Disability, Development and Education,53*, 401–415.

Flaskerud, J. H. (2000). Ethnicity, culture, and neuropsychiatry. *Issues in Mental Health Nursing, 21*, 5–29.

Gartner, J. (1996). Religious commitment, mental health, and prosocial behavior: A review of the empirical literature. In E. P. Shafranske (Ed.), *Religion and the clinical practice of psychology* (pp. 187–214). Washington, DC: American Psychological Association.

Gartner, J. D., Larson, D. B., & Allen, G. D. (1991). Religious commitment and mental health: a review of the empirical literature. *Journal of Psychological Theology, 19*, 6–25.

Haque, A. (1998). Psychology and religion: Their relationship and integration from an Islamic perspective. *American Journal of Islamic Social Sciences, 15*, 97–116.

Haque, A. (2004). Religion and mental health from an Islamic perspective: The case of Muslim Americans. *Journal of Religion and Health, 43*, 45–58.

Haque, A., & Masuan, K. A. (2002). Religious psychology in Malaysia. *International Journal for the Psychology of Religion, 12*, 277–289.

Hill, P. C., & Butter, E. M. (1995). The role of religion in promoting physical health. *Journal of Psychology and Christianity, 14*, 141–155.

Hu, J., Higgins, J., & Higgins, L. T. (2006). Development and limits to development of mental health services in China. *Criminal Behaviour and Mental Health, 16*, 69–76.

Jacob, K. S., Sharan, P., Mirza, I., Garrido-Cumbrera, M., Seedat, S., Mari, J. J., et al. (2007). Mental health systems in countries: Where are we now? *Lancet, 370*, 1061–1077.

Juthani, N. V. (2001). Psychiatric treatment of Hindus. *International Review of Psychiatry, 13*, 125–130.

Kakar, S. (1978). *The inner world: A psychoanalytic study of childhood and society in India*. New Delhi: Oxford University Press.

Kapur, R. L. (1975). Mental health care in rural India: A study of existing patterns and their implications for future policy. *British Journal of Psychiatry, 127*, 286–293.

Kapur, R. L. (1979). The role of traditional healers in mental health care in rural India. *Social Sciences & Medicine, 13B*, 27–31.

Karim, S., Saeed, K., Rana, M. H., Mubbashar, M. H., & Jenkins, R. (2004). Pakistan mental health country profile. *International Review of Psychiatry, 16*, 83–92.

Kasoro, S., Sebudde, S., Kabagambe-Rugumba, G., Ovuga, E., & Boardman, A. (2002). Mental illness in one district of Uganda. *International Journal of Social Psychiatry, 48*, 29–37.

Kennedy, G. J. (1998). Religion and depression. In H. G. Koenig (Ed.), *Handbook of religion and mental health* (pp. 129–145). San Diego: Academic.

Kennedy, J. C., & Olsson, K. (1996). Health care seeking behaviour and formal integration: A rural Mexican case study. *Human Organization, 55*, 41–46.

Khandelwal, S. K., Jhingan, H. P., Ramesh, S., Gupta, R. K., & Srivastava, V. K. (2004). India mental health country profile. *International Review of Psychiatry, 16*, 126–141.

Kiima, D. M., Njenga, F. G., Okonji, M. M. O., & Kigamwa, P. A. (2004). Kenya mental health country profile. *International Review of Psychiatry, 16*, 48–53.

Kirmayer, L. J. (2000). The future of cultural psychiatry: an international perspective. *Canadian Journal of Psychiatry, 45*, 438–446.

Kleinman, A. (1988). *Rethinking psychiatry: From cultural category to personal experience*. New York: Free Press.

Koenig, H. G. (1998). Religious attitudes and practices of hospitalized medically ill older adults. *International Journal of Geriatric Psychology, 13*, 213–24.

Koenig, H. G., George, L. K., Meador, K. G., Blazer, D. G., & Ford, S. M. (1994). Religious practices and alcoholism in a southern adult population. *Hospital and Community Psychiatry, 45*, 225–31.

Koenig, H. G., George, L. K., & Peterson, B. L. (1998). Religiosity and remission of depression in medically ill older patients. *American Journal of Psychiatry, 155*, 536–42.

Kumaraswamy, N. (2007). Psychotherapy in Brunei Darussalam. *Journal of Clinical Psychology, 63*, 735–745.

Lago, C. (2006). *Race, culture and counseling: The ongoing challenge* (2nd ed.). London: Open University Press.

Larson, D. B., Sherrill, K. A., Lyons, J. S., Craigie, F. C. Jr, & Theilman, S. B. (1992). Associations between dimensions of religious commitment and mental health reported in the *American Journal of Psychiatry* and *Archives of General Psychiatry*: 1978–1989. *American Journal of Psychiatry, 149*, 557–559.

Larson, D. B., Swyers, J. P., & McCullough, M. E. (Eds.). (1998). *Scientific research on spirituality and health: A consensus report.* Rockville, MD: National Institute for Healthcare Research.

Levin, J. S., & Chatters, L. M. (1998). Research on religion and mental health: an overview of empirical findings and theoretical issues. In H. G. Koenig (Ed.), *Handbook of religion and mental health* (pp. 34–50). San Diego: Academic.

Levin, J. S., Chatters, L. M., Ellison, C. G., & Taylor, R. J. (1996). Religious involvement, health outcomes, and public health practice. *Current Issues Public Health, 2,* 220–225.

Lyssenko, V. (2004). The human body composition in statics and dynamics: Ayurveda and the philosophical schools of Vaisesika and Samkhya. *Journal of Indian Philosophy, 32,* 31–56.

McCreary, J. R. (1968). Population growth and urbanization. In E. Schwimmer (Ed.), *The Maori people in the nineteen sixties* (pp. 187–204), Auckland, NZ: Blackwood & Janet Paul.

Marsella, A. J., & Yamada, A. M. (2000). Culture and mental health: an introduction and overview of foundations, concepts and issues. In I. Cuéllar & F. A. Paniagua (Eds.), *Handbook of multicultural mental health* (pp. 3–24), San Diego, USA: Academic.

Massard, J. (1988). Doctoring by go-between: aspects of health care for Malay children. *Social Science and Medicine, 27,* 789–797.

Mayeya, J., Chazulwa, R., Mayeya, P. N., et al. (2004). Zambia mental health country profile. *International Review of Psychiatry, 16,* 63–72.

Ministry of Health (2005). *Draft action plan Te Tahuhu – Improving mental health 2005–2015: The Second New Zealand Mental Health and Addiction Plan.* Wellington: Ministry of Health, NZ.

Ministry of Health and Family Welfare (1982). *National Mental Health Programme for India.* New Delhi: Government of India.

Mumford, D. B., Minhas, F. H., Akhtar, I., Akhtar, S., & Mubbashar, M. H. (2000). Stress and psychiatric disorder in urban Rawalpindi: Community survey. *British Journal of Psychiatry, 177,* 557–562.

Mumford, D. B., Nazir, M., Jilani, F. U., & Baig, I. Y. (1996). Stress and psychiatric disorder in the Hindu Kush: a community survey of mountain villages of Pakistan. *British Journal of Psychiatry, 168,* 299–307.

Mumford, D. B., Saeed, K., Ahmed, I., Latif, S., & Mubbashar, M. H. (1997). Stress and psychiatric disorder in rural Punjab: a community survey. *British Journal of Psychiatry, 170,* 473–478.

National Institute of Mental Health (2001). *Strategic plan on reducing health disparities.* Rockville, MD: Author.

NCPHP (2007). http://en.ncphp.government.bg/files/projects/PrimaryHealthCare_Eng.pdf; accessed October 2007.

Ndyanabangi, S., Basangwa, D., Lutakome, J., & Mubiru, C. (2004). Uganda mental health country profile. *International Review of Psychiatry, 16,* 54–62.

Osman, M. T. (1989). *Malay folk beliefs.* Kuala Lumpur: Dewan Bahasa Dan Pustaka.

Overall, J., & Gorham, D. (1962). Brief psychiatric rating scale. *Psychological Reports, 10,* 799.

Oxford Dictionary (1999). (10th ed.). New York: Oxford University Press.

Pargament, K. I. (1997). *The psychology of religion and coping.* New York: Guilford Press.

Patel, V. (2007). Mental health in low- and middle-income countries. *British Medical Bulletin, 81 & 82*, 81–96.

Patel, V., Sumathipala, A., Khan, M. M., Thapa, S. B., & Rahman, O. (2007). South Asian region. In K. Bhui & D. Bhugra (Eds.), *Culture and mental health* (pp. 212–224). London: Hodder Arnold.

Pavagada, R. & DeSouza, R. (2007). Culture and mental health care in New Zealand: Indigenous and non-indigenous people. *Culture and mental health* (pp. 245–259). London: Hodder Arnold.

Pesek, T. J., Helton, L. R., & Nair, M. (2006). Healing across cultures: learning from traditions. *EcoHealth, 3*, 114–118.

Phillips, M. R., Yang, G., Li, S., & Li, Y. (2004). Suicide and the unique prevalence pattern of schizophrenia in mainland China: a retrospective observational study. *Lancet, 364*, 1062–1068.

Pradhan, P. K. (2003). Mental health and social work in Nepal. Retrieved November, 2007, from http://www.jassw.jp/17th_apswc/PDF/sessionD/DE_4_1_pradhan_prabahat_kiran.pdf

Prasadarao, P. S. D. V. (2007). Mental health of older people in Aotearoa, New Zealand: Needs, issues and psychological approaches to management. In I. M. Evans., M. O'Driscoll, J. J. Rucklidge (Eds.), *Professional practice of psychology in Aotearoa New Zealand* (pp. 509–524). New Zealand Psychological Society: Wellington, New Zealand.

Prasadarao, P. S. D. V., & Sudhir, P. M. (2001). Clinical psychology in India. *Journal of Clinical Psychology in Medical Settings, 8*, 31–38.

Pressman, P., Lyons, J. S., Larson, D. B., & Strain, J. S. (1990). Religious beliefs, depression, and ambulation status in elderly women with broken hips. *American Journal of Psychiatry, 147*, 758–760.

Raguram, R., Venkateswaran, A., Ramakrishna, J., & Weiss, M. G. (2002). Traditional community resources for mental health: a report of temple healing from India. *British Medical Journal, 325*, 38–40.

Reddy, M. V., & Chandrashekar, C. R. (1998). Prevalence of mental and behavioral disorders in India: a meta-analysis. *Indian Journal of Psychiatry, 40*, 149–157.

Regmi, S. K., Pokhare, A., Ojha, S. P., Pradhan, S. N., & Chapagain, G. (2004). Nepal mental health country profile. *International Review of Psychiatry, 16*, 142–149.

Rochford, T. (2004). Whare tapa wha: A Maori model of a unified theory of health. *Journal of Primary Prevention, 25*, 41–57.

Sachdev, P. S. (1989). Psychiatric illness in the New Zealand Maori. *Australian and New Zealand Journal of Psychiatry, 23*, 529–541.

Saldivia, S., Vicente, B., Kohn, R., Rioseco, P., & Torres, S. (2004). Use of mental health services in Chile. *Psychiatric Services, 55*, 71–76.

Saraceno, B., van Ommeren, M., Batniji, R., Cohen, A., Gureje, O., Mahoney, et al. (2007). Barriers to improvement of mental health services in low-income and middle-income countries. *Lancet, 370*, 1164–1174.

Sethi, S., & Seligman, M. E. P. (1993). Optimism and fundamentalism. *Psychological Science, 4*, 256–259.

Seybold, K. S., & Hill, P. C. (2001). The role of religion and spirituality in mental and physical health. *Current Directions in Psychological Science, 10*, 21–24.

Sharma, P. V. (2000). *Caraka-Samhita: Text with English translation*. Varanasi: Chaukhambha Orientalia.

Singh, A. (2007). Action and reason in the theory of Ayurveda. *AI & Soc., 21*, 27–46.

Siriwanarangsan, P., Liknapichitkul, D., & Khandelwal, S. K. (2004). Thailand mental health country profile. *International Review of Psychiatry, 16*, 150–158.

Statistics New Zealand. http://www.stats.govt.nz/default.htm; accessed November 2007.

Stekelenburg, J., Jager, B. E., Kolk, P. R., Westen, E. H. M. N., van der Kwaak, A. & Wolffers, I. N. (2005). Health care seeking behaviour and utilization of traditional healers in Kalabo, Zambia. *Health Policy, 71*, 67–81.

Stewart, C. L. (2004). Chile mental health country profile. *International Review of Psychiatry, 16*, 73–82.

Suwanlert, S. (1976). Neurotic and psychotic states attributed to Thai "Phii Pob" spirit possession. *Australia and New Zealand Journal of Psychiatry, 10*, 119–123.

Thoresen, C. E. (1999). Spirituality and health: Is there a relationship? *Journal of Health Psychology, 4*, 291–300.

Tomov, T., Mladenova, M., Lazarova, I., Sotirov, V., & Okoliyski, M. (2004). Bulgaria mental health country profile. *International Review of Psychiatry, 16*, 93–106.

United Nations Thailand (2007). Retrieved November 2007, from http://www.un.or.th/thailand/ population.html.

Weiss, M. G., Isaac, M., Parkar, S. R., Chowdhury, A. N., & Raguram, R. (2001). Global, national, and local approaches to mental health: Examples from India. *Tropical Medicine and International Health, 6*, 4–23.

Wig, N. N. (1999). Mental health and spiritual values: A view from the East. *International Review of Psychiatry, 11*, 92–96.

Williams, D. R., Larson, D. B., Buckler, R. E., Heckman, R. C., & Pyle, C. M. (1991). Religion and psychological distress in a community sample. *Social Science and Medicine, 32*, 1257–1262.

World Health Organization (2003). *Investing in mental health*. Geneva: Author.

World Health Organization (2005). *Mental health atlas, 2005*. Geneva: Author.

World Health Organization (2007a). Retrieved October, 2007, from http://www.who.int/countries/bgr/en/.

World Health Organization (2007b). Retrieved October, 2007, from http://www.who.int/countries/mys/en/.

World Health Organization (2007c). Retrieved October 2007, from http://www.who.int/mental_health/policy/country/chile/en/index.html.

Wright, C., Nepal, M. K., & Bruce-Jones, W. D. A. (1989). Mental health patients in primary health care services in Nepal. *Asia-Pacific Journal of Public Health, 3*, 224–230.

Xia, G., & Qian, M. (2001). The relationship of parenting style to self-reported mental health among two subcultures of Chinese. *Journal of Adolescence, 24*, 251–260.

Yip, K. (2005). Chinese concepts of mental health: cultural implications for social work practice. *International Social Work, 48*, 391–407.

Yip, K. (2006). Community mental health in the People's Republic of China: A critical analysis. *Community Mental Health Journal, 42*, 41–51.

Zayas, L. H., Torres, L. R., Malcolm, J., & DesRosiers, F. S. (1996). Clinicians' definitions of ethnically sensitive therapy. *Professional Psychology: Research and Practice, 27*, 78–82.

Part II

Cross-Cultural Issues in Specific Psychological Disorders

9

Culture and Mood Disorders

Sussie Eshun and Toy Caldwell-Colbert

Cultural influences on mood disorders have been debated and studied extensively in the last half century. The need to focus on the role that culture plays in mood disorders has stemmed mostly from increased migration and rapid globalization. It is estimated that approximately 170 million people live outside their home country and about 700 million people cross-national borders each year (Koehn, 2006). Research studies continue to point to misdiagnosis and significant disparities in assessing and treating mental illness across cultures and ethnic groups. In response to this need, the World Health Organization has sponsored several large-scale studies and launched some initiatives to help enhance treatment of mental illnesses in general.

In this chapter we review cross-cultural/ethnic differences and similarities in prevalence, incidence, and symptom presentation of mood disorders. We also discuss possible cultural factors that mediate reported cross-cultural differences and comment on implications for diagnosis and treatment of mood disorders among people of varying cultural backgrounds.

Defining Mood Disorders

Mood disorders are a group of mental illnesses that affect a person's frame of mind. The *Diagnostic and Statistical Manual–IV-TR* distinguishes two main types of mood disorders: major depression and bipolar or manic-depression (APA, 2000). Depression (or major depressive episode) is characterized by depressed mood, loss of interest or pleasure in most activities, significant appetite disturbance with either weight loss or gain (more than 5 percent in the past month), sleep disturbance, low energy, poor concentration, feelings of guilt or low self-worth, and recurring thoughts about death for more than two weeks (APA, 2000; WHO, 2007). In some cases depressive symptoms include continued somatic reports, such as aches, pains, or cramps that do not go away even with appropriate medical treatment (NIMH, 2007).

Aside from major depression, there are other types of depressive disorders depending on severity and other associated biological or environmental conditions. These include dysthymic disorder, psychotic depression, postpartum depression, and seasonal affective disorder. Dysthymic disorder is marked by less severe symptoms that persist over a long time (two or more years) and psychotic depression is a severe form of depression accompanied by one or more indications of psychosis such as hallucinations and delusions. Postpartum depression occurs when a new mother develops major depression within one month after delivery and seasonal affective disorders is identified by the onset of depression during the winter months when there is less natural sunlight (NIMH, 2007).

Bipolar disorder, also known as manic-depression consists of "cycling mood changes-from extreme highs to extreme lows" (NIMH, 2007). According to the *DSM–IV–TR*, the extreme highs or mania are typically characterized by expansive or irritable mood, increased energy, decreased need for sleep, pressured speech, racing thoughts, inflated self-esteem, feelings of invulnerability, and poor judgment (APA, 2000). Symptoms associated with the extreme lows are the same as major depression described earlier in this section. Overall depressive disorders are more common than bipolar disorders.

Cross-Cultural Difference and Similarities in Mood Disorders

Culture-Bound Syndromes – *Shenjing Shuairuo*

Although the *DSM* and *ICD* diagnostic criteria for mood disorders are used worldwide, recent observations and research in different cultures have resulted in the new diagnostic category of culture-bound syndromes which have been discussed in some of the chapters in this book. Of particular importance here is *Shenjing shuairuo* or neurasthenia, often described as the Chinese version of major depressive disorder. *The Chinese Classification of Mental Disorders*, 3rd ed. (CCMD-3) lists symptoms of *Shenjing shuairuo* as including fatigue, dizziness, headaches, joint and muscle pain, loss of concentration, gastrointestinal complaints, and sleep disturbance (Chinese Psychiatric Society, 2001). Although the CCMD-3 diagnostic criteria for neurasthenia emphasizes somatic complaints, views that major depression and *Shenjing shuairuo* are similar stem from a study by Kleinman (1982). Results from his study indicated that 87 percent of a sample of Hunan Chinese who had been diagnosed with *Shenjing shuairuo* also met criteria for major depression and responded satisfactorily to tricyclic antidepressant medications. Other studies have confirmed that the most commonly perceived symptoms include anxiety, insomnia, and depression (Lee & Wong, 1995).

Some studies have pointed to changes in the prevalence of neurasthenia and linked some of the changes to changes in political regimes in China. Chang et al.

(2005) are among researchers who have argued that *Shenjing shuairuo* could easily be reclassified as other *DSM–IV* disorders, particularly somatoform disorders, and may have little to do with major depression as outlined in western classification codes. They investigated degree of concordance between Chinese patients suffering from *Shenjing shuairuo, ICD-10* Neurasthenia, and one or more *DSM–IV* diagnoses. Data from their study showed that participants diagnosed with *DSM–IV* mood disorders had significantly higher scores for overall distress than those with *Shenjing shuairuo*. However, they found no reliable difference between patients with *Shenjing shuairuo* and those with *DSM–IV* somatoform disorders, leading them to conclude that unlike prior assertions that *Shenjing shuairuo* was more or less the Chinese version of the western major depression, it is more similar to somatoform disorders. In fact, the 3rd edition of the CCMD makes the distinction between major depression and *Shenjing shuairuo* by requiring that individuals diagnosed with the latter have at least 3 of 5 groups of symptoms: physical/mental fatigue or weakness, irritability or worry, excitability, nervous pain, and sleep disturbance.

National and Ethnic Variations in Prevalence and Incidence Rates

Depression affects approximately 121 million people worldwide (WHO, 2007). Depression is the fourth leading cause of disease burden in the world. It is estimated to account for 4.46 percent of total disability adjusted life years (DALYs) in 2000 (Ustun, Ayuso-Mateos, Chatterji, Mathers, & Murray, 2004). Ustun et al.'s analysis of data from the WHO regions, showed that whereas no mood disorders were among the top ten DALYs for Africa, major depression was the fifth leading cause for the Eastern Mediterranean region, fourth for Southeast Asia, first for the Americas, third for Europe, and second for the Western Pacific region. Although the researchers' goal was not to explain the differences in rates of DALYs it is noteworthy pointing out that the results from Africa may be more of a reflection of a stark lack of any reliable data from the region than low rates of depression.

Results from the WHO World Mental Health Survey Consortium indicated that mood disorders were the second common mental health challenge, with 12-month prevalence ranging from low rates of 0.8 percent in Nigeria, 1.7 percent in Shanghai (China), and 2.5 percent in Beijing (China) to high rates of 9.6 percent in the US, 9.1 percent in Ukraine, and 8.5 percent in France (WHO World Mental Health Survey Consortium, 2004). Their results confirm earlier reports of lower rates of depression in nonwestern nations (Biji, Graaf, Hiripi, et al., 2003; Goldberg & Lecrubier, 1995; Simon, Goldberg, Von Korff, & Ustun, 2002; Weissman, Bland, Canino, et al., 1996). Since the European commission funded the Outcome of Depression International Network (ODIN) in 1996, several studies have focused on prevalence rates among European countries. In the first report, prevalence rates were compared between rural and urban communities in Finland, Ireland, Norway, Spain, and the United Kingdom (Ayuso-Mateos, Vazquez-Barquero, Dowrick, et al.,

2001). The researchers found weighted prevalence rates for depressive episodes ranging from a low 1.8 percent in urban Spain to a high of 15.01 percent in urban UK; and rates from dysthymic ranging from 0.2 percent in urban UK to 2.9 percent in urban Ireland. Ayuso-Mateos et al. (2001) explained that their observed differences in prevalence rates reflected cultural differences and/or variations in risk factors and how individuals in the various countries and regions (urban vs. rural) express the mental illness.

Weissman et al. (1996) noted that regardless of observed differences in depression across cultures, females had higher prevalence rates than males in all countries studied. Furthermore, unlike depression, the lifetime prevalence rates for bipolar disorder were similar across nations, with no striking gender differences. In the US, depression is the most commonly experienced mental illness, with prevalence rates of 15 percent for men and 35 percent for women over the course of one's lifetime (WHO World Mental Health Survey Consortium, 1996). Similar findings of gender variations within nations have been documented in comparisons of low income urban women in Brazil, Chile, and India (Blue, Ducci, Jaswal, Ludermir, & Harphan, 1995).

Although studies of mood disorders and other psychological illnesses in African countries are very few, the existence of mood disorders have been documented using western-based assessment instruments in Nigeria (Adewuya, Ola, & Aloba, 2007), Ethiopia (Mogga, Prince, Alem, et al., 2006) Uganda (Nakku, Nakasi, & Mirembe, 2006), and Zimbabwe (Patel, Anas, Broadhead, Todd, & Reeler, 2001), to mention a few. A review of studies from African nations indicate that depression is more common than was once thought and also draw attention to the paucity of research on the assessment and treatment of mood disorders in the sub-Saharan African region as a whole (Tomlinson, Swartz, Kruger, & Gureje, 2007).

Ethnic variations in mood disorders, particularly major depression have also been documented within nations. In the UK, African Caribbean women have been found to have significantly higher rates of depression than white European men and women in a community sample from Manchester (Shaw, Creed, Tomenson, Riste, & Cruickshank, 1999). Cross-ethnic studies in the UK are limited. However the overall consensus seems to that people from minority groups have higher prevalence rates than the dominant group (Bhugra & Mastrogianni, 2004).

Studies of ethnic samples in the US have yielded similar findings of higher rates of depression among ethnic minority groups, with the exception of Asian Americans who have consistently been associated with lower prevalence rates (Jackson-Triche, Sullivan, Wells, Rogers, Camp, & Mazel, 2000). Other investigations have demonstrated that ethnic differences depend on the type of mood disorder. Riolo, Nguyen, Greden, and King (2005) found that while whites had higher lifetime prevalence for major depression, African Americans and Mexican Americans had significantly higher lifetime prevalence rates for dysthymic disorder. Yet still it has been argued that ethnic variations in depression also depend on certain demographic studies, including age, income, and education. Dunlop, Song, Lyons, Manheim, and Chang (2003) reported higher prevalence rates of major depression among Hispanics, followed by African Americans and then European Americans. They further showed that the odds of depressive disorders in older Hispanics were 44 percent greater than in whites. All in all it seems that differences in depression rates between the various ethnic groups, particularly African Americans and European Americans, are reduced significantly when demographic and socioeconomic factors are controlled (Bhugra & Mastrogianni, 2004).

Although few studies provide reliable explanations for cross-national variations in mood disorders, some studies have linked differences in bipolar I disorders across nations to diet, which is an important cultural value. Noaghiul and Hibbeln (2003) found national seafood consumption to be significantly related to lifetime prevalence rates of bipolar disorder. Their results confirm previous studies that showed a negative relationship between seafood consumption and prevalence for affective disorders and major depression across countries (Hibbeln, 1998; Hibbeln & Salem, 1995). They explained that their findings may be linked with Omega-3 fatty acids, which has been reported to decrease the depressive symptoms and also lower the number of severe affective episodes (Stoll, Severus, Freeman, et al., 1999; Su, Shen, & Huang, 2000).

National and Ethnic Variations in Levels of Mood Disorders

Cross-cultural differences in levels and rates of depression have been reported quite extensively. Cultural variations have been reported in comparisons between western and nonwestern cultural groups as well as those among western industrialized nations. Arrindell, Steptoe, and Wardle (2003) compared 14 nations based on Hofstede's (2000) cultural construct of masculine and feminine categories. They found that nations with high masculinity index scores (e.g., Germany, Ireland, and Poland) had significantly higher mean scores on the Beck Depression Inventory than those with low masculinity index scores (e.g., Sweden, Norway, and The Netherlands). They explained that their results may be linked to less masculine nations being more flexible in offering opportunities for self-fulfillment and some other factors that have been associated with positive health. Other results of cross-national variations between western countries have been found in women during pregnancy and postpartum (Gorman, O'Hara, Figueiredo, et al., 2004; Nakku et al., 2006).

Ethnic differences in levels of mood disorders have also been reported. In a comparative study of depressive symptoms between Native Hawaiians, European Americans and Japanese American samples, Kanazawa, White, and Hampson (2007) found that Native Hawaiians had higher levels of depressive symptoms than the other groups. They also reported higher levels of interpersonal problems among depressed Hawaiians, compared to nondepressed Hawaiians. The researchers discussed their findings in light of the importance of "group harmony and the [importance of] extended family" (p. 42).

National and Ethnic Variations in Symptom Presentation

"Culture influences the experience of symptoms, the idioms used to report them, [and] decisions about treatment" (Kleinman, 2004). Decades of research on mood disorders have shown that depression can be recognized fairy well in almost every culture, as long as researchers and practitioners are aware of the unique differences in how natives present their symptoms. Results from a WHO study conducted in Basle (Switzerland), Teheran (Iran), Montreal (Canada), and Tokyo and Nagasaki (Japan) in the early 1980s demonstrated significant similarities as well as differences in depressive symptom presentation (Sartorius et al., 1983). Overall the authors found that core depressive symptoms such as sad mood, anxiety, lack of energy, low self-worth, poor concentration, and loss of interest were reported by majority of participants from the various sites. However, feelings of guilt were more common in Basle and Montreal, while somatic complaints were more common in Teheran.

The focus on somatic complaints as a key symptom of mood disorders in nonwestern cultures has also been debated quite extensively. Differences in somatic complaints as key symptoms of mood disorders have been found mostly among Asian cultures (Kleinman, 1982, 2004; Yoo & Skovholt, 2001). As discussed in more detail later, Chang et al. (2005) demonstrated that *Shenjing shuairuo* was used to describe a broad range of symptoms, "including depressed mood, "vexatiousness" (*fan nao*), anxiety, pain and other somatic discomforts" (p. 213). The authors further suggested that the term *Shenjing shuairuo* may be more of an "idiom of distress particularly among individuals living in rural areas of China" (p. 213).

Whereas some researchers have argued that cross-national differences exist mainly because of how somatization is defined, others have linked the reported differences to variations between western biomedical and nonwestern traditional (or holistic) medical practices (Bhugra & Mastrogianni, 2004). The general consensus is that each major cultural group seems to have its own way of communicating about mood and emotional distress. While some Indians may use somatic idioms like "sinking heat," people from Dubai may describe their distress as "*jesmi metkasser* or broken body," and Nigerians may use an idiom which connotes "heaviness sensation in the head" (Bhugra & Mastrogianni, 2004, p. 16), and Zimbabweans may use a cultural metaphor like *kufungisisa* "thinking too much" to describe and/or explain their depression (Patel et al., 2001).

Other studies have demonstrated cross-cultural differences in coping with depression and psychological distress on the whole. Vandervoort (2001) compared coping strategies for sadness among Hawaiian college students of varying cultural backgrounds. She found that compared with multiethnic individuals, Asians and Europeans were less likely to use "confrontive and positive reappraisal coping strategies." She explained her results in terms of Hawaiian cultural beliefs of optimism and expectation that each negative experience is eventually offset by a positive one. Vandervoort's study is unique in that it is one of few inquiries into persons with multiethnic backgrounds.

This is a group that continues to be on the rise and need to be included in cross-ethnic studies.

Regardless of the continued debate about cultural variations in how symptoms of depression are presented, some facts remain important. It is vital that researchers and mental health providers be aware of cultural idioms or ways of communicating about emotional distress. Such awareness is key to correct diagnosis and treatment of all people. Also, though cultural differences have been emphasized in this chapter it is crucial that practitioners also recognize individual differences within a given ethnic or cultural group and not treat individuals in a stereotypical way because of their culture or ethnicity. Many studies have demonstrated that other demographic factors, including socioeconomic status and religion, also influence the types of symptoms expressed.

Factors Mediating Cross-Cultural Variations in Mood Disorders

Perception of Mental Illness

The stigma associated with mental illness goes beyond the affected individual to their families and caregivers. The illness influences a community's perception of the affected individual as well as the treatment options and decisions made by health care workers (Lancet, 2007). Sartorius and Schulze (2005) explain that stigmatization presents individuals with a vicious cycle which often starts with discrimination from the community and health care providers and results in low self-worth and an increased likelihood of relapse. Parker et al. (2001) describe the stigma of mental illness in Chinese culture where mental illness may be viewed as "evidence of weakness of character ... and cause family shame," which may result in families denying a relative's mental illness (p. 862).

In the US various ethnic groups have been reported to possess varying attitudes and beliefs about depression. For instance, Asian Americans are more likely to experience stigma associated with seeking treatment for mental illness in general (Fogel & Ford, 2005). Similarly, according to a National Mental Health Association survey, approximately 63 percent of African Americans believe that depression is a "personal weakness," compared to the overall survey average of 54 percent. Furthermore only 31 percent of African Americans sampled believed depression was a health problem and approximately 25 percent or less recognized common symptoms of depression (National Mental Health Association, 1996).

Studies that have investigated the reasons for variations in levels of depression across cultural groups have identified three main factors. These include cultural depictions of one self, perceptions about mind–body relations, and expressions and regulations of one's emotions (Tsai & Chentsova-Dutton, 2002). For example, Kanazawa et al. (2007) describe Asian vs. American cultural differences in the presentation of depressive symptoms in terms of "internal disturbances"

among Americans in the dominant group, compared to "interpersonal disturbances" in Asian sub-groups mainly because of an emphasis on autonomy and
self-sufficiency among the former group and interdependence and collective
connectedness among the latter group.

Treatment Intervention and Provider-Related Issues

Individuals suffering from mood disorders may describe their symptoms in a
way that may be different from their health provider, especially where the two
are from different cultural back grounds (Cohen et al., 2005). Commenting
on rates of depression among the Chinese, Parker et al. (2001) highlight a
possible interplay between a tendency for Chinese to minimize their experience
of depression and the likelihood for western cultures to overemphasize aspects
of human experience which may be considered normal in certain cultural
groups. This interplay may suggest that conditions that may be viewed by the
mental health provider as atypical and in need for psychological help may be
perceived by natives as a normal (but challenging) part of life that needs to
be dealt with according to their own norms and traditions.

It has been well documented that individuals from minority groups are less
likely to receive correct diagnosis for depression and hence less likely to be
referred for appropriate treatment by their healthcare providers (Bhui, Bhugra,
Goldberg, Dunn, & Desai, 2001; Sirey, Meyers, Bruce, Alexopoulos, Perlick, &
Raue, 1999). A review of studies suggest that African Americans are more
likely to be admitted to inpatient care, to be committed involuntarily, and to be
referred for medication only or to the emergency room when they seek outpatient care (Spector, 2001; Strakowski, Lonczak, Sax, et al., 1995). The general
finding of ethnic variations in healthcare services may be related to records
indicating that African Americans are less likely to accept psychotherapy or
antidepressant medication as an acceptable form of treatment for depression
compared to Hispanics and non-Hispanic whites (Cooper, Gonzales, Gallo,
et al., 2003). In fact data from the National Comorbidity Survey (Kessler,
McGonagle, Zhao, Nelson, Hughes, Eshelman, et al., 1994) showed that only
15.6 percent of the African Americans who met criteria for mood disorders
sought help from a mental health specialist (e.g., psychologist, psychiatrist, or
social worker), and 28.7 percent consulted with any provider (e.g., general
physician, priest or rabbi, spiritual herbalist).

In the survey on attitudes and beliefs discussed in the previous section, investigators reported that close to 30 percent of African Americans said they would
"handle it" (depression) themselves if they were depressed and a significant
67 percent and more believed that prayer and faith alone will successfully treat
depression "almost all of the time" or "some of the time." Another interesting
finding was that only one-third of the African-American samples indicated that
they would take medication for depression if prescribed by a doctor, compared
to 69 percent of the general population of respondents (National Mental
Health Association, 1996).

Table 9.1 Interventions geared towards reducing disparities in the outcome of depression

Level	Factors to be considered
System	Low socioeconomic status
	Lack of resources to pay for health cost
	Lack of trained mental health professionals
Community	Negative attitudes and perceptions about mental illness
	Stigma attached to health seeking behaviors
	Availability of social support
Provider	Misdiagnosis or lack of recognition of depression
	Poor communication – appropriate use of open- and closed-ended interview questions
	Lack of trust, due to history of race-discordant relationships
Person	Symptom expression and presentation
	Personal beliefs about the etiology of depressive symptoms
	Personal experiences with health providers

Source: Abstracted from Van Voorhees et al., 2007.

Beyond the negative perceptions about treatment among ethnic minority individuals affected by mood disorders, other provider-related factors come to play. Misdiagnosis is one of these factors. It is common knowledge that individuals suffering from bipolar disorders are often diagnosed with major depression in the initial phase of their treatment, but of even more concern are reports that African Americans with bipolar are often diagnosed more so with schizophrenia than the dominant group (Jones & Gray, 1986). It is noteworthy mentioning that misdiagnosis of bipolar disorders is common among other dominant and minority ethnic groups as well (Adebimpe, 1994). Information provided in this section so far is best summarized by the points in Table 9.1.

Another basic but important factor is the disproportionately small numbers of culturally different (or ethnic minority) mental health providers. A report on resources for mental health, based on the World Bank's income groups, indicated extremely low numbers of psychologist and psychiatrists in low income nations (0.04 and 0.1 per 100,000 respectively), compared with 1.8 and 2.7 per 100,000 people in upper-middle nations, and 11.0 and 9.2 per 100,000 people in high income nations (Saxena et al., 2006). Similarly, in the US the Surgeon General's report on mental health indicated proportions of African-American health care givers as follows: 2 percent of all psychiatrists, 2 percent of all psychologists, and 4 percent of social workers. These proportions are even lower for Hispanics, with rates of 29 per 100,000 compared with 175 per 100,000 for non-Hispanic whites (US Surgeon General, 1999). These strikingly low numbers of mental health providers from low income nations and ethnic minority groups pose a problem to the development of effective comprehensive treatment modalities for a significant proportion of the world's population.

Implications for Researchers and Practitioners

Reports from the WHO indicate that although mood disorders can be reliably diagnosed and treated, only a small proportion of suffers receive effective treatment. For instance, estimates suggest that overall less than 25 percent of people suffering from depression have access to effective treatment (WHO, 2007). Other studies have documented that depression is "under-recognized and under-treated throughout the world," with average detection rates of about 50 percent among primary care physicians (for a review, see Bhugra & Mastrogianni, 2004). It has been argued that continued use of diagnostic criteria developed and validated using western samples may lead to misdiagnosis and under-diagnosis of ethnic minorities and nonwestern individuals. Sandhu (1997) summarized this reality in commenting on Asian Americans and Pacific Islanders by saying "there are wide cultural differences in emotional scripts, social bonding practices, and psychological mechanisms to defend against intrapsychic and interpsychic threats among Asian and mainstream American cultures" (p. 14).

Mental health providers are encouraged to go beyond merely cataloging symptoms to educating themselves about their meaning. Tomlinson et al. (2007) and Patel et al. (2001) both point out that although individuals from sub-Saharan Africa may have a tendency to offer somatic (mostly headaches and fatigue), interpersonal- and spiritual-related complaint in their initial presentation of depression, further inquiry on the part of the clinician often yields more emotional and cognitive descriptions. Other examples are from investigations of refugees and migrant populations in New Zealand who did not benefit from common western forms of treatment for depression, and suggest that conceptualizing conditions in terms of demoralization may be more useful for successful intervention, since they did not fit neatly into any of the *DSM–IV* categories (Briggs & Macleod, 2006). The authors define demoralization as "a change in morale spanning a spectrum of mental attitudes from disheartenment (mild loss of confidence) through despondency (starting to give up) and despair (losing hope) to demoralization (having given up)," (p. 513) and argue that it is a different syndrome from major depression as conceptualized in western cultures. Likewise, based on Kanazawa et al.'s (2007) study on depressive symptoms among Hawaiian samples and Patel et al.'s study of Zimbabwean samples, it is fair to caution mental health providers about the significance of interpersonal relationships, the extended family, and collective connectedness among certain cultures who have been traditionally described as collective.

Furthermore, the disproportionately low numbers of qualified mental health providers needs to be seriously addressed. However, given the reality and time involved in increasing numbers of culturally different psychologists, psychiatrists, and other mental health providers, one alternative is to ensure that research published meet criterion for true generalization to all people groups. This could be addressed by adopting some changes that the American Psychological Association has developed to help increase the numbers of ethnic minority peer-reviewers for APA journals (Carpenter, 2001). Inclusion of culturally diverse editors and peer reviewers offers opportunity for reviewers to point out certain issues that may not necessarily be recognized by reviewers from the dominant group, which could further improve the quality and generalizability.

Another point is that research on cross-cultural differences in mood disorders (and other types of mental illness) ought to be interpreted with caution (Patten, 2003). Most of the studies cited in this chapter present cross-national comparisons as almost with the assumption that national samples are homogeneous and therefore representative, but they may not be. Parker et al. (2001) make this argument using the case of Chinese, who being the world's most populous nation, consists of at least 55 ethnic groups and also includes populations living outside the mainland such as Taiwan and Hong Kong who have historically been more exposed to western cultures. However, the argument against assumed homogeneity should be balanced with the fact that mood disorders still remain one of the topmost contributors to the burden of disease in mainland China. Similar arguments could be made for other nonwestern nations and regions, especially those with much stigma attached to mental illness. Additionally, most of the cross-national studies have focused on semantic and technical equivalence and neglected other forms of equivalence (i.e., content, criterion, and conceptual) that have been identified to be important for developing assessment instruments for cross-cultural research (Flaherty et al., 1988).

Summary and Conclusions

The information reviewed in this chapter confirms that mood disorders exist worldwide, are often presented in culturally-relevant ways, and need to be treated effectively to reduce the global burden of disease. In dealing with mood disorders, we are faced with several challenges, including lack of trained providers, under-recognition and misdiagnosis, lack of resources, and serious stigma associated with mental illness in general. The following points are important:

1. The impact of acculturation, distress, and dysfunction from acculturative stress should be assessed,
2. Families and significant people in the lives of the individual affected by mood disorder should be included in the initial conceptualization and treatment planning,
3. The mental health provider's awareness and understanding of cultural idioms or ways of communicating about emotional distress is vital for correct diagnosis and treatment of people from diverse cultural backgrounds,
4. Although cultural differences have been emphasized in this chapter it is crucial that practitioners also recognize individual differences within a given ethnic or cultural group and not treat individuals in a stereotypical way because of their culture or ethnicity.

5. Active promotion of mental health education and other initiatives as has been undertaken by major institutions such as American Psychological Association, American Psychiatric Association, the World Health Organization, and the World Psychiatric Association.

REFERENCES

Adepimbe, V. R. (1994). Race, racism, and epidemiological surveys. *Hospital and Community Psychiatry, 51,* 8–19.

Adewuya, A. O., Ola, B. A., & Aloba, O. O. (2007). Prevalence of major depressive disorders and a validation of the Beck Depression Inventory among Nigerian adolescents. *European Child and Adolescent Psychiatry, 16*(5), 287–292.

American Psychiatric Association (2000). *Diagnostic and statistical manual,* 4th ed., *Text revised (DSM–IV–TR),* Washington, DC: American Psychiatric Association.

Arrindell, W. A., Steptoe, A., & Wardle, J. (2003). Higher levels of state depression in masculine than in feminine nations. *Behaviour Research and Therapy, 41,* 809–817.

Ayuso-Mateos, J. L., Vazquez-Barquero, J. L., Dowrick, C., et al. (2001). Depressive disorders in Europe: prevalence figures from the ODIN study. *British Journal of Psychiatry, 179,* 308–316.

Biji, R. V., Graaf, R., Hiripi, E., et al. (2003). The prevalence of treated and untreated mental disorders in five countries. *Health Affairs, 22*(3), 122–133.

Bhugra, D., & Mastrogianni, A. (2004). Globalisation and mental disorders: Overview with relation to depression. *British Journal of Psychiatry, 184,* 10–20.

Bhui, K., Bhugra, D., Goldberg, D., Dunn, G., & Desai. M. (2001). Cultural influences on the prevalence of common mental disorder, general practitioners' assessments and health-seeking among Punjabi and English people visiting their general practitioner. *Psychological Medicine, 31*(5), 815–825.

Blue, I., Ducci, M. E., Jaswal, S., Ludermir, A., & Harphan, T. (1995). The mental health of low income urban women. In T. Harpham & I. Blue (Eds.), *Urbanisation and mental health in developing countries* (pp. 75–102). Aldershot, UK: Avebury.

Briggs, L., & Macleod, A. D. (2006). Demoralisation – a useful conceptualization of non-specific psychological distress among refugees attending mental health services. *International Journal of Social Psychiatry, 52*(6), 512–524.

Carpenter, S. (2001). Boosting the number of ethnic minority reviewers for APA journals. *APA Monitor, 32*(8).

Chang, D. F., Myers, H. F., Yeung, A., et al. (2005). Shenjing shuairuo and the *DSM–IV*: Diagnosis, distress, and disability in a Chinese primary care setting. *Transcultural Psychiatry, 42*(2), 204–218.

Chinese Psychiatric Society (2001). *The Chinese classification of mental disorders* (3rd ed. (CCMD-3)). Shandong, China: Shandong Publishing House of Science and Technology (in Chinese).

Cohen, C. I., Magai, C., Yaffee, R., & Walcott-Brown, R. (2005). Comparison of users and non-users of mental health services among depressed, older, urban African Americans. American *Journal of Geriatric Psychiatry, 13*(7), 545–553.

Cooper, L. A., Gonzales, J. J., Gallo, J. J., et al. (2003). The acceptability of treatment for depression among African-American, Hispanic, and white primary care patients. *Medical Care, 41*(4), 479–489.

Dunlop, D. D, Song, J., Lyons, J. S., Manheim, L. M., & Chang, R. W. (2003). Racial/ethnic differences in rates of depression among preretirement adults. *American Journal of Public Health, 93*(11), 1945–1952.

Flaherty, J. A., Gavira, M., Pathak, D., et al. (1988). Developing instruments for cross-cultural psychiatric research. *Journal of Nervous and Mental Disorders, 176,* 257–263.

Fogel, J., & Ford, D. E. (2005). Stigma beliefs of Asian Americans with depression in an Internet sample. *Canadian Journal of Psychiatry, 50*(8), 470–478.

Goldberg, D. P., & Lecrubier, Y. (1995). Form and frequency of mental disorders across centres. In T. B. Ustun & N. Sartorius (Eds.), *Mental illness in general health care: An international study* (pp. 323–334), Chichester: John Wiley & Sons, Ltd.

Gorman, L. L., O'Hara, M. W., Figueiredo, B., et al. (2004). Adaptation of the structured clinical interview for *DSM–IV* disorders for assessing depression in women during pregnancy and post-partum across countries and cultures. *British Journal of Psychiatry, 184* (suppl. 46), s17–s23.

Hibbeln, J. R. (1998). Fish consumption and major depression (letter). *Lancet, 315,* 1213.

Hibbeln, J. R., & Salem, N. (1995). Dietary polyunsaturated fatty acids and depression: when cholesterol does not satisfy. *American Journal of Nutrition, 62,* 1–9.

Hofstede, G. (2000). Masculine and feminine cultures. In A. E. Kazdin (Ed.), *Encyclopedia of psychology,* vol. 5, Washington, DC: American Psychological Association.

Jackson-Triche, M. E., Sullivan, G., Wells, K., Rogers, W., Camp, P., & Mazel, R. (2000). Depression and health related quality in ethnic minorities seeking care in general settings. *Journal of Affective Disorders, 58,* 89–97.

Jones, B. E., & Gray, B. A. (1986). Problems in diagnosing schizophrenia and affective disorders among blacks. *Hospital & Community Psychiatry, 37,* 61–65.

Kanazawa, A., White, P. M., & Hampson, S. E. (2007). Ethnic variation in depressive symptoms in a community sample in Hawaii. *Cultural Diversity and Ethnic Minority Psychology, 13*(1), 35–44.

Kessler, R. C., McGonagle, K. A., Zhao, S., Nelson, C. B., Hughes, M., & Eshelman, S., et al. (1994). Lifetime and 12-month prevalence of *DSM–III–R* psychiatric disorders in the United States. Results from the National Comorbidity Survey. *Archives of General Psychiatry, 51,* 8–19.

Kessler, R. C., Nelson, C. B., McGonagle, K. A., Liu, J., Swartz, M., & Blazer, D. G. (1996). Comorbidity of *DSM–III* R major depressive disorder in the general population: Results from the US National Comorbidity Survey. *British Journal of Psychiatry Suppl., 30,* 17–30.

Kleinman, A. (1982). Neurasthenia and depression: A study of somatization and culture in China. *Culture, Medicine and Psychiatry, 6*(2), 117–190.

Kleinman, A. (2004). Culture and depression. *New England Journal of Medicine, 351*(10), 951–953.

Koehn, P. (2006). Globalization, migration health, and educational preparation for transnational medical encounters. *Global Health, 2*(2).

Lancet (2007). Stigma and mental health. *The Lancet.* Online publication. DOI: 10.1016/S0140-6736(07)61245-8. (http://www.thelancet.com).

Lau, A. (2006). Making the case for selective and directed cultural adaptations of evidence-based treatments: Examples from parent training. *Clinical Psychology: Science and Practice, 13*(4), 295–310.

Lee, S., & Wong, C. (1995). Rethinking neurasthenia: the illness concepts of shenjing shuairuo among Chinese undergraduates in Hong Kong. Culture. *Medicine, and Psychiatry, 19*(1), 91–111.

Mogga, S., Prince, M., Alem, A., et al. (2006). Outcome of major depression in Ethiopia, *British Journal of Psychiatry, 189*, 241–246.

Nakku, J. E., Nakasi, G., & Mirembe, F. (2006). Postpartum depression at six weeks in primary health care: Prevalence and associated factors. *African Health Sciences, 6*(4), 207–214.

National Mental Health Association (1996). *American attitudes about clinical depression and its treatment.* March 27, 1996.

NIMH (2007). *Depression.* [http://www.nimh.nih.gov/health/publications/depression/] Retrieved December 27, 2007.

Noaghiul, S., & Hibbeln, J. R. (2003). Cross-national comparisons of seafood consumption and rates of bipolar disorders. *American Journal of Psychiatry, 160*(12), 2222–2227.

Parker, G., Gladstone, G., & Chee, K. T. (2001). Depression in the planet's largest ethnic group: The Chinese. *American Journal of Psychiatry, 158*(6), 857–864.

Patel, V. Anas, M., Broadhead, J., Todd, C., & Reeler, A. (2001). Depression in developing countries: Lessons from Zimbabwe – education and debate. *British Medical Journal, 322*, 482–484.

Patten, S. B. (2003). International differences in major depression prevalence: what do they mean? *Journal of Clinical Epidemiology, 56*, 711–716.

Riolo, S. A., Nguyen, T. A., Greden, J. F., & King, C. A. (2005). Prevalence of depression by race/ethnicity: findings from the National Health and Nutrition Examination Survey III. *American Journal of Public Health, 95*(6), 998–1000.

Sandhu, D. S. (1997). Psychocultural profiles of Asian and Pacific Islander Americans: Implications for counseling and psychotherapy. *Journal of Multicultural Counseling and Development, 25*, 7–22.

Sartorius, N., Davidson, H., Ernberg, G., et al. (1983). *Depressive disorders in different cultures.* Geneva: WHO.

Sartorius, N., & Schulze, H. (2005). *Reducing the stigma of mental illness.* Cambridge: Cambridge University Press.

Saxena, S., Sharan, P., Garrido, M., & Saraceno, B. (2006). World Health Organization's mental health atlas 2005: Implications for policy development. *World Psychiatry, 53*(3), 179–184.

Shaw, C. M., Creed, F., Tomenson, B., Riste, L., & Cruickshank J. K. (1999). Prevalence of anxiety and depressive illness and help seeking behavior in African Caribbeans and white Europeans: two phase general population survey, *British Medical Journal, 318*, 302–306.

Simon, G. E., Goldberg, D. P., Von Korff, M., & Ustun, T. B. (2002). Understanding cross-national differences in depression prevalence. *Psychological Medicine, 32*, 585–594.

Sirey, J. A., Meyers, B. S., Bruce, M. L., Alexopoulos, G. S., Perlick, D. A., & Raue, P. (1999). Predictors of antidepressant prescription and early use among depressed outpatients. *American Journal of Psychiatry, 156*(5), 690–696.

Spector, R. (2001). Is there racial bias in clinicians' perceptions of the dangerousness of psychiatric patients? A review of the literature. *Journal of Mental Health, 10*(1), 5–15.

Stoll, A. L., Severus, W. E., Freeman, M. P., et al. (1999). Omega-3 fatty acids in bipolar disorder: a preliminary double-blind, placebo controlled trial. *Archives of General Psychiatry, 56*, 407–412.

Strakowski, S. M., Lonczak, H. S., Sax, K. W., et al. (1995). The effects of race on diagnosis and disposition from a psychiatric emergency service. *Journal of Clinical Psychiatry 56*(3), 101–107.

Su, K. P., Shen, W. W., & Huang, S. Y. (2000). Are omega-3 fatty acids beneficial in depression but not mania? *Archives of General Psychiatry, 57*, 518–530.

Tomlinson, M., Swartz, L., Kruger, L. M., & Gureje, O. (2007). Manifestations of affective disturbance in sub-Saharan Africa: Key themes. *Journal of Affective Disorders, 102*(1–3), 191–198.

Tsai, J. L., & Chentsova-Dutton, Y. (2002). Understanding depression across cultures. In I. H. Gotlib & C. L. Hammen (Eds.), *Handbook of depression* (pp. 467–491). New York: Guilford Press.

US Surgeon General (1999). *Mental health: Culture, race, and ethnicity.* (http://www.surgeongeneral.gov).

Ustun, T. B., Ayuso-Mateos, J. L., Chatterji, S., Mathers, C., & Murray, C. J. L. (2004). Global burden of depression in the year 2000. *British Journal of Psychiatry, 184*, 386–392.

Van Voorhees, B. W., Walter, A. E., Prochaska, M., & Quinn, M. T. (2007). Reducing health disparities in depressive disorders outcomes between non-Hispanic whites and ethnic minorities: A call for pragmatic strategies over the life course. *Medical Care Research and Review, 64*, 157S–194S.

Vandervoort, D. J. (2001). Cross-national differences in coping with sadness. *Current Psychology, 20*(2), 147–153.

Weissman, M. M., Bland, R. C., Canino, G. J., et al. (1996). Cross-national epidemiology of major depression and bipolar disorder. *JAMA, 276*(4), 293–299.

World Health Organization (2007). *Depression* (http://www.who.int/mental_health/management/depression/definition/) Retrieved December 27, 2007.

World Mental Health Survey Consortium (2004). Prevalence, severity, and unmet need for treatment of mental disorders in the World Health Organization world mental health surveys. *JAMA, 291*(21), 2581–2590.

Yoo, S-K., & Skovholt, T. M. (2001). Cross-cultural examination of depression expression and help-seeking behavior: A comparative study of American and Korean college students. *Journal of College Counseling, 4*, 10–19.

10

Culture and Anxiety Disorders

Simon A. Rego

What is anxiety? Is it an experience common to all people? At what point does anxiety become a disorder? Are the anxiety disorders consistent across cultures? The aim of this chapter is to focus on the role that culture plays on the anxiety disorders in different societies.[1] The major focus will be on comparisons of prevalence rates and symptom presentations, as Psychotherapy was addressed in Chapter 12. While much of this chapter focuses on research conducted with adults, growing evidence suggests that there is a great deal of overlap in the way that anxiety manifests itself in children and adults (cf. Silverman, 1993).

This chapter is divided into sections, each corresponding to one of the major *DSM–IV–TR* anxiety disorders (Panic Disorder and Agoraphobia, Specific Phobia, Social Anxiety Disorder, Obsessive-Compulsive Disorder, and GAD).[2] Within each section, definitions of the disorder will be provided, as well as basic descriptions of symptoms that are commonly reported. Each section will also contain a summary of the most recently available cross-cultural research, with an emphasis placed on the latest epidemiological findings – both within the United States and abroad.[3] Finally, where appropriate, the sections will include information on "culture-bound syndromes" which are defined as: recurrent, locality-specific patterns of aberrant behavior and troubling experience that may or may not be linked to a particular *DSM–IV* diagnostic category (APA, 2000).

It should be noted, however, that scholars have struggled with the concept of culture-bound syndromes (Levine & Gaw, 1995) since the inception of the term. Levine and Gaw (1995) point out that while most authors would agree

---

[1]   This chapter is being presented as an extension of the excellent work on culture and anxiety already done by Good and Kleinman (1985) and Friedman (1997).

[2]   Posttraumatic Stress Disorder (PTSD) has been intentionally omitted, as this disorder will be covered in detail in the following chapter.

[3]   A summary of results from some of the studies reviewed in this chapter is provided in Table 10.1.

that the term "culture-bound syndrome" was intended to describe forms of otherwise common mental illness that are rendered unusual because of the influence of culture, the term has become somewhat of an anachronism. Levine and Gaw (1995) argue that the word "syndrome" implies specific disease entities, not illnesses of attribution of idioms of distress and that the word "bound" implies that the entities described are restricted to a single culture. Levine and Gaw (1995) state that close examination reveals that many of the so-called "culture-bound" syndromes are in fact found in multiple cultures that have some common symptoms only that they are "nonwestern."

Levine and Gaw (1995) make several suggestions as to how we can understand (and classify) these phenomena in such a way that highlights their uniqueness but does not dismiss them as too rare and exotic to warrant attention. These suggestions include recognizing that the culture-bound syndromes are a heterogeneous group of conditions and acknowledging that while the concepts represented may be difficult for the average western clinician to recognize, in their respective cultures, they are neither rare nor unusual. Finally, Levine and Gaw (1995) recommend that those culture-bound syndromes that are "true" syndromes be classified together with their western counterparts. As such, these suggestions have been considered in the development of this chapter.

While the concept of anxiety has been recognized as an important and universal aspect of human existence since the late 1800s, before the publication of the *Diagnostic and Statistical Manual*, 3rd ed. (*DSM–III*; APA, 1980) widespread disagreements existed about how anxiety was best defined. With the operationalization of anxiety disorders in *DSM–III*, however, studies on anxiety and the anxiety disorders increased dramatically and much has now been learned about the nature of anxiety (cf. Barlow, 2002; Beck, Emery, & Greenberg, 1985; Tuma & Maser, 1985). For example, we know that the best-estimate one-year prevalence of any anxiety disorder is around 16.4 percent, making anxiety disorders more prevalent than any other class of disorder in the United States, and representing the single largest mental health problem in the country (Barlow, 2002). And while the prevalence rates of some anxiety disorders (e.g., specific phobias) may diminish with age, the course tends to be chronic and for many, may remain present in a less severe form even if successfully treated (Barlow, 2002). We know that this leads to substantial direct and indirect costs to individuals and health care systems (cf. Greenberg et al., 1999) increased risk of other disorders (e.g., alcohol abuse – see Swendson et al., 1998) and even heightened risk of suicide (Allgulander, 1994).

Despite all of the progress that has been made in the field of anxiety disorder research, relatively little consideration has been given to the way in which anxiety and the anxiety disorders are influenced by culture. As noted by Guarnaccia (1997), while the World Health Organization has conducted major studies on schizophrenia and depression, it has yet to examine the nature of anxiety – other than indirectly in their study of psychopathology in primary care (cf. Gureje et al., 1998). This is somewhat surprising, given the fact that most researchers agree that anxiety and disorders of anxiety are universally present in human societies (Good & Kleinman, 1985) and occur at relatively similar prevalence rates (Barlow, 2002). It is also surprising given that most researchers also agree that the expression of emotion is culturally influenced, and that cultural inter-pretations of anxiety can affect its course, presentation, and ideal methods for treating it (Barlow, 2002). Fortunately, it appears as if a shift is beginning to occur, and we are now seeing an increasing amount of research examining the role that culture plays on the expression of anxiety. A variety of factors may be responsible for this shift, including an increasing trend towards globalization, improvements in technology, communications and access to information, and increasing collaboration between researchers in different countries. The primary factor responsible for this surge in interest in the United States, however, likely came from an entirely different and yet simple factor: need.

Major shifts are occurring in the demographics within the United States. In August 2007, the Associated Press released an article stating that "Whites are now in the minority in nearly one in 10 U.S. counties." And by 2050, most forecasters have suggested that more than half of the population in the United States will be of Hispanic, African-American, Asian, or Native American descent (Friedman, 1997). While this shift will have a major impact on the "culture" of the United States, researchers and clinicians working in health care will also have to adjust the current diagnostic and treatment systems in order to account for the impact of culture. In other words, in order to assess a person's condition, one must not only examine the situation or trigger, physiological symptoms, cognitions, and behaviors, but also account for the person's culture – as the meaningful forms through which distress is articulated and constituted as social reality, can vary in significant ways across cultures and cultural groups (Good & Kleinman, 1985). As noted by Kirmayer (2001), culture-specific symptoms may lead to under recognition or misidentification of psychological distress.

Panic Disorder (PD) and Agoraphobia

The essential feature of PD is the presence of recurrent, unexpected panic attacks followed by at least one month of concern about experiencing additional attacks, worry about the implications of the attack or its consequences, or making a significant change in behavior related to the attacks (APA, 2000). A panic attack consists of a sudden, discrete period of intense fear or discom-fort, that reaches its peak within approximately 10 minutes and is accompanied by at least four of the following 13 symptoms: palpitations, pounding or racing heart, sweating, trembling or shaking, shortness of breath or smothering sensa-tions, choking sensations, chest pain, pressure, or discomfort, nausea or abdominal distress, feeling dizzy, unsteady, lightheaded or faint, feelings of derealization or depersonalization, chills or hot flushes, numbness or tingling, and/or fears of losing control, going crazy, or dying. It should be noted that for a diagnosis of PD, the panic attacks cannot be due to the direct physiologi-cal effects of a substance or a general medical condition and cannot be better accounted for by another mental disorder. It should also be noted that, given the fact that panic attacks can occur across anxiety disorders, a panic attack per se is not a codable disorder.

The essential feature of agoraphobia is the presence of intense anxiety in places or situations from which escape might be difficult (or embarrassing) or in which help might not be available in the event one was to experience a panic attack (or panic-like symptoms). The situations must be either avoided or else endured with intense anxiety and fear, and often require the presence of a companion to be faced. In the most severe cases of agoraphobia, the person may become housebound. As with PD, the anxiety and/or phobic avoidance cannot be better accounted for by another mental disorder, and as with panic attacks, agoraphobia alone is not a codable disorder.

Agoraphobia is being included in this section because in the United States the prevalence of agoraphobia in clinical settings has been estimated to be at 95 percent in individuals also diagnosed with PD. It should be emphasized, however, that when examining the prevalence of agoraphobia in other countries, some cultural groups prescribe much more restricted public roles for certain members of the group – particularly women – than is common in American society (Guarnaccia, 1997). For example, Guarnaccia (1997) cites a study conducted by Mohamed Fakhr El-Islam in Qatar that found only 8 percent of Qatari women with phobias reported agoraphobia (cf. Kirmayer et al., 1995). In addition, he notes "being bound to the home, which is a sign of severe agoraphobia in the West, is a sign of virtue in a Muslim housewife" (El-Islam, as cited in Kirmayer et al., 1995).

The *DSM–IV–TR* states that in the United States, lifetime prevalence rates of PD in community samples have been reported to be as high as 3.5 percent, with one-year prevalence rates between 0.5 percent and 1.5 percent (APA, 2000). Good and Kleinman (1985) note that two, population-based studies (ECA, NCS) did not find any differences in PD prevalence among African Americans, Hispanics, and Whites (Eaton et al., 1991; Horwath, Johnson, & Hornig, 1993). In addition, they conclude that based on data from community studies, there is a remarkable level of consistency in the prevalence of PD across sites – from Connecticut to Puerto Rico (Horwath & Weissman, 1997). Horwath and Weissman (1997), however, have found that there is some indication of an age-by-race interaction effect in PD prevalence in the United States. According to these authors, it appears that older Whites tend to have the lowest lifetime prevalence rates of PD, but with Hispanic females the lifetime prevalence rates tend to increase with age.

A few points should also be made with regard to the data on African Americans with PD. First, as noted by Smith, Friedman, and Nevid (1999), African Americans have been largely underrepresented in treatment outcome studies, tend to have later onset of the disorder, use different coping strategies (e.g., religiosity) relative to Whites, and show less self-blame. Second, while Friedman, Paradis, and Hatch (1994) in general found similar characteristic panic symptoms among African Americans and Whites with anxiety, they note that African Americans had more health care utilization and reported more life stress. Other researchers have reported that higher rates of fears of dying exist among African Americans and that African-American patients also frequently have higher rates of hypertension.

Finally, African-American patients with PD appear to have a higher incidence of sleep paralysis – a condition experienced between sleep and waking that includes a surge of terror accompanied by the inability to move, occasionally with vivid hallucinations. In fact, Paradis and Friedman (2005) found that recurrent sleep paralysis was reported by 59 percent of African Americans with PD – versus only 7 percent of Whites. In accordance with Friedman, Paradis, and Hatch (1994), they found that significantly more early life stressors were reported by African Americans than Whites and concluded that higher levels of psychosocial stressors, including poverty, racism and acculturation, may contribute to the higher rates of sleep paralysis experienced by African Americans.

If we extend our lens outside of the United States, we find that lifetime rates for PD appear to show good agreement in prevalence across countries (Friedman, 1997). For example, Nazemi et al. (2003) conducted a study on panic attacks in university students in Iran. Data were collected using Farsi translations of several empirically supported assessment measures commonly used in the United States (e.g., the Panic Attack Questionnaire, Beck Depression Inventory, etc.). They found that 38 percent of participants reported panic attacks in the past year and that 21 percent reported panic attacks in the month prior to assessment. They noted that men and those with unexpected panic reported greater panic severity and that women with panic attacks reported greater situational fear and avoidance. The authors concluded that their findings provide tentative support for cross-cultural similarity in panic phenomenology and the validity of *DSM (III–R,* in this case*)* PD criteria among university students in Iran.

Interestingly, the lone exception in the consistency of panic prevalence findings has been in Taiwan, where PD appears to occur at much lower rates (Friedman, 1997, citing Horwath and Weissman, 1995). While it is unclear why the rates of panic are lower in Taiwan, it should be noted that rates for most psychiatric disorders are low in Taiwan. Clearly, this is an area for further research.

When considering the role that culture plays on the expression of panic and anxiety, researchers have identified several culture-bound syndromes that appear to be similar to PD. For example, an experience known as *ataque de nervios* ("attack of nerves") has been identified in certain Hispanic cultures (particularly those from Caribbean and Latin America). While an *ataque* contains many of the symptoms found in a "classic" panic attack, it may also contain additional symptoms such as shouting uncontrollably, bursting into tears, cursing, falling to the ground, and memory loss following the attack (Barlow, 2002). An *ataque* generally appears to occur like a panic attack (e.g., under stressful circumstances) and is considered to be a culturally acceptable response to difficult circumstances (Guarnaccia, Rubio-Stipec, & Canino, 1989).

Liebowitz et al. (1994) concluded that *ataque de nervios* overlaps with PD but is a more inclusive construct and state that further study of its interrelation with other psychological disorders is needed.

Hinton (e.g., 2001a, 2001b, 2002) has also described several different syndromes among Khmer refugees that appear to resemble PD. For example, one syndrome, called *Kyol goeu* ("wind overload"), appears to be a fainting syndrome that in turn generates catastrophic cognitions about any autonomic symptoms the Khmer experience when they stand. Hinton (2001a) notes that, as in western patients with PD, the Khmer with *Kyol goeu* present with a set of danger-laden beliefs about the symptoms of autonomic arousal that in turn cause them to constantly scan their body – especially upon standing. And as is the case in western patients with PD, this belief and subsequent hypervigilance then generates, maintains, and produces panic attacks – thus contributing to the high rate of orthostatically induced panic attacks observed in this population.

The second syndrome found in the Khmer and described by Hinton (2001b) has been called "sore-neck" syndrome. In this case, the danger-laden beliefs focus on the neck, with sufferers of a sore neck fearing that wind and blood pressure may burst the vessels. Hinton (2001b) notes that during an acute panic episode, a Khmer may report many – if not all – of the following neck and head complaints: headache, blurry vision, a buzzing in the ear, and dizziness. In addition, he notes that while in the midst of a sore-neck attack, the Khmer frequently report experiencing palpitations and other symptoms of autonomic arousal, such as sweating, shortness of breath, and trembling (Hinton, 2001b). He notes that a sufferer of sore-neck episodes will often meet criteria for PD.

Finally, Hinton et al. (2002) describe the Khmer "weak heart" syndrome – which involves a fear of death from heart palpitations. Here, according to the Khmer conception, a person suffering from a "weak heart" will experience episodes of palpitations on slight provocation (e.g., triggered by orthostasis, anger, a noise, worry, an odor, exercise) and will fear that he or she will run the risk of dying of a heart attack during these periods of palpitations (Hinton et al., 2002). The sufferer typically also has other symptoms that he or she attributes to the alleged cardiac dysfunction, including: fatigue, shortness of breath, and orthostatic dizziness. Hinton et al. (2002) notes that as in "sore-neck" syndrome, this syndrome overlaps considerably with the western illnesses that feature panic attacks – in particular posttraumatic stress disorder and PD.

Finally, in an interesting commentary that connects the culture-bound syndrome work and that of western conceptualization of panic, Hsia and Barlow (2001) compared the Khmer concept of wind overload with the Puerto Rican concept of ataque de nervios. They concluded that the physiological symptoms and cognitions in the syndromes were similar and suggested that these disorders may be fundamentally identical but have culturally mediated presentations. Thus, we have evidence concluding that the western concept of PD is similar to Khmer and Puerto-Rican syndromes of wind overload and *ataque de nervios*, and that the Khmer and Puerto-Rican concepts are also similar to one another.

Specific Phobia (SP)

The essential feature of SP is a marked and persistent fear of clearly discernible, circumscribed objects or situations (e.g., flying, heights, animals, injections, etc.) that is excessive and unreasonable and lasts at least six months (APA, 2000). Exposure to the phobic stimulus must almost always provoke anxiety – which may escalate into panic attack (see the section above on Panic for the *DSM–IV–TR* description of a panic attack). The fear must be recognized as excessive or unreasonable and the person must either avoid the phobic situation or endure it with intense anxiety or distress. The avoidance, anxious anticipation, or distress in the feared situation must either interfere significantly with the person's normal routine, occupational/academic functioning or social activities/relationships or the person must have marked distress about having the phobia. The anxiety, panic attacks, or phobic avoidance associated with the specific object or situation cannot be better accounted for by another mental disorder.

According to the *DSM–IV*, in the United States phobias of objects or situations are quite common in the general population, but rarely result in sufficient impairment or distress to warrant a diagnosis. In community samples, current prevalence rates range from 4 percent to 8.8 percent and lifetime prevalence rates range from 7.2 percent to 11.3 percent. In terms of cultural differences within the United States, SPs appear to be more prevalent in African Americans and Hispanics than in Whites (APA, 2000), even after controlling for demographic and socioeconomic factors (Brown, Eaton & Sussman, 1990). This has led some researchers (e.g., Curtis et al., 1998) to conclude that being African-American or Hispanic is a risk factor for having a greater number of SPs. While prevalence rates may differ, no significant differences between groups in terms of content of phobias. For example, Neal, Lilly, and Zakis (1993) found that the content of fears among African Americans and Whites was similar.

Complicating the issue of the impact of culture on prevalence of SPs, however, is the level of acculturation in the individual. For example, a study by Karno et al. (1989), examined prevalence of phobias in different Hispanic and non-Hispanic groups and found that the prevalence of SPs was 7.8 percent among Mexican Americans who had been born in Mexico, 12.7 percent among Mexican Americans who had been born in the United States, and 6.8 percent among non-Hispanic Whites who had been born in the United States. Similarly, in a related study, Vega et al. (1998) found that recent Mexican immigrants were much less likely to have a SP than Mexican Americans who had lived in the United States for many years or who were born in the United States.

Further complicating the issue of the impact of culture on prevalence of SPs is the fact that researchers examining the prevalence and expression of SPs across countries have discovered differences in the prevalence of SPs. For example, Ingman, Ollendick, and Akande (1999) examined differences in prevalence of specific fears in children from Nigeria and Kenya. While Nigerian children reported higher fear ratings than children from Kenya, children from both countries had higher ratings than children from United States, Australia, and China. In addition, they found an interaction between culture and religion, in that Christian children living in the Nigeria and Kenya had higher levels of fear on certain factors than did Muslim children. Similarly, Chambers, Yeragani, and Keshavan (1986) studied the prevalence of SPs in adults living in India and the United Kingdom and found certain phobias (e.g., animals, the dark, and bad weather) were more than twice as prevalent in India as the United Kingdom. They also note that the pattern reversed for other phobias (e.g., agoraphobia and SAD).

Several studies have also examined the relationship between SPs and the emotion of disgust across cultures. For example, Davey et al. (1998) examined cultural factors in the fear structure of animal fears in people of western and Asian cultures from seven different countries. The researchers found that a core group of animals in the disgust-relevant category (e.g., spiders, mice) were similar across cultures. In addition, Olatunji, Sawchuk, de Jong, and Lohr (2006) looked at the structural relation between disgust sensitivity and blood-injection-injury (BII) fears, using American and Dutch data. They found that the hypothesized relation between "animal reminder" and "core" disgust sensitivity and BII fears yielded a good fit to both the American and Dutch samples, supporting the notion that disgust is a universal emotion that may become associated with stimuli in a consistent way across cultures.

More recently, a major study was conducted to examine phobic anxiety in 11 nations (Australia, East Germany, Great Britain, Greece, Guatemala, Hungary, Italy, Japan, Spain, Sweden, and Venezuela) and to determine the cross-national dimensional constancy of a model of self-assessed fears originally established in Dutch, British, and Canadian samples (Arrindell et al., 2003). The researchers administered the Fear Survey Schedule-III (FSS-III) to 5,491 students and found that a close correspondence was demonstrated across national samples. They noted that in an attempt to maximize sample diversity, students were recruited from universities situated in different regions of each country and in different major courses of study. They found that in each country, the corresponding scales were internally consistent, were intercorrelated at magnitudes comparable to those yielded in the original samples, and yielded the typical sex differences (higher scores for females) found in the original samples. They concluded that the organization of self-assessed fears is sufficiently similar across nations and that cross-national comparisons are feasible.

Numerous culture-bound syndromes that resemble SPs have also been identified in the literature. For example, two of several culturally bound syndromes found in the Chinese culture are called Koro and Pa-Leng/Pa-Feng. In Koro, patients present with acute pain and/or an overwhelming fear of genital retraction (males become convinced that the penis will suddenly withdraw into the abdomen; females believe that their nipples, breasts, labia or vulva will retract). The onset tends to be rapid, intense, and unexpected, and patients expect the consequences to be fatal. Studies on this syndrome cite factors such as illness, exposure to cold or excessive sexual intercourse as precursors to the disorder. Interestingly, as in disorders found in western culture, the identification of the syndrome has led to the creation of many devices intended to stop retraction – despite the fact that the fear typically subsides within a few hours and recurrences pass quickly if supports are available in community.

In Pa-Leng/Pa-Feng, patients report an excessive fear of the cold (Pa-Leng) and winds (Pa-Feng). This syndrome is said to be best understood in terms of yin and yang, with wind and cold both being yin phenomena, and therefore present a threat to a man's yang (positive/male energy). Patients believing that they have an excess of yin will then ruminate over further loss of body heat – which they believe can produce fatigue, impotence or death. As such, males presenting with this syndrome may compulsively dress in heavy or excessive clothing to keep out cold and wind – even on a hot day. They may also avoid wind or drafts and eat foods that are symbolically and calorically "hot" while avoiding foods that are "cold."

Social Anxiety Disorder (SAD)

The essential feature of SAD is a marked and persistent fear of social or performance situations in which the person is exposed to unfamiliar people or to possible scrutiny by others (APA, 2000). The person fears that he or she will act in a way (or show anxiety symptoms) that will be humiliating or embarrassing. Exposure to the feared situation must almost always provoke anxiety, which may take the form of a panic attack. The person must recognize that the fear is excessive or unreasonable, and the feared situations must either be avoided or else endured with intense anxiety or distress. The avoidance, anxious anticipation, or distress in the feared social or performance situation must interfere significantly with the person's normal routine, occupational or academic functioning, social activities or relationships, or the person must have marked distress about having the phobia. Another mental disorder, the direct effects of substance, or a general medical condition must not better account for the fear or avoidance. If the person's fears include most social situations, the specifier "Generalized" may be used.

According to the *DSM–IV–TR*, in the United States, lifetime prevalence rates of SAD in epidemiological and community samples ranges from 3 percent to 13 percent, with the variance in the prevalence rates likely being impacted by the threshold used to determine distress or impairment and the number of types of social situations surveyed. For example, in one study 20 percent of respondents reported excessive fear of public speaking and performance, but only 2 percent appeared to experience enough impairment or distress to warrant a diagnosis of SAD. In terms of cross-cultural comparisons within the United States, Ferrell, Beidel, and Turner (2004) examined the assessment and treatment of children with SAD, and found no differences in symptomatic presentation between African-American and White children. They also found that no significant differences based on race in terms of improvement from treatment.

At a global level, most researchers agree that SAD exists throughout the world, but some disagreement exists in the exact prevalence rates. For example, Iancu et al. (2006) state that SAD is rather rare in Eastern societies, and estimate its prevalence rate at only 0.5 percent in Eastern samples. As pointed out in the *DSM–IV–TR*, however, the clinical presentation and resulting impairment may differ across cultures, depending on social demands (APA, 2000). With this idea in mind, Heinrichs et al. (2006) examined cultural differences in perceived social norms and social anxiety using participants from eight countries. They found that personal and cultural norms showed somewhat different patterns in comparison between types of countries (individualistic/collectivistic), with collectivistic countries being more accepting toward socially reticent and withdrawn behaviors than individualistic countries. In contrast to this, however, they found no difference between individualistic and collectivistic countries on individuals' personal perspectives regarding socially withdrawn behavior.

As mentioned in the previous paragraph, Iancu et al. (2006) noted a difference in the prevalence of SAD in western and eastern societies and therefore decided to examine SAD prevalence in Israel (which they define as "an Asian state characterized by western culture" (p. 399)). They assessed for the prevalence of SAD in a nonclinical sample of Israeli adolescents (soldiers from the Israel Defense Forces) using empirically supported assessment measures and found that probable SAD was present in 4.5 percent of their sample. They also noted that subjects with probable SAD had a rate of comorbidity with SP symptoms of 44 percent. They concluded that their findings corroborate those from other studies in western countries – both regarding the high prevalence of SAD symptoms and its demographic and clinical correlates, as well as regarding the high overlap rate with SP symptoms.

Several culture-bound syndromes that resemble SAD have also been identified in the literature. Perhaps the most extensively studied syndrome is the Japanese syndrome called *taijin kyofusho* (TKS) – a fear that they will displease or embarrass others. TKS can be divided into four subtypes (Suzuki, Takei, Kawai, Minabe, & Mori, 2003) that vary depending on the content of the fear: (1) *sekimen-kyofu* (phobia of blushing), (2) *shubo-kyofu* (phobia of a deformed body), (3) *jikoshisen-kyofu* (phobia of eye-to-eye contact), and (4) *jikoshu-kyofu* (phobia of one's own foul body odor). In TKS, much like SAD, the person has a fear of being observed that results in an avoidance of social situations. In addition, the person may have a strong fear of looking people in the eye and a fear that some aspect of their personal presentation (e.g., odor, blushing, staring inappropriately) will appear reprehensible to others. Where TKS differs from SAD, however, is that in certain subtypes the concern is about doing something or presenting an appearance that will offend or embarrass others – as opposed to being afraid of the possibility of being scrutinized by others and embarrassing oneself (Kirmayer, 1991).

Is TKS really a culturally bound syndrome? Or is it simply a variation of SAD? Suzuki, Takei, Kawai, Minabe, and Mori (2003) argue that the notion that TKS is a culture-bound syndrome cannot be held, as *sekimen-kyofu* could reasonably be subsumed within the category of SAD (since the fear of blushing is a common symptom) and *shubo-kyofu* fulfills the criteria for body dysmorphic disorder in *DSM–IV*. In contrast to these findings, however, Tarumi, Ichimiya, Yamada, Umesue, and Kuroki (2004), examined Japanese university students who reported feeling tense or nervous in social or interpersonal interactions, and found that those who fit the diagnosis of the offensive subtype of TKS had relatively low scores on an empirically supported measure of SAD. Therefore, they concluded that the symptoms of some TKS sufferers do not fall within the SAD spectrum.

Nakamura (2006) investigated the similarity and difference between TKS and SAD based on *DSM* classification. Three evaluators conducted a *DSM–III–R* structured clinical interview (SCID Axis I and II, Japanese version) on outpatients at a hospital in Japan. They found that 65.8 percent of cases given a diagnosis of TKS were also given the diagnosis of SAD. In addition, they found that among a particular subtype of TKS cases (which they called "neurotic"), the percentage was even higher (81.5 percent).

In addition, rather than simply looking at how SAD symptoms overlap with TKS, Nakamura (2006) administered a TKS questionnaire to patients in Canada diagnosed with SAD. They found that many symptoms of TKS (e.g., phobia of their own glance or feeling afraid that one's own glance may make others uncomfortable), which had been considered characteristic of TKS, were also observed in the Canadian subjects. They also found that in both groups symptoms tended to worsen when exposed to: (a) a large group of people rather than a small group, (b) people of the opposite sex rather than of the same sex, (c) peers of the same age rather than the senior or the junior, and (d) acquaintances rather than strangers or intimate persons. Therefore, they concluded that TKS has more in common with SAD than previously considered.

It seems reasonable at this point to conclude that the syndrome is complex, and that it may be better to compare particular subtypes of the syndrome to SAD, or other individual personality factors that can influence the expression of the syndrome, rather than make gross generalizations. For example, Sakurai, Nagata, Harai, et al. (2005) examined the symptomatological structure and clinical subtypes of patients diagnosed with SAD in the Japanese clinical population. They identified three subtypes that they named "scrutiny fears", "conversation fears" and "relationship fears". They found that the first two appeared common to western clinical populations but the third appeared unique to the Japanese. In addition, Dinnel, Kleinknecht, and Tanaka-Matsumi (2002) conducted a cross-cultural comparison of US patients diagnosed with SAD and Japanese patients diagnosed with TKS, in relation to their respective culturally prescribed self-construals as independent and interdependent. They found that TKS symptoms are more likely to be expressed by individuals who are Japanese and individuals who construe themselves low on independence but high on interdependence. In addition, SAD symptoms are more likely to be expressed by individuals who construe themselves low on independence but high on interdependence – irrespective of culture.

Finally, it should be noted that while there is some controversy about the overlap between SAD and TKS, there is evidence that medications can be equally effective with either disorder. For example, Nagata, van Vliet, Yamada, Kataoka, Iketani, and Kiriike (2006) investigated the efficacy of paroxetine (an SSRI) in patients with TKS. Using a 12-week open-label trial, they found that 47 percent of patients were responders to the drug treatment. They concluded that, in accordance with other recent, open-label trials for TKS, selective serotonin reuptake inhibitors (SSRIs) might be as effective as in the treatment of SAD.

Furthermore, in addition to the work being done on TKS, researchers (e.g., Greenberg, Stravynski, & Bilu, 2004) have also described a syndrome that resembles SAD that may be unique to ultra-orthodox Jewish males: *aymat zibur*. *Aymat zibur* ("fear of the community"), is a term used by ultra-orthodox Jews to describe fears of performance – although in its original meaning is meant to express the respect that the leader of prayers is expected to have for his role. In their article, Greenberg et al. (2004) present three cases of ultra-orthodox male referrals to a psychiatrist in Jerusalem in which the content concerns performing: either speaking on religious matters publicly (a role associated with status and authority), or leading prayers and ceremonies (a role of sanctity and duty). The authors note that the cases described were motivated by personal shame – which is similar to SAD of the performance variety found in other cultures – rather than fear and respect. They also hypothesize that the absence of women sufferers may be understood as a consequence of the cultural value placed on modesty in women and there being no expectation of women to participate in study and public prayer. Finally, they note that the absence of complaints of interactional SAD may be a consequence of the general discouragement of socialization not related to religious study.

Generalized Anxiety Disorder (GAD)

The essential feature of GAD is excessive anxiety and worry, occurring more days than not, about a number of events or activities, for at least six months (APA, 2000). The person must find it difficult to control the worry, and the worry and anxiety must be associated with at least three of the following six symptoms: restlessness or feeling keyed up or on edge, being easily fatigued, difficulty concentrating or mind going blank, irritability, muscle tension, or a sleep disturbance. The focus of the anxiety and worry cannot be confined to features of another Axis I disorder, and must not occur exclusively during post-traumatic stress disorder. The anxiety, worry, or physical symptoms must cause clinically significant distress or impairment in social, occupational, or other important areas of functioning. The disturbance must not be due to the direct effects of substance or a general medical condition, and must not occur exclusively during a mood disorder, psychotic disorder, or pervasive developmental disorder.

The *DSM–IV–TR* states that in a community sample, the one-year prevalence rate was approximately 3 percent and the lifetime prevalence rate was 5 percent (APA, 2000). The only note in *DSM–IV–TR* on the role of cultural issues on GAD states that there is considerable cultural variation in the expression of anxiety (e.g., in some cultures anxiety is expressed predominantly through somatic symptoms, in others through cognitive symptoms) and that it is important to consider the cultural context when evaluating whether worries about certain situations are excessive.

In line with this advice, Hoge et al. (2006) compared anxiety symptoms in patients with GAD in urban mental health settings in Nepal and the United States, using an empirically supported measure of anxiety. They found that while there was no difference in the total scores on the measure, the Nepali group scored higher on the somatic subscale (e.g., symptoms such as "dizziness" and "indigestion"), while the American group scored higher on the psychological subscale (e.g., symptoms such as "scared" and "nervous"). The authors conclude that one possible explanation may be due to differences in cultural traditions of describing distress and refer readers to previous cross-cultural studies of depression that also found a greater somatic focus in Asian populations.

Several studies have examined the prevalence of GAD in other countries. For example, in one of the largest studies to date, Maier, Gansicke, Freyberger, Linz, Heun, and Lecrubier (2000) examined the frequency and associated social disability of GAD by analyzing data from the World Health Organization study on "Psychological Problems in Primary Care" (conducted in a standardized manner in 14 countries). The authors found that GAD was common in primary care in nearly all countries, with a mean one month prevalence rate of 7.9 percent. They also found that it was associated with social disability that was as severe as that in chronic somatic diseases.

In further support of this finding, Lim, Ng, Chua, et al. (2005) reported on the prevalence, comorbidity, and risk factors associated with GAD in Singapore. They note that a previous study reported a lifetime prevalence of 1.5 percent in Southeast Asia, which they believe highlighted a low preference for seeking professional help and consultation by persons suffering from mental health problems. In their study, however, they found the lifetime prevalence rate for GAD was 3.3 percent, with current prevalence being 3.0 percent. Similar to western findings of gender differences in prevalence, they found a female to male ratio of 3.6:1. Also as is common in western cultures, they found that GAD was significantly associated with the presence of other psychiatric comorbidities (e.g., major depressive disorder, dysthymia, panic disorder, agoraphobia, and SAD) and that prevalence increased in older individuals.

While several studies have now been conducted on prevalence rates of GAD across cultures, only a few studies have addressed the cultural differences in worry content. For example, Watari and Brodbeck (2000) compared worry in Japanese-American and White older adults and found no significant differences in worry content. They note that overall, health worries appeared to be the most frequently reported.

Similarly, Diaz (2000) examined the theme of worry and GAD criteria in university students and educated professionals living in Peru. Diaz (2000) administered the Spanish translation of two empirically supported self-report questionnaires in a major city in Peru. In addition to finding that the prevalence rates for GAD in Peru were similar to those found in previously studied cultures, she found no significant differences in terms of worry content between subjects meeting criteria for GAD criteria and those not meeting GAD criteria. Diaz (2000), however, did note that Peruvians who met all other *DSM–IV* criteria for GAD rarely endorsed the "uncontrollability" criterion and hypothesized that this may have been an artifact of how the GAD measures used in the study were translated.

Alcaine (2004) then examined the diagnostic translation issue (along with meta-cognitive processes, and relevant cultural issues) in the expression of GAD, using a Spanish-dominant sample in New York City. In this study, an empirically supported, diagnostic self-report questionnaire was compared to a structured clinical interview; with the Spanish translation of the "uncontrollable" criterion manipulated in order to examine response rates and reduce wording that may result in the misdiagnosis of GAD. Alcaine found that the measure was an accurate self-report instrument for identifying GAD, and that the translation for the "uncontrollable" criterion was not significantly problematic.

Obsessive-Compulsive Disorder (OCD)

The essential features of OCD are recurrent obsessions or compulsions that are severe enough to be time consuming or cause marked distress or significant impairment (APA, 2000). At some point during the course of the disorder the person must acknowledge that the obsessions and/or compulsions are excessive or unreasonable and, if another Axis I disorder is present, the content of the obsessions or compulsions cannot be restricted to it. The disturbance must not be due to the direct effect of substance or a general medical condition. If for most of the time during the current episode the person does not recognize that the obsessions and/or compulsions are excessive or unreasonable, the specifier "With Poor Insight" may be used.

The *DSM–IV–TR* states that lifetime prevalence rates of obsessive compulsive disorder in community studies are estimated at 2.5 percent, with 1-year prevalence rates at 0.5–2.1 percent in adults. It also states, however, that methodological problems with the assessment tool used in the community studies raise the possibility that the true prevalence rates are much lower. Yet community studies with children and adolescents have estimated lifetime prevalence of 1–2.3 percent and a 1-year prevalence of 0.7 percent, so this concern may be unfounded. Studies examining the impact of culture on OCD in the United States have not found any differences in prevalence of OCD based on race (Hispanic, African-American, White), although epidemiological data has indicated OCD slightly less common among African Americans than Whites in the general population (Barlow, 2002). This difference does not appear to be significant (Karno et al., 1988), however, leading some researchers (e.g., Castillo, 1997) to suggest that differences in the observed prevalence rates of OCD between cultural groups in the US may be due to greater tolerance in some cultures for behavior that deviates from the norm.

In terms of prevalence of OCD in other cultures, the *DSM–IV–TR* asserts that prevalence rates of OCD are similar in many different cultures around the world. In accordance with this, Weissman et al. (1994) reviewed data on lifetime and annual prevalence rates, age at onset, symptom profiles, and comorbidity of OCD from community surveys of adults (aged 18–65+ years) in seven countries (Canada, Finland, Taiwan, Africa, Puerto Rico, Korea, and New Zealand) and found that the annual prevalence rates are very consistent and stable among these countries – ranging from 1.1/100 in Korea and New Zealand to 1.8/100 in Puerto Rico. The sole exception appeared to be that of Taiwan (0.4/100 population) – which is similar to the findings on PD (see section above).

In addition to the findings on prevalence, Barlow (2002) notes that patients from different cultures display very similar forms of disorder (e.g., washing, checking) and adds that even the frequencies of these forms of OCD are similar across cultures. As an example of this, Insel (1984) reviewed studies from England, Hong Kong, India, Egypt, Japan, and Norway and found that OCD symptoms were typical of United States and European studies.

While prevalence rates, forms, and symptoms of OCD may be similar across cultures, it should be noted that religious and cultural beliefs may influence the themes of obsessions and compulsions in subtle ways (e.g., Orthodox Jews with religious compulsions may have symptoms focusing on dietary practices) and that important life transitions and mourning may lead to an intensification of ritual behavior that may appear to be an compulsion to a clinician who is not familiar with the cultural context. As noted in the *DSM–IV*, culturally prescribed ritualistic behavior should not itself be considered indicative of OCD – unless it exceeds cultural norms, occurs at times and places judged inappropriate by other of the same culture, and interferes with social role functioning.

In addition to religious beliefs, variability in symptom presentation and frequency of themes across national sites may be influenced by other cultural factors (Ghassemzadeh, Khamseh, & Ebrahimkhani, 2005). For example, Barlow (2002) notes that some obsessive fears are culturally specific, such as fear of leprosy in some parts of Africa and many OCD rituals can be attributed to excessive concern with cultural preoccupations (e.g., high percentage of cleaning rituals in Egypt and India may be due to dictates of the Muslim religion in Egypt or emphasis on cleanliness in India). Barlow also notes that even within cultures, historical shifts can occur in the focus of the obsessive fears – such as in the case of obsessive fear of disease – which tend to mirror current media information within the culture.

Barlow (2002) writes that while the prevalence of OCD in Saudi Arabia is similar to other countries, the content of obsessions and nature of compulsions differs (e.g., more related to religious practices associated with strong Muslim beliefs). Lemelson (2003) examined patients suffering from OCD in Bali, Indonesia and found that Balinese culture strongly shaped symptomatic expression – with the most common obsessional themes being those that emphasized patients' obsessional need to know information about their social sized network, such as the identity and status of passers-by. In addition, somatic obsessions and religious themes around witchcraft and spirits were prominent. Fontenelle, Mendlowicz, Marques, and Versiani (2004) examined patients with OCD in Rio de Janeiro, Brazil and compared them with those reported in 15 clinical samples from North and Latin America, Europe, Africa, and Asia. They found a predominance of aggressive and religious obsessions in only the Brazilian and Middle Eastern samples.

In terms of direct comparisons, Karadag, Oguzhanoglu, Ozdel, Atesci, and Amuk (2006) investigated the clinical features of OCD and the possible association between obsessive-compulsive symptoms and culture-related characteristics in a sample of Turkish patients with OCD. Similar to findings in the United States, they found that the onset of OCD symptoms was earlier in males. In terms of particular forms of OCD, they found that the most commonly occurring obsessions were contamination (56.7 percent), aggression (48.9 percent), and somatic (24.1 percent), followed by religious (19.9 percent), symmetry (18.4 percent), and sexual imagery (15.6 percent). While symmetry and sexual obsessions, and checking compulsions and rituals, tended to be more common in male patients, dirt and contamination obsessions and washing compulsions were slightly more common in females. Finally, they note that the vast majority of patients with religious obsessions (83 percent) and half of the patients with sexual obsessions had compulsions that included religious practices – and that patients with sexual and religious obsessions delayed seeking professional help.

Millet, Leclaire, Bourdel, Loo, Tezcan, and Kuloglu (2000) compared the sociodemographic characteristics, clinical, and phenomenological features of obsessive-compulsive symptoms in patients from France and Turkey suffering from obsessive-compulsive disorder. They found that dirt-contamination obsessions and cleaning-washing compulsions were the most common forms in both groups and noted that religious obsessions and praying compulsions appeared more frequently in male Turkish patients. They concluded that cultural factors must be taken into account when subtyping OCD.

Finally, the research has identified culturally bound syndromes that resemble OCD. For example, Chowdhury, Mukherjee, Ghosh, and Chowdhury (2003) reported on the occurrence of a delusion of animal pregnancy in males (and one female) from a part of rural West Bengal, India. They note that this delusion appears to be based on a strong cultural belief that a dog bite may evolve into a puppy pregnancy – even in the human male. A review of psychiatric status showed that there was a clear association of obsessive-compulsive disorder in two of the seven cases (29 percent) reported.

Conclusion

Anxiety disorders are the most prevalent class of disorders in the United States, represent the single largest mental health problem in the country, and cause tremendous direct and indirect costs to individuals and our health system. While the anxiety disorders also appear to occur at relatively similar prevalence rates in other countries, it is clear that ethnicity and culture influence their expression, and thus can have an impact on the presentation, course, and treatment. This notion also appears to hold true for individuals residing within the US, but hailing from different cultures.

With this in mind, it is likely that the concept of "culture-bound syndromes" is a misnomer, and instead represents a phase in research during which we simply lacked the data needed to recognize, evaluate, and compare these "syndromes" to western disorders. It now appears much more likely that these "syndromes" are actually variants of western disorders (or vice versa), with the expression of particular symptoms within each general category of disorder being influenced by the cultural beliefs and practices of the individual and society in which he or she lives. As such, it is important for researchers and treatment providers to pay particular attention to the cultural context (e.g., cultural/religious beliefs, historical shifts within the person's country, recent moves, life transitions, level of acculturation, etc.) when performing an assessment/evaluation, making a diagnosis, and considering treatment interventions.

Mental health professionals should also consider referring to (or consulting with) other providers with expertise on the culture of the individual being evaluated – especially when lacking in experience in working with a particular ethnic or cultural group. In addition, it would be wise to consider consulting with religious leaders or family/community members with expertise on the culture of the individual being evaluated – especially with regard to the issue of whether the individual's behavior violates the social norms of his or her culture.

Although we have seen much progress in the study of the role that culture plays on anxiety disorders, more work is clearly needed. Fortunately, the combination of a rapidly shifting global population along with continuing improvements in technology are enabling increased communication and collaboration between researchers in different countries. For example, the *Journal of Clinical Psychiatry* recently published a special supplement that provides an overview of key data from the European Study of the Epidemiology of Mental Disorders (ESEMeD) – the first large-scale survey to collect comprehensive data on a variety of psychiatric disorders throughout Europe (Alonso & Lépine, 2007).

This survey, which was the result of a joint collaboration between European investigators and the World Health Organization, collected data on more than 21,000 adults representative of a population of more than 212 million people, from six countries (Belgium, France, Germany, Italy, the Netherlands, and Spain). Perhaps more importantly, the data should provide an epidemiologic basis for reform of mental health policy within Europe (Alonso & Lépine, 2007). We are clearly at an exciting point in time for the study and treatment of anxiety disorders across cultures.

Table 10.1   Summary of research findings on cultural differences within the United States and between countries/regions

Disorder	Cultural differences within the United States	Cultural differences between countries/regions
Agoraphobia	No differences reported	Agoraphobia found in only 8% of Qatari women with phobias.
Panic Disorder	No differences in prevalence found between African Americans, Hispanics, and Whites	Lifetime rates for PD consistent across countries – except Taiwan (much lower rates – see OCD).
	No differences in prevalence found across *sites* used in studies	Ataque de nervios in Hispanics.
	May be age by race interaction in Whites (older = lower prevalence) and Hispanics (older = higher prevalence) African Americans underrepresented in treatment outcome studies; show higher incidence of sleep paralysis versus Whites with PD	Kyol goeu, sore neck, and weak heart syndromes in Khmer.
Specific Phobia	More prevalent in African Americans and Hispanics than Whites – but content the same	Prevalence differs by country. E.g., higher in Nigeria and Kenya than USA, Australia, and China; India higher than UK.
	Level of acculturation may be a factor	Religion may be a factor. E.g., Christian higher than Muslim for certain phobias, but Muslim higher than Christian for others. Koro and Pa-Leng/Pa-Feng syndromes in China.
Social Anxiety Disorder	No differences between African Americans and Whites in symptom presentation	Rare in the East.
	No differences in improvement from treatment based on race	Israel, with more Western culture, has rate of SAD like USA.

Table 10.1 (*cont'd*)

Disorder	Cultural differences within the United States	Cultural differences between countries/regions
		Individualistic versus collectivistic cultural norms may have impact.
		Independence versus interdependence may have impact.
		Taijin Kyofusho (TKS) in Japan.
		Aymat zibur in ultra-orthodox Jewish males.
Generalized Anxiety Disorder	No worry content differences reported in Japanese-American and White older adults (with health being the most frequent worry in both groups)	Culture may have impact on expression of anxiety, e.g., Nepal versus USA: no difference in severity, but somatic subscale higher in Nepali group, while psychological subscale higher in American group.
		Common in primary care in nearly all countries surveyed.
		Singapore has current prevalence similar to USA, similar gender differences like that of USA, high levels of comorbidity like in USA, and increased prevalence in older individuals like in USA.
		Prevalence in Peru similar to other cultures.
Obsessive-Compulsive Disorder	No differences found in prevalence based on race (African Americans, Hispanics, Whites all similar)	Prevalence similar and stable in many different cultures around the world – except Taiwan (much lower rates – see PD).
	Slightly less common in African Americans; may be result of cultural differences in tolerance of behavior that deviates from the norm and/or where individuals seek help (e.g., dermatologist versus psychiatrist for excessive hand-washing)	Similar forms and frequency of forms of OCD observed, e.g., UK, Hong Kong, India, Egypt, Japan, Norway, USA, and Europeans all report similar OCD symptoms.
		Cultural and religious beliefs may influence OCD themes in subtle ways. E.g., More religious themes found in Saudi Arabia, although similar overall prevalence; high percentage of cleaning rituals in Egypt and India may be due to dictates of Muslim religion and/or cultural emphasis on cleanliness.

(*cont'd*)

Table 10.1   (*cont'd*)

Disorder	Cultural differences within the United States	Cultural differences between countries/regions
		Bali, Indonesia has high prevalence of need to know theme – regarding social sized network, witchcraft, and spirits.
		More aggressive and religious themes in Brazil and Middle East.
		Turkish patients similar to Americans in terms of earlier onset in males; Turkish patients with more religious themes than French.
		West Bengal, India – animal pregnancy based on delusional belief that dog bite can impregnate humans.

REFERENCES

Alcaine, O. M. (2004). Generalized anxiety disorder among United States Latinos: The uncontrollability, diagnosis, and expression of chronic worry. *Dissertation Abstracts International: Section B: The Sciences and Engineering, 64(12-B)*, 6319.

Al-Issa, I., & Oudji, S. (1998). Culture and anxiety disorders. In S. S. Kazarian & D. R. Evans (Eds.), *Cultural clinical psychology: Theory, research, and practice* (pp. 127–151). New York: Oxford University Press.

Allgulander, C. (1994). Suicide and mortality patterns in anxiety neurosis and depressive neurosis. *Archives of General Psychiatry, 51,* 708–712.

Alonso, J., & Lépine, J-P. (2007). Overview of Key Data from the European Study of the Epidemiology of Mental Disorders (ESEMeD). *Journal of Clinical Psychiatry, 68 (Supplement 2)*, 3–9.

American Psychiatric Association (APA) (2000). *Diagnostic and statistical manual of mental disorders* (4th edn, text revision). Washington, DC: Author.

Arrindell, W. A., Eisemann, M., Richter, J., et al. (2003). Phobic anxiety in 11 nations part I: Dimensional constancy of the five-factor model. *Behaviour Research and Therapy, 41(4)*, 461–479.

Barlow, D. H. (2002). *Anxiety and its disorders: The nature and treatment of anxiety and panic* (2nd ed.). New York: Guilford Press.

Beck, A. T., Emery, G., & Greenberg, R. L. (1985). *Anxiety disorders and phobias: A cognitive perspective.* New York: Basic Books.

Boehnlein, J. K. (2001). Cultural interpretations of physiological processes in post-traumatic stress disorder and panic disorder. *Transcultural Psychiatry, 38(4)*, 461–467.

Brown, D. R., Eaton, W., & Sussman, L. (1990). Racial differences in the prevalence of phobic disorders. *Journal of Nervous and Mental Disease, 178(7)*, 434–441.

Castillo, R. (1997). *Culture and mental illness: A client centered approach*. Pacific Grove, CA: Brooks/Cole.

Chambers, J., Yeragani, V. K., & Keshavan, M. S. (1986). Phobias in India and the United Kingdom: A trans-cultural study. *Acta Psychiatrica Scandinavica, 74*, 388–391.

Chowdhury, A. N, Mukherjee, H., Ghosh, K. K., & Chowdhury, S. (2003). Puppy pregnancy in humans: A culture-bound disorder in rural West Bengal, India. *International Journal of Social Psychiatry, 49*(1), 35–42.

Curtis, G. C., Magee, W. J., Eaton, W. W., Wittchen, H. U., & Kessler, R. C. (1998). Specific fears and phobias. Epidemiology and classification. *British Journal of Psychiatry, 173*, 212–217.

Davey, G. C. L., McDonald, A. S., Hirisave, U., et al. (1998). A cross-cultural study of animal fears. *Behaviour Research and Therapy, 36*, 735–750.

Diaz, M. L. (2000). Exploring generalized anxiety disorder and worry in Peru. *Dissertation Abstracts International: Section B: The Sciences and Engineering, 60*(8-B), 4215.

Dinnel, D. L., Kleinknecht, R. A., & Tanaka-Matsumi, J. (2002). A cross-cultural comparison of social phobia symptoms. *Journal of Psychopathology and Behavioral Assessment, 24*(2), 75–84.

Eaton, W. W., Dryman, A., & Weissman, M. M. (1991). Panic and phobia: The diagnosis of panic disorder and phobic disorder. In L. N. Robins & D. A. Regier (Eds.), *Psychiatric disorders in America.* (pp. 155–203). New York: Free Press.

Essau, C. A., Sakano, Y., Ishikawa, S., & Sasagawa, S. (2004). Anxiety symptoms in Japanese and in German children. *Behaviour Research and Therapy, 42*(5), 601–612.

Ferrell, C. B., Beidel, D. C., & Turner, S. M. (2004). Assessment and treatment of socially phobic children: A cross cultural comparison. *Journal of Clinical Child and Adolescent Psychology, 33*(2), 260–268.

Fontenelle, L. F., Mendlowicz, M. V., Marques, C., & Versiani, M. (2004). Trans-cultural aspects of obsessive-compulsive disorder: A description of a Brazilian sample and a systematic review of international clinical studies. *Journal of Psychiatric Research, 38*(4), 403–411.

Friedman, S. (1997). *Cultural issues in the treatment of anxiety.* New York: Guilford Press.

Friedman, S., Paradis, C. M., & Hatch, M. (1994). Characteristics of African American and White patients with panic disorder and agoraphobia. *Hospital Community Psychiatry, 45*, 798–803.

Friedman, S., Smith, L. C., Halpern, B., et al. (2003). Obsessive-compulsive disorder in a multi-ethnic urban outpatient clinic: Initial presentation and treatment outcome with exposure and ritual prevention. *Behavior Therapy, 34*(3), 397–410.

Ghassemzadeh, H., Khamseh, A., & Ebrahimkhani, N. (2005). Demographic variables and clinical features of obsessive-compulsive disorder in Iran: A second report. In B. E. Ling (Ed.), *Obsessive compulsive disorder research* (pp. 243–271). Hauppauge, NY: Nova Biomedical Books.

Good, B. J., & Kleinman, A. M. (1985). Culture and anxiety: Cross-cultural evidence for the patterning of anxiety disorders. In A. H. Tuma & J. Maser (Eds.), *Anxiety and the anxiety disorders* (pp. 297–324). Hillsdale, NJ: Erlbaum.

Greenberg, D., Stravynski, A., & Bilu, Y. (2004). Social phobia in ultra-orthodox Jewish males: Culture-bound syndrome or virtue? *Mental Health, Religion & Culture, 7*(4), 289–305.

Greenberg, P. E., Sisitsky, T., Kessler, R. C., et al. (1999). The economic burden of anxiety disorders in the 1990s. *Journal of Clinical Psychiatry, 60*(7), 427–435.

Guarnaccia, P. J. (1997). A cross-cultural perspective on anxiety disorders. In: S. Friedman (Ed.), *Cultural issues in the treatment of anxiety* (pp. 3–20). New York: Guilford Press.

Guarnaccia, P. J., Rubio-Stipec, M., & Canino, G. (1989). Ataques de nervios in the Puerto Rican diagnostic interview schedule: The impact of cultural categories on psychiatric epidemiology. *Culture, Medicine and Psychiatry, 13*(3), 275–295.

Gureje, O., Von Korff, M., Simon, G. E., & Gater, R. (1998). Persistent pain and well-being: A World Health Organization study in primary care. *Journal of the American Medical Association, 280*(2), 147–151.

Harmon, H., Langley, A., & Ginsburg, G. S. (2006). The role of gender and culture in treating youth with anxiety disorders. *Journal of Cognitive Psychotherapy, 20*(3), 301–310.

Heinrichs, N., Rapee, R. M., Alden, L. A., et al. (2006). Cultural differences in perceived social norms and social anxiety. *Behaviour Research and Therapy, 44*(8), 1187–1197.

Hinton, D., Hinton, S. Pham, T., Chau, H., & Tran, M. (2003). "Hit by the wind" and temperature-shift panic among Vietnamese refugees. *Transcultural Psychiatry, 40*(3), 342–376.

Hinton, D., Hinton, S., Um, K., Chea, A., & Sak, S. (2002). The Khmer "weak heart" syndrome: Fear of death from palpitations. *Transcultural Psychiatry, 39*(3), 323–344.

Hinton, D., Pich, V., Safren, S.A., Pollack, M. H., & McNally, R. J. (2006). Anxiety sensitivity among Cambodian refugees with panic disorder: A factor analytic investigation. *Journal of Anxiety Disorders, 20*(3), 281–295.

Hinton, D., Um, K., & Ba, P. (2001a). Kyol goeu ('wind overload') Part I: A cultural syndrome of orthostatic panic among Khmer refugees. *Transcultural Psychiatry, 38*(4), 403–432.

Hinton, D., Um, K., & Ba, P. (2001b) A unique panic-disorder presentation among Khmer refugees: The sore-neck syndrome. *Culture, Medicine and Psychiatry, 25*(3), 297–316.

Hoge, E. A., Tamrakar, S. M., Christian, K. M., et al. (2006). Cross-cultural differences in somatic presentation in patients with generalized anxiety disorder. *Journal of Nervous and Mental Disease, 194*(12), 962–966.

Horwath, E., Johnson, J., & Hornig, C. D. (1993). Epidemiology of panic disorder in African-Americans. *American Journal of Psychiatry, 150*(3), 465–469.

Horwath, E., & Weissman, M. M. (1997). Epidemiology of anxiety disorders across cultural groups. In S. Friedman (Ed.), *Cultural issues in the treatment of anxiety* (pp. 21–39). New York: Guilford Press.

Horwath, E., & Weissman, M. M. (2000). The epidemiology and cross-national presentation of obsessive-compulsive disorder. *Psychiatric Clinics of North America, 23*(3), 493–507.

Hsia, C. C., & Barlow, D. H. (2001). On the nature of culturally bound syndromes in the nosology of mental disorders. *Transcultural Psychiatry, 38*(4), 474–476.

Iancu, I., Levin, J., Hermesh, H., et al. (2006). Social phobia symptoms: Prevalence, sociodemographic correlates, and overlap with specific phobia symptoms. *Comprehensive Psychiatry, 47*(5), 399–405.

Ingman, K. A., Ollendick, T. H., & Akande, A. (1999). Cross-cultural aspects of fears in African children. and adolescents. *Behaviour Research and Therapy, 37*, 337–345.

Insel, T. R. (1984). *New findings in obsessive-compulsive disorder.* Washington, DC: American Psychiatric Press.

Karadag, F., Oguzhanoglu, N.K., Ozdel, O., Atesci, F. C., & Amuk, T. (2006). OCD symptoms in a sample of Turkish patients: A phenomenological picture. *Depression and Anxiety, 23*(3), 145–152.

Karno, M., Golding, J., Burnam, M. A., et al. (1989). Anxiety disorders among Mexican Americans and non-Hispanic whites in Los Angeles. *Journal of Nervous and Mental Disease, 177*(4), 202–209.

Kirmayer, L. J. (1991). The place of culture in psychiatric nosology: Taijin kyofusho and DSM3R. *Journal of Nervous and Mental Disease. 179*, 19–28.

Kirmayer, L. J. (2001). Cultural variations in the clinical presentation of depression and anxiety: implications for diagnosis and treatment. *Journal of Clinical Psychiatry, 62(Supplement 13)*, 22–28.

Kirmayer, L. J., Young, A., & Hayton, B. C. (1995). The cultural context of anxiety disorders. *Psychiatric Clinics of North America, 18(3)*, 503–521.

Kyrios, M., Sanavio, E., Bhar, S., & Liguori, L. (2001). Associations between obsessive-compulsive phenomena, affect and beliefs: Cross-cultural comparisons of Australian and Italian data. *Behavioural and Cognitive Psychotherapy, 29*(4), 409–422.

Lemelson, R. (2003). Obsessive-compulsive disorder in Bali: The cultural shaping of a neuropsychiatric disorder. *Transcultural Psychiatry, 40*(3), 377–408.

Levine, R. E. & Gaw, A. C. (1995). Culture-bound syndromes. *Psychiatric Clinics of North America, 18*(3), 523–536.

Liebowitz, M. R., Salman, E., Jusino, C. M., et al. (1994). Ataques de nervios and panic disorder. *American Journal of Psychiatry, 151(6)*, 871–875.

Lim, L., Ng, T. P., Chua, H. C., et al. (2005). Generalised anxiety disorder in Singapore: Prevalence, co-morbidity and risk factors in a multi-ethnic population. *Social Psychiatry and Psychiatric Epidemiology, 40*(12), 972–979.

Maier, W., Gansicke, M., Freyberger, H. J., Linz, M., Heun, R., & Lecrubier, Y. (2000). Generalized anxiety disorder (*ICD-10*) in primary care from a cross-cultural perspective: A valid diagnostic entity? *Acta Psychiatrica Scandinavica, 101*(1), 29–36.

Millet, B., Leclaire, M., Bourdel, M., Loo, H., Tezcan, E., & Kuloglu, M. (2000). Comparison of sociodemographic, clinical and phenomenological characteristics of Turkish and French patients suffering from obsessive-compulsive disorder. *Canadian Journal of Psychiatry, 45*(9), 848.

Nagata, T., van Vliet, I., Yamada, H., Kataoka, K., Iketani, T., & Kiriike, N. (2006). An open trial of paroxetine for the "offensive subtype" of Taijin Kyofusho and social anxiety disorder. *Depression and Anxiety, 23*(3), 168–174.

Nakamura, K. (2006). Taijin-Kyofu-Sho (phobia of interpersonal situation) and social phobia. In C. M. Velotis (Ed.), *New developments in anxiety disorders research.* Hauppauge, NY: Nova Biomedical Books, pp. 199–215.

Nazemi, H., Kleinknecht, R. A., Dinnel, D. L., et al. (2003). A study of panic attacks in university students of Iran. *Journal of Psychopathology and Behavioral Assessment, 25*(3), 191–201.

Neal, A. M., Lilly, R. S., & Zakis, S. (1993). What are African American children afraid of? A preliminary study. *Journal of Anxiety Disorders, 7*, 129–139.

Olatunji, B. O., Sawchuk, C. N., de Jong, P. J., & Lohr, J. M. (2006). The structural relation between disgust sensitivity and blood-injection-injury fears: A cross-cultural comparison of US and Dutch data. *Journal of Behavior Therapy and Experimental Psychiatry, 37*(1), 16–29.

Paradis, C. M., & Friedman, S. (2005). Sleep paralysis in African Americans with panic disorder. *Transcultural Psychiatry, 42*(1), 123–134.

Rector, N. A., Kocovski, N. L., & Ryder, A. G. (2006). Social anxiety and the fear of causing discomfort to others: Conceptualization and treatment. *Journal of Social & Clinical Psychology, 25*(8), 906–918.

Russell, J. G. (1989). Anxiety disorders in Japan: A review of the Japanese literature on Shinkeishitsu and taijinkyōfushiī. *Culture, Medicine and Psychiatry, 13*(4), 391–403.

Sakurai, A., Nagata, T., Harai, H., et al. (2005). Is "relationship fear" unique to Japan? Symptom factors and patient clusters of social anxiety disorder among the Japanese clinical population. *Journal of Affective Disorders, 87*(1), 131–137.

Sica, C., Novara, C., Sanavio, E., Dorz, S., & Coradeschi, D. (2002). Obsessive compulsive disorder cognitions across cultures. In R. O. Frost & G. Steketee (Eds.), *Cognitive approaches to obsessions and compulsions: Theory, assessment, and treatment* (pp. 371–384). Amsterdam, Netherlands: Pergamon/Elsevier Science Inc.

Silverman, W. K. (1993). *DSM* and classification of anxiety disorders in children and adults. In C. G. Last (Ed.), *Anxiety across the lifespan: A developmental perspective* (pp. 7–36). New York: Springer.

Smith, L. C., Friedman, S., & Nevid, J. (1999). Clinical and sociocultural differences in African American and European American patients with panic disorder and agoraphobia. *Journal of Nervous and Mental Disease, 187*, 549–561.

Stein, D. J., & Matsunaga, H. (2001). Cross-cultural aspects of social anxiety disorder. *Psychiatric Clinics of North America, 24*(4), 773–782.

Suzuki, K., Takei, N., Kawai, M., Minabe, Y., & Mori, N. (2003). Is Taijin Kyofusho a culture-bound syndrome? *American Journal of Psychiatry, 160*(7), 1358.

Swendsen, J. D., Merikangas, K. R., Canino, G. J., Kessler, R. C., Rubio-Stipec, M., & Angst, J. (1998). The comorbidity of alcoholism with anxiety and depressive disorders in four geographic communities. *Comprehensive Psychiatry, 39*(4), 176–184.

Tarumi, S., Ichimiya, A., Yamada, S., Umesue, M., & Kuroki, T. (2004). Taijin Kyofusho in university students: patterns of fear and predispositions to the offensive variant. *Transcultural Psychiatry, 41*(4), 533–546.

Tuma A. H., & Maser, J. D. (Eds.) (1985). *Anxiety and the anxiety disorders*. Hillsdale, NJ: Lawrence Erlbaum.

Vega, W. A., Kolody, B., Aguilar-Gaxiola, S., Alderete, E., Catalano, R., & Caraveo-Anduaga, J. (1998). Lifetime prevalence of DSM–III–R psychiatric disorders among urban and rural Mexican Americans in California. *Archives of General Psychiatry, 55*(9), 771–778.

Watari, K. F., & Brodbeck, C. (2000). Culture, health, and financial, appraisals: Comparison of worry in older Japanese Americans and European Americans. *Journal of Consulting and Clinical Geropsychology, 6*, 25–39.

Weissman, M. M., Bland, R. C., Canino, G. J., et al. (1994). The cross national epidemiology of obsessive compulsive disorder. The Cross National Collaborative Group. *Journal of Clinical Psychiatry, 55*, S5–S10.

11

Cultural Factors in Traumatic Stress

Peter D. Yeomans and Evan M. Forman

Posttraumatic stress disorder (PTSD) as a diagnosis was first recognized in the third edition of the *Diagnostic and Statistical Manual of Mental Disorders (DSM–III)* (APA, 1980). In this chapter, we highlight the relevance of and need for a better elucidation of the prevalence of PTSD in diverse settings and discuss its utility as a way of conceptualizing traumatic stress. Next we discuss critiques of this construct. One of the most central critiques lies in the debate as to the degree to which PTSD is a meaningful and useful construct in the context of cross-cultural psychological research and clinical treatment. We reference components of this debate and conclude with some specific recommendations for research and treatment. The PTSD diagnosis includes a prerequisite traumatic event, three subsets of symptom types, a requisite duration of symptoms beyond one month after the associated event, and a significant distress or decrease in functioning. The intrusion subcategory includes dreams or flashbacks reminiscent of the event, intrusive thoughts about the event, and emotional distress and physiological reactivity to cues associated with the event. The avoidance/numbing subcategory includes the avoidance of people and places that are reminders of the event, the inability to remember all the details of the event, feelings of detachment from others, a restricted range of affect, and a sense of a foreshortened future. The hyperarousal subcategory includes an exaggerated startle response, difficulty concentrating or falling asleep, outbursts of anger, and hypervigilance.

Since its inception PTSD has been embroiled in debate over multiple issues. Major controversies about the diagnosis include the political climate in which it was conceived, the recent broadening of the definition of the traumatic event that is required to meet a diagnosis for PTSD, that event's questionable association with symptom manifestation, and the theoretical view of the nature of traumatic memory (Herbert & Forman, 2005; McNally, 2004). For instance Mol et al. (2005) found that PTSD symptoms were as commonly associated with life events such as an illness or problems at work as they were with events that meet Criterion A. The construct has been a source of even greater controversy in its implication that traumatic memories can be actively repressed and then made inaccessible to memory (Bloom, 1997), a notion that is not supported by research on memory (Lynn, Knox, Fassler, Lillienfeld, & Loftus, 2004; McNally, 2004). All of these controversies warrant substantial caution in our application of the PTSD construct cross-culturally. For instance, Terheggen, Stroebe, and Kleber (2001) reported that for Tibetans the most traumatic event was the witnessing of the destruction of religious signs. However such events do not typically find themselves on a traumatic event checklist.

Importance of Understanding Cultural Factors

The need to identify how people respond to traumatic events has become a central issue in both international psychological and humanitarian domains. Medical and mental health professionals find themselves with an increasingly diverse patient pool that may include recent refugees, asylum applicants, and immigrants from regions of the world that have experienced profound disruption, most often in the form of a war or a natural disaster. As an index of the vast numbers of people who have experienced traumatic events, there have been 190 armed conflicts between the end of the Second World War (WWII) and 1990 resulting in 310,000 deaths and many times more nonfatal casualties (WHO, 2002). In contrast to WWII, most of those killed and injured have been civilians (Zwi, 1991). At the close of 2006, there were over 12.8 million Internally Displaced Persons, 9.8 million refugees, and an additional 10.3 million "people of concern" as designated by the United Nations (UNHCR, 2006).

As the West has expanded its role in the provision of various types of resources to impoverished countries and displaced populations, such aid has increasingly included treatment for trauma-related psychological problems. These treatments have been developed in nations of relatively similar culture (United States, Europe, Australia, Israel) and are thus primarily based on industrialized cultures' conceptualizations of trauma and its sequelae, in particular the notion that PTSD is an expected, or at least likely, psychological reaction to extremely stressful events. The vast majority of the treatment methods and models for traumatic stress have been derived from studies of samples from industrialized countries and yet they are increasingly applied to diverse cultural populations. The validity of this conceptualization and even validity of the diagnosis is still in debate as applied to industrialized cultural populations; the degree to which PTSD is universally applicable is even less certain. The reliability and validity of our measurement of PTSD, what diverse groups consider traumatic, how they respond to trauma, and the type of treatment from which they will most benefit, needs continued attention (Marsella, Friedman, & Spain, 1996).

The debate over the appropriate application of these models in culturally different settings is born out of a larger effort to assist individuals and communities in their recovery from devastating impact of human-caused or natural events. Successful conceptualization of a singular model facilitates research and treatment development, yet oversimplification of the model can cause additional problems. For instance, Kleinman (1977) warns us against the "category fallacy" in which we presume that mental health constructs will translate and be evident in other cultures. There are concerns that the PTSD label implies vulnerability within those who may in fact show more resilience (Frey, 2001). Other writers caution that the use of the PTSD diagnosis draws attention away from the political and social causes of an event and distracts us from the true causes of traumatic stress: political violence, economic injustice, and issues of security (Nader, Dubrow, & Stamm, 1999; Wessells, 1999). Biomedical conceptualizations and treatment of distress potentially reduce the critical consideration of economic and political forces that contribute to such distress (Bracken et al., 1995).

Studies of Prevalence

To understand the cultural factors that influence the presentation of traumatic stress, we must first investigate basic prevalence of PTSD in different settings. Evidence of prevalence demonstrates that the construct can be found in that setting, but does not tell us whether it is the most valid representation of traumatic stress. Conclusions about prevalence are often based on the questionable assumption of the validity of assessment techniques and measures. Nonetheless, it is a starting point for understanding how traumatic stress is manifest among different people.

In cross-cultural research, methodology significantly shapes the nature of findings. For instance, an *etic* investigation imposes preestablished constructs and methods from a cultural perspective foreign to the sample under study, whereas an *emic* approach aims to elicit more qualitative information from the subject by using open-ended questions on the principle that responses should not be forced to fit into preconceived foreign models. Both styles of research can contribute to appreciating cultural manifestation of traumatic stress and both have their limitations. An emic approach has the advantage of collecting indigenous models and descriptors of the experience of traumatic stress. Responses are not limited to those of a predetermined questionnaire and there is opportunity to fully assess the breadth of possible manifestations of distress. The main disadvantage lies in the likelihood of overlooking symptoms that are considered too private or insignificant by respondents. In addition, qualitative data offers limited opportunities for statistical analysis. Questionnaire-based (etic) methods, probe for expected signs and symptoms, and also yield quantitative data.

Studies measuring prevalence can be divided between samples of refugees having lived in or recently arrived in industrialized nations, and samples of nationals living in either their country of origin or having been displaced to another culturally similar country (i.e., Rwandan refugees in Burundi). This distinction is important in that it potentially reflects different degrees of acculturation which may influence symptom presentation. It could be argued that as length of stay in industrialized countries increases, immigrants may be relatively more acculturated and therefore their symptoms may more closely resemble the PTSD model. This distinction also many indicate the extent of daily living stressors associated with refugee status that has been shown to contribute to the maintenance or exacerbation of traumatic stress.

Reported prevalence rates are predictably as diverse as the different samples in which they were solicited. For instance reports of PTSD after natural disaster have ranged from 1.5 percent to 67 percent (Wang et al., 2000), and after war or civil unrest as high as 99 percent (Raymond, 2000). Due to the diversity of samples and their concomitant traumatic histories, it is difficult to discern whether such differences are the result of methodological and sampling differences or the studying of a disorder with significant cultural variability. A comparison of traumatic stress reactions between two different cultural groups does not permit confident attribution of these differences to differences in cultural identity unless other factors are controlled for (SES, trauma exposure, urban versus rural). Nonetheless, a brief summary of the diverse findings is provided below.

Recent Immigrants to the Industrialized World

The following studies primarily used etic approaches such as standardized self-report measures, though they were sometimes read aloud to the participants. Carlson and Rosser-Hogan (1994) sampled Cambodian refugees who had lived in refugee camps in Thailand and had emigrated from Thai refugee camps to the US ten years prior to the study. Eighty-six percent of the sample met criteria for PTSD. Forty-three percent also surpassed cut-offs for substantial emotional distress and 40 percent exceeded cut-offs for clinical depression. Al-Saffar, Borga, Edman, and Hallstrom (2003) sampled foreign nationals (Turkey, Iran, Saudia Arabia) who had immigrated to Sweden at least four years prior to the study. All participants had previous trauma exposure, yet response across ethnic differences was highly variable. The study found the presence of PTSD in 69 percent of the Iranians, 59 percent of the Saudis, 53 percent of the Turks, and only 29 percent of the Swedes. Weine et al. (1995) reported PTSD in 25 percent of a sample of Bosnian adolescents recently relocated to the United States. Similar findings were reported among Kurdish youth refugees (Ahmad, 1992). Kinzie et al. (1986) found that 50 percent of a Cambodian refugee sample living in the US met criteria for PTSD. Observed differences across studies are likely due to some combination of factors such as differences in assessment, in culture, or the postconflict situation. Better identifying the specific factors responsible for these differences will require further study.

Establishment of prevalence begs the question of whether the factor structure of a given PTSD measure is comparable across cultures. Beyond evidence of PTSD symptoms across cultures, we must then examine whether certain symptoms predominate or co-occur together. Sack et al. (1997) investigated the factor structure of the Diagnostic Interview for Children and Adolescents (DICA; Welner et al., 1987) with Cambodian youth refugees. Results revealed the same factor structure as found in samples from industrialized cultures. Similarly, the Impact of Event Scale (Horowitz, Wilner, & Alvarez, 1979) revealed the same underlying factor structure when used with Bosnian youth as when used with British youth (Smith, Perrin, Dyregrov, & Yule, 2003). A study that compared Russian and American youth found that while PTSD prevalence rates differed, the proportional severity of the symptom clusters and their correlation with other forms of psychopathology were comparable (Ruchkin et al., 2005). Whereas these findings lack sufficient validity to confirm that PTSD is the best universal description of traumatic stress, they do indicate that PTSD can be similarly measured across different settings.

Nationals Remaining in a Pre-Industrialized Setting

Several studies engaged samples who were either in their home country or had been displaced to a relatively similar cultural setting. However, there remains a paucity of data when it comes to the assessment of traumatic stress reactions in these populations. A comprehensive review assessed for PTSD prevalence rates and found that only 6 percent (8 out of 135) used samples from developing countries (De Girolamo & McFarlane, 1996).

Traumatic stress symptoms were solicited from a small sample of victims of domestic violence among the Ju/'hoansi (Kalahari Bushmen) of eastern Namibia, one of the world's last ethnic groups still transitioning from a hunter-gatherer lifestyle (McCall & Resick, 2003). Thirty-five percent met criteria for PTSD and 85 percent reported at least some avoidance/numbing symptoms, but not to the degree that *DSM–IV* criteria were met (i.e., three or more symptoms). One year after the Rwandan Genocide, 1,830 Rwandan children were interviewed using the Impact of Event Scale about their experiences and their reactions (Dyregrov, Gupta, Gjestad, & Mukanoheli, 2000). Seventy-nine percent of the children exceeded the cutoff for PTSD one year after the Genocide. In Sierra Leone, a study coordinated by the nongovernmental aid organization Medicins Sans Frontières (Doctors without Borders) assessed for the presence of PTSD in a sample of 245 residents and Internally Displaced Person (IDP's) near Freetown (Raymond, 2000). Based on their responses to a structured interview, the authors concluded that 99 percent of respondents met criteria for PTSD. In another study in Sierra Leone, PTSD symptoms were assessed among refugees in a camp in The Gambia (Fox & Tang, 2000). Forty-nine percent of the sample yielded scores indicative of PTSD, while 80 percent met criteria for anxiety and 85 percent for depression. In Northern Uganda, a structured clinical interview was used to broadly compare Sudanese children living as refugees to Ugandan children who had not experienced war and flight (Paardekooper, de Jong, & Hermanns, 1999). The Sudanese reported increased disturbances from memories, suicide ideation, worries about their future, and worries about the risk of siblings being hurt. Even though the Sudanese children did report more symptoms commonly associated with PTSD, the authors appropriately abstained from classifying the symptoms as psychopathology given the lack of validated measures available for use with Ugandan and Sudanese children. Thus, studies utilizing etic methodology conducted in developing (African) countries have reported varying PTSD prevalence rates, ranging from 35 to 99 percent.

Elsewhere, a few prevalence studies examined possible cultural differences (or the lack thereof). The prevalence of PTSD among Filipinos six years after they were displaced by the eruption of Mt. Pinatubo was assessed (Howard et al., 1999). Results showed that prevalence rates for PTSD (and for major depression, generalized anxiety disorder, bipolar disorder, and alcohol abuse) did not vary between culturally traditional (Aeta) and nontraditional groups. PTSD was the most common single diagnosis across the two subgroups (27.6 percent) and was found in 32.2 percent of the Aetas studied. Shrestha et al. (1998) found that Bhutanese refugees who had torture histories had much higher PTSD prevalence rates than a highly similar cohort that lacked a torture history. A large-scale study used comparable assessment methods in four postconflict settings (Algeria, Cambodia, Ethiopia, and Palestine), and reported that PTSD and other anxiety disorders were the most prevalent disorders in all four settings. For those exposed to violence, PTSD was the most prevalent (except in Cambodia; de Jong et al., 2001). Yet, the authors highlight the various contextual differences that were most predictive of traumatic stress. These contextual predictors included torture, psychiatric history, poor living conditions, daily hassles, domestic stress, death in or separation from family, and alcohol abuse (de Jong et al. 2001). Table 11.1 provides a summary of studies of prevalence and their findings.

Research with Emic Approaches

Research using emic approaches are not well suited to assessing prevalence but can better characterize the local manifestation of traumatic stress. Emic approaches cast a broader net and are more likely to capture symptoms that do not fall within predetermined categories. In an ethnographic study with Mexican disaster survivors, participants described 14 of the 17 PTSD symptoms with little or no prompting (Norris et al., 2001a). Additionally, the rank order frequency of PTSD symptoms closely matched that of other postdisaster PTSD studies. Baron's (2002) qualitative analyses and focus groups with Sudanese refugees in Northern Uganda revealed a consistent pattern of symptoms: anxiety, numerous somatic complaints, standard depressive symptoms, estrangement from friends and family, and loss of motivation to care for family and self (Baron, 2002). Although some of these are symptoms of PTSD, others are not, and the list exhibits a broader symptom picture than offered by the diagnosis of PTSD. These same studies found that refugee and IDP complaints

Table 11.1   Summary of findings of cross-cultural adult PTSD prevalence studies

Citation	Sample	Measures	PTSD prevalence
Carlson & Rosser-Hogan (1994)	Cambodian refugees in U.S. ten years (n = 50)	PTSD checklist (DSM-III), HSCL-25	86%
Al-Saffar et al. (2003)	Foreign nationals (Turkey, Iran, Saudia Arabia) more than 4 years in Sweden (n = 115)	SIP	PTSD in 69% of the Iranians, 59% of the Saudis, 53% of the Turks, and only 29% of the Swedes
Weine et al. (1995)	Bosnian adolescents recently relocated to the United States (n = 20)	PSS	25%
McCall & Resick (2003)	Ju/'hoansi (n = 20)	Structured interview	35%
Dyregrov et al. (2000)	Rwandan children (n = 1830) 1 year post-genocide	IES (shortened version)	79%
Raymond (2000)	Sierra Leonean (n = 245)	IES	99%
Fox & Tang (2000)	Sierra Leonean refugees in The Gambia (n = 55)	HTQ, HSCL-25	49%
Howard et al, 1999	Filipinos after Mt. Pinatubo (n = 351)	PCL-S for DSM-IV	27.6%
Shrestha et al. (1998)	Bhutanese refugees (n = 526)	Clinical interview based on criteria	Prevalence (across all symptoms) higher than comparison group
de Jong et al., 2001	Algeria, Cambodia, Ethiopia, and Gaza	CIDI PTSD module	37.4% Algeria, 28.4% Cambodia, 15.8% Ethiopia, 17.8% Gaza
Wang et al. (2000)	China (n = 338)	CIDI PTSD module	24.2%

CIDI = Composite Interview Diagnostic Interview; HSCL-25 = Hopkins Symptom Checklist; HTQ = Harvard Trauma Questionnaire; IES = Impact of Event Scale; PCL-S = Posttraumatic Symptom Checklist; PSS = PTSD Symptoms Scale; SIP = Self rating Scale for PTSD

consistently focused more on concerns for survival (lack of food, poor health care, threat of violence), rather than on traumatic events they had suffered and their ensuing symptoms (Baron, 2002). Moreover, the majority of IDP's and refugees did not develop distressful symptoms as a result of traumatic events (Baron, 2002); the same has been said to hold true for civilians in industrialized settings (Bonanno, 2004). Another study in Uganda reported that whereas PTSD symptoms were often reported, they were less of the focus of distress than were somatic complaints (Bracken et al., 1995). The results from these emic studies suggest that PTSD may be an overly narrow characterization of traumatic stress across these different cultures, and may not be the best descriptor of reactions to trauma in all settings.

One study drew from the advantages of both etic and emic approaches in order to capture the fullest possible representation of traumatic stress. Yeomans, Herbert, and Forman (2008) used a combination of qualitative and quantitative methods to solicit symptoms among internally displaced people in Burundi all of whom had a history of one or (usually) more conflict-related traumatic events. Standardized measures showed that distress was mostly manifest in symptoms of somatization, anxiety, and depression, and less so in specific PTSD symptoms. Content analysis of open-ended questions (that were asked prior to specific symptom solicitation) that probed for reactions to traumatic events revealed these to be, in order of frequency, material complaints, depression, PTSD, and anxiety. Thus, standardized and open-ended methods suggested that Burundians conceptualized their traumatic stress mostly in terms of material complaints – a likely function of both the culture and the economic realities of this sample.

Symptom Variation

Accumulating evidence suggests that there is substantial variability in the expression of specific traumatic stress symptoms between cultures. Among the findings of PTSD prevalence and some indications of similar factor structure in diverse parts of the globe, there is substantial variability in the specific traumatic stress symptoms. Marsella and colleagues (Marsella et al., 1996; Marsella & Christopher, 2004) have argued that intrusive symptoms may be universal whereas avoidance/numbing may be more culturally based (Marsella et al., 1996). This contention has been supported in a number of studies (Dyregrov, Gupta, Gjestad, & Mukanoheli, 2000; McCall & Resick, 2003). Marsella et al. (1996) suggested that PTSD prevalence rates may be highest in cultures where avoidance and numbing behaviors are more common, as such practices may serve to maintain the other symptoms (Foa et al., 1989). Norris et al. (2001) studied the psychological impact of Hurricane Paulina in Mexico and Hurricane Andrew in the United States and found that Mexicans endorsed significantly more intrusion and avoidance symptoms, whereas Americans endorsed more arousal symptoms. The authors suggest that whereas the high PTSD prevalence rates and their correlation to trauma exposure may support the utility of the PTSD construct cross-culturally, they caution against using PTSD solely as a unidimensional construct. The differences found would not have been evident if PTSD had been considered unidimensionally. Notably, Perilla et al. (2002) found that after Hurricane Andrew, non-White Hispanics and English-speaking (more acculturated) Hispanics had comparable levels of PTSD whereas Spanish-preferring Hispanics had significantly higher levels. Such differences across cultural groups who have experienced comparable traumas point toward the possible influence of cultural differences, linguistic differences, and acculturative processes on symptom presentation.

Biological and Environmental Factors

A summary of the literature reveals considerable variability in PTSD prevalence and specific symptom presentation around the world. While observed variability may be attributed to methodological and sampling differences, we still seek to understand whether the results are more indicative of a culturally bound disorder or the inevitable variability of a more universal construct. There is a current trend in the research to investigate biological markers associated with PTSD and to present the presence of those markers as indicative of how PTSD is shaped by biological factors. These include hormonal and neurobiological correlates to PTSD symptoms. For instance, differences between those with and without trauma histories have been detected in cortisol levels, atrophy of the hippocampus (McNally, 2003), and dysregulation of the hypothalamic-pituitary-adrenal system. These biological investigations have also been extended cross-culturally. In one study, Armenian youth with greater earthquake exposure and subsequent PTSD symptoms had more depressed cortisol levels than nonexposed youth (Goenjian et al., 1996). However, it should be noted that the causality governing this relationship is not clear; we do not know if cortisol levels predisposed the youth to acquire PTSD symptoms. The correlation of biological markers to PTSD symptoms does not answer whether PTSD is more biologically or culturally determined. It does suggest that particular biological markers are associated with PTSD across different settings.

Despite the evidence that PTSD is a universal construct, a dissenting minority argues that PTSD remains substantially a cultural construct. According to this position, opportunity for secondary gain and a professional community's expectation of protracted symptomatology may be more the agents of the perpetuation of posttraumatic stress symptoms than the traumatic event itself. The vast reduction in British soldier war neuroses between the first and second world wars provides some support for the notion that posttraumatic stress is a culturally determined phenomenon. The reduction, is largely attributed to the fact that medical providers communicated an expectation of pathology to WWI trauma survivors, but did not do so to WWII survivors (Shephard, 1999). Further supporting the culturally-bound syndrome argument is the changing picture of traumatic stress over time from paralysis to hemianesthesia, fatigue, mutism and intractable trembling to the modern-day PTSD trinity of intrusion, avoidance/numbing, and hyperarousal (Herbert & Sageman, 2004). PTSD may be a product of an era in which we increasingly understand the psychology of an individual in terms of vulnerability instead of in terms of resiliency (Summerfield, 2004). Distress has become equated with psychopathology and the effect of the PTSD diagnosis is to emphasize the "traumatogenic nature" of an event over any resilience and protective factors (Kagee & Naidoo, 2004).

On the other hand, it has been argued that the refutation of the application of the PTSD construct cross-culturally is a manifestation of a larger dynamic in which professionals deny the existence of trauma in highly distressed populations (Dyregrov, Gupta, Gjestad, & Raundalen, 2002). The suggestion is that such perspectives serve to relieve the international community of its sense of responsibility and its substantial guilt over repeated failures to prevent or alleviate suffering. Yet, such accusations potentially inhibit unbiased scientific discovery. Questioning the applicability of PTSD in nonindustrialized settings appears to be valid given the dramatic cultural differences that exist. Though traumatic stress reactions, in general, may have a universal, biological underpinning, vulnerability to trauma, symptom manifestation, and response to treatment are very likely subject to contextual and cultural factors (Marsella, Friedman, & Spain, 1996).

Contextual Factors Influencing How Traumatic Reactions are Reported

Social desirability   Actual reactions to traumatic events are not necessarily the same as those reactions that are reported. While there are occasions when reactions may be underreported, certain methods of assessing responses to trauma may create a context where it is socially desirable to endorse particular symptoms. Even a carefully translated and then validated measure is still subject to an effect of social desirability in which participants' responses are influenced by their perceptions of what a favorable answer might be. Kinzie and Mason (1987) observed that the responses of Indochinese refugees who lacked prior experience with psychological surveys and interviews were largely influenced by politeness and a desire to respond correctly rather than by their true feelings. The use of emic or ethnosemantic methods such as open-ended questions, free-listing, key informant interviews, and pile sorts – all techniques that solicit information without clearly revealing for what the interviewer is searching – may offer certain advantages over standardized measures (Kagee & Del Soto, 2003; Marsella et al., 1996; Wilk & Bolton, 2002).

Power imbalance   A power differential exists in any therapeutic or health care relationship, yet it is particularly acute in the cross-cultural setting. Locals will often ascribe greater value to industrialized culture and the perceived knowledge and resources it embodies. "Hidden power dynamics and the tacit assumptions that western knowledge trumps local knowledge" can influence how participants choose to answer (Wessells, 1999, p. 275). Members of traditional cultures often denigrate and abandon their own models when confronted with those of the West, irrespective of their applicability (Peddle et al., 1999). Reading self-report measures aloud to illiterate populations increases the potential effect of the nature of the relationship between the participant and interviewer (Pernice, 1994). Similarly, it may also be possible that the presentation of expectations for specific symptoms or protracted vulnerability may be especially acute in such settings. Yeomans et al. (2008) found a significant correlation between participant prior exposure to PTSD psychoeducation and the nature and severity of their symptoms.

Secondary gain Beyond the effect of social desirability mentioned above, patients may endorse the symptoms of interest to the outsider with hopes of receiving some sort of secondary benefit. People who are poverty-stricken and whose environment has been destabilized by violence may very necessarily shape their presentation to increase the odds that they will receive the care and attention that is being offered to those determined as in need (Wessells, 1999; Kagee & Naidoo, 2004). Such a dynamic is not limited to nonindustrialized settings, and PTSD has come to play an essential role in insurance claims, asylum applications, veteran benefits, and the assistance of victims in the United States and elsewhere (Frey, 2001). This is not to say that people are necessarily malingering for personal gain, so much as that their symptoms are in part determined by the climate in which they are solicited. De Jong (2005) has countered the secondary gain argument, citing the high prevalence rates among tortured Bhutanese refugees who he argues had no secondary gain to motivate them and who easily recognized PTSD symptoms from a long list of topics.

Cultural Factors

Social and institutional support Social support and family functioning is a well-established protective factor for traumatic stress reactions (Thabet & Vostanis, 1999). The level of support at an institutional level has also been shown to influence the prevalence of PTSD. Nine months after an earthquake in China in north Hebei province, one village that had suffered less damage but had received less reconstruction support had significantly greater PTSD rates than a comparable village that suffered more seriously and had received substantially more reconstruction support (Wang et al., 2000). Satttler et al. (2002) reported that across different Caribbean nations struck by Hurricane Georges, loss of resources and absence of social support was most predictive of Acute Stress Disorder four weeks after the event. Witmer and Culver (2001) argue that family and social variables are critical predictors of distress and reco-very. Thus, both social support and institutional response after the event seems to reduce the level of subsequent traumatic stress. The more quickly the social fabric, the material infrastructure, and a sense of normalcy can be restored, the sooner the reduction in distress.

Notions of personhood and familism The notion of individuality on which the classification of psychopathology is based is relatively unfamiliar in more col-lectivistic conceptualizations of distress (Bracken et al., 1995). Nonindustrialized cultures often take more of a "sociocentric" than an "egocentric" view of soci-ety (Zur, 1996). Differences in the nature of traumatic stress symptoms have been linked to individualistic and collectivistic cultural differences (Elsass, 2001).

Understanding the nature of the traumatic experience must take place within a framework that considers the individual's larger familial and cultural experience (Morsette, 2006).

Cultural meaning of symptoms The literature offers numerous examples of how the subjective meaning of traumatic events or the associated symptoms may mediate the nature of the response to them (Zur, 1996). For instance, Punamaki (1996) found that ideological commitment moderated Israeli youth distress from political hardships. Zur (1996) discusses the Quiché Mayan who report recurrent dreams of those who died as a result of atrocities in Guatemala. These dreams are associated with positive valence for the comfort that they give. Bosnian adolescents understood memories of the events that had befallen them as normal as opposed to pathological (Weine et al., 1995). Furthermore, the absence of faith and conviction in the postmodern era and an increased orientation toward introspection may foster a sense of uncertainty and emotional vulnerability (Pupavec, 2004). The manifestations of traumatic reactions may be very different in settings in which there exists a relative orientation toward stoicism, where a fatalistic perspective dominates, and where primary import is placed on the social network of the family and the community rather than the individual (Summerfield, 2004). In such cases, the exportation of models presuming vulnerability may be contraindicated.

Social acceptance of expressed distress Cultures vary in the extent to which expression of distress is socially sanctioned and reported. For instance, Chinese are generally reluctant to express distress and often attribute such distress to external or physical causes (Wang et al., 2000). Differences in traumatic stress across gender has been observed both the US and Mexico after landfall of comparable hurricanes (Norris, Perilla, Ibanez, & Murphy, 2001). Moreover, the differences in PTSD severity were greater between men and women in Mexico than in the United States. The authors speculate that Mexican culture tends to adhere to more traditional sex roles in which male "machismo" inhibits disclosure of distress. These differences are considered less pronounced in the US.

Functional impairment The degree to which severity of symptoms is related to the inability to meet one's responsibilities of daily living may also vary across cultures, especially in settings where emotional expression is encouraged. Indeed, one of the dangers of a circumscribed interest in traumatic stress symptoms is the failure to fully assess functional impairment, the most often overlooked criteria of a PTSD diagnosis. A study in Nicaragua found that while peasants with traumatic histories reported PTSD symptoms, they were not otherwise distressed and remained highly functional (Summerfield & Toser, 1991). Witmer and Culver (2001) critique studies that presented high rates of PTSD among Bosnian refugees despite reported high rates of functioning (e.g., GAF scores up to 87), pointing to the potential for critical failure when a focus on pathology obviates consideration of resilience. Even the most comprehensive battery of symptom measures may fail to critically assess degree of functional impairment (Kagee & Naidoo, 2004). Figure 11.1 summarizes some of the factors that determine the manifestation of traumatic stress.

Challenges of Assessment and Treatment

As always, the challenge that remains is the integration of theoretical perspectives and empirical findings into practical strategies and emphases for clinical work. This challenge is exacerbated by the complex issue of culture and the necessity of simultaneously attending to both group and individual differences. Ultimately, the client's individuality precedes his or her affiliation with any particular group. At the same time, cultural identity is typically associated with personal experiences and cultural perspectives relevant to conceptualization and treatment. The clinician, despite prevalence rates, biological factors, and cultural variables, must still fundamentally understand the patient's perspective and report. Familiarity with cultural factors that influence traumatic stress presentation leads to fluency with indigenous idioms of distress, alternative models, research methods best suited for cross-cultural investigations, the pitfalls of assessment techniques and specific measures, and culturally sensitive and effective treatments.

Idioms of Distress

Patient conceptualization and perception of traumatic stress is often not seen as related to the trauma history. Research on Bhutanese refugees found that most often distress is conceptualized in terms of angered gods, dissatisfied spirits, or some form of witchcraft (Shrestha, 1998). Youth in Palestine with trauma histories reported a preponderance of conversion fits, behavioral problems, and psychosomatic complaints (Abu Hein et al., 1993). Hinton et al. (2002) described "Weak Heart" syndrome among Khmer refugees that closely resembles PTSD and panic disorder. It should also be recognized that traumatic stress symptoms as we know them may not be the impetus by which people seek treatment (Marsella & Christopher, 2004).

Assessment

The fact that certain cultures do not have words for particular symptoms not only makes using PTSD measures cross-culturally potentially problematic, it could indicate that these reactions are simply not observed in that society. Studies have found the Impact of Event Scale (IES; Horowitz, Wilner, & Alvarez, 1979) impossible to translate because items within the intrusion and avoidance symptom clusters lost their specificity of meaning and became redundant (Terheggen et al., 2001). Three items (avoidance/numbing symptoms) on the Post Traumatic Inventory (PTI; Carlson & Rosser-Hogan, 1994) were eliminated because they could not be translated when used with a Cambodian

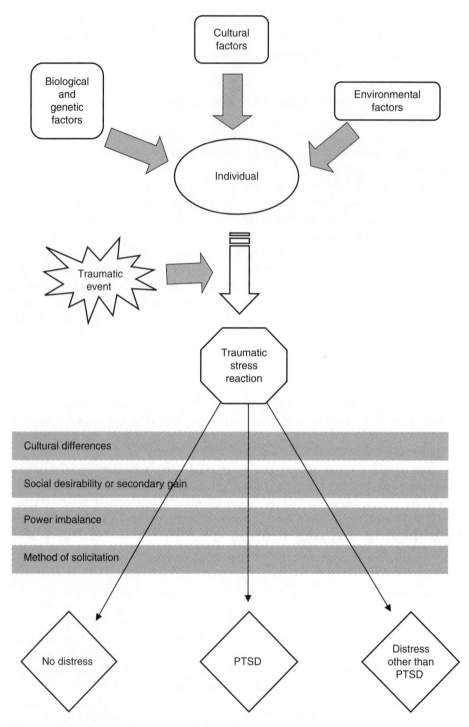

Figure 11.1   Factors shaping specific manifestation of traumatic stress

immigrant population (Carlson & Rosser-Hogan, 1994). As was discussed earlier, the vast majority of measures have not been validated for specific populations. We still have a considerable deficit of assessment tools with unproven reliability and validity in most pre-industrialized settings. We must remember, that even as there may exist a general universal response to trauma, the application of PTSD as a construct as the focus of assessment potentially minimizes the differences that do exist (Kagee & Naidoo). Clearly, given the challenges of successful translation, a PTSD measure should never be considered adequate for making a diagnosis, especially in the cross-cultural context (Green, 1991; Keane, Kaloupek, & Weathers, 1996; Pernice, 1994).

Treatment

The literature remains quite limited as far as the efficacy of different treatments for traumatic stress in diverse cultural settings. The majority of the cross-cultural treatment research has been conducted with immigrant or refugee populations who have left their home country and begun an acculturative process. Predictably, the limitations of many of the studies (e.g., no comparison group) preclude strong conclusions. There is some indication that the current "gold standard" treatment for PTSD of prolonged exposure therapy may also be efficacious cross-culturally yet further investigation is warranted.

A recent review paper found only eight PTSD treatment studies of adult refugee populations. Three of these were essentially case studies and most of the others lacked comparison groups and sizeable samples (for a full review see Nicholl & Thompson, 2004). For instance, one study treated 20 Bosnian refugees with Testimony Psychotherapy, an approach that incorporates substantial elements of imaginal exposure techniques (Weine et al., 1998). Significant decreases in PTSD and other symptom types could not be attributed to the specific intervention given the absence of a comparison group. Another study provided an analysis of CBT treatment compared to exposure treatment alone for a group of traumatized refugees (Paunovic & Ost, 2001). Goenjian et al. (1997) using a grief-focused psychotherapy significantly reduced PTSD symptoms among post-earthquake (1988) Armenian youth compared to a wait-list control. Kosovar youth ($n = 18$) recently arrived in Denmark were treated with a short trauma psychoeducational intervention (Staaehr, 2001). PTSD symptoms as measured on the IES (Impact of Events Scale) indicated significant decreases in symptoms. However, this study also lacked a comparison groups. Another study in Britain with children ($n = 26$) from diverse war-ravaged countries assessed the effect of an intervention that focused on PTSD psychoeducation and coping strategies. Results indicated a significant reduction in PTSD symptoms post-intervention compared to a waitlist control. However, these gains were not maintained at two months post-intervention.

A few studies report on components of humanitarian interventions with samples still in their home country. Trauma treatment and education programs have been developed for Eastern Europe (Bosnia and Croatia) and different regions of Africa (Miller & Rasco, 2004). Given the challenges of such an environment and the meager budget on which many of these programs are administered, there is a paucity of outcome studies in existence. Even developers of recent innovative interventions for refugees acknowledge the legitimate difficulty and the unfortunate dearth of evaluative efforts (Hubbard & Miller, 2004). Of those that do exist, some have opted for anecdotal summaries or more qualitative methods, whereas others have taken more of an empirical approach. Fewer still have been published in peer-reviewed journals. However, a few randomized controlled trials in pre-industrialized settings exist.

A sample of 43 Sudanese refugees in Northern Uganda were randomly assigned to either one session of PTSD psychoeducation, 4 sessions of psycho-education plus supportive counseling (SC), or four sessions of psychoeducation plus narrative exposure therapy (NET; Neuner, Schauer, Klaschik, Karunakara, & Elbert, 2004). NET was associated with significant decreases in PTSD symptoms at post-intervention and at one-year follow up. No significant changes were associated with SC, and psychoeducation was associated with significant increases in PTSD symptoms at post-intervention and one-year follow-up.

Five years after the Rwandan genocide, Staub, Pearlman, Gubin, and Hagengimana (2005) designed and evaluated an intervention for survivors. The intervention took the form of a nine-day training of workshop facilitators and included psychoeducational lectures on PTSD. Traumatic experiences, psychological symptoms, and orientation toward reconciliation were assessed in the participants of the subsequent workshops, not in the facilitators who were in direct receipt of the training. Controlling for Time 1 symptoms and trauma history, results showed that two months after the intervention, trauma symptoms (a combination of PTSD, traumatic grief, self-perceived functioning, Rwanda-specific trauma symptoms) decreased significantly more in the intervention condition than in either of the other two (traditional treatment, wait list control).

Finally, one study examined the specific effect of PTSD psychoeducation among subsistence farmers in Burundi who had little to no prior exposure with nonindigenous constructs of PTSD and traumatic stress (Yeomans, 2007). Participants of a four-day, inter-ethnic healing and reconciliation group workshop intervention showed greater decreases in distress when randomized to a condition that included *no mention* of PTSD symptoms and traumatic stress. All participants had endorsed some degree of symptoms at baseline. Therefore, these results cannot be explained by arguing that psychoeducation served to normalize symptoms that participants already had but were not initially able to recognize or articulate. This suggests that with this population, education about PTSD may have a morbid suggestive effect that can potentially undermine resilience and coping. While additional research is needed to replicate these results, such findings speak for careful consideration of the effects of introducing novel ideas about vulnerability to traumatic stress.

Treatment Guidelines

While the determination of the intervention of choice for cross-cultural treatment of traumatic stress will require additional research and will not likely ever lead to a singular answer, there are some general treatment principles that can be gleaned from the literature. Indigenous customs and local healing practices can be integrated into any foreign intervention (Wessells, 1999). These practices exist, can be identified, and used as a complement to outside models. For instance, the Indigenous Australians consider connection to land, kinship networks, and ritual as critical ingredients for the maintenance of well-being (Petchkovsky & San Roque, 2002). Others emphasize the sociocultural responses such as dances, ceremonies, and rituals, which westerners often overlook – for example the reconstruction of a community center, market, or gathering location. These components could all be integrated into a predominantly cognitive or behavioral treatment mode. However, dependence of cognitive processing to alleviate symptoms could be irrelevant and can undermine the attention to cultural healing rituals (Bracken et al., 1995). Finally, whether the inclusion of traditional healing approaches increases effectiveness of treatment is an empirical question that is in need of additional research.

Assuming that patients have a more collectivist and familial orientation to distress, some may prefer a group therapeutic format to individual psychotherapy. A clinician should be similarly cautioned against focusing on the traumatic event and the specific impact on the individual (Griffiths, 2001). In fact, the field should be wary about using treatment and prevention models that directly or indirectly suggest vulnerability and the likelihood of protracted problems in trauma survivors (Yeomans, 2007). These models, through the powers of suggestion, may be doing harm to those they intend to help. Instead, treatment should emphasize normalization of symptoms and of recovery. Patients from any culture will likely benefit from understanding that what they are experiencing is normal reaction to abnormal events and is expected to remit with time (Herbert & Forman, 2005).

Summary

A growing body of research points to the presence of the syndrome of PTSD in culturally diverse settings. Though utilitarian, the application of the construct of PTSD remains imperfect and associated with dangers that could undermine the greater purpose of providing culturally appropriate care for those who have suffered from war, natural disaster, or other traumatic events. As research continues to explore the degree to which PTSD can be considered a universal construct, we should remain cautious in its application cross-culturally.

A presumption that PTSD is the best model by which to recognize and treat traumatic stress cross-culturally has a number of pitfalls. Too much attention on PTSD constrains the search for a more sophisticated picture of how traumatic stress manifests cross-culturally. We are only beginning to understand how PTSD overlaps with or differs from local idioms of distress. The assumption that PTSD provides the best fit as a model limits our capacity to explore diverse symptoms sets that may also be occurring. The confidence in expectation of a particular symptom set can lead to the confirmation of its presence; some of the best scientists consistently discover exactly what they set out to find. Yet, not only can traumatic stress vary from the textbook PTSD model, evidence indicates that in most cases, traumatic stress symptoms either do not develop or are quickly resolved within the first month.

The overuse of a PTSD model may therefore falsely predict specific symptoms or overpathologize a temporary and normal reaction to a traumatic event. With PTSD comes a presumption of greater vulnerability and the absence of resilience. Marsella and Christopher (2004) argue that the normative response to crisis is the strengthening of communal relationships on the social level and resilience on the individual level. Such a response is beginning to receive more attention in the research (see Posttraumatic growth), but all too often, the PTSD construct presumes protracted vulnerability before it is necessarily evident. The call to reframe our investigations around resilience are slow to catch on (Witmer & Culver, 2001).

There is mounting evidence for biological correlates to PTSD and a growing number of international epidemiological studies concluding that PTSD is found across cultures particularly in samples exposed to violence. Nonetheless, the sole application of the PTSD model may not be the most useful model around which to focus prevention and treatment services across cultures. De Jong (2005), despite having researched PTSD prevalence rates around the globe, articulates the need to put more attention on other mental health issues that remain underinvestigated, such as mood disorders, somatoform disorder, dissociative disorders, and other anxiety disorders. The popularity of the PTSD construct in both academic circles and popular culture can distract us from other factors that may be more essential to formulating patient care cross-culturally. For instance, PTSD was found to be associated with the experience of violence but also with other factors such as living conditions and social instability (de Jong 2005). Similarly, Laban et al. (2005) found that among Iraqi asylum seekers postmigration challenges in the daily life were the best predictors of psychopathology, even more so than traumatic events themselves. Table 11.2 summarizes specific recommendations for both researchers and clinicians.

In summary, much of the literature indicates that in its different variations around the world, PTSD appears to be universally evident (Marsella & Christopher, 2004). Yet, there is also evidence that Criterion A and its associated symptoms may vary and are certainly influenced by cultural factors. Marsella & Christopher (2004) summarize their review of the literature by stating "PTSD cannot be decontexualized from the culture milieu in which it

Table 11.2 Considerations for researchers and clinicians working cross-culturally with PTSD

For researchers:
- Translate and back-translate measures
- Utilize locals at all levels of research team
- Use both qualitative and quantitative methods

For clinicians (and researchers):
- First line of treatment should be meeting material needs and restoring social network
- Be wary of overpathologizing: temper assumption of vulnerability with assumption of resilience
- Cast a broad net in the assessment of symptoms
- Carefully assess functioning independently of symptom endorsement
- Integrate local idioms of distress and treatment methods as appropriate
- Work to reduce clinician-client power imbalance that may be exacerbated by cultural differences.
- Consider cultural differences of fatalism and collectivism versus individualism
- Inquire as to the personal meaning of the endorsed symptoms

occurs, because this isolates it from its etiological roots, experiential referents, and its method of mediation" (p. 527). Treatment must take place within a cultural context but may necessarily integrate modern methods (Dyregrov et al., 2002). The literature documents an increased sensitivity to the risks of treatments without cultural considerations and the overmedicalization of traumatic stress, but we must remain vigilant and continue to recenter our clinical work and research around a contextualized view.

References

Abu Hein, F., Qouta, S., Thabet, A. A. & El Sarraj, E. (1993). Trauma and mental health of children in Gaza. *British Medical Journal, 306,* 1130–1131.
Ahmad, A. (1992). Symptoms of posttraumatic stress disorder among displaced Kurdish children in Iraq: Victims of a man-made disaster after the Gulf war. *Nordic Journal of Psychiatry, 46,* 315–319.
Al-Saffar, S., Borga, P., Edman, G., & Hallstrom, T. (2003). The etiology of posttraumatic stress disorder in four ethnic groups in outpatient psychiatry. *Social Psychiatry and Psychiatric Epidemiology, 38,* 456–462.
APA (1980). *Diagnostic and statistical manual of mental disorders* (3rd ed.). Washington, DC: Author.
Baron, N. (2002). Community based psychosocial and mental health services for southern Sudanese refugees in long-term exile in Uganda. In J. de Jong (Ed.), *Trauma in war and peace: Prevention, practice, and policy* (pp. 157–203). New York: Kluwer Academic/Plunum Publisher.
Bloom, S. (1997). *Creating sanctuary: Toward the evolution of sane societies.* New York: Routledge.

Bonanno, G. A. (2004). Loss, trauma, and human resilience: Have we underestimated the human capacity to thrive after extremely aversive events? *American Psychologist, 59*, 20–28.

Bracken, P. J., Giller, J. E., & Summerfield, D. (1995). Psychological responses to war and atrocity: The limitations of current concepts. *Social Science and Medicine, 40*, 1073–1082.

Carlson, E., & Rosser-Hogan, R. (1994). Cross-cultural response to trauma: A study of traumatic experiences and posttraumatic symptoms in Cambodian refugees. *Journal of Traumatic Stress, 7*, 43–58.

De Girolamo, G., & McFarlane, A. C. (1996) Epidemiology of posttraumatic stress disorder among victims of intentional violence: A review of the literature. In Mak, F. L., & Nadelson, C. C. (Eds.), *International review of psychiatry, Vol. 2.* (pp. 93–119). Washington, DC: American Psychiatric Association.

de Jong, J. T. V. M. (2005). Commentary: Deconstructing critiques on the internationalization of PTSD. *Culture, Medicine, and Psychiatry, 29*, 361–370.

de Jong, J. T. V. M., Komproe, I. H., Van Ommeren, M., et al. (2001). Lifetime events and posttraumatic stress disorder in 4 postconflict settings. *Journal of the American Medical Association, 286*, 555–562.

Dyregrov, A., Gupta, L., Gjestad, R., & Mukanoheli, E. (2000). Trauma exposure and psychological reactions to genocide among Rwandan children. *Journal of Traumatic Stress, 13*, 3–21.

Dyregrov, A., Gupta, L., Gjestad, R., & Raundalen, M. (2002). Is the culture always right? *Traumatology, 8*, 3–10.

Elsass, P. (2001). Individual and collective traumatic memories: A qualitative study of post-traumatic stress disorder symptoms in two Latin American localities. *Transcultural Psychiatry, 38*, 306–316.

Foa, E. B., Steketee, G., & Rothbaum, B. O. (1989). Behavioral/cognitive conceptualizations of post-traumatic stress disorder. *Behavior Therapy, 20*, 155–176.

Fox, S., & Tang, S. (2000). The Sierra Leonean refugee experience: traumatic events and psychiatric sequelae. *Journal of Nervous and Mental Disease, 188*, 490–495.

Frey, C. (2001). Posttraumatic stress disorder and culture. In A. T. Yilmaz, M. G. Weiss & A. Riecher-Rossler (Eds.), *Cultural psychiatry: Euro-international perspectives* (pp. 103–116). Basel, Switzerland: Karger.

Goenjian, A. K., Karayan, I., Pynoos, R. S., & Minassian, D. (1997). Outcome of psychotherapy among early adolescents after trauma. *American Journal of Psychiatry, 154*, 536–542.

Goenjian, A. K., Yehuda, R., Pynoos, R. S., & Steinberg, A. M. (1996). Basal cortisol, dexamethasone suppression of cortisol, and MHPG in adolescents after the 1988 earthquake in Armenia. *American Journal of Psychiatry, 153*, 929–934.

Green, B. L. (1991). Evaluating the effects of disasters. *Journal of Consulting and Clinical Psychology, 3*, 538–546.

Griffiths, P. (2001). Counselling asylum seekers and refugees: a study of Kurds in early and later stages of exile. *European Journal of Psychiatry, 4*, 293–313.

Herbert, J. D., & Forman, E. M. (2005). Posttraumatic stress disorder. In J. E. Fisher & W. O'Donohue (Eds.), *Practice guidelines for evidence based psychotherapy.* New York: Springer.

Herbert, J. D., & Sageman, M. (2004). "First Do No Harm:" Emerging guidelines for the treatment of Posttraumatic Reactions. In G. M. Rosen (Ed.), *Posttraumatic stress disorder: Issues and controversy* (pp. 213–232). Chichester, UK: John Wiley & Sons, Ltd.

Hinton, D., Hinton, S., Um, K., Chea, A. S., & Sak, S. (2002). The Khmer "weak heart" syndrome: Fear of death from palpitations. *Transcultural Psychiatry, 39*, 323–344.

Horowitz, M J., Wilner, N., & Alvarez, W. (1979). Impact of event scale: a measure of subjective distress. *Psychosomatic Medicine, 41*, 209–218.

Howard, W., Loberiza, F., Pfohl, B., Thorne, P., Magpantay, R., & Woolson, R. (1999). Initial results, reliability, and validity of a mental health survey of Mount Pinatubo disaster victims. *Journal of Nervous and Mental Disease, 187*, 661–672.

Hubbard, J., & Miller, K. E. (2004). Evaluating ecological mental health interventions in refugee communities. In K. E. Miller (Ed.) *The mental health of refugees* (pp. 337–374). Mahwah, NJ: Lawrence Erlbaum Associates.

Kagee, A., & Garcia Del Soto, A. (2003). Internal displacement and trauma: The need for a broader paradigm. In C. Brun & N. M. Birkeland (Eds.), *Researching internal displacement: State of the art.* Conference proceedings. *Acta Geographica, Series A*, No. 6, NTNU, Trondheim, 229–243.

Kagee, A. & Naidoo, A. V. (2004). Reconceptualizing the sequelae of political torture: Limitations of a psychiatric paradigm. *Transcultural Psychiatry, 41*, 46–61.

Keane, T. M., Kaloupek, D. G., Weathers, F. W. (1996). Ethnocultural considerations in the assessment of PTSD. In A. J. Marsella, M. J. Friedman, et al. (Eds.), *Ethnocultural aspects of posttraumatic stress disorder: Issues, research, and clinical applications.* (pp. 183–205). Washington, DC: American Psychological Association.

Kinzie, J. D., & Mason, S. M. (1987). The use of self-rating scales in cross-cultural psychiatry. *Hospital and Community Psychiatry, 38*, 190–196.

Kinzie, J. D., Sack, W. H., Angell, R. H., & Manson, S. M. (1986). The psychiatric effects of massive trauma on Cambodian children. *Journal of the American Academy of Child Psychiatry, 25*, 370–376.

Kleinman, A. M. (1977). Depression, somatization and the new cross-cultural psychiatry. *Social Science & Medicine, 11*, 3–10.

Laban, C. J., Gernaat, H. B. P. E., Komproe, I. H., van der Tweel, I., & de Jong, J. T. V. M. (2005). Postmigration living problems and common psychiatric disorders in Iraqi asylum seekers in the Netherlands. *Journal of Nervous and Mental Disease, 193*, 825–832.

Lynn, S. J., Knox, J. A., Fassler, O., Lillienfeld, S. O., & Loftus, E. F. (2004). Memory, trauma, and dissociation. In G. M. Rosen (Ed.) *Posttraumatic stress disorder: Issues and controversies* (pp. 163–186). Chichester, UK: John Wiley & Sons, Ltd.

McCall, G., & Resick, P. (2003). A pilot study of PTSD symptoms among Kalahari Bushmen. *Journal of Traumatic Stress, 16*(5), 445–450.

McNally, R. J. (2003). *Remembering trauma.* Cambridge, MA: Harvard University Press.

McNally, R. J. (2004). Conceptual problems with the *DSM–IV* criteria for posttraumatic stress disorder. In G. M. Rosen (Ed.) *Posttraumatic stress disorder: Issues and controversy* (pp. 1–14). Chichester, UK: John Wiley & Sons, Ltd.

Marsella, A. J., & Christopher, M. A. (2004). Ethnocultural considerations in disasters: An overview of research, issues, and directions. *Psychiatric Clinics of North America, 27*, 521–539.

Marsella, A. J., Friedman, M. J., Gerrity, E. T., & Scurfield, R. M. (1996). Ethnocultural aspects of PTSD: Some closing thoughts. In A. J. Marsella, M. J. Friedman,

E. T. Gerrity, & R. M. Scurfield (Eds.), *Ethnocultural aspects of posttraumatic stress disorder: Issues, research, and clinical applications* (pp. 529–538). Washington, DC: American Psychological Association.

Marsella, A. J., Friedman, M. J., & Spain, E. H. (1996). Ethnocultural aspects of PTSD: An overview of issues and research directions. In A. J. Marsella, M. J. Friedman, E. T. Gerrity, & R. M. Scurfield (Eds.) *Ethnocultural aspects of posttraumatic stress disorder: Issues, research, and clinical applications.* Washington, DC: American Psychological Association.

Miller, K. E., & Rasco, L. M. (2004). *The mental health of refugees: Ecological approaches to healing and adaptation.* Mahwah, NJ: Lawrence Erlbaum Associates.

Mol, S. S. L., Arntz, A., Metsemakers, J. F. M., Dinant, G., Vilters-Van Montfort, P. A. P, & Knottnerus, J. A. (2005). Symptoms of post-traumatic stress disorder after non-traumatic events: Evidence from an open population study. *British Journal of Psychiatry, 186,* 494–499.

Morsette, A. (2006). Cultural differences influence trauma treatment in Native American population. *Traumatic Stress Points, 20,* 7–9.

Nader, K., Dubrow, N., Stamm, B. H. (Eds.) (1999). *Honoring differences: Cultural issues in the treatment of trauma and loss.* Philadelphia: Brunner/Mazel, Inc.

Neuner, F., Schauer, M., Klaschik, C. Karunakara, U., & Elbert, T. (2004.) A comparison of narrative exposure therapy, supportive counseling, and psychoeducation for treating posttraumatic stress disorder in an African refugee settlement. *Journal of Counseling and Clinical Psychology, 72,* 579–587.

Nicholl, C., & Thompson, A. (2004). The psychological treatment of post traumatic stress disorder (PTSD) in adult refugees: A review of the current state of psychological therapies. *Journal of Mental Health, 13,* 351–362.

Norris, F. H., Perilla, J. L., Ibanez, G. E., & Murphy, A. D. (2001). Sex differences in symptoms of posttraumatic stress: Does culture play a role? *Journal of Traumatic Stress. 14,* 7–28.

Norris, F. H., Weisshar, D. L., Conrad, M. L., Diaz, E. M., Murphy, A. D., & Ibanez, G. E. (2001). A qualitative analysis of posttraumatic stress among Mexican victims of disaster. *Journal of Traumatic Stress, 14,* 741–756.

Paardekooper, B., de Jong, J. T. V. M., & Hermanns, J. M. A. (1999). The psychological impact of war and the refugee situation on South Sudanese children in refugee camps in Northern Uganda: An exploratory study. *Journal of Child Psychology and Psychiatry, 40,* 529–536.

Paunovic, N., & Ost, L.-G. (2001). Cognitive-behavior therapy versus exposure therapy in the treatment of PTSD in refugees. *Behavior Research and Therapy, 39,* 1183–1197.

Peddle, N., Monteiro, C., Guluma, V., & Macauley, T., (1999) Trauma, loss, resilience in Africa: A psychosocial community based approach to culturally sensitive healing. In K. Nader, N. Dubrow, & B. H. Stamm (Eds). *Honoring differences: Cultural issues in the treatment of trauma and loss.* Philadelphia: Brunner/Mazel, Inc.

Perilla, J., Norris, F., & Lavizzo, E. (2002). Ethnicity, culture, and disaster response: Identifying and explaining ethnic difference in PTSD six months after Hurricane Andrew. *Journal of Social and Clinical Psychology, 21,* 20–26.

Pernice, R. (1994). Methodological issues in research with refugees and immigrants. *Professional Psychology: Research and Practice, 25,* 207–213.

Petchkovsky, L., & San Roque, C. (2002). Tjunguwiyanytja, attacks on linking: Forced separation and its psychiatric sequelae in Australia' "Stolen Generations". *Transcultural Psychiatry, 39*, 345–366.

Punamaki, R. (1996). Can ideological commitment protect children's psychosocial well-being in situations of political violence? *Child Development, 67*, 55–69.

Pupavec, V. (2002). *Therapeutising refugees, pathologizing populations.* UNHCR, New Issues in Refugee Research, *59*.

Pupavec, V. (2004). Psychosocial interventions and the demoralization of humanitarianism. *Journal of Biosocial Science, 36*, 491–504.

Raymond, N. (2000). The trauma of war in Sierra Leone. *The Lancet, 355*, 2067–2068.

Rosen, G., & Lilienfeld, S. (in press). Posttraumatic stress disorder: An empirical evaluation of core assumptions. *Clinical Psychology Review.*

Ruchkin, V., Schwab-Stone, M., Jones, S., Cicchetti, D. V., Koposov, R., & Vermeiren, R. (2005). Is posttraumatic stress in youth a culture-bound phenomenon? A comparison of symptom trends in selected US, and Russian communities. *American Journal of Psychiatry, 162*, 538–544.

Sack, W. H., Seeley, J. R., & Clarke, G. N. (1997). Does PTSD transcend cultural barriers? A study from the Khmer Adolescent Refugee Project. *Journal of the American Academy of Child & Adolescent Psychiatry, 36*, 49–54.

Sattler, D. N., Preston, A. J., Kaiser, C. F., Olivera, V. E., Valdez, J. & Schlueter, S. (2002). Hurricane Georges: A cross-national study examining preparedness, resource loss, and psychological distress in the U.S. Virgin Islands, Puerto Rico, Dominican Republic, and the United States. *Journal of Traumatic Stress, 15*, 339–350.

Shephard, B. (1999). "Pitiless Psychology": The role of prevention in British military psychiatry in the Second World War. *History of Psychiatry, 10*, 491–510.

Shrestha, N. M., Sharma, B., Van Ommeren, M., et al. (1998). Impact of torture on refugees displaced within the developing world: Symptomatology among Bhutanese refugees in Nepal. *Journal of the American Medical Association, 280*, 443–448.

Smith, P., Perrin, S., Dyregrov, A. & Yule, W. (2003). Principal component analysis of the impact of event scale with children at war. *Personality and Individual Differences, 34*, 315–322.

Staaehr, M. A. (2001). Psychoeducation with Kosovo Albanian refugee children. *Psyke & Logos, 22*, 127–146.

Staub, E., Pearlman, L. A., Gubin, A. & Hagengimana, A. (2005). Healing, reconciliation, forgiving, and the prevention of violence after genocide or mass killing: An intervention and its experimental evaluation in Rwanda. *Journal of Social and Clinical Psychology, 24*, 297–334.

Summerfield, D. (2004). Cross-cultural perspectives on the medicalization of human suffering. In G. M. Rosen (Ed.), *Posttraumatic stress disorder: Issues and controversy* (pp. 233–245). Chichester: John Wiley & Sons, Ltd.

Summerfield, D., & Toser, L. (1991). "Low intensity" war and mental trauma in Nicaragua: a study in a rural community. *Medicine and War, 7*, 84.

Terheggen, M., Stroebe, M.., & Kleber R. (2001). Western conceptualization and eastern experience: A Cross-cultural study of traumatic stress reactions among Tibetan refugees in India. *Journal of Traumatic Stress, 14*, 391–403.

Thabet, A. A. M., & Vostanis, P. (1999). Post-traumatic stress reactions in children of war. *Journal of Child Psychology and Psychiatry, 40*, 385–391.

United Nations High Commission on Refugees (UNHCR). 2006. *2006 Global Trends: Refugees, Asylum Seekers, Returnees, Internally Displaced and Stateless Persons.* New York: Author.

Wang, X., Gao, L., Shinfuku, N., Zhang, H., Zhao, C., & Shen, Y. (2000). Longitudinal study of earthquake-related PTSD in a randomly selected community sample in north China. *American Journal of Psychiatry, 157*, 1260–1266.

Weine, S. M., Becker, D. F., Glashan, T. H., et al. (1995). Psychiatric consequences of "ethnic cleansing": Clinical assessments and trauma testimonies of newly resettled Bosnian refugees. *American Journal of Psychiatry, 152*, 536–542.

Weine, S. M., Kulenovic, A. D., Pavkovic, I., & Gibbons, R. (1998). Testimony psychotherapy in Bosnian refugees: A pilot study. *American Journal of Psychiatry, 155*, 1720–1726.

Welner, Z., Reich, W., Herjanic, B., & Jung, K. G. (1987). Reliability, validity, and parent–child agreement studies of the Diagnostic Interview for Children and Adolescents (DICA). *Journal of the American Academy of Child & Adolescent Psychiatry, 26*, 649–653.

Wessels, M. (1999). Culture, power, and community: Intercultural approaches to psychosocial assistance and healing. In K. Nader, N. Dubrow, & B. H. Stamm (Eds.), *Honoring differences: Cultural issues in the treatment of trauma and loss* (pp. 267–280). Philadelphia: Brunner/Mazel.

Wilk, C. M., & Bolton, P. (2002). Local perceptions of the mental health effects of the Uganda AIDS epidemic. *Journal of Nervous and Mental Disease, 190*, 394–397.

Witmer, T. A. P. & Culver, S. M. (2001). Trauma and resilience among Bosnian refugee families: A critical review of the literature. *Journal of Social Work Research and Evaluation, 2*, 173–187.

World Health Organization (WHO) (2002). *World report on violence and health.* Geneva: Author.

Yeomans, P. D. (2007). The effect of PTSD psychoeducation on the nature and severity of symptoms in a Burundian sample. Unpublished doctoral dissertation, Drexel University, Philadelphia.

Yeomans, P. D., Herbert, J. D., & Forman, E. M. (2008). Symptom comparison across multiple solicitation methods among Burundians with traumatic event histories. *Journal of Traumatic Stress, 21*, 231–234.

Zur, J. (1996). From PTSD to voices in context: From an "experience-far" to an "experience-near" understanding of responses to war and atrocity across cultures. *International Journal of Social Psychiatry, 42*, 305–317.

Zwi, A. B. (1991). Militarism, militarization, health, and the third world. *Medicine and War, 7*, 262–268.

12

Culture and Psychotic Disorders

Kristin M. Vespia

Psychotic disorders such as schizophrenia are generally considered a global concern, one that crosses cultures and nations. Symptoms of psychosis were observed in the ancient civilizations of Greece, Rome, Mesopotamia, and India, and they continue to be present across the world today (Walker, Kestler, Bollini, & Hochman, 2004). These disorders, which are viewed as among the most severe of mental illnesses, can also exact a painful price, including personal distress, difficulty holding a job and maintaining significant relationships, stigma, family and caregiver burden, increased risk for poor physical health, and costs associated with medical care and lost productivity (Knapp, Mangalore, & Simon, 2004; Maxmen & Ward, 1995; Seeman, 2007). One international review of the health care costs of schizophrenia alone suggested it accounts for 1.5–3 percent of a country's medical expenses (Knapp et al., 2004). Others have estimated that the total financial burden associated with schizophrenia may amount to 2 percent of the United States' gross national product (Maxmen & Ward, 1995).

The impact of psychotic disorders can in some ways be quantified, but the term "psychosis" itself may be harder to understand. It has been used since the early days of psychiatric diagnosis, but its meaning has shifted over time. In the *DSM–I* and *DSM–II*, early editions of the American Psychiatric Association's (APA) diagnostic classification system, psychoses occupied the severe end of a continuous scale from mental health to devastating forms of mental illness (Castillo, 1997). More contemporary definitions of psychosis have focused, not on severity, but instead on specific, potential symptoms of these disorders, such as hallucinations (e.g., seeing things that others do not), delusions (e.g., believing others can hear your thoughts), and catatonia (e.g., lack of responsiveness) (APA, 2000). The most current version of the *Diagnostic and Statistical Manual of Mental Disorders (DSM–IV–TR)* provides diagnostic criteria for a number of psychotic disorders. These include, but are not limited to: schizophrenia; schizophreniform disorder; schizoaffective disorder; delusional disorder; brief psychotic disorder; and shared psychotic disorder

(APA, 2000). The *DSM–IV–TR* also provides information about culture-bound syndromes, such as boufée delirante, locura, and spells, that may involve psychotic symptoms or be mistaken for psychotic episodes.

Perhaps because of the significant impact of these disorders on patients, families, and society, they have been the subject of international interest over time. In fact, even though multiculturalism may be considered a relatively recent force within clinical and counseling psychology, the examination of cultural factors and psychotic disorders is not new. Kraeplin studied the existence of dementia praecox (today known as schizophrenia) in Java in 1904 to explore the validity of the condition outside of western cultures (Lin & Kleinman, 1988; Walker et al., 2004). On a larger scale, Kulhara and Chakrabarti (2001) describe the efforts of the World Health Organization (WHO), which has worked since the 1960s to study the existence, expression, and course of schizophrenia in countries across the globe. Published studies of psychotic disorders across racial/ethnic groups within the United States have also been in existence for decades. As an example, Fabrega, Swartz, and Wallace (1968) studied 141 African-American, European American, and Hispanic/Latino hospital patients with schizophrenia to explore whether symptomatic, behavioral, or personality differences might exist based on cultural factors, even attempting to control for potential confounding variables like social class. The authors acknowledged potential methodological and measurement concerns, but some significant between-group variations (e.g., in hallucinations) were documented.

This history of interest in the intersection of culture and psychosis has produced extensive writings and supported the existence of a very complex relationship involving biological, sociocultural, and psychological factors. In fact, one author has even suggested renaming schizophrenia "neuro-emotional integration disorder" in part to highlight its ties to biopsychosocial models (Levin, 2006, p. 327). Although the precise cause of schizophrenia and other psychotic disorders remains an empirical question, numerous biologically based hypotheses have been put forward (Walker et al., 2004). Specific environmental stressors have, however, also been implicated. Socioeconomic status (SES), for instance, may serve as a risk factor in the course of schizophrenia, but it may play a different role for male and female patients (Parrott & Lewine, 2005). Furthermore, symptoms considered to be hallmarks of psychotic disorders, such as delusions and hallucinations, have different meanings cross-culturally and may, at times, represent culturally or religiously appropriate phenomena (APA, 2000; Vega, Sribney, Miskimen, Escobar, & Aguilar-Gaxiola, 2006). It is also well-established that the course of psychotic disorders varies across developed and developing nations, and factors from diet to expressed emotion in families have been investigated as potential explanatory variables (Lin & Kleinman, 1988; Peet, 2004). Even these brief facts, which point to complex relationships among biology, the environment, culture, gender, and social class, indicate that psychotic disorders are a particularly appropriate topic to explore from the perspective embraced by this text: the biopsychocultural approach. This chapter will describe in detail the multi-faceted relationship between cultural factors and psychotic disorders, focusing primarily on the most widely known and researched of these illnesses: schizophrenia. Before turning to a cultural examination, however, the disorders themselves will be described in greater detail.

Diagnosing Schizophrenia and Psychotic Disorders

Schizophrenia is a relatively rare mental illness that is typically diagnosed in late adolescence or early adulthood, often following a gradual development of symptoms, such as withdrawing socially or experiencing blunted or unusual emotional reactions, over a period of years (Maxmen & Ward, 1995; Mueser & McGurk, 2004). Because the disorder often appears in a person's twenties, as he or she is beginning adult life, it can significantly impair the ability to form intimate bonds and achieve the educational or vocational milestones common during this time (Walker et al., 2004). Although complete remission is possible, once diagnosed, it is often a long-term disorder, with the individual either experiencing chronic symptoms or intermittent periods of active symptoms and remissions (APA, 2000; Hegarty, Baldessarini, Tohen, Waternaux, & Oepen, 1994; Walker et al., 2004).

What we know today as schizophrenia was first labeled "dementia praecox" by Emil Kraepelin, who essentially viewed this disorder as one characterized by psychotic symptoms that consistently worsened over time (Walker et al., 2004). Eugen Bleuler would later refer to the condition as schizophrenia, and would describe what he believed were its primary and secondary symptoms (World Health Organization, 1973). For Bleuler, primary symptoms were those present in all patients for the duration of their illness; examples included separation from reality, emotional disturbance, and disordered thinking (World Health Organization, 1973). Secondary symptoms, which he did not believe were present in all patients, and which could be indicative of other mental disorders, included hallucinations and delusions.

Where Bleuler once differentiated primary and secondary indicators of schizophrenia, today the disorder is characterized by positive (an exaggeration of normal thoughts, perceptions, or behaviors) and negative symptoms (a diminishment of normal thoughts, emotions, or behaviors) (APA, 2000). Positive symptoms include delusions, hallucinations, and language or behavior that is disorganized, incoherent, or that fails to respond to outside stimuli. These symptoms can represent difficulties with reality testing (Mueser & McGurk, 2004). Delusions, for example, are said to occur when individuals develop persistent false beliefs. Delusions can be classified into a variety of types, including persecutory (e.g., "Everyone at work is conspiring to get me fired."), grandiose (e.g., "I can heal the sick with just a touch of my hand."),

and delusions of control (e.g., "The CIA is monitoring and determining my thoughts.") (Mueser & McGurk, 2004). Hallucinations, on the other hand, are not beliefs, but perceptual experiences (APA, 2000). These perceptions can be visual or auditory – or even relate to taste, touch, and smell. The key is that they are not shared by others and are not objectively real. For instance, an auditory hallucination might include hearing voices telling you to kill yourself; a visual hallucination might involve seeing dozens of spiders crawling up your arms.

The final positive symptoms of schizophrenia include disorganized speech and behavior (APA, 2000). Individuals may at times speak in ways that are tangential and seem to have no clear relationship to the conversation at hand. They may move from one topic to another with no clear organization, or they may even engage in completely incoherent speech (APA, 2000). The disorganized behavior in schizophrenia can include problems with everyday behaviors, such as basic hygiene and dress. Individuals may also appear agitated or behave in inappropriate or sexualized ways in public by, for example, shouting at passersby on a busy street (American Psychiatric Association, 2000).

The negative symptoms of schizophrenia include flat affect, alogia, and avolition (APA, 2000). Flat affect refers to expressing a reduced range of emotions, which may be accompanied by unresponsive facial expressions (Mueser & McGurk, 2004). Alogia is a significant reduction in speech; the person may produce very few words (Maxmen & Ward, 1995). In a similar vein, avolition means the individual experiences a severe reduction in behavior in general, often failing to participate in everyday activities or social interactions (APA, 2000). This cluster of symptoms may seem less remarkable than hallucinations or delusions, but in fact they are pervasive and closely linked with schizophrenia patients' ability to function effectively in the world (Mueser & McGurk, 2004).

Persons with schizophrenia do not necessarily display all of the symptoms described. With some exceptions, to be diagnosed with the disorder, an individual would need to exhibit two or more of these symptoms for one month (APA, 2000). The symptoms would also have to interfere significantly with the person's work, relationships, or other major areas of his or her life (APA, 2000). Although only one month of active symptoms is required, the *DSM–IV–TR* requires six months of some level of difficulty associated with the disorder to make the diagnosis. For example, persons with schizophrenia who have hallucinations and delusions may not always show evidence of them. They may experience a period before the onset of active symptoms (prodromol phase) or after a time of active symptoms (residual phase) that present a different type or level of difficulties (APA, 2000). Negative symptoms may be part of these phases, or the individual may exhibit less severe forms of positive symptoms, such as holding unusual beliefs, but not experiencing full-blown delusions.

In addition to determining whether a client is suffering from schizophrenia, professionals also assess the particular subtype of the disorder, either Paranoid, Disorganized, Catatonic, Undifferentiated, or Residual, when making a diagnosis

(APA, 2000). These subtypes are based on which symptoms are prominent for the individual. For example, those with paranoid schizophrenia have dominant hallucinations or delusions, while those with disorganized schizophrenia have their most significant difficulty with disorganized behavior and speech.

As noted previously, the *DSM–IV–TR* lists a number of psychotic disorders. The symptoms of some of these conditions, however, share a great deal in common. For instance, schizophreniform and brief psychotic disorders involve essentially the same symptoms as schizophrenia, but their duration is shorter (APA, 2000). Schizoaffective disorder is also characterized by the presence of positive and/or negative symptoms of schizophrenia, but patients frequently (yet not constantly) experience significant, simultaneous mood symptoms, such as a major depressive episode (APA, 2000). In fact, cross-cultural studies of psychosis have often grouped patients with schizophrenia and other conditions within that spectrum (e.g., schizoaffective disorder) together (e.g., Barrio, 2001; Brekke & Barrio, 1997; Parrott & Lewine, 2005). As a result, and because schizophrenia certainly dominates the literature on psychotic disorders, the review of cultural perspectives on psychosis that follows will focus primarily on schizophrenia. The following pages will detail the relationship among culture and the etiology, incidence and prevalence, diagnosis, expression, course, and treatment of schizophrenia and psychotic symptoms.

The Etiology of Schizophrenia: Biopsychocultural Perspectives

As noted previously in this chapter, scholars and clinicians have long expressed interest in the role of culture in psychotic disorders. This fact might be surprising to some because the existence of schizophrenia in countries and cultures around the world has lent support to the widely-held belief that it is, in essence, a disease of the brain (Kulhara & Chakrabarti, 2001; Maxmen & Ward, 1995; Mueser & McGurk, 2004; Walker et al., 2004). The biological underpinnings of schizophrenia are supported by a number of findings. Individuals with first-degree relatives who have the disorder are ten times more likely to be diagnosed themselves (Mueser & McGurk, 2004). Furthermore, specific physiological anomalies have been discovered in schizophrenia patients, including enlarged ventricles and decreased gray matter in the brain, reduced thalamus and hippocampus size, increased levels of dopamine receptors, and abnormalities in PET and functional MRI brain scans when cognitive tasks are performed (Walker et al., 2004).

There are a variety of biological and other theories regarding the etiology of schizophrenia, but there appears to be no one single cause (Walker et al., 2004). And although biological factors cannot be underestimated, environmental forces also play a critical role in its onset and course, as would be expected in the diathesis-stress model (Walker & Diforio, 1997; see also Chapter 9, Gurung & Roethel). Prenatal and delivery complications, such as maternal infections and hypoxia, have been found to be predictors of schizophrenia (Walker et al.,

2004). Stress and stressful life events may also contribute to the onset of the disorder and influence its course, for example, by inducing a relapse or an increase in symptom severity (Walker & Diforio, 1997). In fact, immigration to a new country and living in an urban area are associated with an elevated risk for schizophrenia (Cantor-Graae, 2007). And, of course, because culture is a major environmental variable, and one that might be associated with discrimination or other stressors, a diathesis-stress approach to the disorder would highlight the need to focus on culture to truly understand schizophrenia.

Beyond the actual cause of schizophrenia and other psychotic disorders, readers should also recognize the importance of public perceptions of etiology and potential cross-cultural differences. Furnham and Chan (2004) surveyed 163 people living in Britain and another 176 Chinese individuals from Hong Kong regarding their beliefs about schizophrenia, including its causes. Among other things, the authors discovered the Chinese participants, when asked about the development of schizophrenia, were significantly more likely to agree that factors such as childhood abuse, experiencing family rejection or trauma at an early age, or even stress were possible causes. Those from Britain, by contrast, more strongly endorsed biological causes. Such differences might also be found among cultural groups within a country. Knowing how clients may perceive the cause of their illness is particularly important because those beliefs will likely drive the decision to seek mental health treatment, as well as their intervention preferences.

Incidence and Prevalence Across Groups

Also important to the understanding of a disorder and clients diagnosed with it is an awareness of the frequency with which it occurs. Although schizophrenia is probably the most well-known of the psychotic disorders, it is also exceedingly rare. The *DSM–IV–TR* reports a prevalence range from 0.5–1.5 percent, with estimates of 0.5–5.0 new cases being diagnosed in every 10,000 people each year (APA, 2000). A review of selected international investigations of prevalence indicates that rates tend to fall between 1.4 and 4.6 per 1000 (Jablensky, 2000).

The incidence and prevalence of schizophrenia tend to be similar across sexes and in countries around the world (Jablensky et al., 1992; Mueser & McGurk, 2004). The World Health Organization (WHO) published initial information about its International Pilot Study of Schizophrenia (IPSS) in 1973. The organization was able to examine schizophrenia in the African, Asian, European, North American, and South American continents by establishing centers of study in the cities of Aarhus, Agra, Cali, Ibadan, London, Moscow, Taipei, Washington, D.C., and Prague (WHO, 1973). Cases of schizophrenia were found in each of these sites, lending support to the belief that this is a global disorder (WHO, 1975). Furthermore, a review of the IPSS investigation and more recent international studies of schizophrenia, such as the Determinants of Outcomes of Severe Mental Disorders (DOSMeD) and International Study of Schizophrenia (ISOS), has led to the general conclusion that prevalence and incidence rates of schizophrenia are relatively consistent cross-nationally (Kulhara & Chakrabarti, 2001). In fact, the DOSMeD study originally involved 1,379 participants from 10 nations, including Colombia, Czech Republic (then Czechoslovakia), Denmark, India, Ireland, Japan, Nigeria, Russia (then the USSR), the UK, and the USA (Jablensky et al., 1992). Using their strictest definition of schizophrenia symptoms, incidence rates across centers all hovered at about 1 in 10,000 (from 0.7 in Aarhus, Denmark to 1.4 in Nottingham, UK). When separated by sex, rates varied from 0.8 to 1.7 for men and 0.5 to 1.4 for women.

Questions remain, however, regarding the issue of incidence and prevalence across groups. Reviews suggest the incidence of schizophrenia may be slightly elevated in men, as compared to women, and that women may be diagnosed with the disorder later in their lives (APA, 2000; Jablensky et al., 1992; Lewine, 1981). Examining international findings, more consistent international rates of schizophrenia have been documented when using increasingly narrow and specific diagnostic definitions, as opposed to broader classification schemes (Jablensky et al., 1992; Kulhara & Chakrabarti, 2001).

Studying rates *within* nations also points to complexities and unknowns. A review of incidence and prevalence studies reveals that pockets of unusually high (e.g., specific parts of Finland and Croatia) and low (e.g., Hutterites from South Dakota) rates have been reported (Jablensky, 2000). A frequently investigated example of this phenomenon is African Caribbeans living within the UK. Rates of schizophrenia within this group have frequently been reported as higher than the rest of the population in the UK, even though the incidence of schizophrenia is similar when one compares the White citizens of the UK and individuals from African-Caribbeans' home nations, such as Jamaica (Sharpley, Hutchinson, McKenzie, & Murray, 2001). Such findings have encouraged a number of hypotheses regarding the cause of increased rates in this particular group; however, other researchers have suggested the focus on African-Caribbeans may be misguided. An investigation of schizophrenia in northern London found higher incidence rates for all racial/ethnic minority groups, not simply African-Carribeans, when compared to Caucasians – by an incidence ratio of 3.6 (King, Coker, Leavey, Hoare, & Johnson-Sabine, 1994). Furthermore, a recent meta-analysis of 18 investigations of schizophrenia incidence among immigrants to various countries (published between 1977 and 2003) has supported migration status as a significant risk factor for schizophrenia, noting this risk is even higher for individuals from developing countries and those from nations whose citizens are predominantly Black (Cantor-Graae & Selten, 2005). Providing an explanation for such results is complicated, but finding that skin color exacerbates the risks associated with immigration could point to the role of discrimination (Cantor-Graae & Selton, 2005).

Studies of cultural factors involved in the incidence and prevalence of schizophrenia have existed on the international scene for decades, and the preceding information provides only a glimpse into that literature. In a similar fashion, within the United Sates scholars have expressed interest in differential rates of disease among members of its diverse racial/ethnic groups. Unfortunately, sufficient information is not available to report the prevalence of mental disorders within all of these groups in the United States (U.S. Department of Health and Human Services, 2001). Nonetheless, as will be explored in greater detail below, researchers have discovered that members of minority groups may be at greater risk for a *diagnosis* of schizophrenia, again raising the possibility of sociocultural influences on psychotic disorders.

Diagnosis: Differential Rates Across Cultures

Despite the complications already noted, again, the incidence and prevalence of schizophrenia are generally considered to be similar around the globe (APA, 2000), and overall mental illness prevalence rates are believed to be comparable among racial/ethnic groups within the United States, even if the rates for specific disorders are not fully understood (U.S. Department of Health and Human Services, 2001). These findings, however, are not necessarily consistent with schizophrenia's *diagnostic* rates. In one illustrative investigation researchers reviewed data from 19,219 patients who had sought care from a large health-care organization (Minsky, Vega, Miskimen, Gara, & Escobar, 2003). They found African Americans were significantly more likely to receive a psychotic disorder diagnosis (e.g., 19.1 percent of African-American males versus 9.4 percent and 9.9 percent of Latino and European American males), even though their assessed level of functioning was actually higher than members of the other racial/ethnic groups with that diagnosis.

Although not comparable to the large-scale epidemiological WHO investigations, many studies both of schizophrenia diagnoses and psychotic symptoms in general have discovered higher rates among African-American clients (Blow et al., 2004; Minsky et al., 2003; Mukherjee, Shukla, Woodle, Rosen, & Olarte, 1983; Trierweiler et al., 2000). Similar findings have been reported for Hispanics or Latinos by some authors (Blow et al., 2004; Olfson et al., 2002), but not by others (Minksy et al., 2003). Reviews of research also indicate Asian Americans receive schizophrenia diagnoses at greater rates than members of other racial/ethnic groups (APA, 2000; Bae & Brekke, 2002). The intersection of race/ethnicity and diagnosis within the United States is clear. In fact, in a study of more than 100,000 African-American, Hispanic, and White veterans, researchers found that clients' race was the best predictor of receiving a schizophrenia diagnosis, as opposed to one of bipolar disorder (Blow et al., 2004).

These findings are complicated by a number of factors and do not necessarily point to greater *rates* of psychotic illness among members of minority groups. First, some of these investigations simply examined the existence of psychotic symptoms, not a schizophrenia diagnosis. Hallucinations, delusions, and other symptoms of psychosis are not unique to schizophrenia and may be present in other psychiatric illnesses, such as bipolar disorder and major depressive disorder with psychotic features. Second, diagnostic differences based simply on racial/ ethnic group membership may be confounded by other variables, including acculturation, racial identity, and social class, but these explanatory variables have not been frequently explored in multicultural research (Brekke & Barrio, 1997). Finally, it is difficult to know if the differences described above correspond with true variations in the expression of schizophrenia or with diagnostic biases or lack of cultural competence in assessment, such as failure to recognize the difference between true psychotic symptoms and culturally or religiously appropriate behaviors (Neighbors, Trierweiler, Ford, & Muroff, 2003; Pavkov, Lewis, & Lyons, 1989). Draguns and Tanaka-Matsumi (2003) have also suggested that clinicians are not immune from having social or cultural distance from a client reduce their ability to develop accurate empathy for that individual. Some of the potential explanations for these systematic variations in diagnosis deserve additional attention.

Clinician Attributions and Perceptions of Symptoms

One hypothesis for increased diagnostic rates among many racial/ethnic minority groups is that clinicians perceive these clients and their symptoms differently. Based on reviews of existing research, African Americans, for example, may face an increased likelihood of being viewed through a lens of severity or even danger (Trierweiler, Murhoff, Jackson, Neighbors, & Munday, 2005). Might that tendency correspond with increased diagnoses of schizophrenia? In an examination of 292 inpatients diagnosed with either schizophrenia or a major mood disorder, one group of researchers discovered that clinicians were more likely to report hallucinations and paranoid or suspicious attitudes in African Americans, while they more frequently attributed mood symptoms and negative symptoms to non-African Americans (Trierweiler et al., 2000). The presence of negative symptoms, however, was significantly associated with a diagnosis of schizophrenia for African Americans, but not for other participants in this study. The authors concluded that clinicians viewed African-American patients and their symptoms in a systematically different manner than those from other groups.

In another study of 76 outpatients from an inner-city hospital, 52 of whom had received a misdiagnosis of schizophrenia, African Americans were more likely than Caucasians or Hispanics to receive a misdiagnosis of paranoid schizophrenia (Mukherjee et al., 1983). This result held despite the fact that African Americans were not significantly more likely to report some specific symptoms associated with the disorder, such as delusions of persecution or ideas of reference. Researchers have argued that increased diagnostic rates of this subtype of schizophrenia in African Americans may be due to clinicians viewing normal cultural mistrust as a sign of paranoia (Whaley, 2001a; Whaley, 2001b; Whaley, 2001c). Cultural mistrust and/or cultural paranoia have been described as a normal reaction to persistent exposure to racism (Whaley, 2001b, 2002).

An African-American client may express suspicion when interacting with a White therapist in an assessment interview or describe a feeling of being watched by police, but it is possible that mistrustful behavior is based on a reasonable fear of being misunderstood or subject to racial biases, not on the paranoia associated with mental illness. Of course, true paranoia symptoms (i.e., clinical paranoia) do exist in some African-American clients, and they may also experience a combination of clinical paranoia and cultural mistrust, known as confluent paranoia (Whaley, 2001b). Thus, diagnostic rates for African Americans could be inflated when clinicians do not account for the possibility of expected cultural mistrust, but those rates could be artificially deflated when genuine clinical paranoia is dismissed as a culturally appropriate response (Whaley, 2001b).

Possible misattributions of clients' symptoms are not limited to work with African-American clients, and cultural mistrust is not the only culturally appropriate behavior that might be mistaken for a schizophrenia symptom. As described previously, Minksy and colleagues conducted an investigation of 19,219 patients seeking care from a very large mental health care organization and discovered, consistent with other studies, that African-American clients were more likely to receive a diagnosis of schizophrenia or other psychotic disorder than either European Americans or Latinos, despite their reported higher level of functioning (Minsky et al., 2003). Interestingly, Latino clients in the same study were diagnosed at significantly higher rates than other groups with major depressive disorder. However, they reported not only more depressive symptoms, but more symptoms of psychosis than both African and European Americans. The authors suggested that one hypothesis regarding the discrepancy between Latinos' self-report of psychosis symptoms and clinicians' diagnoses was that they endorsed some culturally appropriate behaviors, such as hearing a deceased loved one's voice, on the research instruments. Skilled clinicians may have realized, however, that these were culturally prescribed behaviors, not signs of psychotic illness. Other studies have found higher rates of schizophrenia diagnosis in Hispanic or Latino clients (Blow et al., 2004; Olfson et al., 2002), and one potential explanation is that clinicians and/or researchers did not appreciate the cultural meaning of participants' expressed symptoms. It is also important to note that similar diagnostic problems could arise with other client groups, such as traditional Native Americans, who might express a belief in supernatural forces that clinicians would view as a psychotic symptom (Herring, 2004).

Of course, these issues of clinician attributions and patient race/ethnicity are not unique to the United States. Some authors have raised diagnostic bias as a potential explanation for the higher rates of schizophrenia among African-Caribbeans in the UK (King et al., 1994), although Cantor-Graae and Selten (2005) argue that strong evidence to support such as a hypothesis is lacking. They note, for example, that their review of existing research demonstrates a similar stability of diagnosis over time for African-Caribbeans and patients from other ethnic groups, and they review a number of other explanatory hypotheses, such as stress associated with discrimination and social inequities (Cantor-Graae & Selten, 2005). These assertions serve to highlight the many challenges associated with isolating the cause of cross-cultural diagnostic variability.

Overlap with Culture-Bound Syndromes

Related to the issue of culturally-prescribed behaviors being perceived as psychotic symptoms is the potential overlap between psychotic disorders and culture-bound syndromes. The *DSM–IV–TR* includes a list of 25 culture-bound syndromes, discrete conditions that appear within specific cultures or localities (APA, 2000). Ghost sickness is one example. Most associated with Native American nations, the condition revolves around an intense focus on death or a specific individual who has died (APA, 2000). In addition to symptoms such as anxiety and suppressed appetite, sufferers may experience hallucinations, experience confusion, or have a preoccupation with danger (APA, 2000). Some of these symptoms might be confused with the disorganized behavior, paranoia, or unusual perceptual experiences sometimes associated with schizophrenia. Other culture-bound syndromes, such as boufée delirante, locura, and koro, also involve the presence of symptoms that might be considered hallucinations or delusions (APA, 2000). Culture-bound syndromes are often associated with groups whose members would be considered persons of color in the United States. If clinicians do not carefully screen for their presence, then it is possible that misdiagnosing such conditions as a psychotic disorder would contribute to increased diagnostic rates of psychotic disorders among racial and ethnic minority groups.

Language Issues and Barriers

Another factor that may contribute to group differences in diagnostic rates of psychotic disorders is language barriers. Members of immigrant groups in particular may face therapeutic encounters in which they cannot converse in their native tongue, and these interactions could contribute to a greater likelihood of misunderstandings within the counseling dyad. A particular problem in the United States has been the lack of Spanish-speaking clinicians (Minsky et al., 2003). Unfortunately, not enough is known about the potential impact of using interpreters or engaging in therapy in one's second language. For example, contradictory results have been reported regarding the use of Spanish in assessment interviews with native Spanish-speaking clients. Some argue that using Spanish increases self-disclosure and expression of symptoms; others report English language interviews elicit those same responses from clients (Minsky et al., 2003). In fact, one investigation of the misdiagnosis of schizophrenia that included Hispanic or Latino clients found that having a clinician who spoke Spanish was not a protective factor (Mukherjee et al., 1983).

Translation and barrier concerns are not the only language issues that have a potential impact on the diagnosis of schizophrenia. Language is a powerful tool, and the power of the label "schizophrenia" may contribute to how it is used in diagnosis (Kim & Berrios, 2001). In many Asian nations, including Japan, language systems employ ideographic Chinese characters. Within that system, the literal Greek roots of the word "schizophrenia" (i.e., "split mind") are depicted directly, and in Japanese this leads to the disorder being expressed as "mind-split-disease" (Kim & Berrios, 2001, p. 181). Kim and Berrios (2001) argue that schizophrenia as an English word does not have that immediate connotation, as its Greek origins and meaning are not directly observable. Although data supporting a causal link are not presented, the authors believe that the direct expression of the disorder in ideographic characters may increase the stigma of schizophrenia and possibly even contribute to Japanese psychiatrists feeling reluctant to share that diagnosis with patients and families. A review of epidemiology studies of schizophrenia in Japan suggests the incidence and prevalence of the disorder is similar to that of other nations (Nakane, Ohta, & Radford, 1992). However, the Japanese Society of Psychiatry and Neurology officially supported a name change in 2002 to "Togo Shitcho Sho" or "integration disorder" (Sato, 2006, p. 53). Sato (2006) reviewed efforts to evaluate the change and indicated that the term, according to one survey, was used in 78 percent of cases only seven months after the name shift. Sato also described reports that the percentage of patients told of their diagnosis increased from 36.7 percent to 69.7 percent between 2002 and 2004.

Symptoms: Differential Expression Within and Across Groups

Given the fact that diagnosis appears to differ based on cultural factors, it should not be surprising that researchers have also discovered some predictable international and multicultural differences in the symptomatic expression of psychotic illnesses. Unfortunately, this particular body of literature has also produced a number of contradictory results. Furthermore, when differences are discovered, it is often challenging for researchers to explain *why* they occur.

Nature, Number, and Severity of Symptoms

International investigations   Reviews of international research suggest that similar psychotic symptoms, such as delusions and blunted affect, exist across cultures (Kulhara & Chakrabarti, 2001). The International Pilot Study of Schizophrenia, as one example, revealed many similarities in the symptoms expressed by 1,202 schizophrenia and schizoaffective disorder patients from sites around the globe (WHO, 1975). Some examples of symptoms that tended to be present in relatively high rates for patients from different countries included diminished insight, affective flattening, and auditory hallucinations (WHO, 1973). On the other hand, cross-cultural differences were also documented. Participants from the Washington, DC area had a relatively low score (48) on diminished insight when compared to other sites (Ibadan, Nigeria at

81 was closest), and those from Agra, India experienced more affective flatness, mood incongruence, and lack of conformity to social norms than other sites (WHO, 1973). Results also indicated that sites tended to cluster together in terms of symptom reports, with Aarhus (Denmark), Cali (Colombia), Ibadan (Nigeria), and Tapei (Taiwan) most closely resembling one another, and Agra and Washington, DC being the most distinct from others (WHO, 1973).

The Determinants of Outcomes of Severe Mental Disorders (DOSMeD) investigation sponsored by the World Health Organization provides another example of a large-scale international investigation of schizophrenia symptoms (Jablensky et al., 1992). As noted previously, the researchers initially interviewed 1,379 patients in ten different countries. They examined cross-cultural differences by reviewing symptom frequency in patients from developed versus developing nations and generally found similarities between these two groups. For instance, negative symptoms, such as withdrawal from social interactions, were more often the initial sign of disturbance in patients than positive symptoms like hallucinations or delusions. Some specific symptom variations were also noted, however. Jablensky and colleagues reported that individuals from developed countries had more primary delusions, as well as more mood symptoms, such as depression, and more thought disorder symptoms, like thought inserting or broadcasting. Persons from developing countries, on the other hand, had higher rates of auditory and visual hallucinations (Jablensky et al., 1992). Unfortunately, even though differences in symptom expression have been documented, these differences are very hard to understand and explain given the presence of a number of confounding variables in existing research, including socioeconomic status differences and the use of varying diagnostic methods or criteria (Kulhara & Chakrabarti, 2001).

Multicultural investigations within the United States Research within the United States also points both to similarities and variations in symptom profiles. The same diagnostic criteria are used across cultural groups (APA, 2000), suggesting a commonality of symptomatic expression. However, some studies have discovered significant differences in symptom frequency or severity between racial/ethnic minority and majority groups within the United States (Olfson et al., 2002; Weisman et al., 2000), while others have not (Bae & Brekke, 2002). Research on this topic has, however, used different methods and assessment instruments. As an example, one investigation of 223 community mental health patients in an urban area found no differences in symptoms between Korean Americans, African Americans, Latinos, and European Americans after additional variables (i.e., education, sex, age) were controlled, but not all researchers control for these potentially confounding variables (Bae & Brekke, 2002).

The studies that have found symptom differences between groups have produced results that might be expected by readers – and some that might surprise them. One investigation of more than one thousand patients in an urban area in the United States revealed higher symptom rates in individuals who had fewer than eight years of education and who themselves, or whose families, earned under $6,000 (Olfson et al., 2002). Given the possible stress associated with both of these factors, increased symptom rates might be expected. On the other hand, a within-group study of Mexican Americans' reported psychosis symptoms (not diagnoses of psychotic disorders) found higher symptom rates in individuals born in the United States, as opposed to immigrants (Vega et al., 2006). This result might surprise some, particularly given the fact that immigration has been considered a potential risk factor for schizophrenia.

Existing sociological theories might help explain the reduced severity of immigrants' symptoms. In 1980, Mirowsky and Ross tested the relative merits of two such theories: the minority status and the ethnic-culture perspectives. The minority status or social stress hypothesis would predict symptom differences among racial, ethnic, or cultural groups, with persons of color experiencing more severe symptoms due to the stresses and possible oppression associated with minority status (Brekke & Barrio, 1997; Mirowsky & Ross, 1980). By contrast, the ethnic-culture or stress buffering hypothesis would suggest that many racial/ethnic minority cultures have protective factors, such as cohesive family structure, that would actually attenuate symptom severity (Brekke & Barrio, 1997; Mirowsky & Ross, 1980). A group of researchers conducted a study in part to help evaluate these competing perspectives as they pertain to schizophrenia (Brekke & Barrio, 1997).

Brekke and Barrio (1997) studied a sample of 184 African-American, Latino, and White patients with a psychotic disorder diagnosis who were receiving community mental health care in an urban area. In addition to gathering information about symptoms, they collected data about participants' socioeconomic status and their sociocentricity, probably more commonly thought of as a collectivist orientation. The researchers recorded the number of days patients lived with their families in the previous six months and administered measures of empathy and social competence. Minority group participants in the study scored higher on empathy and social competence; those differences were greatest between African Americans and Whites. The authors then examined the psychotic symptoms of group members. Both when they controlled for socioeconomic status and when they did not, White participants were found to be *more* symptomatic than members of racial/ethnic minority groups. When the sociocentric variables were controlled for, almost all of these significant symptom differences disappeared. These findings suggest that cultural factors may protect against symptom severity, and that the stress buffering hypothesis may be more applicable for individuals with schizophrenia than the social stress hypothesis. The results may also explain the previously reported conclusion (i.e., Vega et al., 2006) that immigrant Mexican Americans, who probably retained closer ties to their sociocentric cultural traditions, had fewer symptoms than US-born Mexican Americans. Furthermore, this study may provide insight into consistent international findings that patients with schizophrenia in developing nations, which would likely be considered more sociocentric, demonstrate decreased illness severity and better outcomes than those in developed nations (Lin & Kleinman, 1988).

Specific Types of Symptoms

A final topic of interest to researchers regarding psychotic symptoms has been whether *types* of symptoms vary based on cultural factors, both domestically and internationally. Again, there are some contradictory findings. For example, some reviews have suggested that negative symptoms of schizophrenia are more biologically-based and less subject to the effects of environment and culture, but at least one study of 116 schizophrenia patients found higher rates of negative symptoms among Anglo-Americans compared to Mexican Americans (Weisman et al., 2000). Other results have been more consistent. Reviews and studies have reported that Latino clients have more hypochondriacal and somatic symptoms than other groups (Brekke & Barrio, 1997; Weisman et al., 2000). Authors have suggested this finding is consistent with cultural information indicating that Hispanics or Latinos are more likely to express their distress in a physical manner (Weisman et al., 2000).

Hallucinations and delusions have been the subject of many comparative investigations. Although both symptoms are found across cultures, researchers have questioned whether their content or quality could be influenced by environmental factors, including the passage of time (e.g., Stompe, Ortwein-Swoboda, Ritter, & Schanda, 2003). For example, two mental health professionals from a Texas hospital examined records of patients from the 1930s and 1980s to explore differences in the content of their delusions and hallucinations (Mitchell & Vierkant, 1989). They discovered that in many cases the time period and associated cultural milieu did *not* impact delusions. Delusions of persecution in both eras, for instance, most frequently involved fears of being murdered. However, the authors argued that an increasingly violent and negative environment in the 1980s was reflected in patients' more threatening auditory hallucinations (e.g., voices commanding one to hurt or kill). They also noted a greater presence of delusions associated with enormous wealth in the 1930s, a time of significant financial deprivation.

The influence of the immediate environment on symptoms is also supported by a cross-cultural study of the medical records of patients from Pakistan, Pakistanis living in the UK, and White British patients (Suhail & Cochrane, 2002). The investigators found that there were greater differences in the frequency of specific types of delusions and hallucinations between the two Pakistani groups than between the White and Pakistani patients living in the UK. There were also differences in content, with, for example, Pakistani patients residing in their native country being more likely to experience delusions related to Black magic or visual hallucinations of spirits or ghosts. Again, the authors point to the similarity between the two groups living in Britain as evidence that patients' current environment may have a great impact on their symptoms.

Other cultural variations both in content and type of hallucinations and delusions have been reported. An international investigation of a nonrepresentative sample of 1,287 patients from India and the United States with schizophrenia or schizoaffective disorder found that a greater percentage of Americans suffered from auditory, visual, and gustatory hallucinations, while rates of somatic and olfactory hallucinations were similar between groups (Thomas et al., 2007). In a different examination of Anglo-American and Mexican-American schizophrenia patients, Mexican-American clients reported more delusions involving positive family relations, such as worrying about family safety, possibly reflecting a collectivist orientation (Weisman et al., 2000). Anglo-Americans experienced more persecutory delusions and delusions involving science-fiction content, perhaps related to the popularity of the genre in American culture. Kim and colleagues (1993) studied delusions in 771 Korean, Korean-Chinese, and Chinese patients and also discovered culturally relevant themes. As one example, delusions with a family theme occurred in more than half of Korean patients, but in only about 12 percent of Chinese patients, which the authors linked to changes in the extended family system produced by social policy in China (Kim et al., 1993).

The Course of Psychotic Disorders: Differential Outcomes Within and Across Groups

The course of schizophrenia relates to its symptomatic presentation and basically refers to the outcome of the disorder. Is it long-term? Is it likely to enter a complete remission? Does it involve a severe or more benign symptom presentation?

In general, one can conclude that the course of schizophrenia is influenced by environmental, including cultural, factors, but a complex interplay among those factors may exist. One potential interaction involves social class and gender or race/ethnicity. Women tend to be diagnosed with schizophrenia slightly later in life than men (APA, 2000). Their functioning is typically better prior to diagnosis, and they demonstrate better outcomes (Mueser & McGurk, 2004). When looking at SES, individuals with schizophrenia are often subject to social drift, or a decline in socioeconomic status, because their symptoms influence factors like the ability to maintain gainful employment, but poverty can also serve a risk factor in the *onset* of schizophrenia (Johnson, Cohen, Dohrenwend, Link, & Brook, 1999; Parrott & Lewine, 2005). Socioeconomic factors may, however, influence men and women differently. At least one study of 120 patients with schizophrenia or schizoaffective disorder found higher family socioeconomic status was associated with decreased disorder severity in women and increased severity in men (Parrott & Lewine, 2005). Although the authors cannot provide a causal explanation based on their data, they suggest men from higher SES families may experience increased hopelessness and stress as a result of financial advantage (e.g., in the form of expectations for success or high status careers), while women experience the same circumstances as a basis of support – or at least not as a source of stress.

Looking beyond gender, to the extent that socioeconomic status is actually a risk factor for schizophrenia, it may have a particular impact on racial and ethnic minorities in the United States, who are disproportionately represented in poverty rates (U.S. Department of Health and Human Services, 2001). Nonetheless, as reviewed earlier, racial and ethnic minority clients may benefit from stress buffering and cultural factors that reduce symptom severity. How do these factors interact to impact the course of schizophrenia? What provides the strongest influence? These questions are challenging ones to answer, particularly given the lack of within-group research on the course of schizophrenia and other psychotic disorders, such as studies that only involve African-American clients and examine differential courses and effects of schizophrenia based on variations in acculturation, SES, or gender.

Developing versus Developed Nations

Although many questions about culture and the course of psychotic disorders remain, on the international scene one particular finding has been consistently and widely reported: the differential course of schizophrenia in developing versus developed countries (Hopper & Wanderling, 2000; Karno & Jenkins, 1993; Kulhara & Chakrabarti, 2001; Lin & Kleinman, 1988). Since the International Pilot Study of Schizophrenia, which was conducted late in the 1960s, research reviews have reported a better course and outcome for patients in developing nations (Karno & Jenkins, 1993). Long-term follow-up investigations have begun to explore the validity of this finding across time (e.g., Sartorius, Gulbinat, Harrison, Laska, & Siegel, 1996). Hopper and Wanderling (2000) note that better outcomes for individuals from developing countries have been found across three WHO collaborative research studies, and that result has also held for 2 year, 5 year, and 15 year follow-up investigations. To provide more detail, the two-year follow-up from the DoSMED study found that patients from developing nations performed more favorably on a number of measures, including the percentage of patients who experienced a remitting course of their illness during the follow-up period (62.8 percent versus 36.9 percent; Jablensky et al., 1992). Those from developed countries had higher percentages of patients on some of the poor outcome measures, such as the numbers who had either continuous or episodic illness throughout the two years with no remission (38.2 percent versus 21.6 percent) or who showed social functioning deficits for the duration of that time span (41.6 percent versus 15.7 percent; Jablensky et al., 1992).

Potential explanations offered in the literature for these consistent findings regarding developed and developing nations include increased social support, decreased stigma associated with mental illness, an easier return to sustainable work, and greater use of extended family in care of the patient in developing nations (Lin & Kleinman, 1988). One researcher even conducted an analysis of national food consumption patterns and a number of the reported two-year schizophrenia outcomes from the IPSS and DoSMED investigations (Peet,

2004). Peet found refined sugar consumption was associated with poorer schizophrenia outcomes and suggested national dietary habits might help explain national distinctions in the disorder's course.

Another possible issue in the differential course of psychotic disorders is the degree of expressed emotion within the family. Expressed emotion has been described as an important risk factor both for schizophrenia relapse within cultural groups in the United States and for a more severe course of the disorder across developed nations (Lin & Kleinman, 1988; López et al., 2004; Weisman et al., 1993). Expressed emotion (EE) is typically described as a family environment characterized by critical, negative attitudes and comments directed toward the patient, along with emotional over-involvement (Weisman, López, Karno, & Jenkins, 1993). If high EE families are more common within industrialized nations and European American cultural groups in the United States, that might help to explain increased symptoms and more negative outcomes. Unfortunately, results related to EE are not that clear-cut. In their review of international studies of EE, Hashemi and Cochrane (1999) reported that although some studies (e.g., of Mexican Americans and families from India) found comparatively lower numbers of EE families, other investigations of "nonwestern" nations such as Egypt did not produce similar results. Even if consistent rates of EE were discovered, it is important to note that the meaning of these behaviors and their relationship to schizophrenia outcomes might vary across cultures. For example, Hashemi and Cochrane (1999) also provided information on the first author's doctoral thesis – an investigation of expressed emotion among 20 British Pakistani, 20 British Sikh, and 20 White families. High EE levels varied dramatically among these groups (British Pakistani – 80 percent; White – 45 percent; British Sikh – 30 percent), but perhaps the more intriguing finding was that high EE families were a predictor of relapse for the White patients but not for patients from the other two ethnic groups. Thus, as with all of the potential explanatory factors for cultural differences, research on EE holds promise, but again, more within-group and within-nation research could prove illuminating.

Treatment: Differential Options and Responses Across Groups

The final area in which culture might impact psychotic disorders is treatment. Individuals' response and access to care can be influenced by environmental factors, particularly social class and culture.

Options for and Access to Treatment

Access to treatment for schizophrenia is not universal. Poverty is one issue that reduces access. Research has established that course and outcomes of schizophrenia tend to be better in developing countries, but at least one study of individuals from India who did have a poor course of the disorder revealed that they had very poor long-term outcomes (Mojtabai et al., 2001). Mojtabai and colleagues examined 15-year follow-up data on 171 patients originally enrolled in the DoSMED study (Jablensky et al., 1992) and discovered, for example, that 47 percent of those with poor 2-year outcomes ($n = 15$) died before the end of the 15-year period – compared to only 11 percent of the other 156 patients. The authors noted in their discussion of the research that some developing nations struggle with poverty that can contribute to a scarcity of basic necessities, such as food, for persons with mental illness, as well as a lack of formal treatment facilities. Whether in developing or developed nations, the inability to find or afford quality treatment may lead to families taking over care, and if there is no immediate or extended family to accept that burden, individuals may have few alternatives. Resource scarcity within countries or for specific clients may also influence the availability of one of the most common treatments for psychotic illnesses: medications.

Other obstacles to effective treatment also exist. Members of groups that have been traditionally oppressed may opt not to seek care from systems often dominated by majority group treatment providers and philosophies. Authors have pointed out that members of racial/ethnic minority groups in the United States often seek treatment at lower rates than European Americans (Snowden & Cheung, 1990). African Americans may, for example, be reluctant to seek treatment as a result of cultural mistrust (Whaley, 2004). Members of other groups may avoid formal treatment, preferring traditional healing practices consistent with their cultural beliefs (Karno & Jenkins, 1993). For example, the DoSMED study reports that more than one-quarter of patients in Agra, India and Ibadan, Nigeria had their first contact prior to inclusion in the study with a traditional or faith healer (Jablensky et al., 1992). That said, clinicians and researchers need to be cautious about assuming that variations in help-seeking behavior will be found based on cultural group membership or the so-called "developing" versus "developed" nation dichotomy. A recent investigation of 312 schizophrenia outpatients in Nigeria and their attitudes toward antipsychotic medication revealed that participants were generally positive about the drugs, and that some of the same issues that have predicted negative attitudes in western countries (e.g., diminished insight, symptom severity) were also significant predictors in this study (Adewuya, Ola, Mosaku, Fatoye, & Eegunranti, 2006).

Looking beyond obstacles to preferences for treatment, different options tend to be available or emphasized across cultures. Kealey (2005), in her review of cross-cultural studies of schizophrenia, reported that the emphasis on biological causes of schizophrenia in the United States and Europe may contribute to a lack of reliance on psycho-educational family interventions that have demonstrated effectiveness. A different investigation of 24 schizophrenia treatment guidelines from 18 countries across the globe revealed substantial differences in content and recommendations (Gaebel, Weinmann, Sartorius, Rutz, & McIntyre, 2005). The plans varied in suggested medications (e.g., first- or second-generation drugs), dosages, and durations. Only six of the documents provided thorough information about community mental health treatment for schizophrenia, although 50 percent or more suggested some family, psycho-educational, and/or career interventions. The review demonstrated the exist-ence of different national perspectives on the treatment of schizophrenia; unfortunately, however, few guidelines from developing countries could be identified, leading to questions about the generalizability of the review.

Other insights into typical treatment modalities have been provided by cross-national studies of schizophrenia treatment. A comparison of treatment between Germany and Japan is one illustrative example (Hübner-Liebermann, Spiebl, Iwai, & Cording, 2005). The authors studied 865 schizophrenia patients hospitalized in Germany and 50 such patients in Japan – a country known for its large number and use of psychiatric hospital beds. Some of the differences were stark. The average hospital stay in Germany was 52 days, compared to 153 days in Japan. Treatment while in the hospital also varied considerably. Restraints were used significantly more often in Japan (20 percent versus 7 percent), and specific psychotherapeutic interventions were used far less frequently (e.g., 15 percent versus 0 percent for behavior therapy; 76 percent versus 52 percent for occupational therapy). The Japanese and German hospi-tals both overwhelmingly used neuroleptic medications to treat patients, but the Toyko hospital also prescribed benzodiazepines (78 percent versus 17 per-cent) and various tranquilizers (24 percent versus 1 percent) in greater num-bers. Although patients from both facilities still displayed symptoms of illness upon discharge, the Japanese patients showed more improvement. Even though this study only provided information about treatment at two hospitals, its results provide support for a larger point. Perspectives on effective treatment – including appropriate medications and psychotherapeutic treatments and whether patients should be hospitalized or integrated into the community – vary in meaningful ways cross-culturally and across countries. Hübner-Liebermann and colleagues (2005) note, for example, that other researchers have found much longer hospital stays in their psychiatric research in Japan, and that these stays are not simply justified by continuing illness, but by socio-cultural factors like difficulty accessing nonhospital-based treatment alterna-tives and some patients actually asking for continued hospitalization because of worries about bringing shame to their families.

Responses to Treatment

Regardless of the decision to seek treatment and the options available, some group variations exist in responses to care. Reviews of cross-cultural treatment indicate members of different racial, ethnic, and cultural groups demonstrate both diverse attitudes toward taking psychotropic medication and different phys-iological reactions to them (Karno & Jenkins, 1993; Kulhara & Chakrabarti, 2001). Karno and Jenkins (1993) report, for example, that existing evidence sug-gests Asian schizophrenia patients may obtain the same therapeutic results with less neuroleptic medication than Caucasians. Diaz, Woods, and Rosenheck (2005) documented significantly lower psychotropic medication adherence rates in African-American and Hispanic clients (those who were not bilingual) who presented with a variety of conditions and prescribed drugs. The authors point, however, to a need for additional research on this topic with larger sample sizes and more attention to possible explanatory variables, such as acculturative stress.

Responses to psychotherapeutic interventions may also differ. In fact, such variations might be expected given cultural differences in attitudes toward these treatments, as well as the lack of universal application of multicultural counseling skills and culturally relevant treatments. Current evidence on cultural factors in treatment response is mixed. One study of an ethnically diverse sample of 226 patients with schizophrenia or schizoaffective disorder concluded that African-American, Latino, and European American individuals had an equally positive response to a community-based intervention program in terms of work outcome, social functioning, independent living, and self-esteem (Bae, Brekke, & Bola, 2004). The differences reported were only in the pace of change. By contrast, another investigation of 98 patients with schizophrenia and schizoaffective disorder revealed African Americans and Latinos either showed less improvement or worsened, when compared to European American participants, in vocational and social functioning (Phillips, Barrio, & Brekke, 2001). The authors discovered no racial/ethnic differences on outcomes related to hospitalization and independent living, however. One consistent finding related to interventions comes from an international review of family-based treatments. Falloon and his colleagues examined 22 investigations from various countries and found evidence to support the effectiveness of family-based stress management interventions in providing benefits to patients, such as decreased symptoms and improved social and family functioning (Falloon, Held, Coverdale, Roncone, & Laidlaw, 1999).

Implications and Recommendations

The information reviewed in this chapter provides a broad foundation for making recommendations regarding the assessment, treatment, and scholarly investigation of psychotic disorders across cultural groups. Each of these recommendations, along with a brief rationale, will be described in turn.

Assessment

Accurate assessment of psychotic symptoms and disorders is critical if patients are to receive adequate and appropriate treatment. There are a number of recommendations that might improve assessment practices.

1. *Use structured interviews.* Researchers have argued that structured interviews lead to greater cross-cultural diagnostic accuracy, suggesting they should be used whenever possible (Minsky et al., 2003; Mukherjee

et al., 1983). Clinicians should also educate themselves about culturally appropriate interviewing practices (Aklin & Turner, 2006).

2. *Make sure assessment instruments are culturally appropriate.* Given problems that have been reported with clinician attributions and misdiagnosis of psychotic disorders, treatment providers should be sure to use assessment tools that are appropriate for their clients and that include them in their norm groups.

3. *Supplement assessment instruments with measures of cultural mistrust, racial identity, and/or acculturation.* Due to potential difficulties differentiating between true paranoia and cultural mistrust in African Americans, clinicians might also administer measures of mistrust and acculturation (Whaley, 2001b). Acculturation measures might also enhance the assessment of members of other groups and prevent treatment professionals from making cultural generalizations and ignoring within-group differences.

4. *Be aware of culture-bound syndromes and differences in symptomatic expression.* Clinicians may not appreciate specific differences in symptoms across cultures, such as Latino clients more often expressing distress somatically. Assessment and treatment professionals should educate themselves about culture-bound syndromes, cultural differences in symptom expression, and culturally prescribed behaviors that might be misinterpreted as psychotic symptoms.

5. *Follow multicultural assessment guidelines.* Guidelines and educational information exist to assist clinicians in the effective assessment and treatment of culturally diverse clients, and adhering to them may enhance effective practice (e.g., American Psychological Association, 2003).

Treatment

The treatment recommendations which follow relate to some of the same issues raised in the accurate assessment of psychotic disorders, and they again involve practicing in a manner consistent with cultural competence.

1. *Use evidence-based practices.* There is an ever-expanding research base that reviews effective treatment approaches for specific disorders. Although significant caution must be exercised if applying such treatments to members of groups on which they have not been studied, using interventions with research support may decrease negative treatment outcomes.

2. *Involve family and extended support networks in treatment, as appropriate.* Given the relationship between Expressed Emotion (EE) and negative schizophrenia outcomes, and the possibility of family cohesion serving as a protective buffer, family interventions may be very appropriate. Clinicians might also investigate culturally sensitive treatment approaches (e.g., Weisman, 2005) and be open to involving extended support networks, including indigenous healers.

3. *Build on strengths associated with sociocentric values.* Because sociocentric factors, such as empathy and social competence, have been associated with less severe symptoms in racial/ethnic minority clients, using treatment approaches that encourage these values may be beneficial (Barrio, 2001).
4. *Be aware of issues related to acculturation, racial identity, and cultural mistrust.* Factors such as mistrust and viewing psychotherapy as incongruent with cultural values may reduce help-seeking behaviors and increase premature termination. Clinicians need to assess and address such concerns early in treatment.
5. *Follow multicultural treatment guidelines.* As was the case with assessment, clinicians should read and understand guidelines regarding multicultural practice, as well as information about multicultural competence (American Psychological Association, 2003; Sue, Arredondo, & McDavis, 1992).

Research

Finally, good research is required to understand psychotic disorders and their relationship with cultural factors. It is that research that will guide appropriate assessment and treatment of the patients who struggle with these illnesses.

1. *Include potentially explanatory variables (e.g., acculturation) in between-group studies.* More researchers should improve their studies by including variables, such as acculturation and socioeconomic status, which might explain between-group differences and help illuminate the complex relationships among culture, gender, and social class.
2. *Conduct more within-group investigations.* Although understanding between-group differences is important, it can lead to making inappropriate generalizations about group members. Existing information suggests within-group differences might be found based on acculturation, racial identity, urban versus rural setting, SES, gender, and family dynamics. Unfortunately, one of the major gaps in the literature regarding culture and psychotic disorders is the lack of significant within-group studies.
3. *Perform more research with under-investigated groups.* Certain groups, such as Native Americans, appear to be under-investigated and should be the focus of future studies.

Concluding Comments

Existing evidence clearly demonstrates a connection between culture and the diagnosis, symptoms, course, and treatment of psychotic disorders. Given the significant personal and economic impact of these disorders, conducting quality research and providing appropriate assessment and treatment are critical. One of the best hopes for doing so may be approaching the topic using a biopsycho-*cultural* approach.

References

Adewuya, A. O., Ola, B. A., Mosaku, S. K., Fatoye, F. O., & Eegunranti, A. B. (2006). Attitude toward antipsychotics among out-patients with schizophrenia in Nigeria. *Acta Psychiatrica Scandinavica, 113*, 207–211.

Aklin, W. M., & Turner, S. M. (2006). Toward understanding ethnic and cultural factors in the interviewing process. *Psychotherapy: Research, Practice, Training, 43*, 50–64.

American Psychiatric Association (2000). *Diagnostic and statistical manual of mental disorders* (4th ed., Text Revision). Washington, DC: Author.

American Psychological Association (2003). Guidelines on multicultural education, training, research, practice, and organizational change for psychologists. *American Psychologist, 58*, 377–402.

Bae, S.-W. & Brekke, J. (2002). Characteristics of Korean-Americans with schizophrenia: A cross-ethnic comparison with African-Americans, Latinos, and Euro-Americans. *Schizophrenia Bulletin, 28*, 703–717.

Bae, S.-W., Brekke, J. S., & Bola, J. R. (2004). Ethnicity and treatment outcome variation in schizophrenia: A longitudinal study of community-based psychosocial rehabilitation intervention. *Journal of Nervous and Mental Disease, 192*, 623–628.

Barrio, C. (2001). Culture and schizophrenia: A cross-ethnic growth curve analysis. *Journal of Nervous and Mental Disease, 189*, 676–684.

Blow, F. C., Zeber, J. E., McCarthy, J. F., Valenstein, M., Gillon, L, & Bingham, C. R. (2004). Ethnicity and diagnostic patterns in veterans with psychoses. *Social Psychiatry and Psychiatric Epidemiology, 39*, 841–851.

Brekke, J. S., & Barrio, C. (1997). Cross-ethnic symptom differences in schizophrenia: The influence of culture and minority status. *Schizophrenia Bulletin, 23*, 305–316.

Cantor-Graae, E. (2007). The contribution of social factors to the development of schizophrenia: A review of recent findings. *Canadian Journal of Psychiatry, 52*, 277–286.

Cantor-Graae, E., & Selten, J.-P. (2005). Schizophrenia and migration: A meta-analysis and review. *American Journal of Psychiatry, 162*, 12–24.

Castillo, R. J. (1997). *Culture and mental illness: A client-centered approach.* Pacific Grove, CA: Brooks/Cole.

Diaz, E., Woods, S. W., & Rosenheck, R. A. (2005). Effects of ethnicity on psychotropic medications adherence. *Community Mental Health Journal, 41*, 521–537.

Draguns, J. G., & Tanaka-Matsumi, J. (2003). Assessment of psychopathology across and within cultures: Issues and findings. *Behaviour Research and Therapy, 41*, 755–776.

Fabrega, H., Jr. Swartz, J. D., & Wallace, C. A. (1968). Ethnic differences in psychopathology. *Archives of General Psychiatry, 19*, 218–226.

Falloon, I. R. H., Held, T., Coverdale, J. H., Roncone, R., & Laidlaw, T. M. (1999). Family interventions for schizophrenia: A review of long-term benefits of international studies. *Psychiatric Rehabilitation Skills, 3*, 268–290.

Furnham, A., & Chan, E. (2004). Lay theories of schizophrenia: A cross-cultural comparison of British and Hong Kong Chinese attitudes, attributions, and beliefs. *Social Psychiatry and Psychiatric Epidemiology, 39*, 543–552.

Gaebel, W., Weinmann, S., Sartorius, N., Rutz, W., & McIntyre, J. S. (2005). Schizophrenia practice guidelines: International survey and comparison. *British Journal of Psychiatry, 187*, 248–255.

Hashemi, A. H., & Cochrane, R. (1999). Expressed emotion and schizophrenia: A review of studies across cultures. *International Review of Psychiatry, 11*, 219–224.

Hegarty, J. D., Baldessarini, R. J., Tohen, M., Waternaux, C., & Oepen, G. (1994). One hundred years of schizophrenia: A meta-analysis of the outcome literature. *American Journal of Psychiatry, 151*, 1409–1416.

Herring, R. D. (2004). Physical and mental health needs of Native American Indian and Alaska Native populations. In D. R. Atkinson (Ed.), *Counseling American minorities* (6th ed.). Boston: McGraw-Hill.

Hopper, K., & Wanderling, J. (2000). Revisiting the developed versus developing country distinction in course and outcome in schizophrenia: Results from ISoS, the WHO collaborative followup project. *Schizophrenia Bulletin, 26*, 835–846.

Hübner-Liebermann, B., Spiebl, H., Iwai, K., & Cording, C. (2005). Treatment of schizophrenia: Implications derived from an intercultural hospital comparison between Germany and Japan. *International Journal of Social Psychiatry, 51*, 83–96.

Jablensky, A. (2000). Epidemiology of schizophrenia: The global burden of disease and disability. *European Archives of Psychiatry and Clinical Neuroscience, 250*, 274–285.

Jablensky, A., Sartorius, N., Ernberg, G., Anker, M., Korten, A., Cooper, J. E., et al. (1992). Schizophrenia: Manifestations, incidence, and course in different cultures, A World Health Organization ten-country study. *Psychological Medicine, Monograph Supplement 20*, 1–97.

Johnson, J. G., Cohen, P., Dohrenwend, B. P., Link, B. G., & Brook, J. S. (1999). A longitudinal investigation of social causation and social selection processes involved in the association between socioeconomic status and psychiatric disorders. *Journal of Abnormal Psychology, 108*, 490–499.

Karno, M., & Jenkins, J. H. (1993). Cross-cultural issues in the course and treatment of schizophrenia. *Psychiatric Clinics of North America, 16*, 339–350.

Kealy, E. M. (2005). Variations in the experience of schizophrenia: A cross-cultural review. *Journal of Social Work Research and Evaluation, 6*, 47–56.

Kim, K.-I., Li, D., Jiang, Z., Cui, X., Lin, L., Kang, J. J., et al. (1993). Schizophrenic delusions among Koreans, Korean-Chinese, and Chinese: A transcultural study. *International Journal of Social Psychiatry, 39*, 190–199.

Kim, Y., & Berrios, G. E., (2001). Impact of the term *schizophrenia* on the culture of ideograph: The Japanese experience. *Schizophrenia Bulletin, 27*, 181–185.

King, M., Coker, E., Leavey, G., Hoare, A., & Johnson-Sabine, E. (1994). Incidence of psychotic illness in London: Comparison of ethnic groups. *British Medical Journal, 309*, 1115–1119.

Knapp, M., Mangalore, R., & Simon, J. (2004). The global costs of schizophrenia. *Schizophrenia Bulletin, 30*, 279–293.

Kulhara, P., & Chakrabarti, S. (2001). Culture and schizophrenia and other psychotic disorders. *Cultural Psychiatry: International Perspectives, 24*, 449–464.

Levin, T. (2006). Schizophrenia should be renamed to help educate patients and the public. *International Journal of Social Psychiatry, 52*, 324–331.

Lewine, R. R. J. (1981). Sex difference in schizophrenia: Timing or subtypes? *Psychological Bulletin, 90*, 432–444.

Lin, K.-M., & Kleinman, A. M. (1988). Psychopathology and clinical course of schizophrenia: A cross-cultural perspective. *Schizophrenia Bulletin, 14*, 555–567.

López, S. R., Hipke, K. N., Polo, A. J., Jenkins, J. H., Karno, M., Vaughn, C., et al. (2004). Ethnicity, expressed emotion, attributions, and course of schizophrenia: Family warmth matters. *Journal of Abnormal Psychology, 113*, 428–439.

Maxmen, J. S., & Ward, N. G. (1995). *Essential psychopathology and its treatment* (2nd ed.). New York: W. W. Norton & Company.

Minsky, S., Vega, W., Miskimen, T., Gara, M., & Escobar, J. (2003). Diagnostic patterns in Latino, African American, and European American psychiatric patients. *Archives of General Psychiatry, 60,* 637–644.

Mirowsky, J., II., & Ross, C. E. (1980). Minority status, ethnic culture, and distress: A comparison of Blacks, Whites, Mexicans, and Mexican Americans. *American Journal of Sociology, 86,* 479–495.

Mitchell, J., & Vierkant, A. D. (1989). Delusions and hallucinations as a reflection of the subcultural milieu among psychotic patients of the 1930s and 1980s. *Journal of Psychology, 123,* 269–274.

Mojtabai, R., Varma, V. K., Malhotra, S., Mattoo, S. K., Misra, A., Wig, N. N., et al. (2001). Mortality and long-term course of schizophrenia with poor 2-year course. *British Journal of Psychiatry, 178,* 71–75.

Mueser, K. T., & McGurk, S. R. (2004, June). Schizophrenia. *The Lancet, 363,* 2063–2072.

Mukherjee, S., Shukla, S., Woodle, J., Rosen, A. M., & Olarte, S. (1983). Misdiagnosis of schizophrenia in bipolar patients: A multiethnic comparison. *American Journal of Psychiatry, 140,* 1571–1574.

Nakane, Y., Ohta, Y., & Radford, M. H. B. (1992). Epidemiological studies of schizophrenia in Japan. *Schizophrenia Bulletin, 18,* 75–84.

Neighbors, H. W., Trierweiler, S. J., Ford, B. C., & Muroff, J. R. (2003). Racial difference in *DSM* diagnosis using a semi-structured instrument: The importance of clinical judgment in the diagnosis of African Americans. *Journal of Health and Social Behavior, 44,* 237–256.

Olfson, M., Lewis-Fernández, R., Weissman, M. M., Feder, A., Gameroff, M. J., Pilowsky, D., & Fuentes, M. (2002). Psychotic symptoms in an urban general medical practice. *American Journal of Psychiatry, 159,* 1412–1419.

Parrott, B., & Lewine, R. (2005). Socioeconomic status of origin and the clinical expression of schizophrenia. *Schizophrenia Research, 75,* 417–424.

Pavkov, T. W., Lewis, D. A., & Lyons, J. S. (1989). Psychiatric diagnoses and racial bias: An empirical investigation. *Professional Psychology: Research and Practice, 20,* 364–368.

Peet, M. (2004). International variations in the outcome of schizophrenia and the prevalence of depression in relation to national dietary practices: An ecological analysis. *British Journal of Psychiatry, 184,* 404–408.

Phillips, E. S., Barrio, C., & Brekke, J. S. (2001). The impact of ethnicity on prospective functional outcomes from community-based psychosocial rehabilitation for persons with schizophrenia. *Journal of Community Psychology, 29,* 657–673.

Sartorius, N., Gulbinat, W., Harrison, G., Laska, E., & Siegel, C. (1996). Long-term follow-up of schizophrenia in 16 countries. *Social Psychiatry and Psychiatric Epidemiology, 31,* 249–258.

Sato, M. (2006). Renaming schizophrenia: A Japanese perspective. *World Psychiatry, 5,* 53–55.

Seeman, M. V. (2007). An outcome measure in schizophrenia: Mortality. *The Canadian Journal of Psychiatry, 52,* 55–60.

Sharpley, M., Hutchinson, G., McKenzie, K., & Murray, R. M. (2001). Understanding the excess of psychosis among the African-Caribbean population in England. *British Journal of Psychiatry, 178* (suppl. 40), s60–s68.

Snowden, L. R., & Cheung, F. K. (1990). Use of inpatient mental health services by members of ethnic minority groups. *American Psychologist, 45,* 347–355.

Stompe, T., Ortwein-Swoboda, G., Ritter, K., & Schanda, H. (2003). Old wine in new bottles? Stability and plasticity of the contents of schizophrenic delusions. *Psychopathology, 36,* 6–12.

Sue, D. W., Arredondo, P., & McDavis, R. J. (1992). Multicultural counseling competencies and standards: A call to the profession. *Journal of Multicultural Counseling and Development, 20,* 64–89.

Suhail, K., & Cochrane, R. (2002). Effect of culture and environment on the phenomenology of delusions and hallucinations. *International Journal of Social Psychiatry, 48,* 126–138.

Thomas, P., Mathur, P., Gottesman, I. I., Nagpal, R., Nimgaonkar, V. L., & Deshpande, S. N. (2007). Correlates of hallucinations in schizophrenia: A cross-cultural evaluation. *Schizophrenia Research, 92,* 41–49.

Trierweiler, S. J., Muroff, J. R., Jackson, J. S., Neighbors, H. W., & Munday, C. (2005). Clinician race, situational attributions, and diagnoses of mood versus schizophrenia disorders. *Cultural Diversity and Ethnic Minority Psychology, 11,* 351–364.

Trierweiler, S. J., Neighbors, H. W., Munday, C., Thompson, E. E., Binion, V. J., & Gomez, J. P. (2000). Clinician attributions associated with the diagnosis of schizophrenia in African American and non-African American patients. *Journal of Consulting and Clinical Psychology, 68,* 171–175.

U.S. Department of Health and Human Services (2001). *Mental health: Culture, race, and ethnicity – a supplement to Mental health: A report of the Surgeon General.* Rockville, MD: U.S. Department of Health and Human Services, Public Health Service, Office of the Surgeon General.

Vega, W. A., Sribney, W. M., Miskimen, T. M., Escobar, J. I., & Aguilar-Gaxiola, S. (2006, July). Putative psychotic symptoms in the Mexican American population. *Journal of Nervous and Mental Disease, 194,* 471–477.

Walker, E., & Diforio, D. (1997). Schizophrenia: A neural diathesis-stress model. *Psychological Review, 104,* 667–685.

Walker, E., Kestler, L., Bollini, A., & Hochman, K. M. (2004). Schizophrenia: Etiology and course. *Annual Review of Psychology, 55,* 401–430.

Weisman, A. (2005). Integrating culturally based approaches with existing interventions for Hispanic/Latino families coping with schizophrenia. *Psychotherapy: Theory, Research, Practice, Training, 42,* 178–197.

Weisman, A., López, S. R., Karno, M., & Jenkins, J. (1993). An attributional analysis of expressed emotion in Mexican-American families with schizophrenia. *Journal of Abnormal Psychology, 102,* 601–606.

Weisman, A. G., López, S. R., Ventura, J., Nuechterlein, K. H., Goldstein, M. J., & Hwang, S. (2000). A comparison of psychiatric symptoms between Anglo-Americans and Mexican-Americans with schizophrenia. *Schizophrenia Bulletin, 26,* 817–824.

Whaley, A. L. (2001a). Cultural mistrust and the clinical diagnosis of paranoid schizophrenia in African American patients. *Journal of Psychopathology and Behavioral Assessment, 23,* 93–100.

Whaley, A. L. (2001b). Cultural mistrust: An important psychological construct for diagnosis and treatment of African Americans. *Professional Psychology: Research and Practice, 32,* 555–562.

Whaley, A. L. (2001c). Cultural mistrust of White mental health clinicians among African Americans with severe mental illness. *American Journal of Orthopsychiatry, 71*, 252–256.

Whaley, A. L. (2002). Confluent paranoia in African American psychiatric patients: An empirical study of Ridley's typology. *Journal of Abnormal Psychology, 111*, 568–577.

Whaley, A. L. (2004). Ethnicity/race, paranoia, and hospitalization for mental health problems among men. *American Journal of Public Health, 94*, 78–81.

World Health Organization. (1973). *Report of the International Pilot Study of Schizophrenia* (Vol. 1). Geneva, Switzerland: Author. Retrieved January 21, 2007 from the World Health Organization website: http://whqlibdoc.who.int/offset/WHO_OFFSET_2_(chp1-chp8).pdf; http://whqlibdoc.who.int/offset/WHO_OFFSET_2_(chp9-chp11).pdf; http://whqlibdoc.who.int/offset/WHO_OFFSET_2_(chp12-chp15).pdf

World Health Organization (1975). *Schizophrenia: A multinational study*. Geneva, Switzerland: Author. Retrieved January 21, 2007 from the World Health Organization website: http://whqlibdoc.who.int/php/WHO_PHP_63.pdf

13

Culture and Eating Disorders

*Megan A. Markey Hood, Jillon S. Vander Wal,
and Judith L. Gibbons*

Eating disorders have been widely assumed to be products of cultural influences. In fact, some have proposed that anorexia and bulimia nervosa are culture bound-syndromes that are specifically linked to western industrialized cultures (e.g., Prince, 1985). Yet culture, as a concept, is not an adequate explanation. Culture is a multifaceted construct that permeates the everyday settings in which persons live. By "unpackaging" culture, its particular influential features can be examined and explored in terms of the development and expression of disordered eating behaviors and attitudes. The aim of this chapter is to discuss the role of culture in eating disorders by describing the presentation and phenomenology of eating disorders both within and across cultures. In addition, information will be presented on current practices and issues related to assessing and treating eating disorders in various cultural settings. While growing evidence suggests that eating disorders are influenced by a number of genetic (Bulik, Sullivan, & Kendler, 1998; Monteleone, Tortorella, Castaldo, Di Filippo, & Maj, 2007; Wade, Bulik, Neale, & Kendler, 2000) and individual factors such as perfectionism and negative affect (Stice, 2002), this chapter will focus primarily on the role of cultural factors in disordered eating.

Defining Eating Disorders

Eating disorders, like most psychological disorders, have been studied overwhelmingly among persons of European descent as well as among persons living in industrialized nations. With the advent of cross-cultural research on eating disorders near the end of the twentieth century, the accuracy of the current diagnostic criteria in appropriately categorizing different types of disordered eating behaviors and attitudes as "pathological" has been debated (Lee, 1995; Palmer, 1993; Thaw, Williamson, & Martin, 2001). The current standard for diagnosing eating disorders is described by *The Diagnostic and*

Statistical Manual of Mental Disorders, 4th ed., Text Revision (*DSM–IV–TR*; American Psychiatric Association, 2000).

According to the *DSM–IV–TR*, the defining characteristic of all eating disorders is a severe disturbance in eating behaviors. Diagnostic criteria are currently provided for two eating disorders, *anorexia nervosa* and *bulimia nervosa*, and a third general category, *eating disorder not otherwise specified*. In addition, investigational diagnostic criteria are provided by the *DSM–IV–TR* for a fourth eating disorder category, *binge eating disorder*. Research on eating disorders primarily focuses on anorexia and bulimia nervosa, which will be the focus of the discussion in this chapter.

Diagnostically, anorexia nervosa is defined by the following criteria: refusing to maintain body weight at or above a minimally normal weight for age and height; having an intense fear of gaining weight or becoming fat, even though under-weight; having a disturbed view of the way in which one's body weight or shape is experienced, undue influence of body weight or shape on self-evaluation, or denial of the seriousness of the current low body weight; and experiencing amenorrhea (the absence of at least three consecutive menstrual cycles; APA, 2000, p. 589).

Bulimia nervosa is characterized by the following criteria: recurrent episodes of binge eating; recurrent use of inappropriate compensatory behaviors in order to prevent weight gain; engaging in binge eating and inappropriate compensatory behaviors, on average, at least two times per week for three months; and having a self-evaluation that is unduly influenced by body shape and weight. Binge eating episodes are characterized as eating, in a discrete period of time, an abnormally large amount of food for the circumstances and a sense of a lack of control over the eating during the episode. Common compensatory behaviors include vomiting, fasting, excessively exercising, or misusing laxatives, diuretics, enemas, or other medications (APA, 2000, p. 594).

Binge eating disorder is an eating disorder characterized by the presence of binge eating episodes associated with eating rapidly until uncomfortably full despite not feeling physically hungry. Individuals often eat alone due to embarrassment and negative feelings about themselves related to their eating habits. No inappropriate compensatory behaviors are present, such as those found in the criteria for bulimia nervosa. Binge eating episodes occur at least two days a week for six months (APA, 2000, p. 787).

Eating Disorders as Culture-Bound Syndromes

For many years, the disordered eating and disturbances in body image that are characteristic of eating disorders were believed to exist exclusively among non-Hispanic white middle to upper class female youths living in western cultures (Miller & Pumariega, 2001; Wildes, Emergy, & Simons, 2001). This fact led researchers to hypothesize that eating disorders are "culture-bound syndromes," defined as disorders that are confined to certain cultures due to their psycho-social features (Prince, 1985).

According to the *DSM–IV–TR* (APA, 2000), full-syndrome eating disorders (those meeting full criteria for the disorders) are fairly rare, with anorexia and bulimia nervosa being found in approximately 0.5 percent and 1–3 percent of the population respectively. The *DSM–IV–TR* rates apply largely to western nations, although eating disorders have been reported in nearly every area of the world (Anderson-Fye & Becker, 2004; Keel & Klump, 2003). Prevalence rates of eating disorders in nonwestern countries, such as areas of Asia (including Japan, Singapore, and Korea), the Middle East (including Iran), and Africa (including Egypt and South Africa), have been found to be comparable to those in western countries (Anderson-Fye & Becker, 2004). Research on the prevalence of eating disorders in other regions is comprised mostly of case and self-report data, but suggests that disordered eating behaviors exist to some degree in many areas of the world, including China (Lee, Chiu, & Chen, 1989), Israel (Mitrany, Lubin, Chetrit, & Modan, 1995), and countries in South America (Pumarino & Vivanco, 1982; Zuckerfeld, Fuchs, & Cormillot, 1988). Although it has been surmised that the prevalence rates of eating disorders in these regions may be lower than in western societies, partial syndrome eating disorders, or the presence of disordered eating attitudes and behaviors that do not meet diagnostic criteria, may exist at high levels in some countries, including Israel and Argentina (Stein et al., 1997; Zuckerfeld, Fuchs, & Cormillot, 1998).

Rates of eating disorders vary by ethnicity within westernized societies as well. For example, in the United States the rates of eating disorders are different among Caucasian, African-American, Latina, and Native American women, yet no ethnic group is completely immune. When compared to Caucasian women, African-American women tend to have lower rates of anorexia nervosa (Crago et al., 1996) but similar rates of binge eating (Striegel-Moore, Wilfley, Pike, Dohm, & Fairburn, 2000), and Latina women may have slightly higher rates of eating disorders than both of these ethnic groups (Bruce & Agras, 1992). Asian-American women have the lowest rates of eating disorders among the major ethnic groups in the United States (Lucero, Hicks, Bramlette, & Brassington, 1992), while Native American women may have the highest rates (Crago, 1996).

Keel and Klump (2003) examined the cross-historical and cross-cultural evidence for both anorexia and bulimia nervosa. They found that while cases of refusing food to the point of emaciation have been documented throughout various cultures and historical periods, the obsession with weight and shape that is included in the current diagnostic criteria for anorexia nervosa is a more recent phenomena isolated to western culture. The authors suggest that only this portion of the criteria for anorexia nervosa is dependent on culture and that anorexia nervosa itself should not be considered a culture-bound syndrome.

In addition, they interpreted a review of the literature exploring the prevalence of eating disorders in nonwesternized nations as indicating that there is a lack of evidence for the existence of bulimia nervosa in individuals who have not been exposed to western influences, which suggests that bulimia nervosa is most likely culture-bound, supporting the conclusions drawn in some studies (Habermas, 1989). However, other studies, pointing to documentation of bulimia nervosa among groups isolated from western influence, argue otherwise (Lee, 1991; 1995; Mumford et al., 1992). In order to fully understand the complex relationship between culture and eating disorders, specific cultural characteristics must be examined.

Cultural Characteristics

"Unpackaging" culture in order to determine why prevalence rates of eating disorders vary from culture to culture and across historical periods, involves exploring the different pathways by which culture may influence the development and expression of eating disorders. Markey (2004) proposed a tripartite model of the pathways linking culture and disordered eating. In this model, culture leads to disordered eating via three important factors: eating behaviors and patterns that have been passed down from one generation to another, ideal body sizes and shapes, and views of health and wellness.

Eating Behaviors

Food is an important aspect of any culture. From food preferences to food preparation, eating is embedded in culture. Individual eating behaviors are impacted by a number of ecological systems, from family and peer influences to larger societal standards and expectations. As the key behavioral component of eating disorders is the consumption (or lack thereof) of food, eating disorders are impacted by cultural expectations of eating behavior.

Eating socialization begins in the family environment, where children learn eating behaviors at a very young age (Birch & Fisher, 1998). The familial context itself is influenced by its members' past experiences, traditions, and habits (Markey, 2004), which together create a unique environment wherein children learn to associate food with specific thoughts, feelings, and behaviors. Children look to their parents to learn appropriate eating behaviors, and when parents model unhealthy eating habits, children are often at risk for developing these habits themselves. Studies conducted in westernized societies suggest that girls whose mothers model unhealthy weight control behaviors and beliefs about weight and shape may be at higher risk for developing their own unhealthy eating practices (Hill & Franklin, 1998; Levine, Smolak, Moodey, & Hessen, 1994; Pike & Rodin, 1991). Although there is little information on modeling of eating behaviors in nonwesternized societies, social learning theory suggests that similar mechanisms may be in place in these cultures as well.

As children reach the preadolescent and adolescent years and the opinions of peers grow in importance, peer influences on eating attitudes and behaviors similarly become more powerful. Adolescents may look to their friends to learn standards for eating behaviors and attitudes in order to be accepted by the peer group (Paxton, Schutz, Wertheim, & Muir, 1999). Peer pressure and teasing can also increase the likelihood of developing bulimic behaviors and other disordered eating practices (Cattarin & Thompson, 1994; Field, Camargo, Taylor, Bekey, & Colditz, 1999; Levine et al., 1994). In cultures in which peers typically express less concern about weight and shape, such as Latina and African-American cultures in the United States, peer influences may play less of a role in the development of unhealthy eating habits. In countries such as Japan, where parental influences remain more important than peer influences until mid-adolescence (Mukai, 1996), adolescents may also be somewhat more protected from the influence of peers on disordered eating.

On a broader level, eating disorders have been posited to be associated with the prevalence and accessibility of food resources in a culture, though this may not be equally true for anorexia and bulimia nervosa. While the food refusal seen in anorexia nervosa can occur regardless of an individual's access to food, the binge eating characteristic of bulimia nervosa must occur in a context in which the individual has the resources to attain and consume large amounts of food. This may be part of the reason that more cases of anorexia than bulimia nervosa can be found historically, as access to an abundance of food and indoor plumbing is correlated with increased prevalence rates of bulimia nervosa (Keel & Klump, 2003).

More access to high-calorie foods also allows for the inconspicuous accumulation and consumption of food, which may contribute to the fact that bulimia nervosa, unlike anorexia nervosa, is more common in urban rather than rural areas (Hoek et al., 1995). Regions that have limited access to food and few contacts with westernized culture, such as many parts of Africa, generally have few to no occurrences of eating disorders (Keel & Klump, 2003). For example, a teenager living in a rural area in an African nation will have less access to large amounts of food used in binge eating episodes than a teenager living in an urban industrialized nation where convenience foods are readily available.

Ideal Body Size

Preferences regarding weight and shape vary across cultures and ethnic groups (Striegel-Moore & Smolak, 2000) and have been associated with eating disorders due to their impact on body image, or the way individuals feel about their appearance. Theories of eating disorders posit that women who perceive a discrepancy between their own body size and the ideal body size supported by their culture, which is often expressed via the media, parental, and peer influences (Keery et al., 2004), develop body image disturbances that are characteristic of eating disorders.

The mass media have been suggested to be the most powerful means by which sociocultural ideals about beauty and body size are relayed to society (Andersen & DiDomenico, 1992). As a result, the shift over the past half-century or so towards a preference for a thinner figure (Wiseman et al., 1992) has been broadcast to women via a number of media sources, including magazines, movies, and television programs. Cross-sectional, longitudinal, and experimental studies have shown that exposure to western media images contributes to thin ideal internalization and body image dissatisfaction, risk factors for eating disorder development (Cafri, Yamamiya, Brannick, & Thompson, 2005; Groesz, Levine, & Murnen, 2002; Stice, 2002).

Such exposure also directly negatively affects eating disorder symptoms (Hawkins, Richards, Granley, & Stein, 2004; Yamamiya, Cash, Melnyk, Posavac, & Posavac, 2005). Becker et al. (2002) documented the effects of introducing television to Fijian culture, a culture with few reported incidences of eating disorders. Three years after television was introduced to the society, Fijian adolescent females reported increased rates of disordered eating behaviors and attitudes. Qualitative research results from the study indicated that the young girls looked to television as a template for successful living according to western cultural values and standards.

The dual pathway or sociocultural model (Figure 13.1; Stice, 2001; Stice & Agras, 1998) describes the proposed pathways by which the thin ideal, portrayed via media and other sources, is translated into eating disorder symptoms. According to this model, internalization of the thin ideal leads to body dissatisfaction, which in turn leads to negative affect and dieting behaviors. These behaviors then increase the risk for eating disorder symptomatology, specifically bulimic pathology. This model has held up in nonwestern populations (Vander Wal, Gibbons, & Grazioso, 2008; Warren et al., 2005), suggesting that these pathways lead to eating disorder symptoms across cultures.

Not all cultures endorse the so-called thin ideal that is characteristic of eating disorders. For example, in the United States both Latina (Crago et al., 1996; Winkleby et al., 1996) and African-American (Striegel-Moore & Smolak, 2000) cultures have been found to favor larger body sizes and have less narrowly defined body ideals than does Caucasian culture. Cultures that have a preference for larger or curvier body sizes are considered to be protected from some aspects of eating disorders as a result of lower levels of body dissatisfaction (Anderson-Fye, 2004; Furnham & Baguma, 1994), yet rates of binge eating tend to be approximately equal among Caucasian and minority groups in the

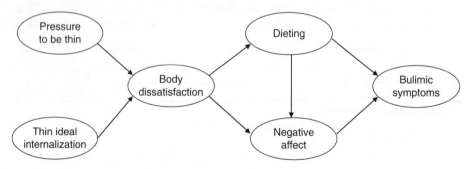

Figure 13.1   The dual pathway model of bulimic symptomatology
Source: Adapted from Stice (2001)

United States. This suggests that body dissatisfaction is not sufficient for the development and manifestation of disordered eating attitudes and behaviors.

Perceptions of Health

Striving for physical and emotional health is generally a goal of all people regardless of cultural background, yet the definition and means of attaining health may vary. Mental health, in particular, is viewed and experienced differently across cultures. While many western cultures define mental disorders by considering a combination of cognitive, emotional, and behavioral symptoms, other cultures may attach meaning only to certain symptoms. For example, in many Hispanic cultures an experience is only considered an illness when it includes visible symptoms, health problems, or pain (Friedman & DiMatteo, 1989). Disordered eating then may only be considered pathological when physical symptoms, such as the amenorrhea and emaciation found in anorexia nervosa, are present. These variations in the conceptualization of mental health appear to affect the ways in which mental disorders, including eating disorders, are expressed as well. Research suggests that the "fat phobia," or fear of gaining weight despite being underweight, that is a diagnostic criterion for anorexia nervosa, may be a culture-bound symptom in that this symptom is not consistently found in eating disorders across cultures (Banks, 1992). For example, studies of eating disorders in China have found that of women experiencing significant disordered eating symptoms, a large number meet criteria for full-syndrome eating disorders except for the "fat phobia" criterion (Lee, 1991).

Cultures in Transition

Just as cultural influences on eating disorders can be studied by looking at the pathways that connect cultural factors and disordered eating within each culture, examining the experiences of individuals who encounter cultural transitions can also provide a wealth of information. One example of a cultural transition includes the changes that occur in societies as they become more industrialized and experience increased exposure to westernized values. An example of a more acute transition between cultures is the immigration experience.

When Cultures Change

Studies consistently show that having contact with or being influenced by western culture significantly increases the prevalence of eating disorders, especially in the case of bulimia nervosa (Keel & Klump, 2003). Western culture is defined as "those core cultural values, mores, and ideas attributable to Western Europe and the United States and characterizing mainstream dominant North American culture" (Anderson-Fye & Becker, 2004, p. 577). Westernization has been associated with increases in disordered eating in a number of countries, including Egypt, China, India, Japan, Malaysia, Pakistan, and Zimbabwe (Anderson-Fye & Becker, 2004). Although westernization is clearly linked to the aforementioned thin ideal, it also refers to a broader set of values that are increasingly being adopted by nonwestern cultures.

As cultures experience economic and political transitions, a number of factors may affect the prevalence rate of eating disorders. The introduction to western media may be a key manner by which western values are transmitted. For instance, in Becker et al.'s (2002) study of the role of exposure to western media in Fiji, the introduction of television was associated with an increase in symptoms of eating disorders and self-induced vomiting to lose weight.

Social modernization is associated with increasingly egalitarian gender role attitudes and gender equity (Inglehart & Norris, 2003). As women gain greater educational opportunities and become more involved in the work force, they may become more vulnerable to messages from the media and larger society regarding the ideal ways to look and behave in order to be successful and accepted. For example, following WWII, Japanese women with eating disorders experienced conflict between traditional and modern values and standards, resulting in identity conflicts (Pike & Borovoy, 2004).

Rapid modernization has also been found to result in difficulties with disordered eating and body dissatisfaction in Asian and Caribbean countries (Katzman, Hermans, Van Hoeken, & Hoek, 2004; Tsai, Curbow, & Heinberg, 2003). However, given the association between more egalitarian gender roles and fewer eating disturbances (Brown, Cross, & Nelson, 1990), the change in gender roles, rather than the nature of gender roles may be of most importance. For example, the increase in rates of eating disorders in Japan since the 1970s has been associated with role conflicts as more women enter the work force while also trying to meet the cultural expectations of the roles of wife and mother (Pike & Borovoy, 2004).

When People Change Cultures

The influence of culture on mental health may be most apparent for individuals whose cultural values and beliefs do not match those of the majority culture in which they live. As discussed in the introductory chapter, *acculturation* involves exposure to the beliefs and behaviors of a new culture, a process that can often cause *acculturative stress*. Immigration to western societies has been linked with an increased risk for developing eating disorders (Mumford, Whitehouse, & Platts, 1991), which suggests that characteristics of western society and the acculturation process both play roles in the development of disordered eating. Some have suggested that as people adapt to new environments, they look to the media and others around them for "cultural guides" to their new settings (Suarez-Orozco & Suarez-Orozco, 2001), which places them at risk for the same negative influences of media experienced by individuals in the new culture.

In addition, the stress of the acculturation process can produce internal conflict as a result of the challenges of social integration, dealing with personal crises, and coping with conflicts between traditional and contemporary values (Anderson-Fye & Becker, 2004), which can put minority groups at higher risk for eating disorders. While some researchers suggest that greater acculturation is correlated with an increased risk of eating disorders (Harris & Kuba, 1997), others indicate that lower acculturation leads to an increased risk of eating problems due the stress of being in conflict with the majority culture (Lake et al., 2000; Root, 1990). For example, Lake et al. (2000) found that among a sample of women attending an Australian university, Hong Kong-born women with traditional ethnic identities endorsed more disordered eating behaviors and attitudes than either Australian women or acculturated Hong Kong-born women. Still others have found that high acculturation may be a risk factor for some minority groups, such as Latinas, but not others, such as Asian-American women (Gowen, Hayward, Killen, Robinson, & Taylor, 1999). Though research on the impact of acculturation on disordered eating symptoms presents a unique opportunity for studying the role of culture and conflicts between cultural values, it is likely that specific aspects of the acculturative process, rather than acculturation per se, convey risk.

Cross-Cultural Assessment of Eating Disorders

Just as culture appears to impact the development of eating disorders, the cross-cultural presentation of eating disorders may pose challenges for those seeking to assess these conditions. Challenges include differential responses to inquiry about eating disorder symptoms, cultural differences in symptom presentation, difficulties in translation and comprehension, and most significantly, issues of cultural and conceptual validity. Even if it is assumed that information can be conveyed accurately, proceeding from a western conceptualization may lead one to overlook relevant risk and protective factors as well as differences in symptom presentation. Knowledge of the cultural context in which measures of disordered eating are applied can advance the understanding of eating disorder development and expression.

Reactions to Symptom Inquiry

Inquiry about eating disorder symptoms may elicit differential responses across cultural groups. In western countries, persons with anorexia nervosa may deny symptoms because they view the symptoms favorably whereas persons with bulimia nervosa may be ashamed (Anderson & Paulosky, 2004). Feelings of shame were identified as one of many barriers to help seeking among Mexican American women with eating disorders (Cachelin & Striegel-Moore, 2006). In Japan, endorsing an eating disorder or a mental disturbance may be perceived as a negative reflection on one's family and community (Yoshimura, 1995).

Under the previous socialist or communist regimes of Eastern Europe, eating disorders were "taboo" in that they were thought to only exist in the Bourgeois class (Boyadjieva & Steinhausen, 1996). In contrast to these experiences of shame, some may view their symptoms with pride, such as those who have joined the pro-eating disorders movement or those who attribute their starvation to religious reasons.

Group membership may also impact response. In the United States, members of ethnic minority groups sometimes feel compelled to "read" the expectations of members of the dominant culture and to act or answer accordingly (Smolak & Striegel-Moore, 2001). For instance, although no differences between Black and White adolescent girls on responses to measures of dieting and body image were found, the Black girls reported more body satisfaction and less dieting than the White girls during focus group study (Parker et al., 1995). Further, persons with eating disorders may not be able to supply comprehensive or accurate information due to the symptoms of these disorders (Anderson & Pauloskey, 2004; Crowther & Sherwood, 1997).

Translation and Comprehension

The cross-cultural assessment of eating disorder symptoms is also hampered by difficulties in translation and comprehension. For instance, the translation of the 26-item version of the Eating Attitudes Test (EAT-26; Garner, Olmsted, Polivy, & Garfinkel, 1982) into Urdu (the national language of Pakistan) was especially difficult because certain terms such as "binge" and "dieting behavior" did not have equivalent expressions in that language (Choudry & Mumford, 1992). Even with an adequate translation, some concepts may be too complex for participants to rate accurately without assistance (Binford, le Grange, & Jellar, 2005; Fichter & Quadfleig, 2000). The concept of binge eating is particularly challenging (Palmer, Robertson, Cain, & Black, 1996) as it is a colloquial term involving the subjective yet defining characteristics of both a loss of control and consumption of a large amount of food in a short period of time (Fairburn & Beglin, 1994). Even if an instrument can be translated, the cross-cultural equivalence of meaning remains a major concern (Smolak & Striegel-Moore, 2001). Grilo, Lozano, and Elder (2005) documented their experience in the translation of the Eating Disorders Examination into Spanish (S-EDE). Those seeking to translate other measures may benefit from their observations.

Cultural and Conceptual Validity

The final and most important challenge involves the cultural and conceptual validity of existing assessment instruments. Even if one can accurately convey the concepts of interest, the measure may not address the range and types of problems encountered by various cultural and ethnic groups (Mumford, Whitehouse, & Choudry, 1992; Smolak & Striegel-Moore, 2001). For example, in a study of the validity of the EDI in Mexico, items relating to perfectionism had to be eliminated because of low correlations with the rest of the scale (Unikel Santoncini, Bojorquez Chapela, Carreño García, & Caballero Romo, 2006). Further, questions may assess not only behavior, but motivation. For example, the rationale for not eating among Chinese anorexia nervosa patients generally does not include a fear of fatness; therefore, endorsement of items that assess food avoidance due to a fear of fatness is unlikely (Lee, Kwok, Liau, & Leung, 2002). It is imperative to investigate the reliability and validity of an instrument among the group to be studied (Fernandez, Malacrne, Wilfley, & McQuaid, 2006).

Differences in symptom presentation may damage a measure's validity. For instance, vomiting is a prominent symptom of bulimia nervosa in the United States, but not in Korea; yet self-torment following eating has been documented in Korea, but not in the United States (Ryu, Lyle, Galer-Unti, & Black, 1999). Whereas western measures of body image emphasize concern with the size of one's stomach and hips, Koreans place more emphasis on the size of one's waist and calves (Ryu et al., 1999). Furthermore, perfectionism may be a less salient factor in old western countries, such as those in Europe, than in the United States (van Strien & Ouwens, 2003). In China (Lee, Ho, & Hsu, 1993) the presence of non-fat phobic patients with anorexia nervosa has been noted. Although this observation had been made in the United States, it was generally dismissed because persons with anorexia nervosa have been found to be poor reporters of symptoms (Crowther & Sherwood, 1997). The differentiation between fat and non-fat phobic (nontypical) anorexia nervosa has recently been discovered to be clinically meaningful with the latter having better treatment outcomes (Strober, Freeman, & Morrell, 1999).

Assessment of Cultural-Level Risk Factors

As mentioned earlier, a number of important cultural risk factors including upward social mobility (Anderson-Fye & Becker, 2004), modernization (Tsai, Curbow, & Heinberg, 2003), industrialization, urbanization, changing family structure (Pike & Borovoy, 2003), and attitudes toward female education (Choudry & Mumford, 1992) are not routinely assessed. Assessment of the context in which eating disorders emerge may help inform theoretical models and choice of treatment options. Present sociocultural models emphasize culture in the context of internalization of the western "thin ideal" (Striegel-Moore & Bulik, 2007). However, these models fail to include the role of the aforementioned characteristics, in large part, due to limited research in this area. Additionally, treatment choice and emphasis is influenced by the context in which eating disorders develop. For instance, a more symptom-based approach such as that afforded by cognitive behavioral treatment formulations may be more appropriate for eating disorders that develop in pursuit of a thin ideal whereas an interpersonal approach may be more appropriate for the treatment of eating disorders that occur in the context of changing career, family, or gender roles.

Cultural differences on measures of eating disorders may inform our understanding of the role of culture in eating disorder expression. For instance, on the Bulimia Test Revised (BULIT-R; Thelen, Farmer, Wonderlich, & Smith, 1991), a measure of bulimic symptomatology, a separate speed/amount of eating factor was discovered for African and Asian Americans but not for Caucasian or Latino Americans (Fernandez, Malacrne Wilfley, & McQuaid, 2006). The authors speculate that the finding of a separate factor for items with the word binge and items referring to binge eating without using the word binge suggests that some groups may distinguish between what they consider to be binge eating and eating large amounts of food in a short period of time. Lee, Lee, Leung, and Yu (1997) observed that some differences in on the Eating Disorder Inventory may reflect cultural rather than pathological differences. Although the core pathology appears cross culturally, the particular manifestation of symptoms differs.

Cross-Cultural Treatment of Eating Disorders

As case reports of eating disorders occur with increasing frequency across the world, perhaps the most important question is how best to treat eating disorders. Due to significant medical complications, treatment should include a full medical evaluation. Readers may turn to Pomeroy (2004) for a broad overview or to Powers and Santana (2002) for detailed medical information. From a mental health perspective, persons treating eating disorders must decide whether to develop and use their own culturally specific treatments, to use empirically supported treatments of predominantly western origin, or to adapt these treatments in some manner to accommodate the specific needs and cultural context of their clients (Hwang, 2006).

A review of the Ovid versions of the Medline and Psych Info databases revealed only one culturally specific treatment for eating disorders. Morita-based therapy is a four-staged Japanese treatment originally developed for the treatment of neurotic spectrum disorders. The basic tenets of this treatment, its application to eating disorders, and preliminary outcomes are described by LeVine (1993). According to the theory, some persons have a hypersensitive degree of self-awareness, engaging in excessively self-critical and self-focused thinking that is often symptom-focused. As a result, patients become reactionary to symptom congruent stimuli and disengaged from other aspects of their lives. The purpose of the therapy is to stop the self-critical introspection and symptom preoccupation.

Empirically supported western treatments, although showing great promise, have not yet been widely disseminated. For those unfamiliar with psychological interventions, it should be noted that these treatments refer to specific manualized protocols and not to treatment orientations or philosophies. Advantages of these protocols include standardization of treatment, ease of communication, improved time usage, and an increased ability to identify core efficacious components whereas disadvantages include difficulties in accessibility, lack of training opportunities, and reduced flexibility in meeting the needs of individual clients (Heimberg, 1998; Lambert, 1998; Wilson, 1998). For each treatment mentioned below, the reference to the corresponding treatment protocol is provided.

A recent comprehensive review of the psychological treatment of eating disorders summarizes the state of the science (Wilson, Grilo, & Vitousek, 2007). Of note, the treatment literature on eating disorders, particularly for anorexia nervosa, is quite limited. The only randomized controlled clinical trials to date have been conducted in westernized nations. The great complexity of these trials, coupled with difficulty in recruiting patients for treatment, has not allowed for the examination of ethnic, racial, or cross-cultural predictors of treatment response. According to Wilson and colleagues, the most efficacious treatment for adolescents with anorexia nervosa is the family-based treatment consistent with the Maudsley Method as detailed by Lock, le Grange, Agras, and Dare (2001). However, they point out that the treatment has not been shown to be effective with adults with a longer duration of symptoms. The authors also note that a second treatment, cognitive behavioral therapy, as described by Garner, Vitousek, and Pike (1997), has shown some effectiveness in limited applications, yet much room for improvement exists. Adjunct therapies, such as the use of medications and nutritional counseling, are considered contraindicated in the absence of concurrent therapy.

According to Wilson and colleagues, the outlook for the successful treatment of bulimia nervosa is considerably more positive. They note that cognitive behavioral therapy, as outlined by Fairburn, Marcus, and Wilson (1993) as well as by Wilson, Fairburn, and Agras (1997), has a great deal of empirical support with the majority of patients showing recovery or marked improvement. They further note that an alternative treatment, interpersonal psychotherapy, as described by Fairburn (1997), shows promise although fewer studies have been conducted. The aforementioned family-based treatment has now been extended to the treatment of bulimia nervosa among adolescents with positive results (le Grange & Lock, 2007). Wilson and colleagues also draw attention to the encouraging preliminary results associated with dialectical behavior therapy, a relatively new treatment originally designed for the treatment of borderline personality disorder (Safer, Telch, & Agras, 2001). They also note that current evidence for the effectiveness of medication is at best minimal.

The literature on the treatment of one of the more recently recognized eating disorders, binge eating disorder, is growing. According to Wilson and colleagues, the most efficacious treatment is cognitive behavioral therapy as detailed by Fairburn, Marcus, and Wilson (1993). Alternative treatments that show promise include interpersonal psychotherapy (Wilfley et al., 1993, 2002) and dialectical behavior therapy (Telch, Agras, & Linehan, 2001). A new treatment, which Wilson characterizes as a second-generation manual-based treatment, is the transdiagnostic approach of Fairburn, Cooper, and Shafran (2003). This new treatment moves away from a specific symptom presentation and focuses on common mechanisms underlying the maintenance of eating disorders while affording a greater degree of flexibility in meeting individual client needs. Such an approach may be more applicable in diverse cultural settings in which the symptom presentation may vary. Readers are encouraged to turn to Wilson et al. (2007), Thompson (2004), and Garner and Garfinkel (1997) for further information.

An important question that arises is the extent to which these treatments may generalize across cultures. A recent review of the efficacy of empirically supported treatments among ethnic minority groups in the United States may inform this question. According to the report, empirically supported treatments for depression, anxiety disorders, attention deficit hyperactivity disorder, and disruptive behavior disorders have shown to be at least as efficacious among ethnic minority families and children as among Caucasian populations living in the United States; among adults, interventions for depression, anxiety, and schizophrenia have also generalized from Caucasians to members of ethnic minority groups (Miranda et al., 2005). The authors conclude that these treatments are likely appropriate for most ethnic minority individuals living in the United States.

The extent to which such treatments should be adapted to increase cultural congruence and thereby treatment efficacy is uncertain. Although adapted interventions have been shown to be efficacious, tests of standard versus adapted care have not been conducted (Miranda et al., 2005). Hwang (2006) discusses the challenges of meeting the mental health care needs of diverse populations, evidence for the effectiveness of adapting known treatments, and models of cultural competency. For eating disorders specifically, members of ethnic minority groups are less likely to seek assistance and when they do, are less likely to receive treatment (Cachelin & Striegel-Moore, 2006; Striegel-Moore & Bulik, 2007). As Hwang points out, individual treatment providers may make personal modifications to known treatments to meet the needs of their clients. However, without systematic modification or a clear conceptual framework, this approach becomes entirely ideographic.

Conceptual frameworks for the adaptation of manual-based treatments have been offered. Sue (1990) discusses three domains that influence nonspecific therapy factors, or those universal factors separate from the content of the actual treatment, including culture-bound communication styles, sociopolitical facets of nonverbal communication, and counseling as a communication style. Bernal, Bonilla, and Bellido (1995) present eight dimensions that must be considered in order to successfully adapt a treatment, including manual-based treatments, to another culture. Although developed for a Hispanic population, the dimensions may have wide-scale applicability, and include language, persons, metaphors, content, concepts, goals, methods, and context. A third model, developed with Asian Americans in mind, is the psychotherapy adaptation and modification framework (PAMF) which is a three-tiered model that begins with a consideration of six salient cultural influences on mental health, including prevalence, etiology, phenomenology, diagnostic and assessment issues, coping styles and help-seeking pathways, and treatment and intervention issues (Hwang, 2006). Careful consideration of these issues is used to inform the second tier, which is comprised of six therapeutic domains, including dynamic issues and cultural complexities; orienting clients to psychotherapy and mental health awareness; cultural beliefs regarding mental illness, its causes, and treatments; the client-therapist relationship; cultural differences in the expression and communication of distress; and addressing cultural issues specific to the population. Specific principles derived from each domain, along with a rationale for the adaptation of treatment, are then provided. Thus far, application of such a model has not been attempted with one of the established manualized treatments for eating disorders.

The cross-cultural treatment of eating disorders is just beginning. Given the increasing number of case reports worldwide, there is a growing need for efficacious treatments. Unfortunately, the field of eating disorders is challenged by the failure to use standardized treatment protocols and by poor study design (Wilson et al., 2007) as well as by challenges similar to those faced by the mental health field as a whole, namely the failure to include sufficient numbers of ethnic minorities in treatment efficacy studies (U.S. Department of Health and Human Services, 2001). Given a lack of culturally specific treatments, beginning with an empirically supported treatment may be the best option. The different foci of these treatments, including the family, interpersonal relationships, behavioral and cognitive change, and even eastern philosophical traditions, provide a reasonable starting point. Second-generation treatments, such as the transdiagnostic approach of Fairburn et al. (2003), may ease this transition given the decreased emphasis on specific symptoms. Adaptations to increase cultural congruency should follow a well-described conceptual framework with noted amendments.

Recommendations for Future Research

The cross-cultural examination and treatment of eating disorders is in great need of further exploration. Epidemiological study of the prevalence of eating disorders is required to assess treatment need, even among countries such as the United States. In nonwestern countries, prevalence studies are hampered by a lack of valid assessment instruments. The validation process should include the careful delineation of the core phenomenology of interest, a careful forward and backward translation process, and evaluation of instrument reliability and validity.

Research on the identification, measurement, and explication of the role of specific cultural characteristics in eating disorder development, maintenance, and treatment is also needed. Present models of eating disorder development may be evaluated, new models developed, and core pathways leading to eating disorder development and recovery may be identified. Similarly, examination of potential cultural-level characteristics that pertain to eating disorders is needed. The introduction of television to Fiji presented a unique opportunity to study the role of the media in eating disorder development. However, other characteristics require definition, refinement, or explication of the way in which they may increase eating disorder risk, such as the association between various facets of acculturation and eating disorder symptomatology.

Finally, research on the treatment of eating disorders, especially for anorexia nervosa, is desperately needed. Although randomized controlled trials are a good choice for more prevalent conditions, use of alternative evaluation strategies such as a series of well-controlled single case studies or fine-grained observational studies may be required. Further, ethnic minority response to established treatments in the United States has been established for a variety of presenting conditions (Miranda et al., 2005). Expanding such research to include eating disorders would constitute a great advancement.

Conclusions

The cross-cultural study, diagnosis, assessment, and treatment of eating disorders is in its infancy. A review of the literature shows that eating disorders are culture-influenced. Although a number of assessment instruments have been developed and even translated, concerns about the cultural validity of these instruments are of paramount concern. The tedious process of instrument development, modification, and evaluation among persons with whom the instruments are to be used remains. Similarly, the details of treatments and the modifications made to existing treatments should proceed in a systematic and careful manner. The cross-cultural study of eating disorders holds great promise for advancing our understanding of the etiology, phenomenology, assessment, and treatment of this class of psychological disorders.

REFERENCES

American Psychiatric Association (2000). *Diagnostic and statistical manual of mental disorders* (4th ed.), *Text Revision*. Washington, DC: Author.
Andersen, A. E., & DiDomenico, L. (1992). Diet vs. shape content of popular male and female magazines: A dose-response relationship to the incidence of eating disorders? *International Journal of Eating Disorders, 11*(3), 283–287.
Anderson, D. A., & Paulosky, C. A. (2004). Psychological assessment of eating disorders and related features. In J. K. Thompson, *Handbook of eating disorders and obesity* (pp. 112–129). Hoboken, NJ: John Wiley & Sons, Inc.
Anderson-Fye, E. P. (2004). A "Coca-Cola"shape: Cultural change, body image, and eating disorders in San Andres, Belize. *Culture, Medicine and Psychiatry, 28*, 561–595.
Anderson-Fye, E. P., & Becker, A. E. (2004). Sociocultural aspects of eating disorders. In J. K. Thompson, *Handbook of eating disorders and obesity* (pp. 565–589). Hoboken, NJ: John Wiley & Sons, Inc.

Banks, C. G. (1992). "Culture" in culture-bound syndromes: The case of anorexia nervosa. *Social Science & Medicine, 34*(8), 867–884.

Becker, A. E., Burwell, R. A., Gilman, S. E., Herzog, D. B., & Hamburg, P. (2002). Eating behaviors and attitudes following prolonged exposure to television among ethnic Fijian adolescent girls. *British Journal of Psychiatry, 180*(6), 509–514.

Bernal, G., Bonilla, J., & Bellido, C. (1995). Ecological validity and cultural sensitivity for outcome research: Issues for the cultural adaptation and development of psychosocial treatments with Hispanics. *Journal of Abnormal Child Psychology, 23*(1), 67–82.

Binford, R. B., Le Grange, D., & Jellar, C. C. (2005). Eating Disorders Examination versus Eating Disorders Examination-Questionnaire in adolescents with full and partial-syndrome bulimia nervosa and anorexia nervosa. *International Journal of Eating Disorders, 37*(1), 44–49.

Birch, L. L., & Fisher, J. O. (1998). Development of eating behaviors among children and adolescents. *Pediatrics, 101*(3 Pt 2), 539–549.

Boyadjieva, S., & Steinhausen, H. (1996). The Eating Attitudes Test and the Eating Disorders Inventory in four Bulgarian clinical and nonclinical samples. *International Journal of Eating Disorders, 19*(1), 93–98.

Brown, J. A., Cross, H. J., & Nelson, J. M. (1990). Sex-role identity and sex-role ideology in college women with bulimic behavior. *International Journal of Eating Disorders, 9*(5), 571–575.

Bruce, B., & Agras, W. S. (1992). Binge eating in females: A population-based investigation. *International Journal of Eating Disorders, 12*, 365–373.

Bulik, C. M., Sullivan, P. F., & Kendler, K. S. (1998). Heritability of binge-eating and broadly defined bulimia nervosa. *Biological Psychiatry, 44*(12), 1210–1218.

Cachelin, F. M., & Striegel-Moore, R. H. (2006). Help seeking and barriers to treatment in a community sample of Mexican American and European American women with eating disorders. *International Journal of Eating Disorders, 39*(2), 154–161.

Cafri, G., Yamamiya, Y., Brannick, M., & Thompson, J. K. (2005). The influence of sociocultural factors on body image: A meta analysis. *Clinical Psychology: Science and Practice, 12*(4), 421–433.

Cattarin, J. A., & Thompson J. K. (1994). A three-year longitudinal study of body image, eating disturbance, and general psychological functioning in adolescent females. *Eating Disorders: The Journal of Treatment and Prevention, 2*(2), 114–125.

Choudry, I. Y., & Mumford, D. B. (1992). A pilot study of eating disorders in Mirpur (Pakistan) using an Urdu version of the Eating Attitudes Test. *International Journal of Eating Disorders, 11*(3), 243–251.

Crago, M., Shisslak, C. M., & Estes, L. S. (1996). Eating disturbances among American minority groups: A review. *International Journal of Eating Disorders, 19*(3), 239–248.

Crowther, J. H., & Sherwood, N. E. (1997). Assessment. In D. M. Garner & P. E. Garfinkel (Eds.), *Handbook of treatment for eating disorders* (2nd ed., pp. 34–49). New York: Guilford Press.

Fairburn, C. G. (1997). Interpersonal psychotherapy for bulimia nervosa. In D. M. Garner & P. E. Garfinkel (Ed.), *Handbook of treatment for eating disorders* (2nd ed., pp. 278–294). New York: Guilford Press.

Fairburn, C. G., & Beglin, S. J. (1994). Assessment of eating disorders: Interview or self-report questionnaire? *International Journal of Eating Disorders, 16*(4), 363–370.

Fairburn, C. G., Cooper, Z., & Shafran, R. (2003). Cognitive behaviour therapy for eating disorders: A "transdiagnostic" theory and treatment. *Behaviour Research and Therapy, 41*(5), 509–528.

Fairburn, C. G., Marcus, M. D., & Wilson, G. T. (1993). Cognitive behaviour therapy for binge eating and bulimia nervosa: A comprehensive treatment manual. In C. G. & G. T. Wilson (Eds.), *Binge eating: Nature, assessment and treatment* (pp. 361–404). New York: Guilford.

Fernandez, S., Malacrne, V. L., Wilfley, D. E., & McQuaid, J. (2006). Factor structure of the bulimia test-revised in college women from four ethnic groups. *Cultural Diversity and Ethnic Minority Psychology, 12*(3), 403–419.

Fichter, M. M., & Quadfleig, N. (2000). Comparing self- and expert rating: A self-report screening version (SIAB-S) of the Structured Interview for Anorexic and Bulimic Syndromes for *DSM–IV* and *ICD-10* (SIAB-EX). *European Archives of Psychiatry and Clinical Neuroscience, 250*(4), 175–185.

Field, A. E., Camargo, C. A., Taylor, C. B., Berkey, C. S., & Colditz, G. A. (1999). Relation of peer and media influences to the development of purging behaviors among preadolescent and adolescent girls. *Archives of Pediatrics & Adolescent Medicine, 153*, 1184–1189.

Friedman, H. S., & DiMatteo, M. R. (1989). *Health psychology*. Upper Saddle River, NJ: Prentice-Hall, Inc.

Furnham, A., & Baguma, P. (1994). Cross-cultural differences in the evaluation of male and female body shapes. *International Journal of Eating Disorders, 15*(1), 81–89.

Garner, D. M., & Garfinkel, P. E. (1997). *Handbook of treatment for eating disorders* (2nd ed.). New York: Guilford Press.

Garner, D. M., Olmsted, M. P., Polivy, J., & Garfinkel, P. E. (1982). The eating attitudes test: Psychometric features and clinical correlates. *Psychological Medicine, 12*(4), 871–878.

Garner, D. M., Vitousek, K. M., & Pike, K. M. (1997). Cognitive-behavioral therapy for anorexia nervosa. In D. M. Garner & P. E. Garfinkel (Eds.), *Handbook of treatment for eating disorders* (2nd ed., pp. 94–144). New York: Guilford Press.

Gary, F. A. (2005). Stigma: Barrier to mental health care among ethnic minorities. *Issues in Mental Health Nursing, 26*(10), 979–999.

Gowen, L. K., Hayward, C., Killen, J. D., Robinson, T. N., & Taylor, C. B. (1999). Acculturation and eating disorder symptoms in adolescent girls. *Journal of Research on Adolescence, 9*(1), 67–83.

Grilo, C. M., Lozano, C., & Elder, K. A. (2005). Inter-rater and test-retest reliability of the Spanish language version of the Eating Disorder Examination Interview: Clinical and research implications. *Journal of Psychiatric Practice, 11*(4), 231–240.

Groesz, L. M., Levine, M. P., & Murnen, S. K. (2002). The effect of experimental presentation of thin media images on body satisfaction: A meta-analytic review. *International Journal of Eating Disorders, 31*(1), 1–16.

Habermas, T. (1989). The psychiatric history of anorexia nervosa and bulimia nervosa: Weight concerns and bulimic symptoms in early case reports. *International Journal of Eating Disorders, 8*, 516–517.

Harris, D. J., & Kuba, S. A. (1997). Ethnocultural identity and eating disorders in women of color. *Professional Psychology: Research and Practice, 28*(4), 341–347.

Hawkins, N., Richards, P. S., Granley, H. M., & Stein, D. M. (2004). The impact of exposure to the thin-ideal media image on women. *Eating Disorders: The Journal of Treatment & Prevention, 12*(1), 35–50.

Heimberg, R. G. (1998). Manual-based treatment: An essential ingredient of clinical practice in the 21st century. *Clinical Psychology: Science and Practice, 5*(3), 387–390.

Hill, A. J., & Franklin, J. A. (1998). Mothers, daughters, and dieting: Investigating the transmission of weight control. *British Journal of Clinical Psychology, 37*(1), 3–13.

Hoek, H. W., Bartelds, A. I. M., Bosveld, J. F., et al. (1995). Impact of urbanization on detection rates of eating disorders. *American Journal of Psychiatry, 152*(9), 1272–1278.

Hwang, W. (2006). The psychotherapy adaptation and modification framework: Application to Asian Americans. *American Psychologist, 61*(7), 702–715.

Inglehart, R., & Norris, P. (2003). *Rising tide: Gender equality and cultural change around the world*. New York: Cambridge University Press.

Katzman, M. A., Hermans, K. M. E., Van Hoeken, D., & Hoek, H. W. (2004). Not your "typical island woman": Anorexia nervosa is reported only in subcultures in Curacao. *Culture, Medicine, and Psychiatry, 28*(4), 463–492.

Keel, P. K., & Klump, K. L. (2003). Are eating disorders culture-bound syndromes? Implications for conceptualizing their etiology. *Psychological Bulletin, 129*(5), 747–769.

Keery, H., van den Berg, P., & Thompson, J. K. (2004). An evaluation of the Tripartite Influence Model of body dissatisfaction and eating disturbance with adolescent girls. *Body Image, 1*(3), 237–251.

Lake, A. J., Staiger, P. K., & Glowinski, H. (2000). Effect of Western culture on women's attitudes to eating and perceptions of body shape. *International Journal of Eating Disorders, 27*(1), 83–89.

Lambert, M. J. (1998). Manual-based treatment and clinical practice: Hangman of life or promising development? *Clinical Psychology: Science and Practice, 5*(3), 391–395.

le Grange, D., & Lock, J. (2007). *Treating bulimia in adolescents: A family-based approach*. New York: Guilford Press.

Lee, S. (1995). Self-starvation in context: Towards a culturally sensitive understanding of anorexia nervosa. *Social Science and Medicine, 41*(1), 25–36.

Lee, S. (1991). Anorexia nervosa in Hong Kong: A Chinese perspective. *Psychological Medicine, 21*(3), 703–711.

Lee, S., Chiu, H. F., & Chen, C. N. (1989). Anorexia nervosa in Hong Kong: Why not more in Chinese? *Bristish Journal of Psychiatry, 154*, 683–688.

Lee, S., Ho, T. P., & Hsu, L. K. (1993). Fat phobic and non-fat phobic anorexia nervosa: A comparative study of 70 Chinese patients in Hong Kong. *Psychological Medicine, 23*(4), 999–1017.

Lee, S., Kwok, K., Liau, C., & Leung, T. (2002). Screening Chinese patients with eating disorders using the Eating Attitudes Test in Hong Kong. *International Journal of Eating Disorders, 32*(1), 91–97.

Lee, S., Lee, A. M., Leung, T., & Yu, H. (1997). Psychometric properties of the Eating Disorders Inventory (EDI-1) in a non-clinical Chinese population in Hong Kong. *International Journal of Eating Disorders, 21*(2), 187–194.

Levine, M. P., Smolak, L., Moodey, A. F., Shuman, M. D., & Hessen, L. D. (1994). Normative developmental challenges and dieting and eating disturbances in middle school girls. *International Journal of Eating Disorders, 15*, 11–20.

LeVine, P. (1993). Morita-based therapy and its use across cultures in the treatment of bulimia nervosa. *Journal of Counseling & Development, 72*(1), 82–90.

Lock, J., le Grange, D., Agras, W. S., & Dare, C. (2001). *Treatment manual for anorexia nervosa: A family-based approach.* New York: Guilford Press.

Lucero, K., Hicks, R. A., Bramlette, J., & Brassington, G. S. (1992). Frequency of eating problems among Asian and Caucasian college women. *Psychological Reports, 71,* 255–258.

Markey, C. N. (2004). Culture and the development of eating disorders: A tripartite model. *Eating Disorders, The Journal of Treatment & Prevention, 12*(2), 139–156.

Miller, M. N., & Pumariega, A. J. (2001). Culture and eating disorders: A historical and cross-cultural review. *Psychiatry: Interpersonal and Biological Processes, 64*(2), 93–110.

Miranda, J., Bernal, G., Lau, A., Kohn, L., Hwang, W., & La Framboise, T. (2005). State of the science on psychosocial interventions for ethnic minorities. *Annual Review of Clinical Psychology, 1,* 113–142.

Mitrany, E., Lubin, F., Chetrit, A., & Modan, B. (1995). Eating disorders among Jewish female adolescents in Israel: A 5-year study. *Journal of Adolescent Health, 16*(6), 454–457.

Monteleone, P., Tortorella, A., Castaldo, E., Di Filippo, C., & Maj, M. (2007) The Leu72Met polymorphism of the ghrelin gene is significantly associated with binge eating disorder. *Psychiatric Genetics, 17,* 13–16.

Mukai, T. (1996). Mothers, peers and perceived pressure to diet among Japanese adolescent girls. *Journal of Research on Adolescence, 6*(3), 309–324.

Mumford, D. B., Whitehouse, A. M., & Choudry, I. Y. (1992). Survey of eating disorders in English-Medium schools in Lahore, Pakistan. *International Journal of Eating Disorders, 11*(2), 173–184.

Mumford, D. B., Whitehouse, A. M., & Platts, M. (1991). Sociocultural correlates of eating disorders among Asian schoolgirls in Bradford. *British Journal of Psychiatry, 158,* 222–228.

Ng, C. H. (1997). The stigma of mental illness in Asian cultures. *Australian and New Zealand Journal of Psychiatry, 31*(3), 382–390.

Palmer, R. (1993). Weight concern should not be a necessary criterion for the eating disorders: A polemic. *International Journal of Eating Disorders, 14*(4), 459–465.

Palmer, R., Robertson, D., Cain, M., & Black, S. (1996). The Clinical Eating Disorders Rating Instrument (CEDRI): A validation study. *European Eating Disorders Review, 4*(3), 149–156.

Parker, S., Nichter, M., Nichter, M., Vuckovic, N., Sims, C., & Ritenbaugh, C. (1995). Body image and weight concerns among African American and White adolescent females. *Human Organization, 54,* 103–114.

Paxton, S. J., Schutz, H. K., Wertheim, E. H., & Muir, S. L. (1999). Friendship, clique, and peer influences on body image concerns, dietary restraint, extreme weight-loss behaviors, and binge eating in adolescent girls. *Journal of Abnormal Psychology, 108*(2), 255–266.

Pike, K. M., & Borovoy, A. (2004). The rise of eating disorders in Japan: Issues of culture and limitations of the model of "Westernization." *Culture, Medicine, & Psychiatry, 28*(4), 493–531.

Pike, K. M., & Rodin, J. (1991). Mothers, daughters, and disordered eating. *Journal of Abnormal Psychology, 100*(2), 198–204.

Pomeroy, C. (2004). Assessment of medical status and physical factors. In J. K. Thompson (Ed.), *Handbook of eating disorders and obesity.* Hoboken, NJ: John Wiley & Sons, Inc.

Powers, P. S., & Santana, C. A. (2002). Eating disorders: A guide for the primary care physician. *Primary Care; Clinics in Office Practice, 29*(1), 81–98.

Prince, R. (1985). The concept of culture-bound syndromes: Anorexia nervosa and brain-fag. *Social Science and Medicine, 21*(2), 197–203.

Pumarino, H., & Vivanco, N. (1982). Anorexia nervosa: Medical and psychiatric characteristics of 30 cases. *Revista Medica de Chile, 110*(11), 1081–1092.

Root, M. P. (1990). Disordered eating in women of color. *Sex Roles, 22*(7–8), 525–536.

Ryu, H. R., Lyle, R. M., Galer-Unti, R. A., & Black, D. R. (1999). Cross-cultural assessment of eating disorders: Psychometric characteristics of a Korean version of the Eating Disorder Inventory-2 and the Bulimia Test-Revised. *Eating Disorders, 7*(2), 109–122.

Safer, D. L., Telch, C. F., & Agras, W. S. (2001). Dialectical behavior therapy for bulimia nervosa. *American Journal of Psychiatry, 158*(4), 632–634.

Smolak, L., & Striegel-Moore, R. H. (2001). Challenging the myth of the golden girl: Ethnicity and eating disorders. In R. H. Striegel-Moore & L. Smolak (Eds.), *Eating disorders: Innovative directions in research and practice* (pp. 111–132). Washington, DC: American Psychological Association.

Stein, D., Meged, S., & Bar-Hanin, T. (1997). Partial eating disorders in a community sample of female adolescents. *Journal of the American Academy of Child and Adolescent Psychiatry, 36*, 1116–1123.

Stice, E. (2001). A prospective test of the dual-pathway model of bulimic pathology: Mediating effects of dieting and negative affect. *Journal of Abnormal Psychology, 110*, 124–135.

Stice, E. (2002). Risk and maintenance factors for eating pathology: A meta-analytic review. *Psychological Bulletin, 128*(5), 825–848.

Stice, E., & Agras, W. S. (1998). Predicting the onset and remission of bulimic behaviors in adolescence: A longitudinal groping analysis. *Behavior Therapy, 29*, 257–276.

Striegel-Moore, R. H., & Bulik, C. M. (2007). Risk factors for eating disorders. *American Psychologist, 62*(3), 181–198.

Striegel-Moore, R. H., & Smolak, L. (2000). The influence of ethnicity on eating disorders in women. In R. Eisler, & M. Hersen (Eds.), *Handbook of gender, culture, and health* (pp. 227–253). Mahwah, NJ: Lawrence Eribaum Associates.

Striegel-Moore, R. H., Wilfley, D., Pike, K., Dohm, F., & Fairburn, C. (2000). Recurrent binge eating in Black American women. *Archives of Family Medicine, 9*, 83–87.

Strober, M., Freeman, R., & Morrell, W. (1999). Atypical anorexia nervosa: Separation from typical cases in course and outcome in a long-term prospective study. *International Journal of Eating Disorders, 25*(2), 135–142.

Suarez-Orozco, C., & Suarez-Orozco, M. M. (2001). *Children of immigration*. Cambridge, MA: Harvard University Press.

Sue, D. W. (1990). Culture-specific strategies in counseling: A conceptual framework. *Professional Psychology: Research and Practice, 21*(6), 424–433.

Telch, C. F., Agras, W. S., & Linehan, M. M. (2001). Dialectical behavioral therapy for binge eating disorder. *Journal of Consulting and Clinical Psychology, 69*(6), 1061–1065.

Thaw, J. M., Williamson, D. A., & Martin, C. K. (2001). Impact of altering *DSM–IV* criteria for anorexia and bulimia nervosa on the base rates of eating disorder diagnoses. *Eating and Weight Disorders, 6*(3), 121–129.

Thelen, M. H., Farmer, J., Wonderlich, S., & Smith, M. (1991). A revision of the Bulimia Test: The BULIT-R. *Psychological Assessment, 3*(1), 119–124.

Thelen, M. H., Mintz, L. B., & Vander Wal, J. S. (1996). The bulimia test-revised: Validation with *DSM–IV* criteria for bulimia nervosa. *Psychological Assessment*, *8*(2), 219–221.

Thompson, J. K. (2004). *Handbook of eating disorders and obesity*. Hoboken, New Jersey: John Wiley & Sons, Inc.

Tsai, G., Curbow, B., & Heinberg, L. (2003). Sociocultural and developmental influences on body dissatisfaction and disordered eating attitudes and behaviors of Asian women. *Journal of Nervous and Mental Disease,191*(5), 309–318.

Unikel Santoncini, C., Bojorquez Chapela, I., Carreño García, S., & Caballero Romo, A. (2006). Validación del Eating Disorder Inventory en una muestra de mujeres Mexicanas con trastorno de la conducta alimentaria [Validation of the Eating Disorder Inventory in a sample of Mexican women with eating disorders.] *Salud Mental, 29*, 44–51.

U.S. Department of Health and Human Services (2001). *Mental health: Culture, race, and ethnicity – A supplement to Mental health: A report of the Surgeon General*. Rockville, MD: U.S. Department of Health and Human Services, Public Health Service, Office of the Surgeon General.

van Strien, T., & Ouwens, M. (2003). Validation of the Dutch EDI-2 in one clinical and two non-clinical populations. *European Journal of Psychological Assessment*, *19*(1), 66–84.

Vander Wal, J. S., Gibbons, J. L., & Grazioso, M. P. (2008). The sociocultural model of eating disorder development: Application to a Guatemalan sample, *Eating Behaviors, 9*(3), 277–284.

Wade, T. D., Bulik, C. M., Neale, M., & Kendler, K. S. (2000). Anorexia nervosa and major depression: Shared genetic and environmental risk factors. *American Journal of Psychiatry, 157*(3), 469–471.

Warren, C. S., Gleaves, D. H., Cepeda-Benito, A., Fernandez, M. C., & Rodriguez-Ruiz, S. (2005). Ethnicity as a protective factor against internalization of a thin ideal and body dissatisfaction. *International Journal of Eating Disorders, 37*(3), 241–249.

Wildes, J. E., Emery, R. E., & Simons, A. D. (2001). The roles of ethnicity and culture in the development of eating disturbance and body dissatisfaction: A meta-analytic review. *Clinical Psychology Review, 21*(4), 521–551.

Wilfley, D. E., Agras, W. S., Telch, C. F., et al. (1993). Group cognitive-behavioral therapy and group interpersonal psychotherapy for the nonpurging bulimic individual: A controlled comparison. *Journal of Consulting and Clinical Psychology, 61*(2), 296–305.

Wilfley, D. E., Pike, K. M., Dohm, F. A., Striegel-Moore, R. H., & Fairburn, C. G. (2001). Bias in binge eating disorder: How representative are recruited clinic samples? *Journal of Consulting and Clinical Psychology, 69*(3), 383–388.

Wilfley, D. E., Welch, R. R., Stein, R. I., et al. (2002). A randomized comparison of group cognitive-behavioral therapy and group interpersonal therapy for the treatment of overweight individuals with binge eating disorders. *Archives of General Psychiatry, 59*(8), 713–721.

Wilson, G. T. (1998). Manual-based treatment and clinical practice. *Clinical Psychology: Science and Practice, 5*(3), 363–375.

Wilson, G. T., Fairburn, C. G., & Agras, W. S. (1997). Cognitive-behavioral therapy for bulimia nervosa. In D. M. Garner, & P. E. Garfinkel (Ed.), *Handbook of treatment for eating disorders* (2nd ed., pp. 67–93). New York: Guilford Press.

Wilson, G. T., Grilo, C. M., & Vitousek, K. M. (2007). Psychological treatment of eating disorders. *American Psychologist, 62*(3), 199–216.

Winkleby, M. A., Gardner, C. D., & Taylor, C. B. (1996) The influence of gender and socioeconomic factors on Hispanic/White differences in body mass index. *Preventive Medicine: An International Journal Devoted to Practice and Theory, 25*(2), 203–211.

Wiseman, C. V., Gray, J. J., Mosimann, J. E., & Ahrens, A. H. (1992). Cultural expectations of thinness: An update. *International Journal ofEating Disorders, 11*(1), 85–89.

Yamamiya, Y., Cash, T. F., Melnyk, S. E., Posavac, H. D., & Posavac, S. S. (2005). Women's exposure to thin-and-beautiful media images: Body image effects of media-ideal internalization and impact-reduction interventions. *Body Image, 2*(1), 74–80.

Yoshimura, K. (1995). Acculturative and sociocultural influences on the development of eating disorders in Asian-American females. *Eating Disorders: The Journal of Treatment & Prevention, 3*(3), 216–228.

Zuckerfeld, R., Fuchs, A., & Cormillot, A. (1988). Characterization and detection of bulimia in the city of Buenos Aires. *Acta Psiquiatrica y Psicologica de America Latina, 34*(4), 298–302.

14

Culture and Suicide

David Lester

The aim of this chapter is to present an overview of some of the topics and issues which are present in the interaction of suicide and culture. A major dichotomy here, of course, is the level of analysis. The interaction can be explored for the aggregate suicide rate of a culture and also for the individual suicide living in a particular society or culture. Let us first look at the interaction at the aggregate level.

Societal and Cultural Suicide Rates

Societal suicide rates differ widely around the world. Male suicide rates in 2000 ranged from 80.4 per 100,000 per year in Lithuania to 0.1 in Egypt; for females, the suicide rates ranged from 16.9 in Lithuania to 0.0 in Egypt. Knowledge of worldwide trends in suicide are limited because many African, Middle East and Central and South American countries do not report their suicide rates to the World Health Organization (now online at www.who.int) and because the suicide rates on the website are rarely up-to-date. For all but one nation, the male suicide rate is higher than the female suicide rate. The lone exception is China where women have a higher suicide rate than men.[1] However, China documents suicide fatalities for only a small percentage of the nation, and so the suicide rates are not accurate for the nation as a whole.[2] These differences in national suicide rates are large and generally stable over time.

Suicide rates also vary widely over the different geographic regions of a nation (for example, over American states and Canadian provinces, suicide rates increase toward the west (Lester, 1985)) and over the different social

---

[1] Phillips, Liu, and Zhang (1999) reported suicide rates of 33.6 per 100,000 per year versus 24.2 for the 1990–1994 period for women and men, respectively.
[2] Suicide rates for China in 2000 were not available from the World Health Organization.

groups within a nation (for example, some groups of both native Americans and native Canadians have very high suicide rates (Lester, 1997a)). The Pima had a suicide rate of about 40 per 100,000 per year in the 1960s and 1970s and the Cheyenne a rate of 48 for the period 1960–1968, whereas the Navajo had a suicide rate of only 13 in the late 1960s (Lester, 1997a).

An obvious explanation of such variations in the aggregate suicide rate is that the reporting and counting of suicides in different nations and cultures differ greatly in accuracy (Douglas, 1967). Indeed, it has been easy to document serious official under-reporting of suicides, for example, in Newfoundland (Malla and Hoenig, 1983) and native Americans in Alaska (Hlady and Middaugh, 1988).

Nevertheless, it is very unlikely that completely accurate reporting of suicides would eliminate the national and cultural differences. The suicide rates of immigrant groups both to the United States and to Australia are strongly associated with the suicide rates in the home nations from which they arrived (Sainsbury & Barraclough, 1968; Lester, 1972). For example, the Irish had a relatively low suicide rate in 1959, 2.5 per 100,000, and Irish immigrants to the United States in 1959, where they encountered the same medical examiners as other immigrant groups, also had the lowest suicide of all immigrants groups from European countries, only 9.8 (Dublin, 1963).

The distribution of suicide rates by age varies with the level of economic development of the nation (Girard, 1993). Male suicide rates increase with age in most nations of the world. For females, the distribution of suicide rates by age varies with the level of economic development of the nation. For wealthy nations, such as the United States and Sweden, female suicide rates tend to peak in middle age. For poorer nations, such as Venezuela, suicide rates are higher for elderly women, while for the poorest nations, such as Thailand, the peak shifts to young women (Girard, 1993).

Explaining International Differences in Suicide

The association of sociodemographic and economic variables with national suicides has been best analyzed using factor analysis. In a study of cross-national suicide rates in 72 countries, Lester (1996) identified 13 independent orthogonal factors for the social variables, only one of which was associated with suicide rates. This factor was economic development, with high loadings from such social variables as low population growth and high gross domestic product per capita. Conklin and Simpson (1987), in a similar study, reported that lower suicide rates were found for nations with less economic development and also where Islam was the dominant religion.

Physiological Differences

One possible explanation for differences in national suicide rates is that different nationalities differ in their physiology. For example, there are clear differences in the frequency of genes in the people from the different nations of Europe (Menozzi, Piazza & Cavalli-Sforza, 1978). Thus, different nations and cultures may differ in their genetic structure and so, for example, differences between cultures in the prevalence of inherited psychiatric disorders may be responsible for the differences in the suicide rates of nations and cultures. There has been speculation that the Finno-Ugrian gene (which is found in Finns and Hungarians) may increase the predisposition to suicide (Lester & Kondrichin, 2004).

One study has attempted to demonstrate an association between physiological factors and suicide rates at the cross-national level. Lester (1987) found that the suicide rates of nations were associated with the proportion of people with Types O, A, B and AB blood – the higher the proportion of people in the nation with Type O blood, the lower the suicide rate. However, few studies have explored the role of physiological differences in accounting for national differences in suicide rates.

Psychiatric Differences

The major psychiatric factors found to be associated with suicidal behavior are depression, especially hopelessness, and psychological disturbance, such as neuroticism, anxiety, or emotional instability (Lester, 2004). Psychiatric disorder appears to increase the risk of suicide, with affective disorders and alcohol and drug abuse leading the list. Nations may differ in the prevalence of these conditions, and such differences could account for the differences in suicide rates. For example, nations certainly do differ in their consumption of alcohol (Adrian, 1984), as well as depression (Weissman and Klerman, 1977).

Social Composition

Moksony (1990) noted that one simple explanation of national differences in suicide rates is that the national populations differ in the proportion of those at risk for suicide. For example, typically in developed nations, suicide rates are highest among the elderly, especially elderly males. Therefore, nations with a higher proportion of elderly males will have higher suicide rates.

Societal Differences

The most popular explanation of the variation in national suicide rates focuses on social variables. Durkheim (1897) hypothesized that the suicide rate is related to the level of social integration (the degree to which the people are bound together in social networks) and the level of social regulation (the degree to which people's desires and emotions are regulated by societal norms and customs). According to Durkheim, *egoistic* and *anomic* suicides result from too little social integration and social regulation, respectively, while *altruistic* and *fatalistic* suicides result from too much social integration and social regulation, respectively. Later sociologists have argued that altruistic and fatalistic suicides are rare in modern societies. Therefore, suicide rarely results from excessive social integration or regulation. As a result, suicide in modern societies seems to increase as social integration and regulation *decrease* (e.g., Johnson, 1965).

A major issue here has been raised by Moksony (1990) and Taylor (1990) concerning whether *specific* social variables are directly related to social suicide rates or whether these specific social variables are measures of more basic, abstract and broad social characteristics which determine social suicide rates. Lester (2004) proposed that the strong associations between social variables argues for the importance of basic broad social characteristics. For example, interstate migration, divorce, church nonattendance and alcohol consumption all inter-correlate highly over the states of America, suggesting the role of a social characteristic, perhaps best called *social disorganization*, as a determinant of societal suicide rates. In this case, regions of the world with high rates of divorce would have high rates of suicide for those in all marital statuses. This is found for the United States where states with higher divorce rates have higher suicide rates among the single, the married, the divorced and the widowed (Lester, 1995a).

Lester (2005) entered percentage Type O blood type, alcohol consumption, percentage elderly, divorce rate and birth rate into a multiple regression for 17 industrialized nations. The multiple R was 0.85. He then used the regression equation to predict the suicide rate of seven other European nations, and the Spearman rank correlation was 0.89. However, using the regression equation to predict the suicide rates in seven non-European nations gave a rank correlation of zero! Thus, the predictors (and, therefore, the causes) of suicide rates in non-western nations may be quite different from those for European nations.

Cultural Influences on the Motives for Suicidal Behavior

Suicidal behavior is differently determined and has different meanings in different cultures, as demonstrated by Hendin's (1964) study of suicide in Scandinavian countries. In Denmark, Hendin noted that guilt arousal was the major disciplinary technique employed by Danish mothers to control aggression, resulting in strong dependency needs in their sons. This marked dependency was the root of depression and suicidality after adult experiences of loss or separation. Reunion fantasies with lost loved ones were common in those committing suicide. In contrast, in Sweden, a strong emphasis was placed by parents on performance and success, resulting in ambitious children for whom work was central to their lives. Suicide typically followed failure in performance and the resulting damage to the men's self-esteem.

In her account of suicide among females in Papua-New Guinea, Counts (1988) has illustrated the ways in which a culture can determine the meaning of the suicidal act. In Papua-New Guinea, female suicide is a culturally recognized way of imposing social sanctions. Suicide has political implications for the surviving kin and for those held responsible for the events leading women to commit suicide. In one such instance, the suicide of a rejected fiancée led to sanctions being imposed on the family which had rejected her. Counts described this woman's suicide as a political act which symbolically transformed her from a position of powerlessness to one of power.

Cultures also differ in the degree in which suicide is condemned. It has been argued that one explanation for the low suicide rate in African Americans is that suicide is a less acceptable behavior for African Americans (Early, 1992). Murder rates are much higher in African Americans, both as murderers and as victims, and a larger proportion of the murders involving African Americans are victim-precipitated, that is, the victims played some role, conscious or unconscious, in precipitating their own demise (Wolfgang, 1957).[3] Gibbs (1988) suggested that African-American culture appears to view a victim-precipitated murder as a more acceptable method of dying than suicide.

Choice of Method for Suicide

The methods chosen for suicide differ between cultures. DeCatanzaro (1981) documented culturally unique methods for suicide, such as hanging by tying a noose around one's neck and running to another part of the house in Tikopia (one of the Solomon Islands in the southwestern Pacific Ocean). Suttee (Sati), which is suicide by burning on the husband's funeral pyre, is found in India, while seppuku, which is ritual disembowelment, is found in Japan. These well-known examples of cultural influences on suicide methods also have culturally determined motives (grief and shame, respectively).

Firearms are the most common method for suicide in the United States and Canada presently, while in Switzerland, whose residents typically own firearms as part of their participation in the civilian militia, hanging is the most common method for suicide. A method may come to symbolize the act of suicide, as in England earlier this century when "to take the pipe" meant to commit suicide by inhaling toxic domestic gas since the gas was brought into houses by means of pipes and this was the most common method for suicide. (After the 1960s, domestic gas became less toxic as a result of the switch from coal gas to natural gas.) Burvill and his colleagues (1983) found that immigrants to Australia shifted over time from using the most common methods of suicide in their home nations to those most common in Australia.

There are differences in the methods for suicide used by women and men. For example, in the United States, women use medications and poisons more often for suicide whereas men use more violent methods for suicide such as firearms and hanging (Canetto & Lester, 1995). This difference in method has

---

[3] Wolfgang estimated that, in about a quarter of all murders in his study, the victim played some role, albeit minor, in precipitating the assault. This was more common when husbands were murdered by their wives than when wives were murdered by their husbands.

been proposed as a reason for the greater likelihood of men dying as a result of their suicidal actions while women are more likely to survive.

Research indicates that increased availability of a method for suicide is associated with an increase in its use for suicide (Clarke and Lester, 1989). For example, Killias, van Kesteren and Rindlisbacher (2001) found that, in nations where a large proportion of the population owned guns, higher numbers of suicide were committed with guns. However, ownership of guns had no association with the total suicide rate. This suggests that, if guns are not freely available, people use guns less often for committing suicide but switch instead to other methods for suicide, such as poisons, hanging, stabbing, jumping, and drowning.

Related to this is the recent proposal for preventing suicide by limiting access to lethal methods for suicide (Clarke and Lester, 1989). Kreitman (1976) documented how detoxification of domestic gas in England and Wales led to a virtual elimination of domestic gas for suicide and a reduction in the overall suicide rate. Lester (1995b) studied this phenomenon in six other nations and found that detoxification of domestic gas reduced the use of domestic gas for suicide in all of the nations and, in those nations where suicide by domestic gas was more common, reduced the overall suicide rate as well.

Suicide in One Culture: The Chinese

Studies by Lester (1994a, 1994b) on suicidal behavior in Chinese illustrates the role of culture, a culture of particular interest because the Chinese are native to many nations (such as mainland China and Hong Kong) and have emigrated in large numbers to nations such as America.

The suicide rates of Asian Americans are relatively low compared with whites in the United States. For example, in 1980, the suicide rates were 13.3 per 100,000 per year for Native Americans, 13.2 for white Americans, 9.1 for Japanese Americans, 8.3 for Chinese Americans, 6.1 for African Americans and 3.5 for Filipino Americans (Lester, 1994c).

Lester noted that the patterns of suicide also differed for these ethnic groups. The ratio of the male to female suicide rates was much larger for whites and African Americans than for Asian Americans for whom the suicide rates of men and women were more similar. In addition, suicide rates increased with age for Asian Americans, whereas the suicide rates peaked in young adulthood for African Americans and Native Americans. Asian Americans used hanging for suicide much more often than whites and African Americans, and they used firearms relatively less often. Lester concluded that the epidemiology of suicide in Asian Americans in the US showed similarities to the results of epidemiological studies of suicide in their home nations, indicating that cultural factors have an important influence on the circumstances of suicidal behavior.

In another study, Lester (1994a) examined the epidemiology of suicide in Chinese in Hong Kong, Singapore, Taiwan, mainland China, Hawaii and the United States as a whole. A couple of examples here will illustrate the results.

The ratio of the male to female suicide rates in 1980 were 1.2 for Chinese Americans, 1.2 for Hong Kong residents, 1.2 for Taiwanese residents and 1.2 for Singapore Chinese, identical gender ratios. Suicide rates peaked in the elderly in all the nations: for those 65 and older in Chinese Americans, 75 and older in Hong Kong and Taiwan and 70 and older in Singapore Chinese.[4]

However, the methods used for suicide did differ for the different groups of Chinese: jumping was more common in the Chinese in Singapore and Hong Kong, hanging in Chinese Americans and poisons in Taiwan, probably a result of the difference between the nations in the availability of methods for suicide.[5] Furthermore, the suicide rates differed: in 1980 the suicide rates were 13.5 in Singapore and Hong Kong Chinese, 10.0 in Taiwan and 8.3 for Chinese Americans.

Thus, the gender and age patterns in Chinese suicide seem to be affected strongly by culture, while the absolute suicide rates and methods used are affected by the nation in which the Chinese dwell.[6] It would be of great interest in future research to identify what aspects of Chinese culture causes these differences – is it the religion, family values, political philosophy, etc?

Culture, Linguistics, and Suicide

As Douglas (1967) pointed out, a shared linguistic terminology for suicidal behavior is associated with shared meanings of the behavior, and there are also shared associated terms and phrases, such as despair, hopelessness, and "life isn't worth living." Douglas emphasized that these terms are not the phenomenon itself but rather are adopted by members of the culture (or subculture) to construct meanings for suicidal behavior. However, since the terms are rarely clearly defined or detailed and since there is often disagreement among commentators on their meaning, it follows that the meaning of suicide is ambiguous. Furthermore, since the terms are used to construct meanings for suicidal behavior, then estimates of the incidence and circumstances of suicidal behavior are in part a social construction.

For example, according to the Mohave, a Native American tribe in the southwest of the United States, a fetus which presents itself in the transverse position for birth, leading to its own death and that of its mother, is viewed as having intended to commit suicide and to murder its mother so that they can be together in the spirit world (Devereux, 1961). Medical examiners and coroners in the rest of the United States would not view such a still-born infant as a suicide.

---

[4]   The nations used different classifications by age.

[5]   For example, Lester (1994c) showed that the used of jumping for suicide in Singapore was strongly associated with the development of high rise apartments.

[6]   Within a nation, the different ethnic groups often differ in their suicide rates. Whites have higher suicide rates than blacks in the United States (13.0 per 100,000 per year versus 6.8 in 1992) and in African nations which report suicide rates such as Zimbabwe (17.6 versus 6.9 in 1983–1986) and South Africa (18.4 versus 3.0 in 1984) (Lester, 1998).

Counts (1980), who has studied the suicidal behavior of women in the Kaliai district of Papua New Guinea, noted that in the past elderly widows sometimes immolated themselves on their husband's funeral pyre. The German and Australian colonial governors considered this behavior to be a form of ritual murder rather than suicide, and they outlawed it. Counts, however, saw neither term (suicide or murder) as appropriate for this custom since it differed so much from what North Americans and Europeans regard as either suicide or murder. Neither term describes the behavior, the interpersonal relationships involved, or the attitudes toward the widow and those assisting in her death, nor do they predict how the community will respond to her death.

Recently, some scholars, especially in Europe, have expressed doubts that people engaging in nonfatal suicidal behavior have self-destruction as their aim, and they have moved to calling the behavior "self-poisoning" or "self-injury" (e.g., Ramon, 1980). The semantic implication is that nonfatal suicidal behavior is not "suicide." Since in most cultures women engage in more nonfatal suicidal actions than do men, this renaming of nonfatal suicidal behavior as self-injury makes "suicidal behavior" less common in women than it was hitherto.

Other suicidologists, on the other hand, include a wider range of behaviors under the rubric of "suicidal behavior." For example, Menninger (1938) classified behaviors such as alcoholism, drug abuse, and anorexia as *chronic suicide* since the individuals were shortening their lives by their behaviors. Menninger also classified behaviors such as polysurgery, self-castration, and self-mutilation as *focal suicide*, in which the self-destructive impulse is focused on one part of the body. These behaviors are often gender-linked. For example, anorexia is more common in women whereas illicit drug abuse is more common in men. Canetto (1991) has speculated that adolescents may respond differentially when under stress, with girls choosing nonfatal suicidal behavior more while boys choose drug abuse more. The use of Menninger's categories would change greatly the relative incidence of nonfatal suicidal behavior in women and men.

The Study of Culture Can Challenge Myths

Many theories of human behavior, including suicidal behavior, are based on physiological factors, such as neurotransmitters levels in the brain or levels of particular hormones. Cultural anthropology helps challenge such theories by showing, for example, that behaviors which we consider gender-specific are not found in every culture. As we have noted above, in the United States and in European nations, nonfatal suicidal behavior appears to occur at a higher rate in women than in men; as a result it has come to be viewed as a "feminine" behavior by the general public (Linehan, 1973) and by suicidologists as well. Other cultures, however, provide examples where nonfatal suicidal behavior, often carried out in front of others, is more common in men rather than women. The Nahane (or Kaska), a Native Canadian tribe located in British Columbia and the Yukon, provide a good example of this.

Observations and communications agree that attempted suicide by men is of frequent occurrence and very likely to appear during intoxication. There is a general pattern for such attempted self-destruction. In the two cases of the sort observed during field work, the weapon selected was a rifle. As he brandishes the weapon the would be suicide announces his intention in an emotional outburst. This becomes the signal for interference to block the deed. One or more men leap forward to wrest the gun from the intended suicide's possession and toss it out of sight. The would be victim is now usually emotionally overwhelmed by his behavior. This pattern is illustrated by Louis Maza's behavior during intoxication. Several times during the afternoon, Louis had manifested aggression toward himself, crying: "I don't care if I'm killed. I don't care my life." After several hours of such emotional outbursts interspersed with quarreling and aggression toward his companions, he seized his large caliber rifle and threatened to kill himself. Old Man threw himself on the gun and as the two men grappled for the weapon, Louis succeeded in firing one wild shot. John Kean and the ethnographer ran to the camp and together wrenched the gun from the drunken man. John fired the shells in the chamber and Old Man tossed the gun half-way down the cutbank. No punishment or other discrimination is reserved for attempted suicides. The individual is comforted and in the future, while intoxicated, he is watched lest he repeat the attempt.

(Honigmann, 1949, p. 204)

Among the Washo, located in Nevada and California, nonfatal suicidal behavior seems to be equally common in men and women.

In one case, a man had been having difficulty with his wife; she was interested in another man. The husband ate wild parsnip, but was saved. As a result his sons brought pressure on the wife and made her behave. The couple stayed together until the husband died ... Pete also says that men attempt suicide more than women, who just leave home when interpersonal difficulties arise. The destruction of the self is an ultimate, and the fact that men are more likely to invoke it than women indicates a lack of male authority in Washo culture.

(D'Azevedo et al., 1963, pp. 50–51)

The Washo man is described as lacking authority and lacking in self-confidence, perhaps because the Washo man has had more difficulty adapting to the changing culture in this century than has the Washo woman. Interestingly, the explanation provided by western anthropologists for the occurrence of nonfatal suicidal behavior among Washo men may be generalizable to societies where nonfatal suicidal behavior is more common in women. It may be that nonfatal suicidal behavior is not simply a "feminine" behavior, but rather a behavior found more commonly in those who are oppressed in a society, perhaps because the oppressed have fewer options for expressing their discontent.

The Impact of Culture Conflict

An issue that has become important in recent years is the impact of the pervasive western culture on the suicidal behavior of those living in less modern cultures. The high suicide rate in some Native American and Canadian groups and in some Micronesian islands has made this an issue of grave concern rather than mere academic debate.

Cultures often come into conflict. For example, the conflict between the traditional Native American culture and the dominant American culture has often been viewed as providing a major role in precipitating Native American suicide. May and Dizmang (1974) noted that there were three major sociological theories which have been proposed for explaining the Native American suicide rate. One theory focuses on *social disorganization*. The dominance of the Anglo-American culture has forced Native American culture to change and has eroded traditional cultural systems and values. This changes the level of social regulation and social integration, important causal factors for suicide in Durkheim's (1897) theory of suicide.

A second theory focuses on *cultural conflict* itself. The pressure from the educational system and mass media on Native Americans, especially the youth, to acculturate, a pressure which is opposed by their elders, leads to great stress for the youths.

A third theory focuses on the *breakdown of the family* in Native American tribes. Parents are often unemployed, substance abusers and in trouble with the law, and divorce and desertion of the family by one or more parents is common.

Acculturation occurs when a culture encounters a dominant alternative culture. The resulting pressure from the dominant culture leads to a variety of changes in the nondominant culture (Berry, 1990): physical changes (such as type of housing, urbanization and increasing population density), biological changes (resulting from changing diet and exposure to new diseases), political changes (such as loss of autonomy for the nondominant culture), economic changes (such as changes in type of employment), cultural changes (in language, religion, education and the arts), social relationships (both within the culture and between the two cultures), and psychological changes at the individual level (in behavior, values, attitudes and motives).

Berry noted that four possibilities are open to the nondominant culture: *integration* – maintaining relations with the dominant culture while maintaining cultural identity; *assimilation* – maintaining relations with the dominant culture but not maintaining cultural identity; *separation* – not maintaining relations with the dominant culture but maintaining cultural identity; and *marginalization* – not maintaining relations with the dominant culture and not maintaining cultural identity.

It would be of great interest to categorize the different Native American tribes as to which strategy appears to have been chosen and to examine the different consequences for the society and for the individuals in the society.

Research on Acculturation

Supportive results for the influence of acculturation on suicide in Native Americans comes from Van Winkle and May (1986) who examined suicide rates in three groups of Native Americans in New Mexico (the Apache, Navajo and Pueblo) and attempted to account for the differences in terms of the degree of acculturation. Overall, the crude suicide rates were 43.3 per 100,000 for the Apache, 27.8 for the Pueblo, and 12.0 for the Navajo.

The Jicarilla and Mescalero Apache of New Mexico were originally nomadic hunters and gatherers, organized into self-sufficient bands whose leaders held limited power. Their religion had no organized priesthood and was not a cohesive force in their lives. Individualism was a highly valued characteristic. Today they live in homes scattered about the reservation or in border towns. They raise livestock, cut timber or work in tribally owned businesses. Formal tribal governments have been established, but religion remains unimportant. Individualism is still valued. However, the raiding parties which formerly provided a some degree of social integration have been eliminated. The Apache appear, therefore, to have few integrating forces in their culture, and Van Winkle and May saw their high suicide rate as a direct result of this lack of integration. The Apache have been in close contact with whites. Their reservations are small and surrounded by white communities. Indeed many Apache live in mixed communities. Thus, the Apache have high acculturation in addition to their low social integration.

The Pueblo traditionally lived in compact towns and engaged in agriculture. Religion permeated their lives and was a strong integrating force. There was an organized priesthood and religious societies which took care of religious and civil matters. Individualism was discouraged and conformity valued. Thus, the Pueblo were the most integrated group, and Van Winkle and May found their intermediate suicide rate a puzzle. They tried to explain the Pueblo suicide rate using the role of acculturation. The Pueblo have had increasing contact with whites since 1959. Many of the Pueblos are near large cities such as Albuquerque and Santa Fe. Thus, they have high social integration and moderate but increasing acculturation. For the larger Pueblo tribes, Van Winkle and May compared the suicide rates of those tribes which had acculturated and those which had remained traditional and found a clear tendency for the acculturated and transitional tribes to have the higher suicide rates.

The Navajo, who have the lowest suicide rate, were nomadic hunters and gatherers who later settled down and turned to agriculture. They are organized into bands, but matrilineal clans exert a strong influence. Although religion is important in their lives, they have no organized priesthood. Individualism is valued but not as strongly as among the Apache. Thus, their social integration appears to be intermediate between that of the Apache and that of the Pueblo. However, the Navajo were the most geographically and socially isolated from whites of the three groups until the 1970s when mineral exploration increased on their reservations and some Navajo began to take wage-earning jobs.

Van Winkle and May's explanation of the suicide rates in the three groups can be summarized as in Table 14.1. It can be seen that acculturation performed better than social integration an as explanation of the differing suicide rates.

Table 14.1   Suicide rates in the Apache, Pueblo, and Navajo groups

	Social integration	Acculturation	Suicide rate
Apache	Low	High	High
Pueblo	High	Moderate	Moderate
Navajo	Moderate	Low	Low

Source: Van Winkle & May (1986).

In contrast, however, Bagley (1991) found in Alberta that it was those native Canadian reservations which were more isolated (and, incidentally, poorer) which had the higher suicide rates. In Taiwan also, Lee, Chang, and Cheng (2002) found that the less assimilated aboriginal groups had higher suicides rates than those groups which were more assimilated in the mainstream culture.

These studies indicate that when different cultures encounter each other, the problems of acculturation can result in stress and its consequences, including increased rates of suicidal behavior, especially in the less dominant cultural group. But acculturation may not always lead to an increased incidence of suicide (and other disturbed behaviors). In the future, anthropologists may be able to identify which cultural characteristics enable some cultures to acculturate with few social and personal problems while other cultures develop many problems.

The Assumption of Cultural Invariability

Investigators often assume that a research finding found in one culture will apply to other cultures. It is, therefore, important to replicate research findings in cultures other than the one in which the results were first obtained to check on this assumption. For example, at the sociological level, Lester and Yang (1991) found that females in the labor force and the ratio of divorces to marriages predicted suicide rates in the United States and Australia from 1946 to 1984, but that the associations were in opposite directions for the two nations. While in the United States the ratio of divorces to marriages was positively associated with the suicide, the association was negative in Australia. At the present time, there is no explanation for such differences.

Stack (1992) found that divorce had a deleterious effect on the suicide rate in Sweden and Denmark, but not in Japan. Stack offered four possible reasons; the divorce rate may be too low in Japan to affect the suicide rate, Japanese family support may be strong enough to counteract the loss of a spouse, ties between couples may be weak in Japan, and the cultural emphasis on conformity in Japan may suppress suicidal behavior.

At the individual level, Lester, Castromayor, and Icli (1991) found that an external locus of control was associated with a history of suicidal preoccupation in American, Philippine, and Turkish students, but that the association was no longer found for American students once the level of depression was controlled. In a comparison of depression and suicide in mainland China and the United States, Chiles et al. (1989) found that suicidal intent was predicted better by depression for Chinese psychiatric patients and better by hopelessness for American psychiatric patients.

De Man and his associates (for example, De Man et al., 1987) have published a number of studies of suicidal behavior in French-Canadians in order to explore the replicability of research findings originally identified for English-speaking cultures. It is important, therefore, for researchers to identify which findings have cross-cultural generality (and to which cultures) and which are specific to one culture.

Suicide among Indigenous Peoples

In some nations there has been a good deal of research on and speculation about suicidal behavior in indigenous peoples, sometimes called aborigines. A great deal of research has been conducted on Native Americans in the United States, and some on aborigines in Australia and Taiwan and on the Inuit in Canada and Greenland.

What is noteworthy, however, is that many nations have indigenous peoples, yet we hear little about their suicidality and other self-destructive behaviors. For example, in Central and South America, almost every nation has an indigenous population: 71 percent in Bolivia, 66 percent in Guatemala, 47 percent in Peru, 38 percent in Ecuador, 14 percent in Mexico, 8 percent in Chile, 2 percent in Colombia, 1.5 percent in Paraguay, 1 percent in Venezuela, and 0.4 percent in Brazil (Anon, 2004). In recent years, these indigenous peoples have become organized politically. They have begun to protest against the governments of their nations, often toppling governments (as in Bolivia and Ecuador) and in rare cases assuming power (as in Bolivia and Peru).

Even in developed nations, the oldest inhabitants are often ignored. In suicide statistics from the United Kingdom, data from England and Wales are reported together. A recent report on suicide in Wales (Lester, 1994d) was rejected by reviewers for the *British Journal of Psychiatry* as being of no interest![7] The United Kingdom has ethnic groups in Wales and the county of Cornwall who predate the Roman, Danish, and French invaders and who have their own languages and ethnic identity. Yet their suicidal behavior has received no attention.

In Africa, the situation is odd in a different way. Setting aside the remnants of the European colonialists, all of the peoples there can be considered indigenous. Yet, when data on suicide are reported, they are reported for the artificial nations that the colonial rulers established with no regard for the tribal groups in each country. For example, suicide rates have been reported for Zimbabwe (Rittey &

---

[7]   It is no wonder that there is a Welsh liberation movement.

Castle, 1972; Lester & Wilson, 1988), yet Zimbabwe has two major ethic groups, the Shona (the dominant ethnic group) and the Ndebele. It would make much more sense to explore and compare suicide in these two ethnic groups.

Some nations are only now beginning to organize their mortality-reporting procedures and structures. In many of these, it will be important to take into account the various indigenous groups in the country, such as China which has a multitude of ethnicities within its borders.

Comparisons of Indigenous Peoples within a Nation

In a couple of nations, it has been possible to compare different ethnic groups within a nation. Lester (1997a) reviewed all of the studies on Native American suicide and summarized the suicide rates by tribe and by era. There was a slight tendency for the suicide rates to rise during the twentieth century and for the tribes to differ greatly in their suicide rate, ranging in the 1970s from 149 per 100,000 per year in the Kwakiutl and 73 in the Sioux to 7 in the Pima and 9 in the Lumbee.

Cheng (1995, 1997) compared suicide in Taiwan in two aboriginal groups (the Atayal and the Ami) with suicide in the dominant Han Chinese. The Atayal had a suicide rate of 68.2 per 100,000 per year, the Ami 15.6 and the Han Chinese 18.0. The suicides in all three groups had a similarly high incidence of psychiatric disorder, and the high suicide rate in the Atayal was attributed to their high rate of alcoholism and earlier onset of major depressive disorders.

We need many more studies comparing the different groups of indigenous peoples within a nation – not simply the crude suicide rates, but also the circumstances, motives, and meanings of suicide in these different groups.

The Human Relations Area Files

Anthropologists have typically studied historical societies or societies which have been relatively less influenced by modernization, often called preliterate, nonliterate or primitive societies, societies composed of whom we would now call indigenous peoples.

There is a superb source of data on indigenous peoples in the Human Relations Area Files (HRAF). The headquarters for this project are at Yale University, but microfiche copies of the results of the project are available at other major universities in the United States and around the world. The staff of the project have collected reports from visitors to these cultures as far back as they can and from all kinds of visitors (such as missionaries, colonial administrators and anthropologists). The content of the reports is coded for topic, and, for example, to see what has been written about suicide in these cultures, the code for suicide is ascertained from the codebook (it is 762), and then the section for 762 can be located for each culture in the HRAF. There are about 330 cultures represented in the HRAF. The files are now available on a CD-ROM, and there is a website for the HRAF (www.yale.edu/hraf/collections.htm).

The files are updated and enlarged continually. To give some examples of the source material, in 1994, the Ainu in Japan had 1,573 text pages from 11 sources that had been coded, the Lapps in Finland 3,284 text pages from 16 sources, the Yoruba in Nigeria 1,637 text pages from 45 sources, and Delaware Indians in the United States 1,733 text pages from 15 sources.

Several projects on suicide can be devised from the HRAF. Some investigators have read the files on suicide for a sample of societies and tried to estimate the suicide rate for each society.

Masumura (1977) had two judges rate 35 nations for the frequency of suicide by having them read the suicide entries in the HRAF, and his ratings are shown in Table 14.2.[8] From this group of cultures, it would appear that, among Native American groups, the Kwakiutl have a relatively high suicide rate and the Pomo a relatively low suicide rate. In a research study on this sample, Masumura found that the estimated suicide rate was *positively* associated with a measure of social integration in opposition to a prediction from Durkheim's (1897) classic sociological theory of suicide.

Ember and Ember (1992) drew attention to the fact that the materials on suicides in the HRAF come from very different time periods. Therefore, they urged that it was important to specify the year from which the data were derived. For example, they rated the Creek suicide rate as 1.74 (on a scale of 0–8) in 1800 and the Omaha as 1 in 1860.

Theories of Suicide

There has been one theory of suicide, proposed by Naroll (1962, 1963, 1969), which was based on a study of these nonliterate societies and tested using data from the societies rather than data from modern nations, the basis for Durkheim's (1897) theory of suicide. Naroll proposed that suicide occurred in those who were *socially disoriented*, that in those who lack or lose basic social ties. But since all of those who are in this condition do not commit suicide, there must also be a psychological factor involved, that is, the individual's reaction to *thwarting disorientation contexts*. Thwarting disorientation contexts are those in which the individual's social ties are broken or weakened and those in which another person thwarts the individual and prevents him or her from achieving desired and expected satisfactions or in which they experience frustration. This thwarting must be interpersonal and not impersonal. Storm damage to one's dwelling is not thwarting but, when another person sets fire to it and destroys it, it is thwarting. The widow is not thwarted, but the divorced spouse is thwarted. Under the conditions of thwarting disorientation, individuals are more prone to commit suicide in such a way that it comes to public notice, that

---

[8] Each judge rated the suicide rate of each society on a scale of 0–4, and their ratings were summed.

Table 14.2   Estimates of relative suicide rates for 35 non-literate societies by Masumura (1977)

Group	Suicide score (range 2–8)	Group	Suicide score (range 2–8)
Ainu	6	Kutenai	4
Andamanese	2	Kwakiutl	8
Araucanians	5	Lango	8
Ashanti	6	Maori	8
Bakongo	6	Navajo	2
Banks Islanders	7	Norsemen	5
Bushmen	6	Omaha	4
Chippewa	7	Pomo	2
Chukchee	8	Rwala	7
Creek	6	Samoans	8
Crow	6	Sema Naga	6
Dahomeans	6	Semang	2
Fang	6	Toda	6
Hottentot	6	Trobrianders	8
Iban	7	Tuareg	4
Iroquois	5	Vedda	4
Jivaro	7	Yahgan	2
Kazak	6		

Source: Masamura (1977).

is, *protest suicide*. Naroll felt that this theory, better than other theories, explained suicide committed by indigenous peoples.[9]

Lester (1997b) noted that the Mohave have a clearly specified theory of suicide – namely that suicide in their people is increasingly due to a breakdown in ties to the community and tribe as a whole and to an increasing dependence on a primary relationship with a lover or spouse. Lester tested this hypothesis that suicide would be common in nations with higher levels of individualism, and the results confirmed this hypothesis.

Comment

There has been a failure of suicidologists to study suicidal behavior in many indigenous peoples. On occasions they ignore indigenous peoples completely, such as the Welsh and Cornish peoples in the United Kingdom or the Basques in France and Spain. On other occasions, as in Africa, they study suicide in the artificially created nations (created by the colonial rulers) rather than in the more meaningful ethnic groups. Occasionally, when suicide is studied in these

[9]   Lester (1995c) has compared and contrasted Naroll's theory with those of Durkheim (1897) and Henry and Short (1954).

nations, the investigators omit to mention the ethnic background of the people (e.g., Sefa-Dedeh & Canetto, 1992).

Second, this section has drawn attention to the Human Relations Area Files (HRAF) with its rich source of data on indigenous peoples, including suicide. Data from the HRAF were used to illustrate how suicide rates can be estimated and how the data can be used to test theories of suicide.

Finally, examples were given of theories of suicide which derive from studies of suicide in indigenous peoples rather than from studies of suicide in western nations.

Psychotherapeutic Implications

All of this scholarly discourse is important at the theoretical level, but it may be asked whether there are implications for counseling and psychotherapy. It is sometimes argued that only "like" can counsel "like," that is, that only homosexuals can counsel homosexuals, women counsel women, ex-addicts counsel addicts, and so on. Is the same true also for different cultures? The majority of counselors and psychotherapists deny this, claiming that a good counselor or psychotherapist can counsel any kind of patient. However, to counsel someone very different in background from oneself may require that the counselor learn about the background and culture from which the individual comes. Sue and Sue (1990) have addressed the issues that psychotherapists of one culture must confront when counseling clients from different cultures, such as racism and cultural differences in verbal and nonverbal communication styles.

Zimmerman and Zayas (1995) have illustrated this point in their discussion of treating the suicidal adolescent Hispanic female. They noted that, in New York City, the values of the adolescent latina often clash with those of her more traditional mother. Both mother and daughter experience problems in communication and a rupture in their relationship. Thus, the problem of acculturation exacerbates the normal adolescent turmoil. The latina's mother wants her daughter to succeed in this new culture, yet she also wants her daughter to maintain traditional cultural attitudes and roles. The adolescent latina feels overwhelmed by this conflict and, in extreme cases, makes a suicide attempt in an effort to reduce the tension felt in this conflict. After a suicide attempt, the psychotherapist must explain the conflict to the mother and daughter and help them find ways to re-establish mutual understanding and empathy.

It is possible, of course, that psychotherapists could identify the nature of the problems confronting suicidal people and their families each time they encounter such a family, but the psychotherapeutic process is facilitated if psychotherapists have some notion of the cultural issues which they are likely to encounter.

Sue and Sue (1990) presented the case of Janet, a Chinese-American female college senior majoring in sociology, who came to the college counseling center complaining of depression, feelings of worthlessness and suicidal thoughts. She had difficulty identifying the causes of her depression, but she seemed quite hostile to the psychotherapist who was also Chinese-American.

Discussion of this revealed that Janet resented being seen by a Chinese psychotherapist, feeling that she had been assigned to one because of her own race. Janet disliked everything Chinese, including Chinese men whom she found sexually unattractive. She dated only white men, which had upset her parents. However, her last romance had broken up partly because her boyfriend's parents objected to him dating a Chinese woman.

Janet clearly had difficulties stemming from her continuing denial of her Chinese heritage. She was being forced to realize that she was Chinese for she was not fully accepted by white America. Initially she blamed the Chinese for her dilemma, but then she turned her hostility toward herself. Feeling alienated from her own culture and rejected by the white culture, she was experiencing an identity crisis with a resulting depression.

The psychotherapist in such a case must deal with cultural racism and its effects on minorities. Positive acculturation must be distinguished from rejection of one's own cultural values, as well as typical adolescent rebellion from one's parents. Psychotherapists can work with such a client more effectively if they are conversant with the cultural history and experiences of Asian Americans.

Although the problem of acculturation has been proposed as one of the major causes of depression and suicidal behavior among Native Americans, the majority of research reports on Native American individuals who attempt or complete suicide mention precipitating causes such as grief over loss and quarrels with relatives and friends. Rarely is cultural conflict listed among the precipitating causes. Of course, it may be that the problems of acculturation raise the stress level of individuals so much that stressors, which under ordinary circumstances would not precipitate suicide, now do so.

A few brief case histories have been published which do illustrate the problems of acculturation and culture conflict. For example, Berlin (1986) described the case of a bright young Native American woman who completed undergraduate school and qualified as a teacher and who was admitted to graduate school. Her clan, however, told her that she was required to teach on the reservation. Her desire to go to graduate school was seen as striving to be better than her peers, and this was unacceptable and forbidden. The young women had a psychiatric breakdown and was hospitalized. In a similar situation, the tribe and another family could not decide whether to let a young woman go to graduate school for an MBA after she obtained her undergraduate degree and, during the long wait for a decision, she attempted suicide.

In this latter case, the young woman, whom Berlin called Josie, had alcoholic parents who frequently sent her and her brothers and sisters to live with relatives while they went on drinking sprees. A teacher realized Josie's potential and received permission for Josie to live with her. With this teacher's help, her academic performance improved, and she went to college. Josie now resented that her parents, who had neglected her, were involved in decisions about her life. The clan leadership and tribal council were relatively enlightened about the issues and eventually gave permission for Josie to attend graduate school. While at graduate school, Josie underwent psychotherapy to deal with her depression and anger and other personal problems. After graduation, she returned to the tribe to manage their business office, marrying a young man who had fought a similar battle in order to obtain an MSW degree.

Conclusions

There are large cultural differences in the incidence of suicidal behavior, and culture influences also the methods used for committing suicide and the reasons for doing so. Although these cultural differences may be a result of physiological differences between the members of the different cultures, the more plausible explanations involve psychological and social variables, such as the abuse of alcohol and the level of social integration and regulation. When competing cultures interact, there may be increased stress (and, as a result, an increase in suicidality) in the less dominant culture.

It should be noted also that, in societies which are culturally heterogeneous, such as the United States, Canada, and Australia, it cannot be assumed that suicides from the different cultural groups are similar in rate, method, motive and precipitating factors. Those working to prevent suicide in such societies must take these cultural influences into account (Sue and Sue, 1990; Zimmerman and Zayas, 1995).

This chapter has attempted to raise and briefly discuss several of the issues involved in the interaction of culture and suicide, and suggestions have been made for future research.

1. Suicide statistics should be collected from more nations in the world than at present and the WHO data set should be kept updated in a more timely manner than it is at the present time.
2. Research is needed to determine which aspects of suicidal behavior are culturally invariant and which are not.
3. Research is needed to check on the generalizability of research findings in one culture to other cultures.
4. The role of culture conflict in determining both societal suicide rates and individual suicidal behavior needs more in-depth study, as well as research to test what are the mediating factors (for example, social disorganization or family breakdown).
5. Research on acculturation should extend beyond Native American groups and the First Peoples of Canada to other groups and should explore the roles of the different types of adaptation to the dominant culture (integration, assimilation, separation and marginalization).
6. Many nations have indigenous peoples, most of whom have been ignored by researchers studying suicide. They merit study.

7. Theories of suicide, academic and folk, often differ in nonwestern and indigenous cultures from those proposed by the classic European and American social scientists. These theories should be documented and tested.

These issues should be viewed not as problems, but rather as opportunities to plan and execute innovative and exciting research and to work more effectively with suicidal clients from diverse cultures.

REFERENCES

Adrian, M. (1984). International trends in alcohol production, trade and consumption, and their relationship to alcohol-related problems, 1970 to 1977. *Journal of Public Health Policy, 5,* 344–367.

Anon. (2004). A political awakening. *The Economist, 370*(8363), 35–37.

Bagley, C. (1991). Poverty and suicide among native Canadians. *Psychological Reports, 69,* 149–150.

Berlin, I. N. (1986). Psychopathology and its antecedents among American Indian adolescents. *Advances in Clinical Child Psychology, 9,* 125–152.

Berry, J. W. (1990). Acculturation and adaptation. *Arctic Medical Research, 49,* 142–150.

Burvill, P., McCall, M., Woodings, T., & Stenhouse, N. (1983). Comparison of suicide rates and methods in English, Scots and Irish immigrants in Australia. *Social Science & Medicine, 17,* 705–708.

Canetto, S. S. (1991). Gender roles, suicide attempts, and substance abuse. *Journal of Psychology, 125,* 605–620.

Canetto, S. S., & Lester, D. (1995). *Woman and suicidal behavior.* New York: Springer.

Cheng, A. T. A. (1995). Mental illness and suicide. *Archives of General Psychiatry, 52,* 594–603.

Cheng, A. T. A. (1997). Personality disorder and suicide. *British Journal of Psychiatry, 170,* 441–446.

Chiles, J. A., Strosahl, K., Ping, Z. Y., et al. (1989). Depression, hopelessness and suicidal behavior in Chinese and American psychiatric patients. *American Journal of Psychiatry, 146,* 339–344.

Clarke, R. V., & Lester, D. (1989). *Suicide: Closing the exits.* New York: Springer-Verlag.

Conklin, G. H., & Simpson, M. E. (1987). The family, socioeconomic development and suicide. *Journal of Comparative Family Studies, 18,* 99–111.

Counts, D. A. (1980). Fighting back is not the way: Suicide and the women on Kaliai. *American Ethnologist, 7,* 332–351.

Counts, D. A. (1988). Ambiguity in the interpretation of suicide. In D. Lester (Ed.), *Why women kill themselves* (pp. 87–109). Springfield, IL: Charles Thomas.

D'Azevedo, W. L., Freed, S. A., Freed, R. S., et al. (1963). *The Washo Indians of California and Nevada.* Salt Lake City, UT: University of Utah.

De Man, A. F., Balkou, S., & Iglesias, R. I. (1987). A French-Canadian adaptation of the scale for suicide ideation. *Canadian Journal of Behavioural Science, 19,* 50–55.

DeCatanzaro, D. (1981). *Suicide and self-damaging behavior.* New York: Academic Press.

Devereux, G. (1961). *Mohave ethnopsychiatry.* Washington, DC: Smithsonian Institution.

Douglas, J. D. (1967). *The social meanings of suicide*. Princeton, NJ: Princeton University.

Dublin, L. I. (1963). *Suicide*. New York: Ronald.

Durkheim, E. (1897). *Le suicide*. Paris: Felix Alcan.

Early, K. E. (1992). *Religion and suicide in the African-American community*. Westport, CT: Greenwood.

Ember, C. R., & Ember, R. (1992). Warfare, aggression, and resource problems. *Behavior Science Research, 26,* 169–226.

Gibbs, J. (1988). Conceptual, methodological, and sociocultural issues in black youth suicide. *Suicide & Life-Threatening Behavior, 18,* 73–89.

Girard, C. (1993). Age, gender, and suicide. *American Sociological Review, 58,* 553–574.

Hendin, H. (1964). *Suicide and Scandinavia*. New York: Grune & Stratton.

Henry, A. F., & Short, J. F. (1954). *Suicide and homicide*. New York: Free Press.

Hlady, W. G., & Middaugh, J. P. (1988). The underrecording of suicide in state and national records, Alaska, 1983–1984. *Suicide & Life-Threatening Behavior, 18,* 237–244.

Honigmann, J. J. (1949). *Culture and ethos of Kaska society*. New Haven, CT: Yale University Press.

Johnson, B. D. (1965). Durkheim's one cause of suicide. *American Sociological Review, 30,* 875–886.

Killias, M., Kesteren, J. van, & Rindlisbacher, M. (2001). Guns, violent crime, and suicide in 21 countries. *Canadian Journal of Criminology, 43,* 429–448.

Kreitman, N. (1976). The coal gas story. *British Journal Preventive and Social Medicine, 30,* 86–93.

Lee, C. S., Chang, J. C., & Cheng, A. T. A. (2020). Acculturation and suicide. *Psychological Medicine, 32,* 133–141.

Lester, D. (1972). Migration and suicide. *Medical Journal of Australia, 1,* 941–942.

Lester, D. (1985). Variation in suicide and homicide rates by latitude and longitude in the US, Canada and Australia. *American Journal of Psychiatry, 142,* 523–524.

Lester, D. (1987). National distribution of blood groups, personal violence (suicide and homicide), and national character. *Personality & Individual Differences, 8,* 575–576.

Lester, D. (1994a). The epidemiology of suicide in Chinese populations in six regions of the world. *Chinese Journal of Mental Health, 7,* 21–24.

Lester, D. (1994b). Differences in the epidemiology of suicide in Asian Americans by nation of origin. *Omega, 29,* 89–93.

Lester, D. (1994c). Suicide by jumping in Singapore as a function of high-rise apartment availability. *Perceptual and Motor Skills, 79,* 74.

Lester, D. (1994d). Predicting the suicide rate in Wales. *Psychological Reports, 75,* 1054.

Lester, D. (1995a). Explaining the regional variation of suicide and homicide. *Archives of Suicide Research, 1,* 159–174.

Lester, D. (1995b). Effects of the detoxification of domestic on suicide rates in six nations. *Psychological Reports, 77,* 294.

Lester, D. (1995c). Thwarting disorientation and suicide. *Cross-Cultural Research, 29,* 14–26.

Lester, D. (1996). *Patterns of suicide and homicide in the world*. Commack, NY: Nova Science.

Lester, D. (1997a). *Suicide in American Indians*. Commack, NY: Nova Science.

Lester, D. (1997b). Note on a Mohave theory of suicide. *Cross-Cultural Research, 31*, 268–272.

Lester, D. (1998). *Suicide in African Americans*. Commack, New York: Nova Science.

Lester, D. (2004). *Thinking about suicide*. Hauppauge, NY: Nova Science.

Lester, D. (2005). Predicting suicide in nations. *Archives of Suicide Research, 9*, 219–223.

Lester, D., Castromayor, I. J., & Icli, T. (1991). Locus of control, depression, and suicidal ideation among American, Philippine, and Turkish students. *Journal of Social Psychology, 131*, 447–449.

Lester, D., & Kondrichin, S. V. (2004). Finno-Ugrians, blood types, and suicide. *Perceptual & Motor Skills, 98*, 814,

Lester, D., & Wilson, C. (1988). Suicide in Zimbabwe. *Central African Journal of Medicine, 34*, 147–149.

Lester, D., & Yang, B. (1991). The relationship between divorce, unemployment and female participation in the labour force and suicide rates in Australia and America. *Australian & New Zealand Journal of Psychiatry, 25*, 519–523.

Linehan, M. (1973). Suicide and attempted suicide. *Perceptual and Motor Skills, 37*, 31–34.

Malla, A., & Hoenig, J. (1983). Differences in suicide rates. *Canadian Journal of Psychiatry, 28*, 291–293.

Masumura, W. T. (1977). Social integration and suicide. *Behavior Science Research, 12*, 251–269.

May, P. A., & Dizmang, L. H. (1974). Suicide and the American Indian. *Psychiatric Annals, 4*(11), 22–28.

Menninger, K. (1938). *Man against himself*. New York: Harcourt, Brace & World.

Menozzi, P., Piazza, A., & Cavalli-Sforza, L. (1978). Synthetic maps of human gene frequencies in Europeans. *Science, 201*, 786–792.

Moksony, F. (1990). Ecological analysis of suicide. In D. Lester (Ed.), *Current concepts of suicide*, (pp. 121–138). Philadelphia: Charles.

Naroll, R. (1962). *Data quality control*. New York: Free Press.

Naroll, R. (1963). Thwarting disorientation and suicide. Unpublished discussion paper, Northwestern University.

Naroll, R. (1969). Cultural determinants and the concept of the sick society. In S. C. Plog & R. B. Edgerton (Eds.), *Changing perspectives in mental illness* (pp. 128–155). New York: Holt, Rinehart & Winston.

Phillips, M. R., Liu, H., & Zhang, Y. (1999). Suicide and social change in China. *Culture, Medicine & Psychiatry, 23*, 25–50.

Ramon, S. (1980). Attitudes of doctors and nurses to self-poisoning patients. *Social Science and Medicine, 14A*, 317–324.

Rittey, D. A. W., & Castle, W. M. (1972). Suicides in Rhodesia. *Central African Journal of Medicine, 18*, 97–100.

Sainsbury, P., & Barraclough, B. M. (1968). Differences in suicide rates. *Nature, 220*, 1252.

Sefa-Dedeh, A., & Canetto, S. S. (1992). Women, family and suicidal behavior in Ghana. In V. P. Gielen, L. L. Adler & N. A. Milgram (Eds.), *Psychology in international perspective*, (pp. 299–309). Amsterdam: Swets & Zeitlinger.

Stack, S. (1992). The effect of divorce of suicide in Japan. *Journal of Marriage and the Family, 54*, 327–334.

Sue, D. W., & Sue, D. (1990). *Counseling the culturally different.* New York: Wiley.

Taylor, S. (1990). Suicide, Durkheim, and sociology. In D. Lester (Ed.), *Current concepts of suicide* (pp. 225–236). Philadelphia: Charles.

Van Winkle, N. W., & May, P. (1986). A native American suicide in New Mexico, 1959–1979. *Human Organization, 45,* 296–309.

Weissman, M. M., & Klerman, G. L. (1977). Sex differences and the epidemiology of depression. *Archives of General Psychiatry, 34,* 98–111.

Wolfgang, M. E. (1957). Victim-precipitated criminal homicide. *Journal of Criminal Law, Criminology & Police Science, 48,* 1–11.

Zimmerman, J. K. & Zayas, L. (1995). Suicidal adolescent latinas. In S. Canetto & D. Lester (Ed.), *Women and suicide* (pp. 120–132). New York: Springer.

Author Index

Subject Index